WOMEN OF THE WORLD

The British People and the League of Nations: Democracy, Citizenship and Internationalism, c.1918–1945

WOMEN OF THE WORLD

The Rise of the Female Diplomat

Helen McCarthy

B L O O M S B U R Y
LONDON · NEW DELHI · NEW YORK · SYDNEY

First published in Great Britain 2014

Copyright © 2014 Helen McCarthy

The moral right of the author has been asserted

No part of this book may be used or reproduced in any manner whatsoever without written permission from the publisher except in the case of brief quotations embedded in critical articles or reviews

Every reasonable effort has been made to trace copyright holders of material reproduced in this book, but if any have been inadvertently overlooked the publisher would be glad to hear from them

Bloomsbury Publishing Plc
50 Bedford Square
London
WC1B 3DP

www.bloomsbury.com

Bloomsbury is a trademark of Bloomsbury Publishing Plc

Bloomsbury Publishing, London, New Delhi, New York and Sydney

A CIP catalogue record for this book is available from the British Library

ISBN 978 1 4088 4005 4

10 9 8 7 6 5 4 3 2 1

Typeset by Hewer Text UK Ltd, Edinburgh
Printed and bound in Great Britain by CPI Group (UK) Ltd, Croydon CR0 4YY

For James, Florence and Beatrice

Contents

Preface

One generally did not meet many diplomats growing up in a lower-middle-class family in suburban Essex. With its grammar schools, fine Norman castle and weekly roller disco, Colchester was as pleasant a place as any in which to pass one's childhood. But it was not frequented much by members of Her Majesty's Diplomatic Service. I did not know anyone who knew a diplomat, and nor did any of my friends or relatives.

I was aware, of course, that such people existed. One read about them in novels and history books, or saw them in films and TV programmes, usually depicted as silver-tongued bullshitters or eccentric fools (Lord John Marbury, the unhinged British ambassador to Washington featured in *The West Wing*, is perhaps the perfect epitome of the latter). But I did not encounter my first real, flesh-and-blood British diplomat until after I had left university and was midway through a gloriously self-indulgent year attending classes at Harvard's Kennedy School of Government. Included in the school's regular events programme was a series of seminars on the theme of contemporary diplomacy, one of which was addressed by a youngish British diplomat called Carne Ross from the UK's Permanent Mission to the United Nations in New York. His subject was the negotiations surrounding the drafting of an important Security Council Resolution concerning sanctions on Iraq. To be honest, I do not remember much about what was said; it seemed to hinge upon the placing of a comma in the crucial clause of the resolution. But I remember a great deal about Carne Ross. He was everything I expected a diplomat to be: handsome in an unflashy way (think Boden catalogue rather than Calvin Klein billboard); authoritative without being abrasive; principled but not pious; owner of an understated but unmistakeably steely intellect, and oh-so-slightly diffident in overall demeanour.

A few months later I attended another Kennedy School seminar, this one addressed by Carne's boss, Sir Jeremy Greenstock, then Britain's ambassador to the UN. Again, the substance of his remarks eludes me (much talk of Britain 'punching above its weight' I seem to recall), but Greenstock's elegant conversation – loaded with silken vowels and lightly freighted with purring consonants – only reinforced my growing conviction that Britain's diplomatic corps were a really rather special breed.

And as if just to prove that diplomats are like buses (you spend a lifetime waiting for one and then three come along at once), soon after I found myself rather serendipitously invited to a function at the British embassy in Washington hosted by the then ambassador, Sir Christopher Meyer. As he addressed the assembled guests, Meyer struck me as rather more of a leg-puller than Greenstock or Ross, more of a hail-fellow-well-met kind of character, but no less impressive for it. As the sun set behind us on the embassy lawn and we were summoned to dinner by an immaculately dressed butler, I came to an important conclusion: diplomats were bloody brilliant people.

There was, nonetheless, no question of my ever becoming one. I had a terrible ear for languages and found travel outside the UK mildly stressful, even in Anglophile Massachusetts. I was, for instance, totally discombobulated by the discovery that ATMs in the US spit your cash out *before* they've returned your card, a minor detail which I imagine anyone seriously cut out for diplomacy would take in their stride, but which for me became a near-daily reminder of my outsider status which I could never quite shrug off.

This low-key, rumbling sense of cultural alienation was a far greater deterrent to joining the Foreign Office than anything to do with being female, although I remember thinking at the time how it was almost certainly no coincidence that my first three contacts with the diplomatic world had all come in masculine form. The reasons, it seemed, were not difficult to fathom: the brash, macho world of politics was a pretty unkind place for women full stop; and diplomatic careers, with the endless string of overseas postings and round-the-clock entertaining, appeared to lie at the tougher end of the spectrum, particularly for women wishing to balance work with family life.

It was only some years later, while researching my doctorate on internationalism in the 1920s and '30s, that I began to reflect more deeply on the reasons behind women's historic under-representation within the diplomatic world. This, I discovered, was not simply a function of their traditional absorption in childrearing and homemaking; nor was it a straightforward analogue of the broader feminist struggle to win civil, political and economic equality. Women's admission to the diplomatic profession in Britain was not achieved until 1946, almost thirty years after the vote was won, and some twenty years after female candidates had become eligible for top grades of the Home Civil Service, as well as most other high-flying professions. Why so late? What was so special about the representation of national interests abroad that only men were believed capable of doing it? And what happened in 1946 to make the government change its mind?

As I mused upon these problems other questions presented themselves: were women really entirely absent from diplomacy before mid-century? Were there other ways in which they might have influenced foreign affairs, perhaps as wives, patrons or confidantes? And what about after the bar was lifted? How many women joined the Diplomatic Service in the post-war years? Who were they? How did they survive in what was hitherto an exclusively masculine profession? Did they shake things up or try to fit in with the existing culture? Has the presence of women changed the way diplomacy is done?

On further probing, I discovered that there was practically no existing research on this subject, save a few light-hearted books on diplomatic wives, some biographies of well-known figures such as Gertrude Bell and Freya Stark, and a preliminary research note produced by the Foreign Office back in the 1990s. This was despite the availability of an extraordinarily rich treasure trove of archival material – personal papers, diaries and memoirs – not to mention the as yet unrecorded testimony of those members of the post-war pioneer generation still living. Plenty of male diplomats had written their memoirs or set down their thoughts for posterity in interviews, but as for their female colleagues: one was met only with silence.

As a subject for a book, it seemed tantalising, but I foresaw problems. Was I the right woman for the job? I knew practically nothing about the history of diplomacy. I was not one of those scholars who could navigate the Foreign Office files housed at the National Archives in Kew as if it were their local supermarket. I had no personal connections to the Diplomatic Service, and could not tell a *chargé d'affaires* from a *chef de protocol*, let alone explain the difference between a memorandum and a minute. Yet on further reflection, it struck me that my outsider status could bring advantages, as I would be studying this intriguing, alluring world with fresh eyes and an open mind, free from any fixed notions of how diplomacy works, what diplomats do, or indeed how diplomatic history ought to be written. If that was not sufficient inducement, there was the additional knowledge that if I did not write this book, someone else eventually would – a thought too awful to contemplate. So I decided to take a deep breath, muster my courage, and jump in. The result is *Women of the World*.

PART ONE

Unofficial Envoys

Berlin, 1878

Shortly before two o'clock on 13 June 1878, a succession of finely dressed plenipotentiaries alighted from their carriages outside the Chancellor's mansion in Berlin, primed to redraw the map of south-eastern Europe in the wake of the Russo-Turkish War. Once the fluttering German standard had been hoisted up the flagstaff to cheering crowds, the delegates entered the palace and were ushered into an opulent ballroom, where they partook of some port wine and a dainty biscuit or two and presently found their places around a vast semi-circular table. Once seated, all eyes turned to their host, Prince Bismarck, who declared the proceedings to be open.[1] The Congress of Berlin had begun.

A month later, the great powers in attendance were ready to agree upon the complex contours of a new political geography for the Balkans, which balanced the territorial ambitions of the region's two imperial titans, Russia and the Ottoman Empire. The court artist Anton von Werner captured the scene as the last few signatures were affixed to the treaty during the final session of the congress in a magnificent portrait. Two dozen or so figures fill an elegant, high-ceilinged room, some seated, some standing around a long table covered in green baize. The viewer's eye is immediately drawn to the statuesque bearing of Otto von Bismarck, who shakes the hand of the Russian delegate, Count Schuvalov, whilst the Austro-Hungarian representative, Count Andrássy, looks on. In the background, Schuvalov's colleague, M. D'Oubril, signs the treaty, flanked from behind by the French and

Italian delegates. On the left of the canvas we see the British Prime Minister, Benjamin Disraeli, sharing a friendly exchange with the third Russian representative, Prince Gorchakov, whilst across the room his deputy, Foreign Secretary Lord Salisbury, converses in a relaxed manner with the Turkish members.

The image is the epitome of nineteenth-century diplomatic culture: an aristocratic gathering in sumptuous surroundings in the mould of 1815, when the European powers first convened a grand congress in Vienna to mark the end of the Napoleonic Wars. Von Werner's painting, however, which was intended to celebrate Bismarck's triumph of personal diplomacy, inevitably conceals as much as it reveals. In the first place, it gives the viewer little clue as to the deteriorating health of several key participants: the octogenarian Gorchakov was senile and wheelchair-bound; Disraeli was suffering from bronchitis, asthma and failing kidneys; the French ambassador, the Comte de St Vallier, was riddled with liver disease, whilst Andrássy was coughing up blood. Even Bismarck himself was laid low at the beginning of the congress with rheumatism, fearing he could work for only a few hours at a time. The portrait also betrays little of the shabby treatment meted out to the Turkish delegates, who were repeatedly snubbed or silenced and were left in no doubt of their inferior status in European eyes. They were, at least, in the room, unlike the representatives of the various Balkan states, whose ravaged territories formed the central subjects of discussion at the congress. These wretched souls were granted only a few precious minutes to state their case in front of the plenipotentiaries before being ejected from the conference hall. They, like the countless other hangers-on who descended upon Berlin – from Ottoman bondholders and railway magnates to press correspondents and Orthodox Christians – were left to loiter outside by the buffet thoughtfully provided by the German hosts, hoping to catch some scraps of gossip from the delegates during breaks in the plenary sessions.

In another respect, however, von Werner's portrait is wholly accurate: totally absent is any trace of a feminine presence. In its business aspects at least, the Congress of Berlin was an exclusively masculine affair. True, ladies were plentiful at the receptions and dinners laid on by the participating embassies; Lady Russell, the British ambassadress, and Countess Karolyi, her Austrian opposite number, vied for the prize for staging the most brilliant soirees, while the German crown princess graciously extended her hospitality to the representatives at a sumptuous feast on the final night of the Congress. Frederick Hamilton, a young British attaché, recalled seeing 'indefatigable feminine autograph-hunters' stalking the delegates at these evening entertainments in pursuit of signatures, determined to fill every leaf on the white vellum fans produced by an enterprising tradesman as a souvenir of the congress.[2] One further female personage not physically present in Berlin but deeply engrossed in its proceedings was Queen Victoria, who received long, amusing epistles on a daily basis from Disraeli, packed with gossip and witty pen-portraits of the leading personalities. Always her favourite Prime Minister, Disraeli delighted the Queen with his audacious brinkmanship, at one point calling for a special train to be prepared for his immediate departure – an effective ruse which forced Bismarck to cease blocking discussion of matters central to British interests. Upon his return, Victoria offered Disraeli honours and titles galore; he finally settled on the Royal Garter on condition that Lord Salisbury receive one too (a move which prompted some wags to quip that the Prime Minister had achieved not, as in his own words, 'peace with honour', but 'peace with *honours*').

But in the plenary sessions, and, more importantly, the late-night interviews between individual players where the real work of the congress was conducted, there was no place for the ladies. 'All questions are publicly introduced,' Disraeli wrote famously of Bismarck's conference method, 'and then privately settled.' Women had scant opportunity to intervene at either stage of this process. By the late nineteenth century, the influence that well-connected aristocratic ladies might have wielded in earlier times, when the rules governing diplomacy were far from settled, was on the wane. At home in Britain, the First and Second Reform Acts had enshrined the principle that membership of the political nation was open to men alone. Similarly (and inevitably), representing that political nation overseas was agreed to require qualities and attributes which only men could supply.

Women stood excluded from the diplomatic profession, as they did from so many professions in the late-Victorian era. Their role at Berlin in 1878 was as witness to history, not history's maker. And yet for all that, they were not mute witnesses, though they had not as yet learnt how to make their voices heard.

I

The Natural Order of Things

Esme Howard was standing knee-deep in water and seriously reconsidering his decision to go fishing without waders that morning when the news arrived that he had successfully passed the examination for the Diplomatic Service. It was a cold spring day in 1885 and the River Barle, which runs from the plains of Exmoor down to the Devonshire coast, was thick with salmon – an angler's dream. Howard was more than ready to indulge himself. It was his first proper holiday in over a year, following months of intensive coaching at Mr Scoones's famous crammer in Covent Garden, a venerable institution much frequented by young upper-class males with designs on the Civil Service. Howard's preparation for a career in diplomacy had, however, begun long before that. It was during his final schooldays at Harrow that he chose to forgo the gilded existence of a Cambridge undergraduate and to proceed, without delay, to acquiring the languages which had become a requirement of entry to Britain's diplomatic corps. There followed two years of a roving, peripatetic existence lodging in the homes of German artists, French clergymen and Italian spinsters, mastering their tongues and soaking up their culture. This latter task was, naturally, not without its pleasures. In Paris, Howard became a regular visitor to the Louvre, a habitué of the city's many theatres, and an occasional dinner guest at the British embassy on the exclusive Rue du Faubourg. Similarly, in Florence, he was rarely without an invitation to the balls, salons and clubs where the most brilliant company was to be found.

The telegram that arrived on that chilly morning in 1885 thus promised to bring to a close a long period of youthful uncertainty, preferably with glory. Howard seized it from the messenger boy and quickly scanned its contents. He was, it informed him, one of just four successful candidates that year, having earned a 'fair average' in every subject apart from précis writing, where he came top. 'I suppose,' Howard later reflected, 'that this indicated that I had a rather exceptional gift for picking out the pith and marrow of any diplomatic paper and I imagine that this stood me in good stead in later years.' With somewhat greater humility he added: 'I never expected to pass my first examination but, having done so, it all seemed, like nearly everything that has happened to me in life, to be a part of the natural order of things.'[1]

Many in late-Victorian Britain would have agreed that all was well in a world in which the nation's foreign affairs were conducted by men like Esme Howard. Modern diplomacy evolved in the nineteenth century as a profession for men, but it was only a small, privileged minority of men who could hope to join its ranks. This might have been the era of the industrial revolution and a triumphant bourgeoisie, but European politics retained much of its aristocratic flavour, and the business of diplomacy in particular continued to rely on an intangible but indispensable commodity: prestige. The rarefied world that Howard was soon to enter centred on the key political capitals of Paris, Vienna, St Petersburg and Berlin, cities that were home to a powerful cosmopolitan elite, unified by chains of inter-marriage more tangled than a ball of knotted wool and by codes of etiquette passed down more or less intact from the baroque court. With social weight and political power so closely aligned, diplomats shadowed the movements of high society, attending salons, balls and clubs during the season, and abandoning the city for fashionable spa towns or country retreats during the summer months.

In these circles, power was constantly on show, a kind of never-ending political theatre in which the imperial courts topped the bill. In Vienna, the seat of the Hapsburg rulers of Austria-Hungary, lavish balls were a way of life for the aristocracy, held at all times of the day. George Buchanan, posted there in the 1870s, attended one at Prince Schwarzenberg's palace which commenced at eleven in the morning and drew to a close at six in the evening.[2] Henry Bruce, posted to the Austrian capital thirty years later, was an avid fan of the court balls regularly thrown by the Emperor for the diplomatic corps, never failing to be dazzled by the beauty of the Hofburg's pink marble hall illuminated by candlelight.[3] The scene in Berlin was equally opulent. At his first ball at the Old Schloss in the 1880s, Vincent Corbett filed with his diplomatic colleagues through endless suites of reception rooms, noting the smart military officers in colourful gala dress along the way, until he reached the ornate throne room where members of the royal family eventually made their entrance – the ageing Empress creating quite a spectacle in her diamond-encrusted wheelchair.[4] Similar feasts for the eyes were on hand in St Petersburg, where entertaining at the Tsar's Winter Palace took place on an extravagant scale. As a young attaché, Frederick Hamilton had the good fortune to be present at one of Alexander II's famous *Bals des Palmiers,* at which a hundred enormous palm trees, grown especially for the occasion at the royal summer retreat at Tsarskoe Selo, were imported by road during the dead of winter to decorate the vast interior of the Nicolas Hall.[5] It was not unusual for the Tsar to entertain upwards of 4,000 guests at his regular court balls, at which the congregated ambassadors and their wives would dance the opening mazurka alongside the imperial family. This was followed by general dancing and a sit-down dinner at midnight, with every guest attended by a servant in gold-lace livery and each course announced by bugle fanfare.[6]

Going out and mixing in such elevated company was a fundamental part of the diplomat's job. The exercise of influence and the acquisition of information were rarely best achieved at one's desk in the chancery, and young attachés were expected to forge personal ties in whatever setting the occasion demanded. As well as dressing for dinners and balls, this frequently required them to take up various outdoor pursuits. George Buchanan, for instance, regularly hunted with the Austrian Chancellor, Count Andrássy, at Gödöllő, near Budapest, whilst Charles

Hardinge played tennis with the German ambassador in Constantinople and, a few years later, with the German crown prince and princess when he was posted in Berlin. Frederick Hamilton also became acquainted with the German royal family through manly exertions in the open air, rowing with the future Kaiser, William II, in the British embassy's four-oar boat, which was moored on the lake at Potsdam.

Ambassadors placed great premium on these informal contacts, demanding that their junior officers meet their social duties in full. Hardinge was sternly rebuked by his chief, Lord Dufferin, for retiring early from a ball at the Italian embassy in Constantinople: 'he expected all his young men to attend every dance and make themselves popular in Society by dancing till the end of the evening'.[7] Buchanan, by contrast, needed no such exhortation. In Rome in the 1870s, he often danced until five in the morning at one of the great palaces, 'the scene of constant entertainments'. Henry Bruce similarly enjoyed living it up in Vienna. A typical night for him started with a couple of receptions at neighbouring embassies followed by dinner and bridge at some fashionable apartment, and often concluded with a high-spirited game of passage football back at the chancery, or hot chocolate in the early hours at the Café de L'Europe.

———

Only young men accustomed to leading such a privileged lifestyle and at ease in the company of emperors and dukes could hope to operate effectively in this exclusive milieu. It was little wonder, then, that governments preferred to recruit their representatives from the same social class as the exalted persons with whom they were to deal. A diplomat's social position in England, as one Foreign Office chief explained to a Committee of MPs in 1861, 'should correspond with that which he will hold abroad':

> the members of our diplomatic body abroad are to mix in the best society; and you must therefore have people who are qualified by their social position in this country to enter into that society, otherwise your service there will be ill looked upon, and your attachés will be perfectly useless.[8]

Sir Andrew Buchanan (father of George), reflecting on his experience as ambassador at St Petersburg, echoed the sentiment: 'A man who had not a certain social position could not get into society,' he opined; 'I might introduce him into society, but people would not encourage him to come to their houses.' The ideal diplomat, in Buchanan's view, was the true gentleman, 'a man who has lived in good society at home, and who consequently can appear in good society abroad without attracting any remarks or observations'.[9] Appointing a man of uncertain social origins was a risky enterprise. 'Foreigners are particularly punctilious in those subjects,' warned Sir Augustus Paget, envoy-extraordinary in Italy: 'I generally find that when a new man is appointed to my legation, one of the first questions I am asked is, who is he; what are his relations; what class of society does he belong to, in short.'[10]

Quite apart from these considerations of rank, there were the more practical concerns of how to finance the lifestyle becoming of a representative of the Crown. Men joined the Diplomatic Service as unpaid attachés and could expect only meagre salaries for many years thereafter. Private means to supplement official pay were, therefore, indispensable, particularly if the young diplomat was to reside in the fashionable quarter of town, dress himself in suitable attire, join the smartest clubs and generally eat, drink and entertain in accordance with his position. Some cities were known to be fiendishly expensive; 'a young man cannot live', Sir Andrew Buchanan declared, 'in society at St Petersburg without a carriage'.[11] His son, George, only survived on his second secretary's salary of £1,000 in Vienna by cadging lifts in the ambassador's two-horse carriage ('one-horse carriages were tabooed in society') and through the kindness of friends, who put their theatre and opera boxes at his disposal. Paris was also notorious for soaking up men's personal fortunes; even the ambassador's salary of £10,000 was considered woefully inadequate by Earl Cowley, who occupied the post for fifteen years from 1852 and never sank less than £3,000 of his own wealth into embassy running costs per annum. Much of this was spent on entertaining, which was, in these capitals, a game of national one-upmanship which Britain could ill afford to lose. 'Giving dinners is an essential part of diplomacy,' Sir George Hamilton Seymour famously told a Parliamentary Select Committee in 1850: 'I have no idea of a man being a good diplomat who does not give good dinners.' He defended this view when called before MPs ten years later: 'At Vienna, and at St Petersburg, and other places,' Seymour observed, 'many of the people with whom the English minister is put in competition, are people of very great fortunes, and therefore his style of living must have some reference to the style of those magnates.'[12]

The illustrious social pedigree of Britain's diplomatic corps in the nineteenth century was certainly impressive. More than two-thirds of all senior appointments made between the 1850s and the eve of the First World War were of men belonging to the aristocracy or gentry, or closely connected to one or both.[13] This narrow, landed bias was even more pronounced in the diplomatic corps of the other great powers, with the possible exception of republican France. The Austrian diplomatic service, for instance, only admitted the sons of titled families, whilst the Russian system explicitly excluded merchants, peasants and anyone who paid taxes. Many British diplomats profited professionally by marrying foreign-born wives with titles; in 1860 Paget wed the elaborately named Walpurga Ehrengarde Helena de Hohenthal, the eldest daughter of an Austrian count. Some even claimed direct blood-ties with continental nobility: Claud Russell was a relative on his mother's side of the Vicomte de Peyronnet, whilst Charles Bentinck was both a kinsman of the Dutch Counts Bentick and a German *Reichsgraf* (and appeared accordingly as Count Bentick in the official Foreign Office list until 1914).[14]

It was not impossible for a lower-born man to make his way in diplomacy. The ranks of the early nineteenth-century service included such men as Sir Edward Thornton, son of an innkeeper, and Robert Liston Elliot, whose father kept a chemist's shop on Fenchurch Street. But these men were outliers in a field in which social position and diplomatic rank were intimately correlated. Those with fathers in trade were vastly outnumbered by the offspring of government ministers, Members of Parliament, senior public servants and high-ranking military officers. As for promotional prospects, men with landed backgrounds were more likely to win coveted posts in major European capitals where fortune and rank counted above all things, while their colleagues from humbler families had to make do with lower-status appointments to such places as Peking, Rio de Janeiro or Colombia.[15] Even here, however, a certain degree of social elegance was required when mixing with the status-conscious European colony or entertaining distinguished guests. Sir Rutherford Alcock, Britain's minister at Peking, for example, played host in 1871 to two French princes, the Duke of Edinburgh and his retinue, plus a large number of naval officers and English tourists. 'I do not think that any well-frequented hotel could be better filled than the British legation,' he remarked.[16]

A man keen to serve overseas but lacking a set of impeccable social credentials would find it easier to blend into the Consular Service, long regarded as diplomacy's poor relation. With the promise of inferior pay, a smaller pension, dire career prospects and, more often than not, deeply unpleasant climates, the Consular Service attracted an odd assortment of loners, chancers and climbers to its ranks. These included famous men of the age like David Livingstone and Richard Burton, but more typical were the exhausted colonial administrators looking for a sleepy retirement post, or the clapped-out backbenchers seeking a face-saving move from political life, or the long-serving public officials felt to deserve a pat on the back for services rendered, or the duller sons of clergymen and army officers who did not stand a chance of passing the Diplomatic Service exam. All these and more could be discovered in the Victorian Consular Service. They moved in a very different kind of society from their diplomatic peers: rough, rugged and made up of merchants, seamen, travellers and locals, who loitered in seedy port towns or trading outposts. Occasionally, a consul would secure a move into the Diplomatic Service, usually appointed for his specialist knowledge or highly valued linguistic skills: Alcock in Peking was one example; Sir William White in Constantinople was another. But these occasions were rare. Few consuls could hope to retire with such professional distinction. Elegance and position were the social lubricants that kept the wheels of diplomacy turning in the nineteenth century and members of the Consular Service could typically offer neither of these.[17]

One of the means by which the Foreign Office sustained the social uniformity of its personnel was ancient, simple and foolproof: nepotism. The first hurdle faced by any aspiring young diplomat was to obtain a nomination from the Foreign Secretary of the day, who treated the Foreign Office largely as his personal fiefdom. This was readily given to any candidate who was known personally to the minister, or whose good family name could be vouched for by trusted authorities, and it was unusual for requests to be received from wholly unsuitable quarters. The Earl of Clarendon, who served as Foreign Secretary in the 1850s, recalled receiving letters 'from persons who were what is, in common parlance, called the upper ranks of society, persons who could afford to give their sons the necessary income while they remained unpaid attachés at a foreign court'.[18] This system of patronage survived into the early twentieth century, ensuring that only those with the right connections stood any chance of entering the Service. Sir John Tilley obtained a nomination from Lord Salisbury through the good offices of an under-secretary who happened to be related to Tilley's mother.[19] James Rennell Rodd secured his nomination in 1880 from Salisbury's successor, Lord Granville, whose nephew was a close friend from Oxford and whom Rodd had met on several occasions at the latter's house.[20] Those with an established family history of service in diplomacy found the path to nomination even smoother. The Foreign Office list for the late nineteenth century reads like a genealogy of diplomatic dynasties: Cowleys, Russells and Malets abound. George Buchanan was, quite literally, born into the profession, his mother having given birth at the British legation in Copenhagen, where his father, Sir Andrew, was then minister.

Alongside wealth and family connections, the English public school – that great Victorian institution which moulded Britain's male elite – supplied another guarantor of gentility. Public schools were held in high regard by Foreign Office chiefs, not because they produced great scholars, but because they purportedly bred 'character', the ultimate attribute of any public servant. At these august establishments, a boy learned to be 'independent, manly and unselfish'; he acquired the 'habits of acting in a right, a large, and comprehensive manner'; he bowed to the 'duties and obligations' of the 'little world' of the school, and he developed the skills of forbearance and tact when dealing with his fellows. Flogging and fagging, hazing and games, gave boys 'all the manly and gentlemanlike qualities, which are essential in diplomacy'.[21] Moreover, the public school cultivated thoroughly *English* Englishmen 'of thoroughly English opinions' (regardless of exactly where they had been born), an important consideration when one's business was to send impressionable young men into alluringly foreign society.[22]

By the 1860s, a consensus was building within the Foreign Office in favour of university-educated men for much the same reason. 'One of the great objects should be to keep your attachés and secretaries Englishmen for as long as you can,' argued Henry Elliot, late minister at Naples in 1861; 'if you send them abroad too soon, they become foreigners before they are well into the service.'[23] A few years spent at some institution of higher learning – most commonly Oxford or Cambridge – thus provided an ideal finishing school for the would-be diplomat. The formal knowledge he might pick up along the way was of only secondary importance. Officials looked rather askance at any man with too brilliant a scholarly career behind him (when Henry Bruce asked an ambassador of his mother's acquaintance whether he should leave Eton early to learn languages abroad, he was told that it was 'much more important that I should stay on and row in the Eton Eight'). What mattered was that his character was sound and that he was schooled in the 'art of personal intercourse' upon which effective diplomacy relied.[24]

This narrow circle of schools and Oxbridge colleges produced (and faithfully reproduced) a diplomatic cadre united by educational privilege. Eton was the pre-eminent feeder school well into the twentieth century: as late as 1919, David Kelly felt a profound sense of inferiority on account of having attended a mere London day school (St Paul's) instead of one of the elite group 'from which practically the whole Foreign Office and Diplomatic Service were at that time recruited'.[25] When it came to university, Balliol was the Eton of the colleges; during

Rennell Rodd's time there in the late 1870s, there were no fewer than three other future ambassadors in his year (Cecil Spring-Rice, Arthur Hardinge and Louis Mallet), with George Curzon, a future Foreign Secretary, in the year below. From an early age, these young men were groomed for power and instilled with an unshakeable belief in their superior ability to rule. Henry Bruce had little to show by way of book-learning from his years at Eton, but what he departed with instead was:

> the sense of independence and of responsibility which made and still makes a British public-school boy fit to take his place in the world, fit, if called upon, to govern a province at an age when many a Continental boy, though able to run rings round his British counterpart in academic knowledge, can hardly travel to the next station down the line without a label round his neck.[26]

In 1856, and under pressure from Parliament for greater professionalism across the public service, an examination was introduced for candidates wishing to enter the Diplomatic Service or Foreign Office (the latter was recruited separately, as Foreign Office clerks had no obligation to serve overseas). This reform made no demonstrable difference to the class of men who were admitted to either. A nomination from the Foreign Secretary was still obligatory, and in subject matter the exam mirrored the classical education which was the typical fare of the public schools. It was valued by Foreign Office chiefs more for its efficiency in keeping out 'persons notoriously incompetent' than in driving up the intellectual calibre of recruits.[27] The introduction of a qualifying test, however notional, was nonetheless of significance, as it signalled the beginning of diplomacy's slow transformation from a preserve of the aristocratic dilettante to something approaching a fully fledged profession.[28] Earlier in the century, it was commonplace for upper-class youths to attach themselves to an embassy for a year or two, using their diplomatic status as a calling card in Society, and doing very little – if any – gainful work for the British Crown. Although usually unpaid, this state-sponsored gap year for unoccupied aristocratic males was deeply frowned upon by the 1850s, by which time more formal career structures were emerging across all the European diplomatic services. Diplomacy, the Earl of Clarendon declared in 1861, was 'no longer the idle and sleepy profession it used to be . . . there is reputation and distinction to be gained in it, and young men of intelligence, or their parents for them, have been attracted to it more as a career than formerly they used to be'.[29]

A corollary of this new approach was that by the later nineteenth century, aspiring diplomats were required to study foreign languages with far greater application than before. Esme Howard's two years of lodging with French pastors and German painters in preparation for the exam was not untypical. Vincent Corbett learnt enough French in his six months in Caen to read racy novels and converse 'with tolerable fluency', although his German studies in a small town near Cassel were momentarily derailed by an evening of heavy drinking with students from the local school of forestry. Having failed the exam on his first attempt, Corbett returned to Germany the following summer, but would probably have learnt more had he spent fewer Sunday afternoons sampling the local wines with his fellow lodgers, which included William Tyrrell, later ambassador to Paris. Henry Bruce also shared his billet in Hanover with other candidates for the Diplomatic Service, where their hostess, 'a stately dame' with two daughters, 'jabbered German at us all day long'. He far preferred the bearded widow whose *pension* became his temporary home in Florence, although was unnerved by the maid, Giola, who entered his room at all times of day without knocking, including bath times.

Back in London, most young men subsequently found their way, like Howard, to Scoones's crammer on Garrick Street. William Baptiste Scoones knew more than any other man in England about how to get his students safely through the Diplomatic Service and Foreign Office exam. When John Tilley tried for the Foreign Office in 1893, all but one of the successful candidates recruited over the preceding twenty years had passed through Scoones's trusty hands. His crack team of tutors drilled their students in recommended texts like Adam Smith's *Wealth of Nations* and J. S. Mill's *Principles of Political Economy*, and taught them 'all the tricks of tackling examination papers and the correct answers to recurrent "catch" questions in French, German and Latin'.[30] Some stayed for a few months, others for a year or more, tackling their studies with varying degrees of dedication. Howard lived in a house on Half Moon Street belonging to his father's former butler and with iron self-discipline allowed himself little time for living it up in town. Vincent Corbett, by contrast, failed the exam on his first attempt having overslept after a night of poker, missing the English dictation paper as a result. He returned to Scoones the following year, but pleasures again took precedence over study, this time in the form of riotous nights at the Fielding Club, a well-known haunt of Oscar Wilde and Lord Queensberry. Henry Bruce kept up a similarly Woosteresque lifestyle whilst at Scoones, spending a third of his annual allowance on tickets for the Gaiety Theatre and dining weekly with friends at the Savoy. Both men finally passed the exam on their third try, a triumph which prompted Bruce to motor drunkenly to Eton in the early hours with his pals, some twenty miles away (unfortunately, the car gave out halfway along the route, forcing the party to cadge a lift with a passing farm cart and then catch a commuter train at Slough – 'in our rumpled evening finery, unshaven and dropping by that time with sleep' – back to London the following morning).

Getting into the Diplomatic Service was, then, an expensive business. Parents were expected to finance several years of lengthy study trips abroad and stints of cramming at Scoones – on top, of course, of the routine costs of educating their sons at a good public school and, more often than not, at university too. It was not unusual for candidates, even those who applied themselves rather more soberly to the task in hand than Corbett or Bruce, to take the exam several times before securing a place. Rennell Rodd missed out on his first attempt due to illegible handwriting ('a severe blow to my vanity') and was forced to try again the following year (when, gratifyingly, he came top). The examination gradually became more taxing intellectually, and by 1880, it was properly competitive, with a fixed number of candidates vying for each vacancy. Thereafter followed a series of reforms designed to add further rigour to the recruitment process: in 1892 the exams for

Foreign Office clerkships and Diplomatic Service attachéships were combined; in 1905 the minimum age for entry was raised to twenty-two in a bid to attract more university graduates; and in 1907 control over nominations was transferred to a new selection board, which substituted the old begging letters sent to the Foreign Secretary with an interrogation of the candidates in person.

This hardly eliminated the power of patronage, though. The minister's private secretary sitting on the board and the Secretary of State still retained final approval of all nominations. Open competition, now firmly established across the Home Civil Service, remained anathema to Foreign Office chiefs: who knew how many middle-class upstarts might try their hand at a career in diplomacy? Moreover, the fact that attachés new in post could still expect to receive no salary for the first two years was a potent deterrent to young men of modest means. A private income of anything less than £400 a year was deemed insufficient by the selection board, meaning in practice that nominations were bestowed upon sons of only the wealthiest families. As late as 1914, David Kelly was dismayed to find, upon arriving at the selection board wearing an ordinary suit, that the dozen or so other candidates were, to a man, dressed in tailcoats. Fortunately for Kelly, the board forgave this sartorial faux pas and issued his nomination, but it was an early and revealing indication of just what kind of profession he was shortly to join.

All newcomers spent their first days in the job at the Foreign Office in London, despatched to one of the departments housed in Gilbert Scott's grand Italianate palace, which occupied a large plot of land between Whitehall and St James's Park. Scott had been thwarted in his desire to erect a Gothic temple by Lord Palmerston, whose tastes were firmly classical; but the resulting building, which opened for business in 1868, and which was home also to the India, Colonial and Home Offices, was nonetheless a marked improvement on the cramped conditions which earlier generations of clerks had endured when the Foreign Office was based in small, mean, decrepit buildings on Downing Street.[31] There, it had been repeatedly necessary to prop up the buckling floor with beams when foreign dignitaries came calling, and on one famous occasion the ceiling bulged and descended on to the exact spot where, only moments before, the Foreign Secretary Lord Malmesbury had been sitting. By mid-century, all were agreed that housing a great office of state in such incommodious and ramshackle quarters was positively damaging to the international prestige of the nation. On a more practical note, roomier offices were urgently needed to accommodate the additional clerical staff engaged to deal with a dramatically expanding volume of overseas business. As new missions sprang up in such places as South America, the Levant and the Far East, and the coming of the telegraph eased their communications with London, the amount of paperwork passing through the Foreign Office soared. In 1853, its clerks handled around 35,000 despatches over the course of the year. Half a century later, that figure was approaching 100,000.[32]

Despite this upturn in activity and increased manpower, those recruited in the last decades of the nineteenth century joined, by the standards of Whitehall more generally, a small and tightly knit community. Even by the time of the First World War, the workforce of the Foreign Office in London numbered no more than 176 souls, including lowly office keepers and messengers. Ministers and senior officials took the trouble of making the acquaintance of junior staff when they arrived, and it was the accepted practice, within departments, to address colleagues by their surnames only, a far homelier and more collegial form of greeting than the frightfully stiff 'Mr' or 'Sir' common in the Home Civil Service. At moments of great crisis or war, men could be found at their desks into the early hours of the morning, but in normal times the hours of work were highly agreeable: clerks were not expected to appear before noon or stay much beyond seven or eight, leaving their evenings free for other pursuits – and invitations were usually plentiful. The daily routine was enlivened by the presence of canine companions (Bruce brought his bulldog into work with him every day) and diplomatic colleagues on leave, who would drop in regularly for tea and gossip. Even departmental heads might enter into the fraternal jollity. Francis Bertie, later ambassador to Paris, used to showcase his talents at high kicks and slicing candles in two with a sword whilst Head of the Eastern Department in the 1890s (although he could also be cruel: John Tilley recalled how 'The Bull' would fling files on the floor for his underlings to re-sort if he found even a single paper out of place).[33]

The relationship between senior clerks and their juniors was somewhat akin to that between a house master and his pupils, or between a prefect and a younger boy. The collective ethos and traditions of the Foreign Office were transmitted not by formal instruction or stringent supervision, but, as in the best schools, by observation, experience and, occasionally, hard knocks. Very quickly, new men would learn to recognise the grey liveries of the Queen's Messengers as they dashed in to pick up the 'bag'. After a few weeks, they would become personally known to the long-serving doorkeepers, who would greet them by name (no one bothered much about security back then). They would in time come to know the legendary figures of the Foreign Office: Mr Hertslet in the Library, whose father had been librarian before him and who, it was said, donned a frock coat when speaking to the Secretary of State on the telephone; the permanent secretary, Sir Thomas Sanderson, known as 'Lamps' on account of his enormous round spectacles, and described by one of his successors as 'a survival from the mild hilarities of nineteenth-century *Punch*'; or Eyre Crowe, a career clerk, whose flaming red hair, crushed under an ancient Borsalino hat, was hard to miss as he tramped through the corridors and out onto Horse Guards Parade punctually at one for lunch at the Carlton Club.[34] Those with first-hand knowledge of the man told of his insatiable passion for order, from the appropriate length of a minute, to the width of blotting paper, or the method for fastening a ribbon around a dossier. 'His life,' as one colleague put it, 'was the Foreign Office and nothing but the Foreign Office.'[35]

These eccentric characters, combined with a congenial, clubbish atmosphere, somewhat compensated for the monotonous nature of the work dished out to new men, at least before the reforms of 1903–5. This consisted in the main of docketing and filing away correspondence from overseas missions as it came in; ciphering and deciphering an endless stream of telegrams; sealing bags and envelopes; and copying out inordinate volumes of papers by hand. Typewriters, although known to exist, were rarely sighted by officers before the First World War. Robert Vansittart once spied one sitting under a tarpaulin 'like a gun at Dover Harbour', but was warned off by his head of department, who 'burst in exclaiming: "Leave that thing alone! Don't you know we're in a hurry?"'[36] Most communications would be laboriously copied out using indelible ink and then pressed onto a gelatine pad to make duplicates for distribution to under-secretaries, ministers and, most importantly, the Queen (Victoria refused to read typed documents and always received the top copy with the darkest and silkiest ink). After 1905, these routine duties – what some contemptuously described as 'bottle-washing' – were transferred to an expanding class of lower-division clerks, who were recruited via a less demanding exam and enjoyed almost no prospect of promotion to the prestigious first division where Foreign Office careers were made. Under this new system, members of the latter, even in the junior grades, now had an opportunity to offer ministers proper advice on substantive policy issues. Relieved of low-level paperwork, they were free to draft memoranda on the pressing questions of the day and cultivate a genuine expertise more in line with their intellectual abilities.[37] These reforms produced a welcome change for Foreign Office clerks, who expected to spend most of their careers in London.

Recruits to the Diplomatic Service, by contrast, usually received their first overseas posting after only six or so months of slogging it out in a department. Most men hoped for a golden ticket to one of the plum posts in Europe. George Buchanan, in fact, was in London for just a few weeks before being called to Vienna by his father, who was head of mission there. It was, Buchanan recalled, 'a delightful post' for a young attaché, and as an ambassador's son he enjoyed automatic acceptance into Society. Robert Vansittart was similarly fortunate to win a prime first posting, in his case to Paris. Here, having discovered in the chancery two earnest young secretaries willing to shoulder most of the work, he was able to devote much time to the agreeable pursuits of horse-racing and play-writing. The hours of work in overseas missions were not dissimilar to those in London, although the volume of business needing immediate attention could fluctuate dramatically. At the end of the Congress of Berlin in 1878, Frederick Hamilton sat down with fourteen others at the British embassy to translate the 15,000-word treaty from French into English, starting work at 6 p.m. and completing it at five the next morning. Similarly, Charles Hardinge slaved away until 3 a.m. every night processing telegrams at the embassy in Constantinople during the lead-up to Britain's invasion of Egypt in 1882, although helpfully his ambassador, Lord Dufferin, 'always sent us an excellent supper at midnight'.

Often these flurries of activity would be followed by long stretches of relative tranquillity, and in the less important posts – in South America, for example, or a small German principality – diplomats could find themselves with ample time for leisure. How exactly this spare time was filled varied from place to place. In the big European capitals, there was no shortage of diversions. On top of the official functions and court entertainments, young attachés joined clubs, went to the races, visited the theatre and dined out with fellow members of the diplomatic corps. In St Petersburg in the 1870s, embassy staff amused themselves by tobogganing down forty-foot hills of ice in the winter, and accompanied their chief during warmer months on bear-hunting expeditions, necessitating a five-hour train ride into the countryside. Charles Hardinge found plenty of time whilst in Berlin to indulge his artistic leanings, regularly sketching the lakes at Potsdam and organising an ambitious excursion to capture the landscape from Dresden and the Black Forest to as far as Prague. When Society abandoned town for the summer months, ambassadors usually went too, leaving their juniors at something of a loose end. In Rome in the late 1880s, Vincent Corbett began these lazy days with a swim every morning in the Tiber, and concluded them with 'pleasant and irresponsible evenings' at his club. Later in the summer, Corbett would join the ambassador at his hotel in Sorrento, bathing or sailing in the bay and playing baccarat after dinner. In smaller posts, where social amenities were less plentiful, outdoor pursuits often dominated. In Japan, George Buchanan kept a small stud of racing ponies, whilst in Bulgaria he organised a weekly hockey match at which members of the diplomatic corps, plus the Bulgarian foreign minister, could regularly be seen charging up and down the field outside the British legation, even in heavy snow.

If the community found in the Foreign Office in London was akin to that of a public school or gentleman's club, the embassy or legation functioned more like a surrogate family. In the early nineteenth century, this was quite literally the case. An aristocratic youth would be 'attached' to the household of an ambassador, dining with his family and sleeping under his roof. Sir Minto Farquhar recalled enjoying an open invitation to the ambassador's table whilst serving under the elder Lord Cowley and his successor, Lord Melbourne, in Vienna in the 1830s. This system, he believed, had

> a most excellent effect upon the embassy itself, for we all lived there like one family . . . I think it produced a good feeling on the part of the attachés towards their chief, for I believe that there was nothing which they might have asked that their attachés would not have done, not only as a public duty, but as a great pleasure to themselves.[38]

This familial intimacy became rather less intense as professionalism set in after mid-century, but it continued to characterise relations between many an attaché and his chief. Sir Edward Malet was a committed prac- titioner of the old traditions. In Berlin in the 1880s he established a club room for the bachelor members of the embassy and invited them to dine with him three nights out of every five, all year round. Likewise, Lord Dufferin extended a fatherly welcome to his staff in Rome, where junior officers were always addressed as 'dear child'. When not out carousing, Bruce spent many a cosy evening in with the ambassador in Vienna, Lord Goschen, playing hunt the thimble or doing acrostics; after trans- ferring with Goschen to Berlin, Bruce became a firm favourite, on most days sharing with the ambassador a four-course gourmet lunch prepared by the embassy's two French chefs, accompanied by a different wine for each course ('and there was no dodging any of it', he recalled).

Much hinged on this relationship. Ambassadors acted as patron and protector to younger men, supplying introductions to powerful friends abroad and often helping to secure their next posting. This closeness tended to further entrench the dominance of the upper-class type; as Sir Andrew Buchanan noted in 1871, 'I always live with my secretaries on terms of the greatest intimacy, confidence and friendship; and it is not everybody that I should like to receive in my house on those terms.'[39] Of course, some attachés clashed with their chiefs, and some heads of mission resented footing the bill for feeding their juniors, or refused to do so altogether. Occasionally the intensity of the quasi-paternal bond could become stifling: Henry Bruce suffered a nervous breakdown towards the end of his Berlin posting, partly triggered by how heavily Goschen had come to depend on him, even demanding that Bruce arrange the *placement* at dinner and supervise his domestic servants. On the whole, though, diplomats of all ranks – ambassadors and attachés alike – found comfort and consolation in the bosom of their embassy family. The close fellowship of co-patriots greatly lightened the burden of living far from English shores. Sitting in the chancery next to his colleagues, men who had attended the same schools, the same universities and the same classes at Scoones, the late nineteenth-century diplomat might have felt, with some satisfaction, that he had found his proper place in the world. God was in his heaven and old Etonians ruled the Diplomatic Service.

Yet for all this, male camaraderie alone could not nourish and sustain the ties which bound British diplomatic communities together overseas. For that, diplomats turned to another source altogether, a group with no formal stake in this elite masculine profession, but whose presence was indispensable. Where, then, in the natural order of things, stood the women?

2

Through the Mill

Lady Mary Fraser could be something of a snob. The most tedious task by far which befell her as wife of the secretary of embassy in Vienna in the early 1880s was the procuring of invitations for itinerant Britons who turned up clutching letters of recommendation from the Foreign Office in London. Holders of these 'soup tickets' – as they were derogatorily known in the Service – caused Lady Mary no end of worry, especially the women, as one never quite knew whether they could be trusted not to appear at a royal garden party 'in a serge skirt and cotton blouse'. On one occasion Lady Mary was obliged to present at court a lady of uncertain origins who arrived at the palace 'in a short all round frock, displaying the last thing anybody expected to behold just then, – a neat pair of ankles'. Horrified, Lady Mary marched her companion towards the imperial dais to be received by the Empress Elisabeth, trying as hard as she could to shut out 'the glances of amazement which followed us up that room'. Visitors of this kind, Lady Mary remarked, 'do no kind of credit to their introducers'.

Observing correct etiquette at all times had proved similarly testing in an earlier posting to Peking. There, Lady Mary struck from her visiting list the wife of a French diplomat, an American divorcée 'of darkly suspicious antecedents', who, it transpired, had shot her first husband dead. 'Her appearance and atmosphere, the perfumes she used and the gowns she wore, would have made it impossible to bow to her in Europe,' Lady Mary wrote disparagingly. Moreover, she played the piano just a little *too* well, leading Lady Mary to conclude that her proper spousal duties were being badly neglected: 'I have my doubts as to whether a woman who is not obliged to earn her living profession-ally has quite a right to practise six hours a day while servants look after her children and her husband is trying to write despatches in a contigu-ous apartment.'[1]

These observations might seem catty and superior to modern eyes, but in truth, Lady Mary was simply performing the role expected of her as a high-ranking diplomatic wife. Keeping up appearances was only Rule One in the unofficial handbook that women who married into the Service had to learn – and learn quick. Their routine responsibilities were seemingly endless. Wives arranged for the safe transportation of children, servants and belongings from post to post. Once in situ, they searched for suitable lodgings and hunted down the necessary furnishings to make a proper English home. During the day, they supervised a team of cooks, maids, nannies and gardeners, whilst in the evening they played gracious hostess at embassy functions. They gave away prizes at the Queen's birth-day party and distributed children's treats at Christmas. They volunteered for good causes and joined committees ad infinitum. All this and more diplomatic wives did; willingly, uncomplainingly, reluctantly, or down-right resentfully, they submitted, as Mary Fraser's husband phrased it when they first arrived in Vienna, to being 'put through the mill' for the good of their country.

As a result, women were everywhere and nowhere in the world of old diplomacy. No official function, from the set-piece court ball to the intimate dinner at-home, was complete without a feminine presence. Quite apart from wives, the society inhabited by diplomats was over-flowing with ladies – queens and princesses, aristocrats and salonnières – whose company was keenly sought. Out of these delicate mouths came some of the most brilliant conversation, fascinating gossip and valuable secrets to be had anywhere in town. And yet, for all this, women were not men's equals in diplomacy. They did not represent their sovereigns: only men could do that. They did not sign treaties or conclude negotiations: only men could do that. They were not summoned to urgent conferences at times of great crisis: only their husbands' presence was required at such moments. They were not privy to conversations over cigars at the dinner table after the ladies had retired, or to the masculine confidences exchanged over whisky in the clubs to which their husbands belonged. The place of women in the history of nineteenth-century diplomacy is paradoxical. They were both present and not present – an ambiguity which might, indeed, be said to capture much of the Victorian woman's experience, not only of diplomacy but of public life in general.

It was not, of course, always this way. In the early modern court, women who ruled as monarchs in their own right were entitled to treat foreign policy as their royal prerogative. Queen Elizabeth I instructed her ministers with the self-belief of one who knew that the hand of providence was behind her. The doctrine of divine right ensured that Elizabeth would rule as well as reign, regardless of sex. As sovereign, she hand-picked every ambassador and expected to receive full reports concerning all weighty matters in which England's interests were at stake. She sought counsel from a wide circle of advisors, nearly all male, but freely disregarded any view which failed to coincide with her own. Elizabeth could not, of course, wholly dismiss the fact of her femininity. As a single, childless woman, her matrimonial prospects fuelled endless speculation and political faction, not least due to the considerable diplomatic consequences of marriage to a foreign prince. Such a possibility brought England's alliances on the continent, her hard-won Protestant identity and the future of her throne into play. Yet Elizabeth did not permit these considerations to dent her authority. Male monarchs, after all, were not untroubled by such political dilemmas when choosing a consort, and where matters of the heart collided with great questions of state, Elizabeth proved as shrewd a political operator as any. In short, Elizabethan foreign policy was very much the personal creation of Elizabeth. It cannot be understood or explained without her.[2]

Three centuries on, Britain was once again ruled by a strong-willed woman of impressive longevity who lent her name to an era. Like

Elizabeth, Queen Victoria was deeply engrossed in her nation's foreign affairs. She was encouraged and guided in this during the early years of her reign by her husband, Prince Albert, a native of Saxe-Coburg, whose preoccupation with the fate of central Europe was quickly shared by the young queen. It was after his death in 1861 that Victoria's head for diplomacy became truly her own. She pored over Foreign Office despatches, weighed in on ambassadorial appointments and made successive prime ministers fully cognisant of her personal views on every major foreign policy question. Victoria's zealous regard for the prestige of the British flag was vented with particular force in the late 1870s, when she urged bold action to protect vital trade routes in the eastern Mediterranean from the Russian menace through alliance with the Ottoman Empire. When Russia threatened to intervene (ostensibly, at least) to protect persecuted Christians in Bulgaria, Victoria flooded her Prime Minister, Benjamin Disraeli, with daily letters and hourly telegrams and threatened abdication if he insisted on following 'a miserable cotton-spinning milk and water, peace-at-any-price policy which the Queen will not submit to'.[3]

Yet Victoria, unlike Elizabeth, was no absolute monarch. She could make her feelings known, but she was unable to dictate policy; she was a constitutional monarch with a Parliament, Cabinet and Prime Minister to reckon with, not to mention that nebulous but undeniably potent entity: public opinion. Rarely did all these volatile components concur exactly with Victoria's instincts and all too often – particularly under Whig or Liberal administrations – the Queen found herself in direct conflict with her ministers. What Victoria *could* do, however, and which the childless Elizabeth could not, was to project British influence in Europe through the matrimonial careers of her numerous offspring. The union of her eldest daughter, Vicky, to Prince Frederick of Prussia in 1858, was pursued by the Queen and Prince Albert with high hopes of securing a liberal future for a soon-to-be unified Germany. This was followed by Princess Alice's marriage to Louis of Hesse four years later. All told, Victoria placed her direct descendants on no fewer than ten European thrones and dozens of lesser royal houses.[4] The exact political significance of these matches is difficult to judge.

English-style liberalism was a fragile seed amidst Bismarck's campaign of 'iron and blood' in Germany, whilst the fiendishly complex family trees of the rest of Victoria's brood frequently fostered discord and division rather than harmony and warm feelings towards Britain. Marriage was evidently a very imperfect tool of diplomacy in late nineteenth-century Europe, and, ultimately, far inferior to those available to a queen regnant like Elizabeth three centuries before.

Neither Elizabeth nor Victoria was involved, of course, in the day-to-day aspects of diplomacy. In both eras, those tasks were formally delegated to ambassadors and envoys, all invariably male. In the early modern period, however, the diplomatic profession was ill-defined and the absence of formal, Crown-sponsored credentials was no bar to entry. Crucially, this created possibilities for well-placed women of rank to enter the fray. Before the nineteenth century, international politics were inter-dynastic politics, meaning that wives, mothers, daughters and sisters were often crucial intermediaries who, through their correspondence or personal relationships with members of rival courts, could materially influence events – from building alliances to waging wars. Wives, especially, were often in possession of the most sensitive secrets and were fully briefed on political affairs, even issuing instructions on their husbands' behalves during periods of absence. Noblewomen at foreign courts, moreover, could gain intimate and extended access to a female sovereign through the office of lady-in-waiting, which admitted its holder to the royal bedchamber where lasting connections and bonds of trust could be forged. This potentially made an ambassadress an extremely powerful figure. By the seventeenth century, the dynastic capital of wives weighed heavily – sometimes decisively – in the selection of ambassadors for service at foreign courts. If a prospective ambassadress's kinship connections made her likely to succeed in ingratiating herself with the Queen (especially a queen dowager or queen regent), the odds on her husband's appointment were immeasurably improved.[5]

This world of courtly influence and inter-dynastic politics was, naturally, much changed by Victoria's time. The loss of direct political influence for the monarchy occurred perhaps with greater speed in

Britain than elsewhere (explained, at least in part, by Victoria's long period of mourning following Albert's death). The royal courts of continental Europe, by contrast, retained their irresistible political pull for much longer. But even these were eventually incorporated into formalised bureaucracies, an evolution which recast the dynamics of diplomacy along more recognisably modern lines. The question of who was or was not a diplomat became far less open to debate after the Congress of Vienna of 1814–15, where a codified hierarchy of diplomatic rank – starting with ambassadors and moving down to chargés d'affaires – was agreed, together with fixed codes of protocol and precedence. The convening of international conferences to settle great questions, such as those thrown up by the aftermaths of war, became the norm. By 1878, when the Congress of Berlin met to bring the Eastern crisis to a satisfactory conclusion, elaborate and well-oiled machinery for running negotiations was in place. Untried diplomatic methods thus became established diplomatic tradition, and with every international gathering, every bilateral negotiation, every official entertainment, the European diplomatic corps came to recognise itself more and more as a serious profession.[6]

What did these transformations mean for women? On the face of it, one might assume that a more formalised structure for diplomacy spelt death for that informal influence which noblewomen had wielded in earlier times. One might further assume that, in Britain, the rise of a new ideology of 'separate spheres', which prescribed an ideal of privatised feminine domesticity founded on hearth and home, would have diminished the possibilities for women's political self-expression, including in the realm of diplomacy. There is some truth in these assumptions, but they do not tell the whole story. It was certainly the case that a chasm between politicking and propriety began to open up beneath British women's feet in the decades following the French Revolution. Fears for the safety of the social and domestic status quo made politics a perilous terrain for women, who had to step carefully in order to keep to the narrow path of what was called 'legitimate influence'. Yet many women found this a less restrictive byway than expected; it was possible to deploy feminine virtue as rhetorical cover for a whole range of public activities, be it philanthropy, anti-slavery agitation or patriotic propaganda directed against the French (just so long, of course, as they studiously avoided anything with even a whiff of feminism – that dangerous revolutionary ideology – about it). Even the most impassioned advocates of woman's 'special mission' recognised that, by sticking to these rules, its dutiful pursuit did not preclude a publicly spirited interest in politics; this, as arch-moralist Sarah Stickney Ellis remarked, was 'a serious subject, and one which ought to appeal to every mother's bosom'.[7]

The notion of separate spheres seems especially unhelpful in the case of women of rank and wealth, who, of all classes of females, were the most likely to be found moving in diplomatic circles in the nineteenth century. This type of woman continued to enjoy much latitude within a political system which, if increasingly representative in form, remained unmistakeably aristocratic in style. As in earlier periods, aristocratic women entered the game of politics not for individual glory on the field, but as team players, with the collective interests of their family or dynasty uppermost in their minds. The Society hostess was a pre-eminent figure in mid-Victorian politics, and her efforts to advance the careers of male kith and kin could extend well beyond the purely national political scene. The services of the Foreign Secretary's wife, for instance, were indispensable for cultivating new allies for her husband and nurturing existing ones. Everywhere it was agreed that Lord Palmerston, who served as Foreign Secretary on three separate occasions (and Prime Minister on one), was extraordinarily fortunate to have a wife so skilled in the art of entertaining. Lady Palmerston was the acknowledged queen of the London social scene. An invitation to one of her soirées meant membership of the elite club which encompassed mid-Victorian high society, whilst to be admitted to Lady Palmerston's legendary tea room, the inner sanctum where she received only her most valued guests, was incontrovertible proof of having arrived on the political map. As befitted the wife of the Foreign Secretary, these were truly cosmopolitan affairs, with foreign diplomats and their wives pressing up against ministers and backbenchers in the crush to pass the vestibule and jostling with pressmen and bankers in the slow-moving queue on the grand staircase. The historian can only guess at how many useful introductions, interesting conversations and mutually advantageous understandings were transacted within the walls of Carlton House Terrace or Cambridge House on Piccadilly, where Lady Palmerston conducted her unique brand of tea-table diplomacy.[8]

Later in the century, Lady Derby could not rival her predecessor when it came to large-scale entertainments, but she nevertheless made her presence felt through the cultivation of close contacts with powerful men. Not only was Mary Derby wife of the Conservative Foreign Secretary between 1874 and 1878, but she was stepmother through a previous marriage to Lord Salisbury, who conducted most of the diplomatic legwork for Britain at the Congress of Berlin and who would go on to fill the office of Foreign Secretary in four different ministries, three of which he simultaneously led as Prime Minister. Alongside these highly placed male kin, Mary Derby kept up a regular correspondence with senior diplomats, such as Lord Cowley and Sir Robert Morier. She received frequent reports from the latter in Berlin, who believed that his advice would be more readily noted by Lord Derby if placed before him by his wife 'between tea and seltzer water time', instead of on his desk by an underling at the Foreign Office.[9] During the Eastern Crisis of 1876–8, Lady Derby extended her diplomatic network to include Count Schuvalov, the Russian ambassador, to whom she fed a great deal of confidential information concerning Cabinet discussions over the unfolding power play in the eastern Mediterranean. Like her husband, an advocate of conciliation with Russia, Lady Derby's interventions enraged the bellicose Queen Victoria; they also did little ultimately to advance Lord Derby's cause with his ministerial colleagues, and he resigned soon afterwards, having made no progress in dissuading Disraeli from pursuing an anti-Russian course.[10] Nonetheless, Mary Derby's ability to insert herself into foreign policy debates at the highest level proves that aristocratic women in Britain were no strangers to diplomacy. Even if they played the game on behalf of others, they understood its rules well enough, and it was a foolish man who believed he could win on his own.

Young men posted abroad also learnt to appreciate the usefulness of female allies. Just as foreign dignitaries flocked to parties at Cambridge House, so did British diplomats hurry to the salons of Lady Palmerston's counterparts in continental Europe. James Rennell Rodd consistently sought out the company of women, keenly aware of their status as the opinion-leaders of Society and distributors of patronage. In Berlin, he eagerly attended Princess Radziwill's exclusive gatherings, conscious that his hostess's opinion 'conceded or denied a social passport to the latest-joined attaché'. Later in Cairo, he was a regular guest of the Princess Nazli, one of the few Egyptian ladies permitted to receive European gentlemen: her 'budget of information was always interest-ing'. Finally in Rome, Rennell Rodd frequented the weekly receptions of the old Duchess Massimo and the Marchesa Pallavicini, where 'an after-glow of the old stately life' was perceptible as late as 1902.[11] If diplomacy involved knowing and being known by the right people, then these *grandes dames*, with their extensive social networks, would prove most valuable friends to any ambitious young man.

Court entertainments were, like salons and receptions, mixed occa-sions carefully orchestrated along gender lines. At court balls in Vienna, guests stood in a wide circle formation; the men gathered along one side, the women on the other, awaiting the entrance of the Emperor and Empress, who would slowly make their way round the lines exchanging predictable pleasantries. Another Viennese tradition was the *Comtessin Zimmer*, a room reserved at every ball for the exclusive use of the unmarried girls; there they would retreat after each dance, flush-faced and giggling, sometimes with partners in tow, and safe from the watchful eyes of mothers or older married sisters. Balls were, of course, perfect venues for making advantageous matches, an activity largely under feminine supervision. But even here, diplomats had to be on their guard. John Gregory recalled an incident in Vienna when Princess Fürstenberg espied the young man she had earmarked for her daughter's hand waltzing with another partner: 'Unhesitatingly the old lady, in a fit of uncontrolled jealousy, rushed into the fray and tore down the hair of the offender.' Fortunately, one of the ladies of the British embassy was on hand to restore peace; Gregory wondered, perhaps not entirely in jest, whether 'her intervention had more lasting effect on Anglo-Austrian relations than a thousand official *démarches* at the Ballplatz about subjects in which not a soul was interested'.[12]

It was, perhaps, appropriate that a lady of the diplomatic corps should have been the one to intervene, for although young diplomats might seek powerful female patrons, it was their wives who were expected to take the lead in cultivating feminine society. The paying and receiving of calls filled many hours of a diplomatic wife's day and followed a strict code of etiquette. On Thursdays in Vienna, Mary Fraser was forced to endure the tedious niceties of 'Place Day', when the ladies of the corps were expected to visit Countess Goess, the Empress's *grande maîtresse*, at home. On entering, each lady performed a 'plongeon' (a shallow curtsey), shook her hostess's hand, and then either retreated to the outer ring of chairs or, if her rank permitted, took the place of whichever lady was presently seated on the sofa next to the Countess. 'No tea was served,' Fraser recalled, 'and the conversation was utterly impersonal, three interesting subjects, the Imperial family, politics, and gossip, being tabooed. One never did overtime on those visits!'[13] Meriel Buchanan, whose father was ambassador to St Petersburg before and during the First World War, would regularly accompany her mother on visits to the Empress and countless grand duchesses:

Always it was the same procedure: a few minutes' wait in a warm, scented ante-room, a ceremonious opening of doors, a series of curtsies, ten minutes' conversation, a gracious dismissal, more curtsies, more opening and shutting of doors, somebody helping one into coat and overshoes, a drive back to the Embassy.[14]

In countries where women were traditionally secluded, such as Turkey or Egypt, it was wives alone who could make the acquaintance of the ladies of the court. When Madame Turkhan Pasha, the wife of a

Turkish diplomat, called upon his wife in Constantinople, John Tilley had to leave the house whilst his manservant hid, and the whole visit was conducted under the surveillance of an elderly duenna (or chaperone), who sat in the next room with the door open.[15] Similarly in Cairo, Rennell Rodd's wife, Lilias, 'paid visits to a certain number of cultivated and agreeable Egyptian ladies', whose salons, apart from that of Princess Nazli, were off limits to any male diplomat.[16]

Paying these courtesies was a necessary part of the spousal role and indispensable to the never-ending task of projecting British prestige, upon which successful diplomacy ultimately rested. Many a wife, however, found these social occasions draining. The demands on her were immense: the pressure to appear in exactly the right attire, to use the correct form of words when addressing great personages, to remember names and faces and make introductions, to sustain pleasant conversation with people of the slightest acquaintance, to dance the prescribed dances and to dance them gracefully, and generally to reflect creditably upon her husband at all times. Even the smallest worries could destroy a wife's equilibrium. At the Emperor's New Year's Day reception in Tokyo, for instance, Mary Fraser anxiously eyed the highly polished floor of the throne room, fearing the havoc it might play with her rheumatism. Thankfully she managed to get through 'all the curtseys without accidents'.[17] Even in the relative safety of her home, a wife could never be sure that an important visitor would not drop in unannounced. One morning in Berlin, Lady Anne Macdonell was in the midst of having her hair shampooed when a maid dashed in with the unwelcome news that the crown princess was in the next room.[18] Mary Fraser's toilette was similarly disturbed in Tokyo by the arrival of a company of Japanese ladies wishing to pay their respects.

The terrifying spectre of social failure could haunt diplomats' daughters, too. Meriel Buchanan, who accompanied her father, Sir George, on all his postings, never felt quite at ease in his world. Accompanied by governesses and constantly watched over by her mother, Meriel dutifully acquired the standard accomplishments expected of a young lady of the Edwardian upper class. In Darmstadt, she rode horses; in Rome, she took weekly dancing lessons; in Berlin, she fenced; at The

Hague, she was forced to learn golf. Never a beauty, Meriel did her best to look presentable in the fashions of the day – high-necked muslin blouses reinforced with whale-bone, floor-length skirts, enormous hats tied under the chin with a chiffon veil – and coaxed her hair into puffed-out piles on top of her head. She attended balls and danced with young men, but continually exasperated her mother whose hopes of arranging a smart marriage for her only daughter gradually turned to despair. Buchanan found an escape from these ordeals in writing. In 1912, thanks to the intervention of one of the wives at the American embassy in St Petersburg, who was herself a published writer, Buchanan won a contract for her debut novel, *White Witch*, a romantic tale of young love amongst the European aristocracy, and for a follow-up, *Tania: A Russian Story*, set in St Petersburg's high society, which Buchanan knew so well. Neither was tremendously successful, but Buchanan went on to establish a modest reputation as a writer of non-fiction, most of it, like her novels, linked to her personal experiences in central and eastern Europe.[19]

Meriel Buchanan was not alone in seeking distraction in literary endeavours. Lady Currie, who accompanied her second husband as ambassadress first to Constantinople (1893–8) and then to Rome (1898–1902), was already a minor poet and novelist of some renown, having published more than half a dozen books – mainly slim volumes of gentle, sentimental verse – under the pen name of Violet Fane. Her literary productions continued after her marriage to Sir Philip, including a literal translation of the memoirs of Marguerite de Valois, Queen of Navarre, further works of poetry and several essays. Lady Currie evidently preferred the company of her pen to that of her guests. One of her husband's officers in Constantinople recalled that 'diplomatic duties wearied her sorely, and the sound of her tiara rattling against the mirror which hung behind her usual seat after dinner, as she gently sank into slumber, was the well-known signal to her guests that it was time for them to go home'.[20] In Rome, where Meriel Buchanan knew her, Lady Currie 'seemed always oppressed by the many social duties imposed on her as Ambassadress', and appeared positively glad when the death of Queen Victoria in January 1901 brought to a halt all official entertaining.[21]

By contrast, James Rennell Rodd's wife, who was a talented sculptress, was able to devote half the day to her beloved art, until her husband's promotion to chief of mission turned her official spousal duties into a full-time job. Unlike Lady Currie, however, Lilias Rennell Rodd eagerly embraced her elevated status as ambassadress in Rome, having assiduously lobbied the Foreign Office over the years for her husband's various promotions and transfers (some called her 'Black Lily' on account of her steely wifely ambition).[22] Here, in Italy's cultural capital, the possibilities for uniting a passion for art and literature – which her husband fully shared – with Britain's diplomatic interests were considerable. Rennell Rodd was himself determined to make the British embassy a centre of classical learning and in this Lady Rodd was in her element. In 1910 she devised and directed a series of dramatic scenes taken from classical mythology, although the planned performance in the embassy's lush gardens had to be called off due to the death of Edward VII. Undeterred, Lilias dreamt up an even greater project in 1913: a historic ball featuring a 'pageant of the ages'. The participants were carefully grouped into historical eras, supplied with costumes copied from pictorial records, and drilled in the dance steps of their respective centuries. Rennell Rodd welcomed guests in the famous court suit of Sir Walter Raleigh, identical to the original save for the cheap beads substituting for real pearls, whilst Lady Rodd reserved for herself the honour of leading the procession into the ballroom. Draped in blue and gold cloth, and with a crown of turquoise befitting the Queen of the Gods, she was followed by a troop of Olympian deities which included Apollo (Osborne, one of the embassy secretaries), Mercury (Rennell Rodd's eldest son), Ulysses (the head of chancery, Mounsey), and numerous Greek maidens (assorted nieces and adopted nieces of the Rennell Rodd clan). After that came a group of Italian nobles impersonating the court of Ludovico Sforza, the fifteenth-century Milanese tyrant; then a scene from *The Arabian Nights*, headed by Prince Lichtenstein, the naval attaché at the Austro-Hungarian embassy; then a minuet performed by eight dancers in costume from the reign of Louis XV; and on and on with Bedouin warriors, Mandarins, Venetian doges and finally Lansquenet

soldiers bringing up the rear. It must have made for an extraordinary sight: in one corner, Sir Walter Raleigh accompanied by Sir
Francis Drake, deep in conversation with Ivan the Terrible, and in
another, Leonardo da Vinci conversing with Helen of Troy whilst
Dante looked on.[23]

Other ambassadresses found less picturesque but similarly diverting
ways of advancing British interests through the social side of embassy
life. The fun-loving Hariot Dufferin was a keen player of amateur
theatricals. She won plaudits in Constantinople for her lead in Sheridan's
The Critic in 1881, and a few years later in Cairo performed in a play
penned by Sir Edward Malet, the British consul-general, before an
audience of 160 which included the Egyptian khedive.[24] Ten years later,
and at the behest of the Hungarian ambassador in Rome, Lady Dufferin
took to the stage again, this time playing opposite Rennell Rodd, who
was then a junior secretary, in a light-hearted romantic comedy entitled
Happy Pair. The ambassador was delighted and Lady Dufferin had a
whale of a time, although James Rennell Rodd found rehearsing the
love scenes, which his boss Lord Dufferin insisted on directing, an
excruciating ordeal.[25]

An episode of perhaps greater historical significance involving a
British ambassadress was the day that Lady Ampthill, posted with her
husband to Berlin, rescued Prince William of Hohenzollern, the future
Kaiser, from certain death in the lake at Potsdam. An expert sculler,
Lady Ampthill had agreed to coach the prince, who was keen to build
up the strength in his famously withered arm. On the appointed morning, the ambassadress drew up in a light Thames-built skiff, but instead
of stepping gently in, Prince William leapt athletically from the jetty,
immediately capsizing the boat and plunging both into sixteen feet of
water. The Prince was unable to swim, but, undaunted, Lady Ampthill
sped to his side and managed, despite her voluminous skirts, to keep
him afloat until help arrived.[26] (It is tempting to imagine how the
course of twentieth-century history might have been altered had the
heroic Lady Ampthill failed.)

Diplomatic wives could further boost Britain's standing abroad as
figureheads for worthy causes. As women of high status,

ambassadresses were frequently invited to patronise this hospital or that children's home, or to put the (often considerable) facilities of their embassies and residences to philanthropic uses. Here, again, Lady Dufferin outperformed her peers. In 1883 alone she raised more than £8,500 by organising a ball in aid of the poor of Alexandria, a garden fete to drum up funds for the English Church in Constantinople, an open-air concert for earthquake victims in Smyrna, and a large bazaar, the proceeds of which went to families made homeless by forest fires in Haskeui.[27] As vicereine in India, and encouraged personally by Queen Victoria, Lady Dufferin surpassed even this achievement, founding the National Association for Supplying Female Medical Aid to the Women of India in 1885, a body which campaigned for higher standards of maternity care. An old hand by now at committee work, Lady Hariot managed to persuade every province to adopt her scheme of rigorous training for nurses, midwives and female doctors, and improved hospital facilities for expectant mothers. As a voluntary initiative which addressed a very real need, attracted wealthy Indian donors and wisely avoided Christian proselytising, the Dufferin Fund (as it became known) made a serious contribution both to the development of Western medicine in India and to the stability of British colonial rule. Although criticised in some nationalist quarters for its apparent reluctance to train Indian – as opposed to white British – women, the fund demonstrated just how much influence an energetic and determined spouse could exert. Lady Dufferin left India in 1888 notably more popular than her husband, who had antagonised local opinion by levying income tax, raising salt duties and annexing Burma. One nationalist newspaper even went so far as to suggest that, rather than marking the viceroy's departure with the customary statue in the Calcutta Maiden, the city's largest park, Lady Dufferin ought to receive this honour instead.[28]

Diplomatic wives performed this eclectic repertoire of duties because they recognised them as such: their *duties* – to husband, of course, and to country, but also to the extended families that they acquired at each new posting. Every household needed a mistress, including diplomatic ones. Many a male memoir pays fond tribute to a beloved 'chiefesse', whose benevolent presence and feminine compassion smoothed even the most troubled of waters. For James Rennell Rodd, there was none to rival Lady Ethel Cromer, wife of the celebrated consul-general in Egypt, whom he watched in action in the 1890s:

> Under her gracious and tactful guidance a social order was established there which set and maintained a high standard in the British community. The desire to merit and retain her esteem was a constant and an active influence. Wherever there was trouble or distress her watchful sympathy was at once revealed, and she had the gift of expressing feeling in sincere and spontaneous terms which went to the heart.[29]

Cromer was utterly broken by Lady Ethel's death in 1899. Such, however, was the quasi-familial affection that he inspired amongst his staff that Lilias Rennell Rodd, full of concern for the old man's welfare, invited him for Christmas and plotted to lift his spirits by means of a kind-hearted ploy involving her three-year-old son, Francis ('an extraordinarily winning child of whom Cromer was very fond', according to his father). Instead of receiving Lord Cromer in the usual way, the Rennell Rodds left little Francis alone in the drawing room, dressed in his favourite pink pyjamas and seated in an enormous armchair. Lord Cromer was duly shown in to be greeted by this diminutive host, and when Lady Rodd and her husband appeared a few minutes later, they found their guest 'quite content with the boy sitting on his knee, pulling up his small pyjamas and observing "much hair on leg".'[30]

It was through such quiet and unspectacular acts of kindness that wives could give the diplomatic family its heartbeat and helped draw its members into bonds of common sympathy. In St Petersburg during Lent, when the dancing season had ended, Lady Dufferin held parties for the embassy staff, featuring English parlour games such as Blindman's Bluff, Musical Chairs and Hunt the Slipper. In Vienna, Lady Goschen enjoyed equally homely amusements, joining her husband and members of the chancery in the evenings for acrostics and

'Word Making and Word Taking' (seemingly a precursor of Scrabble).[31] Although barred from their husbands' clubs, wives could and did share in many of the other relaxations of the embassy's male staff, including rugged outdoor pursuits. Lady Dufferin joined a bear-hunting expedition deep in the Russian countryside in 1880, finding herself at the end being tossed in the air by the villagers in line with local custom ('They seized me very nicely, holding down my petticoats, and not letting go of me, but only dancing me up and down'). The whole thing, Lady Dufferin recalled, 'was delightful', although on hearing of her adventure the other diplomatic ladies in St Petersburg 'thought I was mad'.[32]

As well as regularly playing hostess to her husband's staff, a high-ranking wife was responsible for the welfare of newly arrived spouses. In China, Lady Mary Fraser was much encouraged by the warm welcome she received from her chiefesse, Mrs Wade, who was 'everything that the wife of an official in the East should be, thoroughly and fundamentally British, cheery, kind, intelligent, a woman who never made a mistake'. In Vienna, Fraser was equally indebted to Lady Elliot for guiding her through 'the labyrinth of Austrian society', a task greatly aided by the fact that the British ambassadress 'was so generally beloved that people were very good to me for her sake'.[33] Younger wives were frequently awestruck by the ease and self-assurance of these old hands. At her presentation in Rome, Anne Macdonell was 'quite lost in admiration' upon spying Lady Paget, the British ambassadress, who, with her graceful movements and elegant dress, 'was the most beautiful person I had ever seen'.[34] Even a fairly experienced wife could pick up useful information through a quiet chat with a senior spouse. Having dined en route to St Petersburg with Lady Odo Russell (soon to be Ampthill), the ambassadress in Berlin, Lady Dufferin, quickly realised that her new posting would require a great deal more exertion on her part than had been the case in Canada, where her husband had served as governor-general between 1872 and 1878. On arrival at St Petersburg, Lady Dufferin was also grateful to Lady Augustus Loftus, her outgoing predecessor, 'who kindly told me some of the things I wanted to know, and recommended some of her servants whom we take on'.[35]

This kind of practical assistance could be invaluable. Finding and furnishing a suitable residence, for instance, was always first on any new wife's list, and here guidance was crucial. Lady Layard, the ambassadress in Madrid, helped Anne Macdonell secure lodgings for her family in a beautiful house on the Calle Campomanes, although the absence of running water meant arranging a daily delivery from a local Spaniard who filled 'two huge earthenware receptacles, like the proverbial oil jars in Ali Baba's story – one for drinking purposes, the other for cleaning'. Lady Layard was unable, however, to procure a reliable cook, and the woman Macdonell finally engaged was less than satisfactory. She appeared each day with fowls and vegetables 'and queer joints of veal' under her arm, insisted on having her hair done by an open window in the kitchen, and enraged the lady concierge by flirting outrageously with her husband. Worse was to come in Rio de Janeiro, however, where the Macdonells were posted in 1885. The city was in the clutches of the yellow fever, which made the charming villa they hired in the hills outside neighbouring Petropolis initially appear an ideal choice. Relying on a mule to bring the household all its food supplies from town each day, however, was risky, and when the seasonal rains washed away the primitive roads, the family were reduced to eating rice and macaroni, or braving the monkey soup and roast parrot that their resourceful chef managed to rustle up (Lady Anne decided, perhaps wisely, to go hungry). They moved to Petropolis soon after, but the family's troubles were not over. At a fete in Rio to mark Queen Victoria's Jubilee, Lady Anne caught a chill which developed into malaria and, after many bedridden weeks, she was finally shipped back to England.

These were, without question, the least enviable aspects of diplomatic life. Male officers were not spared ill-health or material privations, of course, but wives usually bore primary responsibility for sorting out messes when things went wrong. The fact that these Victorian matriarchs did all this whilst enduring frequent pregnancies (Lady Dufferin produced nine children; Lady Ampthill and Lady Rodd six apiece; Anne Macdonell five) would earn any twenty-first-century mother's admiration and respect. True, they usually had nursemaids to take charge of the more onerous sides of infant care, but no servant could ease the physical ordeal of carrying multiple babies to term during freezing Russian winters or insufferable Washington summers. And no maid could remove the pain of losing a child, sadly not a rare occurrence in the lives of diplomatic families. Mary Fraser's heart went out to the English wife who reportedly burst into tears in front of the Austrian Empress when asked if she had any children: 'She had lost her two little ones the year before.'[36] The joys and sorrows of motherhood formed a firm bond between diplomatic wives which could even transcend nationality. Fraser befriended the German ambassadress in Vienna, who had two boys around the same age, and their children happily played together at each other's houses. Similarly, Lady Dufferin's brood were regular visitors at the home of Countess Schuvalov, wife of the Russian foreign minister in St Petersburg. At Christmas in 1879, she threw a party for them, the principal game of which, Hariot Dufferin recalled, 'consisted in throwing 100 india-rubber balls at each other'. This was followed by 'Round and Round the Mulberry Bush', a cup of hot choco-late and a biscuit, and then time for home.[37]

A wife who could do all this, bear all this, and keep smiling was a valu-able asset indeed for any ambitious diplomat. For men who had risen above the junior attaché grade, the presence of a loyal spouse was regarded as highly advantageous. For top jobs in the major European capitals, an ambassadress with serious social clout could play a decisive part in ensuring the success of a mission. Her absence was viewed as deeply regrettable. Lord Lyons almost missed out on the Paris ambas-sadorship in 1867 for this very reason, Lord Clarendon (the Foreign Secretary) listing as his key drawbacks 'extreme shyness, want of initia-tive, fear of responsibility and still greater fear of marrying'.[38] Twenty-five years on, Charles Hardinge felt able to accept the post of head of chan-cery in Paris (and later the secretaryship of the embassy in St Petersburg) partly on the strength of his wife's recently elevated status as lady-in-waiting to the Princess of Wales: 'the fact of her holding that position at the Court at home', he noted, 'was of great assistance from a social point of view abroad'.[39] (Lilias Rennell Rodd referred to Hardinge's promotion in rather more barbed terms: 'I suppose it is his wife's influence with the Princess of Wales which has done it,' she wrote to her husband.[40]) It was a measure of the value placed on this spousal contribution that the Foreign Office continued to report formally on officers' wives in personnel files until the 1980s.

Inevitably, few if any wives attained perfection in discharging their expected duties. They were human beings, after all. Even Lady Dufferin (whom the *Oxford Dictionary of National Biography* describes as 'the most effective diplomatic wife of her generation') could have her off-days.[41] Receiving guests every Thursday in St Petersburg from 1.30 to 6 p.m., she recorded in her journal in 1879, was 'rather a fatiguing performance when so many of the visitors are unknown to one'. Returning all these calls as etiquette demanded was an even greater trial. 'I am in despair,' she wrote; 'I have at least 600 to pay, and I feel bewildered.'[42] Nonetheless, at least Lady Dufferin could fall back at such times on her polished social skills acquired through a genteel upbringing and long experience of moving in high society. Other wives were not so lucky. Lady White, wife of Sir William, Britain's ambassador in Constantinople between 1886 and 1891, was born plain Katherine Kendzior, the daughter of a German tobacconist – and she was never allowed to forget it. The elevation of one of such humble origins to the rank of ambassadress was highly unusual for the times. It was explained in part by the almost equally unconventional career of her husband, who entered the Consular Service at the relatively late age of thirty-three and was amongst only a small handful of consuls who crossed the rickety bridge into the mainstream Diplomatic Service. Wives inevitably found themselves on the receiving end of the residual snobbery directed towards such upstarts. According to Charles Hardinge, who served under Sir William in Constantinople, Lady White was 'a common woman greatly lacking in dignity and *savoir-faire*'. She was apparently seen in the embassy kitchen collecting scraps from the supper table after a ball, and Hardinge once spied her in the main street of Pera buying live turkeys 'and feeling which was fattest'. This undignified behaviour, he recalled with distaste, 'did not redound to her credit as Ambassadress'.[43]

All the same, Sir William White did at least *have* a wife to serve as his official hostess. It is impossible to know how many British diplomats were drawn into affairs involving unsuitable partners with whom matrimony was out of the question. We do know, however, of one case, that of Lionel Sackville-West and the Spanish dancer, Pepita Oliva, thanks to the detective work of their granddaughter, the novelist Vita Sackville-West.[44] Upon clapping eyes on the dark-eyed and ravishingly beautiful Pepita at a theatre in Paris in 1852, the young attaché Lionel fell deeply in love, and the two started an affair which was to last for more than twenty years and produce five surviving children. Pepita was already married, although estranged from her husband. She was also a Catholic and descendant of gypsies – hardly ideal material for the wife of a British diplomat. Lionel made one wild attempt to wed Pepita in Málaga and had to be forcibly prevented from committing known bigamy by the local English consul, who locked him up for three days before sending him home. Thereafter, Pepita had no choice but to accept her shadowy status as diplomatic mistress, rather than official wife. She was never presented to Lionel's chancery colleagues (although they knew of her existence well enough) or invited to formal receptions or dinners where members of the diplomatic corps were present. Nor did she have any use for the smart cards she had printed with her fictitious (and, in any case, wholly inaccurate) name of Countess West, for Pepita could hardly pay calls on the other diplomatic ladies. Even their children suffered, snubbed at parties and deprived of playmates from the 'good' families in the neighbourhood.

Oddly enough, Lionel's diplomatic career did not appear to have been seriously affected by his unconventional private life. This is almost certainly explained by the pains he took to efface from his official existence any trace of his domestic arrangements. It could be a very different story for men who openly paraded their mistresses, especially if they had wives of their own. Mary Fraser's husband was posted to Vienna as replacement for an officer who had mired himself in scandal of exactly this kind. He had fallen victim 'to the charms of a lady better known for beauty than virtue', and made the fatal mistake of being seen with her in company. Lionel Sackville-West had the decency, at least, to remain unmarried whilst conducting his love affair with Pepita. On her death in childbirth in March 1871, however, his carefully constructed private world fell apart, and what happened next is of no small significance for the history of women in pre-war diplomacy. Pepita's children were initially taken into the care of a family friend, and then later sent to school in Paris. In 1880, when Lionel's eldest daughter, Victoria, was eighteen, they were brought over to England to meet their assorted uncles and aunts, who received these dark-haired, Frenchified nieces and nephews with varying degrees of warmth. At the more welcoming end of the spectrum was Lionel's older sister, Mary Derby, the same Lady Derby who had defied the Queen during the Eastern crisis and could boast of powerful contacts throughout the foreign policy establishment. It was after the confirmation of Lionel's next appointment as minister in Washington that Lady Derby made her move. Victoria Sackville-West, she observed, was a young woman of beauty and charm. Never mind that she spoke broken English with a French accent. If guided wisely, she could become of great use to her bachelor father, and, in the process, wash away the stains of her illegitimate birth. The British legation in Washington needed a hostess and Victoria, Lady Derby announced, was the ideal candidate.

On the face of it, this was a highly unorthodox solution, for Victoria was an ingénue who had not even been presented at court. Nonetheless, her aunt arranged a private audience at Buckingham Palace (the Queen's previous ire towards the Derbys having evidently cooled), and a committee of Washington's most influential ladies subsequently agreed that the young Victoria would be allowed to join their circle as chiefesse of the British legation. Once arrived, Victoria was an instant hit. Her disarming naivety, youthful imperiousness and mildly exotic manners formed a winning combination. She was constantly in demand and received a string of marriage proposals (all of which were declined), including one from the President, the widower Chester Arthur. Victoria did not allow herself to be overwhelmed by the endless invitations and compliments. She soon evolved a system whereby no visitors would be admitted to her presence at the legation without an appointment, a bold departure from the open 'at-homes' that most diplomatic wives dutifully hosted week in and week out. Victoria also refused to bow to the well-established practice of 'bunching', whereby any young man wishing to dance with the object of his affections at a ball was expected to send her a bouquet of flowers in advance; these would be transported to the venue on the night and displayed, allowing all to see which young lady was most desired by the bachelors of Washington. Victoria was having none of it, summarily returning any floral advances which appeared at the legation. As her daughter, Vita, noted, this defiant act was quickly emulated by the other young ladies, 'which proved a welcome economy to all the smart young men, who hitherto gauged a girl's popularity by the number of bouquets she received, and which they could ill afford repeatedly to send'.[45]

Given the circumstances of her birth and upbringing, Victoria Sackville-West was hardly typical of British diplomatic womenfolk. Yet the fact of her existence is a salutary reminder that the Diplomatic Service, for all its codes and conventions, could throw up instances of feminine influence and intervention in some of the most unexpected places. Even as diplomacy was reined in by nineteenth-century protocol and bureaucracy, it could never be wholly contained by it. Diplomatic relations were the cumulative product of an infinite number of conversations and confidences which took place wherever diplomats and politicians gathered together. Where those men gathered, more often than not, women gathered too.

The problem for the historian, of course, is how to interpret women's presence in these social worlds of diplomacy. We know that women hosted salons which young attachés were eager to attend; that they fixed introductions and buttered up allies; and that they helped to knit the embassy family together and provide for their husbands all the comforts of an English home. Given their education and self-evident intellect, it seems inconceivable that women like Mary Fraser or Hariot Dufferin did not develop independent views on the political questions of the day, or that they failed to communicate those views to their husbands by the fireside or over pillow talk. But only in isolated cases, such as that of Lady Derby in 1877, or Lady Dufferin in India in the mid-1880s, does there exist concrete evidence of women's direct contribution to the promotion of British national interests in a diplomatic setting. Naturally, wives were doing this indirectly all the time. Every gracious handshake or elegant curtsey, every witty exchange or well-executed conversation with a foreign dignitary, was part and parcel of the symbolic projection of British prestige.

There are even some glimpses of women lending a more practical hand. Some wives served as private secretaries to their husbands, a job which entailed copying out letters, filing away correspondence and perhaps also keeping accounts and managing diaries. John McNeill, who was attached to the British mission in Persia in the 1820s, delegated these tasks to his wife, Elizabeth, whose discretion, it was said, 'was such that he could entirely trust her with all his diplomatic difficulties'.[46] Mary Fraser felt that she knew the inside of the British chancery in Vienna well enough to refute in her memoirs the suggestion that diplomats routinely sought to intercept the correspondence of other embassies. In Sofia, Meriel Buchanan and her mother actually helped out with deciphering telegrams for several months in 1908, when the pressures of paperwork generated by Bulgaria's declaration of independence proved too much for the understaffed chancery.

From this we must assume that both women received at the very least a rudimentary training in ciphering and deciphering official communications. How many other wives might have slid into a desk next to the attachés and secretaries to lend support during tough times? Frustratingly, the historical record remains stubbornly silent on this point. The memoirs of wives typically open with journeys to new postings, then move on to relay impressions of foreign society and its leading personalities and to describe domestic difficulties and family affairs, before concluding with tearful departures and onward travel to their next destination. Even where an author proves herself expertly conversant in the politics of the day, she rarely expresses any personal view as to the right course of action for British policy. Judging by the

fierce criticism routinely directed at women who wrote openly and
without inhibition on 'political' matters, this reticence was in all likelihood a form of self-imposed censorship. We can never be sure, but it
seems unlikely that the women who married or were born into the
Victorian Diplomatic Service were oblivious to the prevailing prejudices of their age, which held politics to be a masculine domain. It
seems even less likely, given their class privileges and comfortable social
position, that such women would seek actively to challenge these prejudices. It was not wives who would presently be found questioning the
male monopoly over the diplomatic profession, but feminists and
professional women determined to see women's political talents openly
recognised and their unpaid labours formally rewarded. The coming of
war in August 1914 seemed to offer an opportunity for exactly this, but
whether it would resolve the paradox of women's ambiguous presence
in the world of diplomacy was yet to be seen.

3

War

Writing to her sister in March 1917, Bertha Phillpotts confessed to feeling 'much intense satisfaction, after all one has read in the English papers, in doing a tiny bit of war work'. The 'tiny bit' in question was a clerical post at the British legation in Stockholm, where Bertha had been employed for over a year. Her formal duties involved translating articles from the Swedish press, but in practice she quickly found herself becoming something of a maid-of-all-work:

> My main duty is to read about 8 or 9 papers daily & cut out snippets & stick them on to pieces of paper & give them to the Minister or to Owen, according to their nature. In order to give the minister his early I arrive here at 9! After I have done all that & filed the snippets of preceding days, & produced a few old ones on request, I become a cipher-er, or else I compose small & unimportant dispatches or telegrams on the things in the paper.[1]

In addition, Bertha served as private secretary to the head of mission, Sir Esme Howard, and found herself doing endless 'odd jobs' for her brother, Owen, who was Howard's assistant commercial attaché.[2] Bertha also took in hand the poor ventilation arrangements in the office, reporting her victory in 'airing the Chancery: the windows have to be shut when it is empty, & when people are in it they never open the windows, so the air is quite dense'.[3]

How did forty-year-old Bertha Phillpotts come to be sitting in a muggy garret on the top floor of the British legation in wartime Stockholm? Those who knew her could hardly have predicted such a turn of events in what was, up to that point, a quiet and scholarly life spent largely in the contemplative precincts of various Oxbridge women's colleges. Born in 1877, the middle daughter of a Bedford schoolmaster, Bertha showed early academic promise, winning in 1897 a scholarship to Girton College, Cambridge, to read modern and medieval languages. Thereafter, she embarked upon a lifelong study of the history, archaeology and literature of Scandinavia, becoming one of the very few women to enter this select and rarefied field and later to be honoured with some of its most prestigious prizes and professional distinctions.

Ironically, however, Phillpotts's intimate knowledge of the region and its culture was probably less decisive in bringing about her appointment to the Stockholm legation in 1916 than the maddening ineptitude of her brother, who had been employed there since shortly after the outbreak of war. Owen Phillpotts was charismatic and clever but phenomenally disorganised and lacking in common sense. His untidiness at the chancery was legendary, with few daring to go near his roll-top desk, which was always piled high with apple peel, cigarette ends and bits of sealing wax, and carelessly strewn with confidential telegrams and memoranda. Owen landed himself in serious trouble in Gothenberg in 1915 when some sensitive documents which he had left in his overcoat in a hotel cloakroom went missing and subsequently surfaced in a violently pro-German newspaper. The consequences could have been dire: Sweden was a neutral power whose geographical position made her a vital link in the chain of communications with Russia, Britain's major ally. Yet the details of the affair as it later unfolded were farcical, involving a run-in with a mob of street urchins, an abortive break-in, which left Owen locked inside his own flat, and a female reporter posing as a chambermaid. Sir Esme was understandably livid, but Owen managed to keep his job. When Bertha visited Stockholm the following year, she was sincerely importuned by Howard to stay on at the legation to take her brother in hand.[4]

The circumstances of Bertha Phillpotts's appointment were, thus, peculiar, but perhaps not all that surprising. Despite the wartime short-ages of manpower at the Foreign Office, women were not formally admitted to the Diplomatic Service, so it was only through an irregular arrangement of this kind – Phillpotts was not given a proper salary until 1917 – that such an appointment was possible. Despite their readi-ness to serve, the British wartime state was a reluctant employer of educated middle- and upper-class women like Bertha Phillpotts, and the Foreign Office seemed especially disinclined to make proper use of the expertise and experience on offer, whether in London or overseas. Such women could follow a more conventionally feminine path by joining the Voluntary Aid Detachments in northern France, enlisting with the Red Cross, or replicating at home the makeshift soup kitchens and nursing stations organised by diplomatic wives abroad. When it came to matters of high policy or sensitive negotiations with allied powers, women remained on the fringes of diplomacy, just as they had before 1914.

Nonetheless, the war did not leave the ruling male hierarchy wholly undisturbed. In the first place, the explosion of paperwork in London meant that Foreign Office chiefs were faced with little choice but to recruit large numbers of female workers to pick up the slack. As a result, Gilbert Scott's Victorian palazzo was no longer a virtually woman-free zone, and for some of these temporary typists and secretaries their incursions into the lower levels of clerkdom were to prove lasting gains. Moreover, the First World War was to provide a stage for a certain Miss Gertrude Bell, a woman who played a part of real political significance in Britain's prosecution of the war, and who, with her physical tough-ness and lively intellect, appeared to confound the old Victorian stereotypes of fragile and domesticated femininity. Phillpotts and Bell, although very different characters, both represented a tantalising glimpse of what diplomacy might conceivably look like were women to be permitted entry to its exclusive ranks.

———

Like many other Britons taking a well-earned break during the long bank holiday weekend of August 1914, Foreign Office clerk Hughe

Knatchbull-Hugessen was snatching a few hours of repose in the hot sunshine of that fateful summer when a telegram arrived summoning him urgently to London. He caught the first train to Victoria Station, which he found teeming with Germans desperate to leave England, and jumped into a taxi cab which whisked him through deserted streets towards Whitehall. The scene inside the Foreign Office was chaotic. A system of day-and-night shifts had been hastily introduced to deal with the torrent of communications now pouring in from overseas posts at such a rate that even the most senior clerks were dragooned into manning the cipher machines. When Knatchbull-Hugessen reported for duty in the cipher room later that night, he had to wade through a sea of discarded waste paper to reach his colleagues, who were stationed behind desks dictating codes, furiously scribbling down telegrams, or thundering out multiple copies on typewriters. The noise was excruciating; every telegram had to be copied sixteen times for distribution to under-secretaries and Cabinet ministers, and it was only the heaviest-armed stenographer who could do battle with the thick sheaf of carbon paper stuffed into these overworked machines. Taking charge of the graveyard shift from midnight to 8 a.m., Knatchbull-Hugessen was presently called in by his superiors and instructed to oversee the despatch of a very special telegram to all overseas posts. It was a message from the Foreign Secretary, Sir Edward Grey, and it contained Britain's declaration of war with Germany.[5]

The Foreign Office, like other arms of the wartime state, underwent an administrative revolution after August 1914. Entirely new departments sprang into being: there was the War Department, an amalgam of the old Eastern and Western Departments, dealing with key political, military and naval questions; the Department of Political Intelligence, which collected vital information on political conditions overseas; the News Department, created to manage the press and enforce censorship; and, perhaps most importantly of all, the Contraband Department, whose job was to tighten the economic screws on enemy nations. The latter eventually became a fully fledged Ministry of Blockade, sprouting numerous offshoots including the Foreign Trade Department based at Stafford House and the War Trade

Intelligence Department, accommodated in a building located, handily enough, in the lake in St James's Park, now drained of its contents
in case the shimmering waters should direct German bombers to the
surrounding offices during night-time raids. This unusual address was
also to be the eventual home of the Passport Office, which rapidly
expanded from its pre-war establishment of one second-division clerk
and a doorkeeper, who had quietly carried out their business from two
small rooms near the back entrance to the Foreign Office. Inside Scott's
Victorian palazzo, every inch of unused space was commandeered for
war purposes. Huts went up in the central courtyard; resident clerks
handed over their sitting rooms; library store rooms were invaded;
attics reclaimed; a bunker constructed in the basement for the Prime
Minister's personal use; and the ornate suite of reception rooms where
many a foreign dignitary had supped wine was now filled with trestle
tables and clattering typewriters.[6]

Naturally, this ballooning bureaucracy needed to be adequately
staffed. Foreign Office clerks were initially exempted from active
service on the grounds that their trained brains would be much
needed in Whitehall. Even as late as 1917, when British losses in
northern France were multiplying, only a small number of Foreign
Office personnel were released for duty under orders from the War
Office. All the same, the demand for additional manpower was pressing, and from 1915 there was an influx of retired diplomats and
distinguished volunteers from academia, the latter willingly abandoning the comforts of the senior common room for the stringencies
of war work. Attendance at High Table must, in fact, have dropped
considerably, such were the number of Oxbridge dons destined for
the Foreigh Office. There were the historian Arnold Toynbee and
classicist Alfred Zimmern, both already well-regarded writers on
foreign affairs; there was a youthful E. H. Carr, freshly minted with
a Cambridge double first and later to write one of the founding texts
of international relations; there was the scientist and future Master
of Corpus Christi, Cambridge, Will Spens; and there were countless
historians: Sir James Headlam-Morley and Lewis Namier took up
posts in political intelligence; George Butler joined the News

Department, and Henry Carless Davis became vice-chairman of the War Trade Intelligence Department.[7]

To fill these temporary posts, male recruits had to prove they were unfit for military service or over-age. Naturally no such restrictions applied to women, who were debarred from taking up arms for their country, and therefore formed an obvious source of substitute labour. Although almost wholly absent from the very highest decision-making circles, a small number of women did eventually win temporary posts in the wartime state commanding at least a modicum of authority. Some, for example, were concerned with the overall organisation of the female workforce, inspecting armament factories, running the Women's Land Army or advising industry on how best to replace male workers. Others investigated claims for separation allowances submitted by soldiers' wives, administered old age pensions or crunched consumption statistics for the Ministry of Food. Those with linguistic skills were employed as translators, whilst women possessing scientific expertise were highly sought after for technical posts at the Ministry of Munitions. Some educated middle- and upper-class women who came with personal recommendations found posts in the Secret Intelligence Services, working as postal censors for MI9, registry supervisors at MI5, or personal secretaries to high-ranking intelligence chiefs.[8]

The picture was broadly similar at the Foreign Office, which recruited a handful of university women to its ever-growing bureaucracy. Hilda Johnstone, a History lecturer at Manchester, found a post at the War Trade Intelligence Department, as did both the Oxford-trained anthropologist Barbara Freire-Marecco and University College London graduate Theodora Bosanquet (previously secretary to Henry James and later literary editor of *Time and Tide*). Fellow graduate Dorothy Bigby's temporary employment in 1915 turned into a permanent fixture. She went on to run the British delegation's registry in Paris during the famous Peace Conference of 1919, and thereafter became a staff officer and later registrar in the Librarian's Department.

These appointments were, nonetheless, feminine islets in a vast sea of male authority. It was much further down the chain of command, in the typing and secretarial pools, that the majority of temporary female employees were to be found. As in other government departments, the Foreign Office engaged the services of large numbers of young women clerks to tame the flood of war-related paperwork. Their presence across Whitehall was striking for its unprecedented numerical strength after 1914, although women had, in fact, been employed in the Civil Service for several decades. The Post Office took the bold step of recruiting female clerks back in the 1870s, where they processed telegrams and worked the new telegraph system. Other departments gradually followed suit, with the new 'typing grade' occasioned by the introduction of this admirable invention to government departments eventually becoming a more or less feminine preserve. Women posed little threat to the career prospects of male clerks, as they were segregated into separate grades, received lower salaries and most resigned or were dismissed upon marriage. In fact, women proved such a satisfactory source of low-level labour for the British state that by the eve of the war there were no fewer than 6,800 female clerks and typists on the government payroll, plus a massive 58,000 women employed in the Post Office and another thousand working as cleaners and attendants.[9]

The Foreign Office, despite its superior attitude towards the Home Civil Service and its administrative innovations, was not left untouched by this white-blouse revolution. Typewriters, as already noted, were looked on with suspicion and dismay by many officers, but an important precedent was set in 1889 when the services of a lady typist, Miss Sophia Fulcher, were tentatively engaged for non-confidential copying. She could hardly have felt herself one of the boys, however, as she was initially installed in an attic room with boxes of files sent up via a contraption that closely resembled a dumb waiter, necessitating virtually no personal contact with any male officer.[10] By the mid-1890s, Miss Fulcher had been joined by a handful of female colleagues, who remained tucked away from prying male eyes, and further appointments over subsequent years meant that the Foreign Office's typing pool had swelled to eleven ladies on the outbreak of the war, most of them young, unmarried women in their twenties.

A feminine presence at the Foreign Office was not, then, wholly unheard of in pre-war days, even if these exotic creatures were rarely glimpsed by most male officers. That presence, however, after August 1914, became far more conspicuous. Foreign Office chiefs soon overcame their initial reluctance to entrust unknown females with sensitive communications, and lady typists became an established feature of the wartime cipher section, along with the girls from the Stationery Office drafted in to work the duplicator machines (which supplemented the cumbersome carbon paper method). Upstairs, meanwhile, in the banqueting room, a large team of women swelled the ranks of the Contraband Department, whilst out in the courtyard, dozens of female clerical assistants huddled in huts wrestling with the mighty paperwork of the Passport Office.[11]

There is tantalisingly little known about these female clerks and their lives. We might assume that they generally harked from the same lower-middle- and middle-class milieu as their Edwardian counterparts: from families too poor to fund a leisured lifestyle, but too genteel to consider sending their daughters into a factory or domestic service. We might also assume that, like MI5, the Foreign Office preferred to recruit women from 'good' families whose discretion and patriotism could be assured. Beyond this, however, little can be reliably deduced. The plain woman clerk did not inspire the same public fascination or provoke the same moral fears as other categories of female war worker. Unlike the girls in the armaments factories, she did not wear trousers, operate heavy machinery or craft components designed to maim and kill. Unlike female bus conductors, ticket inspectors and members of the auxiliary armed forces, she did not contribute to the outlandish spectacle of uniformed women on Britain's streets. She was not photographed and exhibited by the Ministry of Information as an extraordinary product of the war effort. By contrast, the woman in the office was, in 1914, a familiar, respectable and unthreatening figure. Sadly, the fullest extant source for the Foreign Office comprises the fragmented and – to modern eyes – deeply patronising recollections of the chief clerk, John Tilley, who noted of the temporary female staff that:

many were naturally amateurs; some had difficulty . . . in acquiring habits of precision, and in the registries were said to be apt to think one number on a paper as good as another. Others were hard to persuade that, once engaged, they could not go off at once when their mothers and aunts and children were sick or otherwise in need of their help.[12]

Tilley also relates tales of female superintendents terrified by the presence of mice in the banqueting room and of ladies cowering in the basement during air raids, all amusing anecdotes for the reader, but which reveal little of the fabric and feel of daily life as actually lived by the thousands of women who kept the wartime machinery of government running: the commute to work by tram, tube or omnibus through streets thronged with Tommies on leave or convalescent soldiers clad in distinctive hospital blue; a simple lunch in a cheap restaurant or a Lyons tea house, followed by a quick look in the shops for a ready-made dance frock that would leave just enough over to meet the rent; most evenings spent in a city of shadows and stillness, with London's streetlights dimmed to elude the German bomber and even Big Ben standing silent with his clock face in darkness; some nights spent in cellars and underground stations, hiding from Zeppelins and wondering what fraction of the terror experienced by loved ones on the Western Front they were now feeling in their subterranean sanctuaries.

All this, combined with food queues, fuel restrictions, rising prices and inescapable fears for the safety of brothers and sweethearts overseas, made civilian life in wartime London a battle fought with body and soul.[13] But perhaps for women employed at the Foreign Office, these struggles were lightened by the thrill of walking into Scott's imposing Italianate palace each morning, passing the doorkeepers and clattering through long, marble corridors, greeting colleagues and exchanging news, and finally drawing up a chair and settling down to type out documents which, just perhaps, might land on the desks of important men with important decisions to make. If, for most, the wages were modest and the work routine, the setting and scale of the greater collective enterprise of which these women could feel themselves part was anything but.

———

Thousands of miles away in Petrograd,* Meriel Buchanan also sensed herself to be on the edge of historic events. As ambassador to one of Britain's major allies, her father had become a constant visitor to the Imperial Palace, where he spent long hours exhorting the Tsar to stiffen his allegiance to the Triple Entente and resist any separate deal with Germany. These were tumultuous months and years for Russia, with revolutionary sentiment everywhere rumbling underfoot; but even Sir George Buchanan, close as he was to the imperial family, could not convince Nicholas II that without serious social and political reform the Romanovs' days were numbered. When the storm broke in March 1917, leading to the Tsar's abdication and the installation of the Provisional Government, Sir George remained in the thick of things, delicately broaching the subject of the royal family's safe passage from Russia. Thereafter Sir George doggedly refused to abandon his post, continuing to build relations with the interim government headed by Alexander Kerensky and to safeguard the British colony even as the threat of a Bolshevik rising grew ever more likely. He finally gave up the game and left the city with his family in January 1918, two months after Lenin's march on the Winter Palace, leaving a couple of junior officers to do what they could to sustain unofficial diplomatic contacts with the new regime.

Meriel Buchanan experienced all this, of course, at one remove. She watched her father dash out of the embassy to attend important meetings and she saw him return hours later, often tired and despondent. Occasionally he would impart fragments of the consequential conversations which had taken place, but, unlike her father, Meriel's war was not filled with weighty reckonings and finely calibrated political decisions. Instead, it started in August 1914 with a casual visit to a nearby hospital, where Buchanan timidly offered her services to the superintending matron and was told to report to the outpatient department.

* The city was renamed Petrograd at the outbreak of the war on the grounds that 'St Petersburg' sounded too Germanic.

There, to her dismay, she was met 'by an overpowering smell of unwashed humanity, uncared-for suppurating sores, and various kinds of ointments and disinfectants'.[14] Resisting the urge either to cry or to be sick, Buchanan gamely plunged into a cheerless regime of washing and bandaging strangers' limbs that was to fill her mornings for the next month. Soon after, Buchanan moved to a neighbouring hospital where the British colony had taken over a wing for wounded soldiers. There the routine was slightly more varied: she spent the hours between 9 a.m. and 1 p.m. cleaning wounds and changing dressings before breaking for lunch – usually fish or cabbage soup with slices of black bread, followed by 'some rather doubtful-looking meat, whose origin one was too tired and too hungry to question'. Then it was back to work:

> scrubbing, polishing, disinfecting, and perhaps later on the removal of a piece of shell or shrapnel from some shattered limb, a renewed cleaning of white enamel tables and instruments, into the bathroom to wash piles of bandages, down the passage to hang them up to dry, and take down the ones that had been washed the day before. A cup of tea and bread and jam, a tour through the wards to help make the beds and take temperatures, and home down the long Pokrovsky Prospect with its crowded yellow trams, across the Nicholas Bridge, and along the wide, almost deserted quays to the Embassy.[15]

When not occupied at the hospital, Buchanan joined her mother's regular work parties, which took place in the embassy ballroom, now filled with trestle tables and pieces of red carpet to protect the shiny parquet floor from scrapes. Here, twice a week, smartly dressed British ladies settled down to roll bandages, prepare dressings and sew pyjamas for distribution at the city's hospitals or transportation via ambulance trains to the Eastern Front. Buchanan also helped out at the maternity hospital that her mother opened in spring 1915 to care for the numerous expectant mothers who flooded into the city with the first wave of war refugees. Buchanan's old leisurely life of at-homes and dress-fittings was well and truly a thing of the past: by the mid-point of the war, she was tying up bundles of second-hand clothing for impoverished families, working shifts at a feeding centre set up by British volunteers at the Warsaw railway station, and spending a day a week scrubbing the lice-infested bodies of refugee children.

In Rome, Lilias Rennell Rodd's duties as ambassadress were also much altered by the declaration of hostilities, although she spent rather less time than Meriel Buchanan in the presence of unpleasant odours and dirty bedpans. Instead, she sank her artistic talents into a range of activities to aid those wounded, disabled or otherwise impoverished by the war, which Italy officially joined on the Allied side in May 1915 after a short period of neutrality. As with her pre-war pageants, Lady Rodd did nothing by halves. Her first project, a small charity shop stocked with 'useful and pretty things', proved so successful that it was forced to move to larger premises on the Via Veneto, where she added a hugely popular tea room known as La Belle Alliance. As her husband recalled:

> Lampshades and screens executed by artists under her guidance from Japanese, Byzantine and classical designs, painted dress materials, artistic toys, small pieces of furniture copied from good designs and painted or lacquered in the Venetian manner secured a ready market, while their production gave employment to many who at that time found little demand for their craftsmanship. Old Japanese embroideries, of which she had a considerable stock, were eagerly bought. Venetian glass had become difficult to obtain, owing to the closing of the furnaces, but she had fortunately laid in an ample supply. Judicious purchases were made of old furniture and discarded church candlesticks, which were restored or copied by clever workmen. Well-known artists offered pictures and sketches. A number of friends were busy producing handbags and bead-necklaces.[16]

With business booming, La Belle Alliance moved to its final location in some outbuildings in the embassy's gardens, where a rota of Italian and British ladies dispensed tea and cake to a constant stream of appreciative customers.

But that was only the beginning of Lilias Rennell Rodd's good works. She poured the considerable funds from her shop into training and work schemes for disabled veterans. She held regular concerts in the embassy ballroom, now converted into an auditorium, staged numerous plays, some of which she wrote herself, and hosted countless bazaars, lotteries and fairs in aid of the Red Cross. At one such event, Lady Rodd persuaded each Allied nation to erect a themed pavilion in the embassy gardens; the British tent was attended by ladies in costume copied from a Gainsborough painting, but even these elegant English belles could not outdo their US colleagues, whose 'American bar' reaped the largest profits of all thanks to the presence of 'an attractive group of barmaids'.[17] The ambassadress's final triumph was a British-Italian exhibition of Arts and Crafts, which took place immediately after the Armistice and generated a handsome profit by showcasing a tasteful selection of goods produced by the finest craftsmen of both nations. For all this, the Italian government honoured Lilias Rennell Rodd with a gold medal in grateful recognition of her devoted service to its countrymen (and in so doing provided yet another example of how valuably a wife could contribute to restocking the reserves of diplomatic goodwill between her nation and its allies).

It was perhaps unsurprising that the wives and daughters of the British Diplomatic Service should throw themselves into war relief work with such dedication. Many boasted, as previously noted, a strong track record of involvement in charitable organisations, and in chan-nelling their philanthropic energies into the war effort they mirrored the patriotic style displayed by women of their class back in Britain. The daily press at home was crammed with images and stories of soci-ety ladies packing parcels for men at the front, organising first-aid workers, entertaining the troops and welcoming refugees. Many middle- and upper-class women joined the Volunteer Aid Detachments (VADs) despatched to nurse the wounded in northern France, and a handful of aristocratic ladies deployed their considerable powers of persuasion to raise funds for new military hospitals, such as the one established by the Duchess of Westminster in the casino at Le Touquet.[18] The pioneering doctor and suffragist Elsie Inglis went even further, establishing the Scottish Women's Hospitals for Foreign Service at the beginning of the war, whose all-female medical teams travelled into France, Serbia and Russia to run relief hospitals for Allied soldiers.[19]

Naturally, most diplomatic womenfolk who, like Meriel Buchanan, were drawn to relief work of a medical nature, lacked formal training, but there were exceptions. Lady Helen Duncombe, who in 1890 married Vincent D'Abernon, a future British ambassador to Germany, found her skills as a nurse anaesthetist in high demand during the war. She spent four months in 1916 assisting French surgeons at the base hospitals near Verdun, and later became a Red Cross commandant at a clearing station in Dolegna in northern Italy, caring for soldiers wounded in the Second Army's offensive of August 1917. She was billeted with fellow VADs in a tumbledown villa swarming with flies, although she soon found that there was little time for sleep or relaxation once the casualties started to pour in – as many as a thousand a day during the heaviest period of fighting. Working gruelling eight-hour shifts with only a few hours of repose in between, Lady D'Abernon dressed and bandaged cracked skulls and mutilated limbs, administered tetanus shots, offered hot coffee or scraps of ice to hopeless cases left in ambulances for onward transportation, and helped poor souls blinded by gas to write letters home to their families. It was distressing and exhausting work, but it did not end with Italy's abandonment of the Isonzo a month later, for October 1918 saw Lady D'Abernon back in France, employed as an anaesthetist at a small field hospital at Vic-sur-Aisne near the front. The accommodation was even worse than in Dolegna, consisting of a damp bed under a leaking roof in a loft overrun by rats. It was at least preferable to the hospital ward – in actual fact, a tent erected on soggy clay. There D'Abernon and her three colleagues tended to forty-five men stretched out on hard, makeshift beds, some writhing in agony, others numbed into silence by the extent of their injuries. She worked flat out for over a month, rarely snatching more than two or three hours of sleep a day, the heavy fug of human suffering always close about her. With the Armistice declared on 11 November, Helen D'Abernon gratefully left this vale of tears for Paris, and was soon enveloped in the luxurious comforts of the British embassy. But the haunting and haunted faces of those whose lives the war had claimed she would not easily forget.[20]

Initially at least, the war service of Gertrude Bell was cast in the same mould of upper-class, feminine, voluntary endeavour. In November 1914, forty-six-year-old Bell arrived at Clandon Park in Surrey, home of family friend Lord Onslow and one of the many great houses transformed by their aristocratic owners into military hospitals during the First World War. Clad in a specially purchased Red Cross uniform and desperate to get stuck into some absorbing work, Bell was disappointed to discover that she would not be doing any proper nursing, which remained in the hands of the trained VADs. Instead she filled the hours by chatting in French to the patients (all Belgian), distributing reading matter and completing routine paperwork. This usually got her to 5.30 p.m., when she would retire to her room for a solitary dinner and an hour or two of letter-writing before bed. It was a strangely mundane existence for the brilliant, multilingual Oxford graduate known to the world as a courageous mountaineer and traveller of far-off lands. Bell's 1907 work, *The Desert and the Sown*, based on a journey through Palestine and Syria, had established her as a travel-writer of the first order, as well as a noted authority on the politics, culture and geography of the Middle East. Further travels and publications cemented this public reputation and secured her election to the Royal Geographical Society in June 1913 (which had only very recently opened its membership to women). Six months after receiving this honour, Bell was on the road again, this time undertaking a perilous expedition on camel back to the remote desert city of Hayyil, overcoming obstructive Ottoman officials, befriending Arab tribesmen and picking up useful intelligence about the ruling dynasty, the Rashids, along the way. Her daring adventure, which saw Bell held prisoner for a nerve-racking eleven days in the fortress city, later earned her the Royal Geographical Society's much coveted Gold Medal.[21]

It was for her unique perspective on the region, which at this time fell under the authority of the Ottoman Empire, Germany's ally (and therefore Britain's enemy) that the War Office had written to Bell in August 1914, soon after the declaration of war. Would she kindly produce a memo on the likely Arab response in the event of a British offensive against the Turks in the south-eastern Mediterranean? Bell obliged; she was well accustomed to supplying the government with intelligence on Arabia, where Germany's growing influence had been a cause for concern for several years. During her earlier travels, Bell fed the Intelligence Division of the Admiralty with information about political developments and the bent of local opinion, and handed over maps and drawings of potential military significance. She knew what officials at the War Office needed from her and quickly produced a detailed, nuanced and authoritative report which made a general case for the existence of substantial pro-British feeling in both Syria and Mesopotamia. Her report was sent on to Cairo, the centre of Britain's wartime intelligence-gathering operation in the region, and was also put before the Foreign Secretary, Sir Edward Grey, to whom the Bell family was well known – Gertrude's father, the industrialist Sir Hugh Bell, having served with him on the board of the London and North Eastern Railway for many years.

Despite this official recognition of Bell's expertise, it was another year before she would find herself on the spot, putting that expertise to proper use, and even longer before the British state would decide it was willing to offer her permanent employment. Other archaeologists and travellers with specialist regional knowledge, such as David Hogarth, Leonard Woolley and T. E. Lawrence, were quickly snapped up for overseas intelligence work at the beginning of the war. Bell, by contrast, followed the worthy but highly conventional example of other upper-class ladies by donning a nurse's uniform and putting herself at the disposal of the wounded and needy. Fortunately, she only had to endure the mind-numbing routines of Clandon Park for a few weeks. On 21 November, a letter arrived containing an offer of immediate employment at the Red Cross Wounded and Missing Enquiry Department (W&MED), based in Boulogne. It was not Cairo, but it would at least bring Bell closer to the action and allow her to sink her teeth into some serious war work.

As she discovered on arrival the following week, the W&MED was established to answer queries from families who had lost contact with their menfolk at the front, and, if possible, to trace and identify the missing soldiers as either wounded or dead. At least, that was what it was *supposed* to be doing, but Bell soon found that the staff were woefully ill-equipped to deal with the huge volume of letters from anxious relatives which arrived in box-loads several times a day. There was no proper filing system in place, no links set up with the military hospitals through which up-to-date lists of the wounded could be compiled, and no sense of professionalism amongst the volunteer staff. Bell soon took things in hand, insisting on the creation of an alpha-betical card index of names which could be quickly checked when letters arrived, even though this labour took over lunch hours and tea breaks for several days. She also assembled a team of male volunteers to make enquiries at the local hospitals, women being forbidden from doing so by the Red Cross (although Bell happily disregarded this 'silly' rule and sauntered into the wards after the office had shut). By the beginning of December she was confident, as she told her step-mother, Florence, that in time 'we ought to have one of the best run offices in France'.[22]

Despite having no prior experience of office work, Bell proved to be a talented administrator with a flair for managing people and processes and an eye for detail ('If we are not scrupulously exact,' she wrote home, 'we are no good at all and it weighs on me').[23] Her fertile mind dreamt up ever more ingenious schemes for gathering information on missing soldiers, and so determined was she to create a model adminis-tration, that she spent the £50 her father sent her for Christmas on filing cabinets, ledgers and furnishings for the office. She was delighted by the praise heaped on her achievements by Red Cross chiefs and expressed her desire for ever greater responsibilities: 'The more work they give, the better I like it.'[24] By mid-January, Bell had more staff, bigger premises and a profound sense of the value of her work to fami-lies left sick with worry over the unknown fate of their loved ones. As she wrote to her father: 'We are doing something, we really are. And people are grateful – you should read the letters that come in every day. Even to relieve the flood of misery a little is something.'[25] When, at the end of March 1915, a new central W&MED office was opened in

London to coordinate the entire operation, there was no question as to which Red Cross worker was most qualified to run it. Bell returned to England and to a staff under her command of twenty clerks, four typists and two Boy Scout messengers ('who are an infinite joy').[26]

In charge was where Bell liked to be. Back in January when the Boulogne office was expanding, she had written to her stepmother: 'I have got the thing going on such a good system here that I'm sure I can take in the whole work and do it efficiently if they give me the clerical staff. And I shall like doing it.'[27] But despite her elevation to office chief, these were, in truth, dark days for Gertrude Bell. Unbeknownst to all but her most intimate friends, she was suffering from a broken heart. She had, since 1912, been in love with a married man, Dick Doughty-Wylie, a professional soldier and military consul whom Bell had first met at Konya in Turkey during her travels five years earlier. The two conducted an intense but unconsummated affair, each writing the other long, angst-ridden letters and snatching a few joyful days here and there in London or at the Bells' family home at Rounton Grange in the North Riding of Yorkshire. Her war work in Boulogne was a welcome distraction from painful thoughts of the dilemma she had turned over in her mind for months: either brave the opprobrium of family and friends as Dick's mistress, or live a lonely, but respectable, life without her soulmate by her side. In April 1915, the decision was, cruelly, taken out of her hands. Dick died a hero's death during the British landings at Gallipoli, a piece of news which Bell learned in the worst possible way, as a scrap of gossip across the table at a lunch party with acquaintances in London.

Bell's letters to her family during the following months only hint at the black emptiness which had entered her soul. She tried to lose herself in her W&MED job, stepping up her hours and volume of work, but was irritable and short-tempered with her staff. 'I am having a horrible time,' she wrote in August, 'with a lot of new people, all to be taught and all making mistakes at every moment. There is no one in whose hands I could leave the office even for a day.'[28] To her stepmother she complained: 'I've been bitterly alone this month. It's intolerable not to like being alone as I used, but I can't keep myself away from my own thoughts, and they are still more intolerable.'[29] Nothing could console her, and she rebuffed all offers of help: 'Nobody does any good really; it sounds ungrateful, but it is so. Nothing does any good.'[30]

––––––

A way out of the darkness came in November 1915. David Hogarth, the archaeologist whose sister, Janet, was an old Oxford friend and was now working at the W&MED, wrote to Bell with a proposition. Would she come out to Cairo to lend a hand with his fledgling Arab Bureau, an elite unit under the auspices of the Foreign Office tasked with coordinating intelligence, political and propaganda work across the Middle East? It had taken more than a year, but finally the opportunity was there, and Bell could at last return to the part of the world which had captured her heart so many years ago. There was never any question as to her answer. Hogarth's sister remembered going into the office one morning and being immediately accosted by Bell, who seized her arm and said: 'I've heard from David; he says anyone can trace the missing but only I can map Northern Arabia. I'm going next week.'[31]

Although this moment is often presented as a decisive turning point in Bell's career, the exact particulars of her new employment were left rather unclear. 'I'm off on Friday morning,' she wrote to her stepmother on 16 November,

> but I think it more than likely that when I reach Egypt I shall find they have no job that will occupy me more than a fortnight, and I may be back before Xmas. It's all vaguer than words can say. I have no instructions; I'm sent out by the Admiralty to see if they have any work for me in Egypt. As for any further journey nothing definite is said and I think the chances are strongly against it.[32]

She arrived in Cairo after a stormy crossing from Marseilles to be met by Hogarth and Lawrence, the latter whom she knew from an earlier stay at the archaeological dig at Carchemish (she thought him 'exceedingly intelligent') and the three repaired to the Grand Continental Hotel, where the whole bureau was housed.[33] Bell's new colleagues were an eclectic and romantic group of scholars, diplomats, journalists and former MPs, brought together by Hogarth and serving under the command of Sir Gilbert Clayton, the Director of Military Intelligence in Cairo. Nominally, the unit was under the control of the Foreign Office, but its members, who dubbed themselves 'The Intrusives', saw their activities as standing at something of a distance from the regular lines of authority. They shared Clayton's desire for a more assertive British policy in the Middle East and advocated the stirring up of an Arab revolt against the Turks as a means of hastening an Allied victory and safeguarding Britain's strategic interests in the region – which, crucially, included trading routes to India and the oilfields of Persia.[34]

Although only too aware from first-hand experience of the factions and rivalries that divided the peoples of Arabia amongst themselves, Bell broadly supported this policy line. Her expansive political imagination could envisage a future Arab state, prosperous and self-governing under a benevolent British tutelage in the short term, and a powerful friend and independent ally to the British Empire in the long term. After years of shocking neglect and poor governance under the Ottomans, the region could be reborn and helped to take its first tottering baby steps by the world's consummate masters of state-building – and taking her place amongst them, Miss Gertrude Bell. Before all of this, however, she had more practical matters to attend to. Her first task was to catalogue the numerous tribes of the Arab lands, detailing their numbers, history and political allegiances. 'It's a vague and difficult subject which would take a lifetime to do properly,' she wrote to Florence Bell on 6 December: 'I should think it will be about a month before I can get it into any sort of shape, but it rather depends on what information one can collect here.' A week later, and Bell felt 'a little more as if I were getting hold of things'. She started each morning with breakfast and a quick Arabic refresher lesson, followed by a stroll to her office next door at the Savoy and a full day of working on tribal histories or annotating telegrams ('the latter is great fun') with a break for lunch. Most evenings she dined with colleagues at the Continental or was a guest of the High

Commissioner, General McMahon; she then managed to fit in a little more Arabic study and another hour of drafting before bed. 'I think I'm right to be here,' she wrote to her stepmother.[35]

This was a world away from the mud and muddle of Boulogne and from fussing Red Cross volunteers in London. There she was a woman in charge. Here, in Cairo, she was a staff officer of ambiguous status operating in an exclusively masculine environment. Yet Bell was no stranger to male officialdom. Brought up as she had been in a rich, politically well-connected family – her grandfather, Sir Lowthian Bell, amassed a fortune through iron manufacturing, represented Hartlepool in Parliament and won a baronetcy in 1885 – she enjoyed ample opportunities as a girl and young woman to make the acquaintance of powerful men, including many from the world of diplomacy. Her uncle, Frank Lascelles, was shooting up the diplomatic career ladder when she visited him in Bucharest in late 1888, at the age of twenty. Kitted out with trunk-loads of fashionable gowns, the young Gertrude blended comfortably into the cosmopolitan high society she encountered in the Romanian capital, and made two important friendships which were to serve her usefully in later years: one was with Valentine Chirol, ex-Foreign Office and soon-to-be foreign correspondent of *The Times*; the other was with Charles Hardinge, on leave from the embassy in Sofia and later to become permanent secretary at the Foreign Office and finally Viceroy of India.

Following her Bucharest sojourn, Bell entered diplomatic circles again in 1892, when she was her uncle's guest in Tehran, a trip which kindled the flames of her growing fascination and affection for the Middle East. Five years after that, Bell was visiting her uncle once more, this time in Berlin, where Lascelles was ambassador. There Bell went skating with the junior secretaries, dined out with the city's leading personalities, danced with officers at court balls and was formally received by the Emperor and Empress. This endless round of entertainments and ceremonials might, in fact, have become Bell's permanent existence had fate not intervened to prevent her from marrying a young diplomat, Henry Cadogan, whom she met and fell for in Tehran. Parental reservations (Cadogan reportedly was a gambler and had heavy debts) forced Bell to delay the planned nuptials and return to England, and then tragic news from Persia removed the possibility for good: Cadogan had fallen into an icy river whilst out fishing and had later died of pneumonia. How differently Bell's life might have unfolded had she become a diplomat's wife in 1893.

Instead, past experiences and personal connections with top diplomats stood Bell in good stead as she sought to stake out her position in wartime Cairo. She successfully prolonged her stay in early 1916 by arranging a journey to Delhi with a view to improving the coordination of the Arab Bureau's intelligence work with that of the Government of India. Officials in Delhi were perturbed by the prospect of an Arab uprising; they feared its effects on the millions of Indian Muslims living under the British Raj, and, moreover, were extremely reluctant to spare any further Indian troops for a major offensive in the Middle East. Bell's task was to assuage these fears and offer reassurance, a delicate mission which she felt was far better carried out by 'a quite unimportant and unofficial person' like herself, who would lose little face were it to fail.[36] The chances of success, however, were boosted by the fact that her old friend from Bucharest, Charles Hardinge, was installed at the viceroy's palace and, better still, Chirol was in Delhi as well. His good offices helped to secure Bell an invitation to stay at the Viceregal Lodge (in three lavishly furnished tents in the garden) and multiple opportunities for conversing one-to-one with the viceroy, whom she thought 'delightfully wise'.[37]

The appreciation was evidently mutual. Towards the end of her visit, once Bell had conferred with government officials, inspected their files and 'pulled things straight a little as between Delhi and Cairo', Hardinge made a suggestion which was to open a new chapter of Bell's already eventful career. She should proceed to Basra, the military headquarters for Britain's Mesopotamian campaign, and there serve as liaison officer for Egypt and India, working under Hardinge's chief political officer, Sir Percy Cox. As a woman, Hardinge warned, she was likely to meet with a frosty reception, but it was up to her to win Cox and his colleagues over by proving her mettle. Bell respected the viceroy's frankness. 'As we have often said,' she wrote to her father, 'all you can do for people is to give them the opportunity of making a plan for themselves. The V. has done that amply.'[38]

Still, it was with a mixture of delight at being in 'my own country once more' and trepidation at the reception which awaited her at general headquarters that Bell arrived in Basra in March 1916: 'it remains to be seen whether they find a job for me or send me away without delay'.[39] Hardinge's predictions turned out to be only partly correct. Cox, who had met Bell years earlier when he advised her against making any expedition to Hayyil (advice she flatly ignored), was sceptical but fair. He took her to lunch with the generals of the Indian Expeditionary Force, formidable old gents who had little time for blue-stocking spinsters, and Bell stunned them with her intellect, humour, political judgement and strategic sense. Impressed, Cox was prepared to accept Bell as his colleague and make full use of her extraordinary knowledge of and instinctive feel for the region and its peoples. There followed a year of exhausting but absorbing work. She produced a comprehensive handbook on the tribes of Arabia, travelled into the interior to check maps and chat with friendly tribesmen, cosied up to Basra's leading notables and arranged visits from powerful sheikhs, fitting in, where she could, morning rides into the desert and walks at sunset through palm groves. 'The days pass like lightning,' she told her stepmother in April.[40]

Gradually, Bell grew more confident in the value of her contribution. 'I do know these people, the Arabs,' she wrote to her father; 'I've been in contact with them in a way which is possible for no official, and it is that intimacy and friendship which makes me useful here now.'[41] Sir Percy clearly agreed, quickly making her an assistant political officer and later regularising her status as an officer of the Indian Expeditionary Force D with the title of Oriental Secretary and a salary of 300 rupees a month. When the British forces pushed the Turks back to the north, in April 1917, she accompanied Cox to Baghdad, the city which would remain her home until her death almost a decade later. By now, Bell's chief was ready to fight for his sole female officer in the face of chauvinistic military authorities. According to Cox, General Maude, who was in command of Mesopotamian operations, on hearing of Bell's presence, expressed considerable misgivings at the news, as he feared her arrival might form an inconvenient precedent for appeals from other ladies, but I reminded him that her services had been specifically offered to me by his predecessor as an ordinary member of my Secretariat; that I regarded her and treated her no differently from any male officer of my Staff, and that her particular abilities could be very useful to me at the present moment.[42]

The years which followed established Gertrude Bell as a serious player in the politics of the Middle East. After the Allied victory and the fall of the Ottoman Empire, it was to Bell that Mesopotamia's tribal leaders, landowners and holy men flocked in order to set out their position as to what kind of state should fill the vacuum left by the Turks. It was Bell who understood the pressing need for agricultural reform and investment in schools, hospitals and roads in order to win the people's trust in British methods and British leadership. And it was Bell who, throughout, never lost sight of her central purpose: to create a stable, ordered government which would leave the region and its people more prosperous and, yes, 'more civilised'. She fought for this cause at the Paris Peace Conference in 1919, and at the Cairo Conference of March 1921, called by Winston Churchill, then Colonial Secretary, to determine the political destiny of Iraq (as Mesopotamia became known), now held in trusteeship by the British as a mandate under the League of Nations. Bell distilled her encyclopaedic knowledge of regional governance in her 1920 masterpiece, 'Review of the Civil Administration of Mesopotamia', which was published by the British government as a White Paper, and remained in post as Oriental Secretary after the creation of a provisional Arab government and the coronation of King Faisal in August 1921. She became a close confidante of the royal family and, revisiting her earlier love – archaeology – drafted an antiquities law which would enable the excavation and preservation of Iraq's many ancient treasures.

With her unique story, Gertrude Bell might seem to jump from the pages of history as a woman unhampered by the conventional constraints of her sex. Her powerful personality, physical toughness and extraordinary capacity for hard work allowed her to disregard or overcome many of the prevailing assumptions of the day about feminine inferiority. She displayed a quality which many believed only men could possess: an implicit confidence in her own political judgement and capacity to lead. Bell sought power because she believed she had what it took to wield it effectively. And wield it she did.

But for all that, Bell could not operate in a world of men as if her femininity was of no consequence. Throughout her years working for the British state in the Middle East, she remained at all times under male authority. As a woman, her presence in the formal structures of government was an anomaly, permissible only because of her unrivalled specialist knowledge and the personal support of powerful allies. She joked to her stepmother in December 1918 that she was 'second choice for High Commissioner here, so I'm told!' There was never any real possibility of a woman filling this post, although Bell added, apparently with seriousness, that it was 'really just as much a female job . . . as a male, because it's mainly concerned with the handling of people individually'.[43]

This statement is a rare instance of Bell openly reflecting on her femininity, entertaining the notion that, as a woman, she might approach her work differently from male colleagues and have something different to contribute to the task of political administration. Seldom in her letters or diaries did Bell attribute any significance in her dealings with fellow officers or Arab acquaintances to her peculiar status as Britain's only female official in Iraq. Bell was famously hostile to feminism and opposed the campaign for women's suffrage before the war, believing she needed neither to become the 'person' she wished to become. And in one sense she was right. Bell did not depend, like other women of her class, upon a husband for status; she often found her colleagues' wives dull and frivolous. Sir Percy's wife, Lady Cox, she thought 'absolutely no good to any mortal soul – she is so damned stupid. I think I never came across any woman with so completely vacant a mind.'[44] Bell preferred, in fact, the company of non-European women, whom she frequently entertained to tea at her house in Baghdad and invited to lectures and film shows. Possibly Bell felt more comfortable in the company of women who stood outside her own culture and would accept her authority as a bearer of Western civilisation, regardless of sex.

In other respects, however, Bell was wrong, for only feminism and collective political power would (eventually) win women the right both to pursue professional ambition and to obey their hearts. Bell never married; it is possible that she died a virgin. But her capacity for forming deep emotional attachments was great, as her correspondence with Dick Doughty-Wylie reveals, whilst her fondness for the various little nieces and nephews that swelled the Bell tribe over the years is palpable in her family letters. Had Bell wed Cadogan in 1893, and borne him children, or eloped with Dick during the war, it is unimaginable that opportunities for power and influence in Iraq would have come her way. And quite possibly Gertrude, the married woman, would not have pursued them. Her love of cigarettes aside, she was no bohemian, and held quite conventional views on marriage and family life (which go some way to explaining the depth of her anguish over the prospect of an adulterous liaison with Dick). On outward appearances, Bell seemed the model Edwardian lady. Even in the desert, her trim figure was always immaculately turned out, and throughout her years in Iraq, Bell went to great pains to secure a ready supply of elegant gowns, undergarments, hats and accessories from London which offered not the tiniest clue as to the extraordinarily original personality which lurked underneath.

The pleasure Bell took in selecting and wearing beautiful clothes was evidently genuine. But her sartorial elegance was also a handy defence mechanism against those who resented the presence of a woman in their midst, and who might have tried to undermine her with the typical misogynist slurs of 'unwomanly' or 'unfeminine' behaviour. Sir Mark Sykes MP, who was closely involved in Middle East policy until his death in 1919, once described Bell as 'a flat-chested, man-woman, globe-trotting, rump-wagging, blathering ass', but it was a view that few shared.[45]

Bell's ability to blend conventional femininity with 'masculine' qualities such as intellect and courage was much commented on – and admired – in tributes paid to her after her death. Hogarth wrote of her 'masculine vigour, hard common sense and practical efficiency – all tempered by feminine charm and a most romantic spirit', while Chirol noted that 'with all the qualities which are usually described as virile she combined in a high degree the charm of feminine refinement'.[46] This, it would seem, was the greatest possible compliment that might be paid to a woman in public life in post-First World War Britain.

We know so much about Gertrude Bell because of her own devouring need to capture in writing every colour and shade of the hand that life had dealt her, whether in letters to family and friends, private diaries or published works. A large swathe of her personal correspondence was edited for publication by her sister, Elsa, shortly after her death, which is when the 'legend' of Gertrude Bell might be said to have begun. Successive volumes of letters became instant bestsellers and the basis for full-length biographies; the first of these appeared in print in 1941 and the most recent was published some sixty-five years later. Of Bertha Phillpotts, another highly educated woman who served Britain over-seas during the war, we know much less. Her letters home from Stockholm sketch out a life of clerical duties, endless housekeeping, a painful right hand, and excessive concern for the welfare of her brother, Owen, who was always losing his handkerchiefs, staying out too late or complaining about having no *Punch* to read. They display none of the ego or political vision of Bell's fertile mind. As a Girton colleague commented after Bertha's death in 1932, 'her heart was still in Icelandic literature and philology. She would never by her own choice have sought out an administrative position. She liked to work quietly by herself, as a scholar does.'[47] It was perhaps unsurprising, therefore, that, unlike Bell, Phillpotts made no effort to prolong her war service after the Armistice, returning to Britain in 1919 to become principal of Westfield College for women, and later mistress of her alma mater, Girton College, Cambridge.

Phillpotts's story is certainly less thrilling than Bell's, but it was ultimately more typical of the war-service trajectories of the educated
middle- and upper-class women of Britain. Most left their temporary
government posts or swapped their nurses' uniforms for civilian dress,
some perhaps with regret but little bitterness towards the competing
claims of the returning heroes. The way was now open for feminists,
who had suspended all campaigning for the vote during the war, to
take up the fight for women's employment rights. At the Foreign
Office, the legacy of the war for women was mixed. A team of female
clerks was sent to Paris as part of the British delegation to the Peace
Conference, and a handful found longer-term employment as secretaries and clerical assistants both in London and abroad. Yet Phillpotts
and Bell were unusual (perhaps unique) for having served their country
during the war in responsible posts overseas, Bell all the more so for her
staying power beyond 1919 and the breadth of her influence over policy
in the Middle East.

Ironically enough, it was exactly this singularity which would
produce clashing assessments of Bell's significance in later debates over
women's suitability for diplomatic careers. For some, she proved how
brightly a woman could shine when given the chance; for others, she
was a rare gem whose sparkle few other Englishwomen could hope to
emulate. The Great War unsettled many of the old axioms of nineteenth-century diplomacy and redrew the political map of Europe. But
for Britain at least, the formal exclusion of women from the Diplomatic
Service was one pre-war practice which, save for these few exceptions,
was left virtually untouched.

PART TWO

The Battle for the Foreign Office

Paris, 1919

The visitor to Paris rarely sees the city to its best advantage in early January, and certainly not during a winter like the bleak, washed-out winter of 1919, when the boulevards stood leafless and damp, the banks of the Seine were barely visible beneath swollen grey waters, and the dominant colour in the slow-moving crowds was the black of women's mourning dress. Paris was a city of ghosts. How many had perished in the fire of the mighty German cannon, which now lined the Champs-Elysées like great slain beasts, no one knew. Captured and brought home as trophies of war, these iron monsters, like the ugly glass panes temporarily lodged in the windows of Notre Dame to save the originals from enemy bombardment, served only to remind Parisians of the price of victory, denominated in blood.

Yet even as the people of France, in step with the bereaved of other nations, buried their dead, the thoughts of the world turned to the living. Here, in this city, drained of its habitual splendour by wintry rains, Europe would embark upon a new beginning. Already statesmen were gathering from far and wide. They brought with them vast armies of advisors, secretaries, interpreters and stenographers who installed themselves in smart hotels, assembled makeshift offices, briefed friendly journalists and gasped at the price of a simple two-course meal. Over the next six months, the victors and vanquished of humankind's first total war created a city within a city. Anxious to secure a settlement acceptable to publics back home, they met for breakfast, lunch and dinner. They compared drafts in palatial halls at the Quai D'Orsay, met petitioners in hotel lobbies and argued over maps by firelight in private suites. This was the Paris Peace Conference at work.[1]

Some four hundred Britons became official citizens of this temporary metropolis. They were housed in two grand hotels: the Majestic, where they slept and ate and entertained, and the Astoria, where they worked in small bedrooms hastily converted into offices. Every precaution was taken to keep the delegation's secrets safe, from the burly detectives posted at the Majestic's front door, right down to the concierge and kitchen staff imported from the Midland Hotel in Manchester, which gave the busy dining room the incongruous feel of a railway terminus somewhere in northern England. Meals were procured here through a cumbersome system of coupons, and frequently featured vegetables which had, as Robert Vansittart, a later permanent secretary, remarked, 'endured the British ordeal by water'.[2] Yet despite it all, the residents of the Majestic found ways to enjoy themselves, with weekly dances, regular concert parties and amateur theatricals providing light relief from the sombre business of the day (not to mention the champagne and vintage port to be had by those making appropriate overtures to the suggestible butler).

This was far from being a monastic society. Esme Howard remembered seeing 'dames of all sorts' passing through the Majestic.[3] Most were secretaries or typists populating outer offices or filing furiously in the registry which occupied the entire top floor of the Astoria. Each kitted out with a brand new wardrobe funded by a generous clothing allowance (this was Paris, after all), these young women brought some much-needed glamour to the social life of the Majestic. But they pulled their weight, too, often staying up late to take dictation from *digestif*-swilling chiefs, or dashing over to the neighbouring Hôtel de Crillon several times a day clutching messages for the American delegation.

Equally visible, but more pleasantly leisured, were the wives and daughters of the delegation's leading men. Denied rooms at the Majestic due, it was rumoured, to loose tongues amongst the womenfolk present at the Congress of Vienna a century before, these ladies were, nonetheless, frequently seen gracing the hotel's dining room and in attendance at the elegant receptions and balls which leavened the stodgier aspects of the conference proceedings. David Lloyd George, the British Prime Minister, brought his daughter and mistress along for the ride, electing to stay in a luxurious apartment lent for the occasion by the wife of a wealthy merchant banker, where the strains of Welsh hymns could be heard wafting through the floorboards late into the night. Others enjoyed the brilliant female society which descended upon Paris during the conference months. Harold Nicolson spent many an evening in the presence of distinguished or well-connected companions. In addition to the flying visits of his novelist wife, Vita Sackville-West, Nicolson's diary records that he dined with Margot and Elizabeth Asquith (wife and daughter of the former Liberal Prime Minister); Lady Muriel Paget (in town to raise money for her Czecho-Slovak Relief Fund); the Society hostess Maggie Greville (in town for the gossip); and various members of Parisian bohemia, including the poetess Anna de Noailles. ('She looks like a hawk from some hieroglyph in a Temple at Luxor,' Nicolson wrote in the entry for 17 March.[4])

Both at work and at play, the peacemakers of 1919 were, then, rarely without feminine company. But which of these women featured in anything more than a mere bit-part in the political theatre which played day after day and night after night between January and June? Where, behind the formal language of the treaties proposed, negotiated and concluded, could traces of a feminine hand be found? Perhaps in the Mesopotamian and Syrian settlements, where Gertrude Bell, who arrived in February fresh from Baghdad, immersed herself 'deep in propaganda' with the French and Americans, her objective a satisfactory balance of power between nascent Arab nationalism and British imperial interests. Or perhaps in the deliberations of the Romanian and Yugoslav commission, whose weary task of arbitrating territorial claims was enlivened by the irresistible entreaties of the golden-haired and vivacious Queen Marie of Romania ('she is very naughty,' said Lloyd George, 'but a very clever woman').[5] And, perhaps, somewhere behind the British premier's own weighty utterances concerning every substantial decision of those six momentous months lay the brains of Frances Stevenson, his devoted private secretary, mistress and later wife: history – and Stevenson's diaries – do not tell us.

What history does confirm is the absence of any serious deliberations over the rights of women by the conference, despite the march of feminist movements in dozens of countries, and the presence of a well-organised suffragist delegation on the spot in Paris. Having met informally with these campaigners in February, the US President Woodrow Wilson raised, somewhat sheepishly, the question of votes for women before his fellow plenipotentiaries. After an awkward silence, the representatives shuffled slowly to their feet one by one to explain in elegant phrases that whilst they could not deny the real force of the ladies' case, it could not *possibly* be considered a matter for *international* agreement. Wilson did not push it, and the subject was closed. All the feminist societies could content themselves with was a small concession concerning women's equal eligibility for posts at the League of Nations, the new peace-keeping machinery agreed by the Allies earlier in the year.

And so it was that when, on 28 June, the Treaty of Versailles, the blueprint of a new European order, came to be signed, the faces around the table belonged – as they had in Berlin forty years before – to men and men alone. As the delegates transacted business, women spectated. The wives of the highest-ranking officials enjoyed a fine view of proceedings from their seats inside the Hall of Mirrors. Frances Stevenson, by contrast, lacking formal spousal status, was relegated to the back row, where the whole event was 'little more than a crowd, with something happening at the other end of the room'.[6] She was, at least, in the hall, unlike the hard-working secretaries and typists of the British delegation patiently standing on the terrace outside, who had been conveyed earlier from the Majestic packed like cattle into three grimy lorries.

This was women's meagre share in a diplomatic event which changed the world irrevocably; but for how much longer would the ordering of global affairs be left in the hands of men? Shortly before the signing, Sir Maurice Hankey, the British delegation's self-important secretary, told his wife that he would be needed by the Prime Minister after the ceremony and warned that she had better return to their car and 'expect a very long wait'.[7] For the women of Britain, it would prove a long wait indeed.

4

Ammunition

In September 1933, Charles Howard Smith, an assistant under-secretary at the Foreign Office, wrote to all serving ambassadors with an unusual request. 'What we want,' he began,

> is that you should lay aside all predilections which you may have in the matter and give your completely unbiased opinion whether a woman could as efficiently perform the duties of a diplomatic or consular officer in the country in which you reside as a man: whether she would be treated with the same respect and attention as diplomatic and consular officers can usually count on, and generally give your views on the whole subject, bearing in mind that, if women were admitted to the Diplomatic and Consular Services, they could not, in fairness, expect only to serve in those posts which are most highly civilised, but would have to take their turn in the more outlying places.[1]

Innocently worded, at least on first glance, Howard Smith's missive drew forth a voluminous and spirited response. Many ambassadors wrote personally and at great length. The ministers in Brazil, Colombia, France, Italy, Switzerland and the USA managed eight pages apiece; Sir Eric Phipps's letter from Berlin ran to nine, whilst Sir Claud Russell, the ambassador to Portugal, won first prize for verbosity, filling fifteen pages sprinkled liberally throughout with obscure classical aphorisms (a touch that Howard Smith doubtless appreciated, given that he, seven years later, would deliver a speech entirely in Latin during his posting as ambassador to Iceland). With a few exceptions, these old hands were staunchly opposed to the employment of female diplomats. Posting women to China, Howard Smith was informed, would be 'unsuitable and highly inadvisable'.[2] Sending them to Yugoslavia would be 'disastrous' and to Liberia 'absolutely out of the question'.[3] Women were 'obviously unsuited' to consular work in Greek ports, whilst the employment of female consuls in Brazil would be 'unthinkable and even criminal'.[4] The consequences of admitting women would be 'deplorable' to the efficiency of the diplomatic service in Norway, whilst in Saudi Arabia, such a posting would be 'incompatible, to use no stronger term, with the maintenance of British prestige in this and neighbouring countries'.[5]

For Howard Smith, who had pledged to gather 'all the ammunition that I can get' against the case for sex equality – which, following persistent lobbying from women's societies, was now being actively considered by a departmental committee – these uncompromising statements were an invaluable addition to his arsenal.[6] Despite the entrance of high-profile female diplomats such as Bolshevik Russia's Alexandra Kollontai and America's Ruth Bryan Owen onto the international scene, the Foreign Office only reluctantly conceded that the time had arrived to consider the question of careers for women in the British Diplomatic Service. For men like Howard Smith, this was a deeply distasteful notion which, if allowed to become reality, would do untold harm to a profession founded on fine masculine qualities – character, integrity, loyalty, clubbability – and threaten to disrupt the domestic arrangements which, thanks to the continuing goodwill of wives, supported it. The battle for the Foreign Office had begun. It was a fight that Charles Howard Smith had every intention of winning.

———

As jubilant crowds gathered in Trafalgar Square to toast the Armistice, down the road in Whitehall officials were scratching their heads. Now that the war was over, they faced the daunting task of dismantling the vast governmental machinery put in place since 1914, which, alongside securing victory, had provided gainful employment for thousands of British women. What should become of these willing patriots, who had rallied so splendidly in their country's hour of need? It seemed obvious that jobs in any reconstructed Civil Service should be reserved for the returning heroes, for whom a regular salary and guaranteed pension was the least their nation could offer in return for the living hell they had endured on the Western Front. Yet it was equally obvious that the world – and the respective place of the sexes within it – as it existed in August 1914 had vanished for good. Women's labour had been pressed into service to an unprecedented degree over the intervening years; it had transformed the look and feel of the British state. Was it fair – was it wise – to discharge these workers so hastily?

The members of the women's committee appointed to advise Christopher Addison, Minister for Reconstruction, knew their answer to these questions. 'Injury will be done to the public service,' they warned in a report published shortly after the Armistice, should the government decide to turn the clock back to the bad old days when openings for women were restricted to the typing pool and a handful of supervisory posts. Yes, they accepted that demobilised soldiers must have their fair share of the jobs, but it would be madness to lose capable workers simply on grounds of sex, and even greater folly to send away those women who had demonstrated 'administrative capacity of high grade' during the war. The great ship of state had navigated the British people through a tempest; but there were still troubled waters ahead, and every hand, regardless of sex, would be needed to hold the tiller steady. The committee's message to Addison was uncompromising: in the short term, make women who had proved their worth eligible for permanent government posts along-side ex-servicemen; and in the long term, open all Civil Service grades to women on the same terms as men.[7]

Such bold advice was in keeping with the expectant mood of the times. The Fourth Reform Act, which enfranchised female household-ers (or the wives of householders) aged over thirty – about 8.5 million women in total – was both the crowning achievement of the pre-war suffrage movement and a curtain-raiser for the next act in the long struggle for women's equality. Sensing an appetite for change amongst first-time female voters, the Labour Party used its newly won status as His Majesty's Official Opposition to introduce the Women's Emancipation Bill to Parliament. If passed, the bill would have immediately extended the suffrage to *all* women, regardless of age (this was not to happen until 1928); it would have permitted women to sit in the House of Lords (a reform eventually passed in 1958); and, finally, it would have outlawed sex discrimination in all judicial and civil appointments. This last provision rang warning bells in Downing Street, for it carried with it several disturbing implications for the government's current employment practices. The first was equal pay for all female employees; the second was the abolition of the marriage bar (the rule which required women to choose between having a job and having a husband); and the third was the prospect of women serving overseas as diplomats and colonial administrators.

All three possibilities were distinctly unwelcome. Pay differentials and marriage bars were excellent ways of controlling the government wage bill and reserving promotion routes for men, who, officials reasoned (inaccurately, as it happens), bore sole responsibility of providing for hungry mouths at home. As for women serving overseas, the proposition was so utterly fantastic and so obviously misguided that it could not possibly be taken seriously, could it? Parliament did not think so; the question received only the briefest of comment during debates on both the Women's Emancipation Bill and the alternative legislation introduced by government – the less ambitiously titled Sex Disqualification (Removal) Bill – to ensure the former's defeat. Even those who defended women's right to jobs in the Home Civil Service drew the line at sending them abroad. 'There are, of course,' remarked the Liberal peer Lord Haldane, 'many appointments into which nobody wishes to put women. For instance, there are appointments in India, and others of a special kind, for which women ought not to be eligible merely because they have passed an examination.'[8] Perhaps most surprisingly, even former suffragists put up little fight over this piece of blatant discrimination. The feminist Ray Strachey, speaking

for a delegation of thirteen women's societies* which visited the Leader
of the Commons, Bonar Law, in August 1919, confessed that 'they fully
realised that it might be inadvisable for certain posts to be held by
women at present, for example in India'.[9]

In truth, Strachey and her colleagues were probably keeping their
powder dry for the larger battles they saw looming on the horizon.
When the government bill was passed at the end of 1919, it made no
provision for women's entry to the House of Lords and it included an
insidious get-out clause which gave the state a free hand in prescribing
women's general 'mode of admission' to the Civil Service. The women's
societies were aghast. A bill which had offered the promise of equality
now left women in almost as precarious a position as before: sex was to
be no disqualification to women's appointment and promotion in
public service, except on occasions when the government decided that
it was. Understandably, feminists like Strachey directed their fire on
what they saw as the gravest implications of this shabby piece of political manoeuvring: namely, unequal pay and discrimination against
married women. The reservation of overseas posts to men was, of
course, deplorable, but, given the apparent consensus of opinion in
favour, there seemed little prospect of reversing this policy in the short
term. Better to focus on getting women through the examinations for
the senior ranks of the Home Civil Service – for which, at last, both
sexes were eligible – than to waste precious energy on hopeless causes.
Once women had made good in Whitehall, one feminist periodical
remarked, it seemed reasonable to assume that 'the question of their
appointment to posts abroad could be more easily advocated'.[10]

Such pragmatism was further justified by the entrenched position of
the Foreign Office, whose inhabitants were not well disposed towards

* The societies were the British Federation of University Women, Federation of Women
Civil Servants, Association of Women Clerks and Secretaries, Civil Service Alliance,
Association of Senior Women Officers in the Central and Divisional Offices of the
Ministry of Labour, Civil Servants Typists' Association, Association of Temporary
Clerks in Government Offices, National Union of Clerks, Association of Women
Sanitary Inspectors and Health Visitors, National Council of Women, National Union
of Societies for Equal Citizenship, Women's Local Government Society, and the
London Society for Women's Service.

radical administrative experiments, not least those involving female diplomats. The whole set-up of Britain's overseas representation had received a thorough drubbing by the Royal Commission on the Civil Service when it reported back in December 1914. The £400 property qualification required of new recruits to the Diplomatic Service, the commissioners argued, had limited entry 'to a narrow circle of society' and should be replaced with proper salaries paid to new entrants. Nominations, they added, should be determined by a formally consti-tuted board of selection and *not* through a nudge and a wink from the Foreign Secretary of the day. Furthermore, officers needed to possess far greater understanding of economic matters than they did at present, given the ever-increasing influence of commerce and industry over diplomatic relations. Finally, and most controversially, the commission recommended that the diplomatic establishment in London and the diplomatic corps overseas be amalgamated into one single service, so that every officer would be obliged to spend years both at home and abroad, thus avoiding narrow specialisation.[11]

Predictably, these recommendations caused great consternation at the Foreign Office, particularly amongst those men who had spent comfortable careers issuing telegrams from their desks in London, and who felt not the slightest urge to discover what their diplomatic colleagues got up to in foreign capitals. The recommendations were disturbing for another reason, too, as they appeared to lend credence and respectability to criticisms emanating from more outspoken quar-ters on the political left. Radicals had long railed against 'aristocratic monopoly' at the Foreign Office. It was back in the 1790s that Charles James Fox demanded a true government of the people which would do away with bumbling diplomacy and foreign policies which served the interests not of the many but of the few.[12] Such critiques won followers throughout the nineteenth century but only truly came of age during the First World War, a conflict which radicals in the Labour Party and beyond blamed upon unaccountable elites 'working in secret and deal-ing in darkness' with 'vast issues of life and death'.[13] Labour's own ambitions for international accord and friendship amongst the peoples of the world could never be realised so long as foreign affairs remained 'in the hands of the British Junkers'.[14] Now, in 1919, with toppling empires giving birth to liberal constitutions and democratic governments across Europe, the days of the 'old' diplomacy were surely numbered. For critics on the left, the time had come to refashion Britain's Diplomatic Service along modern, democratic lines and to sweep away the pernicious system of patronage which had allowed Foreign Office chiefs to handpick recruits in their own image.

Such a savage reading of diplomatic traditions would, one might suppose, have easily incorporated some reference to the casual discrimination which barred women from pursuing careers in diplomacy. Yet removing sex discrimination, as opposed to the social elitism which operated to the detriment of working-class men, was conspicuously absent from left-wing demands for an egalitarian Diplomatic Service staffed by 'the best brains in the country'.[15] Admitting women under the caste-like conditions currently in force would, as radicals saw it, do nothing to advance the working-class struggle. Why, then, create jobs for the daughters of bishops and Oxford dons who saw the world through the same privileged eyes as their brothers and fathers?

Radicals thus saw no greater need for sex equality at the Foreign Office than its own residents, whose energies were, in any case, absorbed in leading a rear-guard action against the Royal Commission's recommendations – back on the table now that the war was over. Following a series of ill-tempered internal tussles, it was agreed that the property qualification and unpaid posts would go, that the entrance exam would be revised, and that some limited interchange between London and overseas posts would take place at junior level. But even with these grudgingly conceded reforms in place, the Diplomatic Service retained its aura of exclusivity (and Foreign Office chiefs continued to preside over the nation's foreign affairs without ever treading on foreign soil).[16] Any observer scrutinising the social make-up of its personnel in the 1920s would have found little trace of the new democracy taking form in post-war Britain. For that, both women and the working classes would have to wait.

In revolutionary Russia, less patience was required. In the autumn of 1922, Joseph Stalin sent Alexandra Kollontai to Oslo (then known as Christiana) to take up a post as second-in-command of the Soviet Union's trade delegation to Norway. Within months, Lenin's former Commissar of Social Welfare was heading the mission, and in February 1924, when the Norwegian government extended formal diplomatic recognition to the Soviet regime, Kollontai became the world's first female head of mission.* She was fifty-one years old.

It was perhaps to be expected that Bolshevik Russia should have earned this particular distinction. Under communism, the sexes were – in theory, at least – equal. Women were eligible for all public offices and admitted to every profession; abortion was legalised and divorce obtainable by mutual consent. Kollontai, Russia's most prominent female politician, seemed to embody this new Soviet Woman. Born into a wealthy, landed family in 1872, Kollontai rejected the life of genteel respectability for which young women of her class were destined, in order to answer the call of revolutionary politics. She spent many years in Europe as an exile, studying Marxism and developing her ideas about women's subjugation under capitalism, before returning to Russia in March 1917 after the fall of the Tsar and joining Lenin's first Bolshevik government later that year. As commissar, Kollontai advocated universal maternity services and communal childcare provision as the very foundation of women's emancipation, and was later instrumental in the creation of the Women's Bureau, which worked to raise the political consciousness of the ordinary Russian woman.

Clever, accomplished, fluent in eleven languages and steeped in

---

* She was not the first formally accredited female diplomat; arguably this honour should go to Nadejda Stancioff, born into a prominent diplomatic family, who was appointed secretary at the Bulgarian legation in Washington in 1921. See Mari A. Firkatian, *Diplomats and Dreamers: The Stancioff Family in Bulgarian History* (Lanham, MD, 2008).

European culture, Kollontai was ideally placed to help Stalin in his bid to establish 'normal' diplomatic relations for Soviet Russia with the rest of the world in the post-revolutionary years.[17] She immediately put these talents to use in Oslo, driving a hard bargain over concessions for Norwegian fishermen in Soviet waters, hammering out a deal to establish a joint Soviet-Norwegian shipping company, and persuading the Norwegian government to upgrade the Russian trade delegation to legation status. During her next posting, which took her to Mexico in 1926, Kollontai opened talks on Soviet contracts for Mexican lead, whilst hosting film screenings at the embassy to audiences of writers, artists and intellectuals keen to learn more about cultural life under communism (the artist Diego Rivera became a good friend and gave Kollontai one of his paintings as a farewell gift). After another stint in Norway, Kollontai became ambassador to Sweden, where she worked hard to break down anti-Soviet feeling and notched up a number of diplomatic wins, including agreement on long-term credit loans to Russia and the return of gold reserves hidden by Kerensky's Provisional Government in Swedish banks. On top of her ambassadorial duties, from 1934 Kollontai made twice-yearly trips to Geneva, where she sat as the sole woman member on the Soviet Union's delegation to the League of Nations.

Despite frequent heart trouble, Kollontai served her government with the energy of a woman half her age. One American journalist thought there was 'something electric and modern about her, impossible to define – something swift and efficient in keeping with our post-war age'.[18] A typical day for Kollontai started with gentle exercises to military music followed by a quick shower and a coffee, after which it was time to knuckle down to work. Her staff in Oslo clocked up ten-hour days, but Kollontai was often seen at her desk drafting despatches late into the night, deep in concentration. She always dressed simply, in black or dark blue, with no make-up to enhance her large blue-grey eyes, and no jewellery save for a silver chain attached to her spectacles. At the embassy, Kollontai's sympathetic manner and egalitarian instincts made her a popular figure. Visitors noted with surprise the friendly, communal suppers at which Russia's lady ambassador shared her table with her staff, right down to the doorman and cook. Yet Kollontai was equally at ease amongst the *chers collègues* of the diplomatic corps; she was a generous hostess and gracious guest, her cultured conversation and mastery of the expected etiquette confounding popular stereotypes of wild, bloodthirsty Bolsheviks bent on revolution. Such was Kollontai's renown, that in 1936 an international congress of businesswomen voted her the world's second most outstanding woman (number one was Frances Perkins, President Roosevelt's Secretary of Labor).

The precedent set by Kollontai's ambassadorial career did not go unnoticed by the British Foreign Office, but its implications for British women were unclear. Of the handful of ambassadors who, in response to Howard Smith's circular of September 1933, did not write back with barely concealed derision or scorn, Sir William Strang, head of mission in Moscow, was by far the most confident in his conviction that women *could* serve effectively in the USSR. Given Kollontai's record and the entirely unremarkable presence of women at the Commissariat for Foreign Affairs, Strang reported, there could be no objection to a British female diplomat on the part of the Soviets. 'Such an appointment,' he added, 'might indeed seem to them to be rather in keeping with the peculiarities of this post.' She would have no trouble doing business with her opposite numbers or going out and about with foreign journalists, such were the 'normal free and easy Moscow habits'.[19] Howard Smith received Strang's endorsement with equanimity, choosing to treat it not as evidence in favour of the feminist case but as the exception which proved the rule. 'Your letter is most interesting and it will be exceedingly useful,' he wrote back; 'It just shows what a very different country Russia must be from the rest of the world.'[20]

Further evidence of Kollontai's singularity was supplied by the letters from Oslo and Stockholm. Britain's ambassador to Norway thought Kollontai could not, as a woman, have retained her post had she been anything other than 'a very exceptionally capable lady'.[21] His counterpart in Sweden described Kollontai as an 'uncommon woman' who was 'remarkably intelligent', but agreed that even in egalitarian

Scandinavia, Kollontai was handicapped by her sex.* The only evidence cited in respect to this point was Kollontai's tendency to invite male officials to a private tête-à-tête over luncheon instead of dinner, but it was grist enough to Howard Smith's mill.[22]

Kollontai's example thus failed to derail Howard Smith's quest for ammunition; but for those British women's societies hoping to bring public opinion round to the idea of female diplomats, Kollontai was a problematic role model for other reasons, too. In the first place, there was the small matter of her revolutionary politics. Bolshevism had few adherents in Britain, regarded by many as the new sinister spectre threatening to overturn Europe's fragile social and political order. Even with a Labour and trade union movement staunchly devoted to parliamentary democracy, fears of the communist bogey-man ran high. As a woman doing a man's job, Kollontai was a doubly unsettling figure. The right-wing press invariably dubbed her a 'Woman Red', and took every opportunity to shock readers with cari-catured accounts of her 'advanced' views on sexual relations. In reporting her appointment to Mexico in 1926, for example, the *Daily Mirror* portrayed Kollontai as more fanatical propagandist than professional diplomat, 'the torchbearer of Bolshevism in the Western Hemisphere', who advocated 'communal courtship' and believed marriage to be an unnecessary institution.[23]

Of course, Kollontai had her admirers. Her experimental novella, *Love of Worker Bees*, was translated and published in English in 1932, earning fine reviews from such literary luminaries as Winifred Holtby and Rebecca West. Yet such praise, if anything, only drew attention to Kollontai's highly unconventional route into diplomacy. Despite her

---

* In fact, only a few years later there would be four female heads of mission across the Scandinavian states, with Kollontai joined in Stockholm at the end of 1936 by Spain's Isabel de Palencia, whilst Mexico's Palma Guillén and the USA's Ruth Bryan Owen (see below) led their countries' respective missions in Copenhagen. It is surely significant that de Palencia and Guillén were, like Kollontai, appointed by post-revolutionary regimes keen to advertise their apparently advanced attitudes towards the equality of the sexes. For Guillén, see James D. Huck, 'Palma Guillén, Mexico's First Female Ambassador and the International Image of Mexico's Post-Revolutionary Gender Policy', *MACLAS: Latin American Essays*, 13 (1999), pp. 159–71.

linguistic skills and political talents, Kollontai was a reluctant diplomat, posted to Oslo by Stalin more for the convenience of putting physical distance between himself and a known critic of his regime than for her fitness to represent Russia abroad. Kollontai's history with Lenin and her support for those demanding greater democracy inside the Communist Party made her an enemy in the eyes of the autocratic Stalin, albeit one whom it was (for the time being, at least) better to neutralise than to eliminate altogether. Kollontai accepted her involuntary exile, resigned to biding her time in Oslo until conditions at home permitted her return. 'I really believed that this appointment would be purely formal,' she wrote in her memoirs, 'and that therefore in Norway I would find time to devote to myself to my literary activity.'[24] Holed up in a hotel in the tourist resort of Holmenkollen, Kollontai did complete several works of fiction during the early months of her posting, but once promoted to head of mission, those hours of quiet repose were quickly eaten up by official business.

Kollontai's loyal work for the regime was noted in Moscow but did not remove the black mark against her name. There was good reason to think that Stalin posted her next to Mexico City with full knowledge of the dangers the altitude (more than 2,000 metres above sea level) would pose to her failing health. He never hesitated to pack other opponents off to Siberian outposts to endure hostile, arctic conditions when it suited him, pleasantly unsurprised when they failed to return. Kollontai found herself struggling to breathe within hours of arriving in Mexico City and, despite cheering crowds, took to her bed, waking later that night with heart palpitations. She wrote plaintively to a friend: 'I am a denizen of the Leningrad marshes. I miss moisture. I long for the water.'[25] Kollontai only survived by negotiating a transfer after barely six months, boarding a steamer in June 1927 and rejoicing as it chugged into the chilly waters of the English Channel. Back in Scandinavia, as Kollontai's public stature increased over the next decade, her anxieties for friends in Moscow grew ever more profound; when the notorious show trials commenced in 1936, to be followed by further purges of party officials and army officers suspected of disloyalty, Kollontai became fearful for her own life, convinced that every communication from Moscow was a summons to her death. When Stalin's war on his enemies at home intensified in 1938, Kollontai withdrew from diplomatic society, finding silence and solace preferable to public appearances at which she might be pressed to justify (or, more dangerously, to condemn) the bloody events taking place in Russia.[26] By playing safe, Kollontai survived, rendering her country further valuable diplomatic service during the Second World War before finally returning to her beloved homeland to live a quiet, uneventful life until her death in 1952. She received no official obituary in the Soviet press.

Kollontai's story was, then, even in 1933, when Howard Smith was fitting out his arsenal, a complicated one. More encouraging for proponents of female diplomats was the news in February that year of Ruth Bryan Owen's appointment as the USA's minister to Denmark, the first American woman to head a mission overseas. Democratic, capitalist, English-speaking: the USA offered a far more compelling analogue to Britain than Bolshevik Russia; here, perhaps, British feminists would find the evidence required to clinch the argument for women's admission to the British Diplomatic Service. The US State Department's early history as an employer of women was not wholly dissimilar to that of the Foreign Office, beginning in the nineteenth century with the introduction of cleaning ladies and typists, and progressing to women's appointment to more responsible posts as archivists, legal advisors and low-ranking clerks in overseas legations. Thereafter the British and American paths appeared to diverge, with Lucile Atcherson, a gutsy suffragist from Ohio, making history in 1922 by becoming the first woman appointed to the prestigious officer class (the equivalent of Britain's administrative grade) of the US Foreign Service, almost a quarter of a century before any British woman would pass this milestone. Atcherson was followed by Pattie Field in 1925 and by a further four successful female candidates by the end of the decade.[27]

Appearances, however, could be deceptive. The US Foreign Service exam had – in theory – been open to all, regardless of sex, for some years, but whilst a sizeable number of women in the 1920s passed the preliminary written test with flying colours, only a handful convinced the board of examiners of their suitability for overseas service during the final interview. The men in whose hands these decisions lay barely concealed their scepticism towards women's fitness to 'discharge the exacting and peculiar duties' of a Foreign Service officer, as Wilbur J. Carr, director of the Consular Service, put it in 1924. Carr and his colleagues even floated the idea of an executive order, issued by the President, to exclude women from presenting themselves as candidates (it would be a 'great convenience' to the board of examiners, he noted). To his credit, the Secretary of State, Charles Hughes, quashed this suggestion, but left the way open for questions about geographical mobility – which, it was assumed, would be trickier in a woman's case – to be factored into the board's final decision. It was this consideration which probably explained women's low pass rate in the oral examination and supplied the grounds on which the board failed a number of otherwise well-qualified female candidates. The remarks of Hugh Gibson, ambassador to Switzerland, upon hearing of Atcherson's posting to his legation in Berne, distilled the contempt which many in the US Foreign Service felt towards the rookie female officers. Atcherson's desk, Gibson wrote jokingly to Hughes in 1925, had been placed, due to pressures on space, in a dusty room previously used for storing old files – and 'anything once put in the file room has never been found again'. Pattie Field's boss in Amsterdam, Consul-General William Gales, was scarcely less unpleasant. He pleaded with the department to reconsider her assignment: 'A woman would not fill the requirements here and would be worse than useless.'[28]

By the time of Ruth Bryan Owen's appointment in 1933, there were just two American women serving abroad as diplomats and eight employed as consuls or trade commissioners, plus a further four who had resigned after earlier periods of service (including both Atcherson and Field). The numbers involved were paltry. Still, in the eyes of British women's societies, who watched the advances made by their English-speaking sisters across the ocean with avid attention, they represented a breakthrough. Here was another advanced, Western nation prepared to send women to represent its interests overseas – and not just to relatively 'safe' European capitals, but to places as far afield as China, Syria, Cuba and Chile. 'In upbringing, education and independence American women are similar to English women,' remarked the Council of Women Civil Servants, a body representing senior female officials, 'and, if they can be entrusted with work in these Services, we feel that British women are worthy of equal confidence.'[29]

Given women's uneven progress in the US Foreign Service over the previous decade, Ruth Bryan Owen's appointment as head of mission was, then, closely watched on both sides of the Atlantic. Owen had not herself risen through the ranks as a career diplomat but was a political appointee, invited to serve by Franklin D. Roosevelt, for whom she had enthusiastically campaigned during the presidential election of 1932. A born Democrat, she was the daughter of William Jennings Bryan, three-times presidential nominee and Secretary of State under Woodrow Wilson. Accompanying him as a child aged six on one of his visits to Congress, Owen would return in her own right in 1928 as congress-woman for Florida's fourth district, working for her constituents at her father's handsome mahogany desk and under his watchful eyes which gazed out of the portrait that never left Owen's office. The British press, however, were on the whole less interested in these details of Owen's political lineage than they were intrigued by her earlier marriage to a British officer in the Royal Engineers and her war service as a volunteer nurse to the British forces in Egypt and Palestine. Such loyalty to her late husband's country of birth evidently endeared Owen to the residents of Fleet Street, who praised her gracious manners and demure demeanour, noting approvingly that diplomatic duties had left these feminine charms entirely intact. The gossip column of the *Daily Express* drew a telling contrast with Kollontai when it described how, during a meeting of the diplomatic corps in Copenhagen, Owen, operating on the principle of 'ladies first', swept past her senior colleagues in a streak of silver-embroidered black velvet to greet the King of Denmark and chat 'diplomatic nothings' into his ear. In neighbouring Sweden, the column observed, 'no feminine precedence is claimed by the Soviet Minister' when in the presence of royalty, for Kollontai 'sees no reason for "ladies first", [and] considers "lady" a repulsive epithet anyway'.[30]

Grateful, no doubt, to be spared such aspersions concerning her femininity, Owen might, all the same, have felt just a hint of annoyance at the condescending tone of much of this press comment. Male diplomats were quoted in stories about treaties, summits and high political intrigues; female diplomats, it appeared, were more interesting for their wardrobe (in Owen's case, black velvet with pearls), their offspring (four children and three grandchildren), and their views on whether women really could excel in this most masculine of professions. On the latter point, Owen always tried to avoid controversy: 'If women are suited, by reason of particular qualities or because of experience,' she told one reporter primly, 'they will be given those [diplomatic] appointments.'[31] 'Competition,' she informed another, 'can always be trusted to bar out the incompetent. Those who cannot do the work will be weeded out automatically.'[32]

Yet unthreatening appearance and soothing manner aside, this forty-seven-year-old widow and grandmother was no fool. Owen was a fighter and a survivor. She had weathered a political storm in 1928 when her eligibility to run for Congress was challenged on the charge that Owen had forfeited her US citizenship by marrying a foreigner eighteen years earlier. Owen faced down her enemies in front of the House of Representatives, which found in her favour and later gave her a much sought-after spot on the prestigious Foreign Affairs Committee, where she quickly mastered the intricacies of American foreign policy. Moreover, Owen had powerful friends who looked after her interests after she lost her congressional seat in 1932. Having narrowly missed a place in Roosevelt's Cabinet, Owen's suitability for a top diplomatic appointment was forcefully advocated by the First Lady, Eleanor Roosevelt, and by Molly Dewson, head of the Women's Division of the Democratic National Committee. Both lobbied assiduously for Owen's posting, drawing the President's attention to her talents as a public speaker, her many accomplishments as a congresswoman, and her first-hand knowledge of Danish society and culture acquired during a two-month motor tour of Denmark in 1931.

Their representations did the trick. Two years later, Owen returned, stepping on to the wharf at Copenhagen's bustling port in June 1933 and into, as she noted with delight, 'the pages of my Hans Christian Andersen book!'[33] Once in post, Owen did not dawdle whilst awaiting instructions from her superiors but attacked her work with gusto, setting in train new projects and initiatives designed to boost US interests in Denmark. Her calls for renewed trade talks won few supporters back in Washington (where the Danes were in the doghouse for imposing tariffs on US goods), but her investigation of America's public image as portrayed in the Scandinavian press caught the approving eye of Cordell Hull, Roosevelt's Secretary of State. Owen's extensive collection of news clippings revealed some alarming distortions and misconceptions – not least the excessive coverage enjoyed by Al Capone and his gangster associates – and convinced Hull that a wider study of the foreign press was urgently required. A true pedant when it came to correcting inaccuracies in the Copenhagen press, Owen took the problem of improving America's standing in the eyes of the Danish people extremely seriously. She never missed an opportunity to generate good news stories, from reading fairy tales to schoolchildren in passable Danish, to joining an official seven-week expedition to Greenland in 1935. According to her biographer, she practised a type of 'people's diplomacy', believing that warm, lively engagement in all aspects of Danish society was the best means of fostering goodwill towards America.[34] If the effusive and appreciative reaction in Denmark to news of her departure in 1936 was anything to go by, Owen pulled this off with aplomb.

But how was Ruth Bryan Owen's appointment received in the British Foreign Office? Did the case of America's first female chief of mission create any greater ripples of anxiety than had Russia's Kollontai? The sanguine response of the British minister in Copenhagen to Howard Smith's circular of 1933 suggested that defenders of the status quo could rest easy. Owen was not debarred from routine formal gatherings on account of her sex, the ambassador observed, but her influence was highly questionable. 'She is not a figure commanding undoubted respect,' he wrote, 'and nor, does it seem to me, are her words received with the same attention as those of her countrymen at other posts.' This he blamed partly on the Danes, who, despite being 'in the van of what is sometimes called "sex-emancipation"', remained allergic to women in high-ranking political posts, and partly on Owen's tendency (shared, in his view, by many members of the fairer sex) for excessive sentimentality. This latter quality caused the ambassador to doubt whether Owen would ever be deemed capable of 'setting forth impartially and objectively her country's point of view' or 'carrying on difficult and protracted negotiations involving sustained concentration and effort'. Moreover, as a woman, Owen was bound to encounter difficulties when seeking informal access to her diplomatic colleagues: 'I should myself undoubtedly feel a certain hesitation in asking Mrs Owen . . . to dine alone with me, particularly in a public place, at any rate more than once a year; whereas I might readily do so in the case of a male colleague.'[35]

In his affable reply to this pleasing missive, Howard Smith raised a further objection: namely, Owen's status as a political appointee rather than a career diplomat. Such postings were common in the higher ranks of the US Foreign Service but were frowned upon in Britain, where an ambassador was expected, like the fine wines on his table, to mature slowly over decades of loyal service within the diplomatic family. Owen's case was, in this respect, not an instructive one and could therefore be easily dismissed: 'she is not a diplomatist *de carrière*,' Howard Smith remarked, 'and will presumably go when the Democratic party goes in America'.[36]

In fact, Owen went much sooner than that. In the early summer of 1936, now aged fifty-one, she announced her engagement and imminent marriage to Borge Rohde, a captain in the Danish King's Life Guards. Dripping in powder-blue chiffon to match her betrothed's colourful military uniform, Owen wed Rohde at a church in Hyde Park – Roosevelt's home town in New York State – with the President, First Lady and press in attendance. Her colleagues at the State Department were unlikely to have been amongst the well-wishers, Owen having failed to notify them of her impending nuptials before they were reported in the press. This oversight may have helped to solidify opinion against her when the matter of Owen's continuing employment was raised for discussion. Plenty of male diplomats married foreigners without fear of the consequences, but under Danish law, Owen, having married a Dane, was now herself a Dane. Could an official envoy of the United States share the nationality of the country to which she was posted? Owen evidently thought she could and expected to be kept on. The State Department, however, had other ideas. Under pressure to resign, Owen finally appealed to Roosevelt for advice; she would do nothing, she declared, to endanger his re-election campaign, which was now in full throttle. The President took the easy way out and Owen dutifully resigned. She had been in post just over three years.

Thus the diplomatic career of America's first female head of mission was cut short by nationality laws which discriminated against married women – the same laws which had nearly scuppered Owen's political career back in 1928. Reflecting on this inauspicious ending, the *New York Times* remarked that unless in future the State Department forbade all diplomatic marriages to foreigners, 'in no sense can a woman appointee go as far as a man in the field of international relations'.[37] What this well-meaning editorial failed to acknowledge, however, was that marriage of any kind was off limits to female career diplomats in the US Foreign Service (and would remain so until 1971). As for political appointees like Owen, those who followed in her footsteps remained husbandless; Florence Harriman, posted to Norway in 1937, was long widowed and gave romantic trysts with members of the Norwegian court a miss. It was the same story with Washington socialite Perle Mesta, who was sent by President Truman as ambassador to Luxembourg in 1949 (and would be played, a year later, by Ethel Merman as the fictitious lady diplomat of Irving Berlin's musical, *Call Me Madam*). In short, the Americans were reluctant pioneers of diplomatic careers for women. Those hunting for cast-iron precedents would have to look elsewhere.

———

Back at the Foreign Office in London, these experimental postings of women diplomats by Britain's enemies and allies were watched with interest but little alarm. Foreigners could go their own way. What mattered was the path that Britain chose to follow, and by late 1933, when Howard Smith was firing off salvos to ambassadors from Brussels to Beirut, the question of women's eligibility for the Diplomatic and Consular Services was firmly back on the table. It had returned thanks to a single recommendation contained within the voluminous report of the Royal Commission on the Civil Service (the second to be appointed in under twenty years), published two years earlier. Chaired by the distinguished judge, Lord Tomlin, the commission was asked to make special reference to the conditions of women's employment, a subject on which the five female and nine male commissioners duly began to hear evidence in the autumn of 1929. Feminists, who had continued to grumble sotto voce over the male monopoly on overseas posts during the 1920s, now saw their chance to force the issue back into the public eye.

Yet as the commission's proceedings progressed, it soon became clear that sex discrimination at the Foreign Office was merely the unsightly scab on a much deeper scar. At least in the Diplomatic Service the reservation of posts to men was openly admitted. Arguably more disturbing was the discovery that home departments had been testing the get-out clause in the 1919 equality legislation to the limit. The Ministry of Defence, it appeared, would brook no feminine presence in anything other than the lowly typist grades, the Ministry of Labour refused to recruit female Customs and Excise officers, the Office of Works employed no women in responsible posts, whilst the Post Office clung to the old segregated structures, channelling female employees into a separate – and, inevitably, more poorly paid – women's branch. Supervisory posts in the Forestry Commission, the Royal Mint and the Board of Control, jobs inspecting railways, mines or livestock, governorships of prisons and asylums – all were, in practice, off limits to women. The reason for this was simple. All these jobs involved in some shape or form the supervision of men. In 1929, a full decade after women had secured their political rights and entered Parliament, the thought that a male employee might reasonably be expected to take orders from a female superior was sheer fantasy. It remained an affront to the natural order of things, in which men called the shots in the workplace and women, where they wielded formal authority at all, did so over female subordinates only.[38]

The earlier hope that women would 'make good' in Whitehall thus was confounded. Yes, there were women in the prestigious administrative grade, but the figures wheeled out by the Council of Women Civil Servants revealed that they were few and far between: only thirteen women at assistant principal grade, six at principal grade, two at assistant secretary level, and no women at all in any higher posts, meaning, as the council spelled out, that women were 'almost entirely absent from the grade responsible for the formation of policy'.[39] Several witnesses probed further into this failure by women to storm the corridors of power. Prejudice certainly barred the way for those who safely cleared the first hurdle by passing the competitive examination held annually to recruit new members to Britain's policy-making elite. But few women got that far. In 1932 only six of the 379 candidates were female, and not one of them made the grade.

The marriage bar was undoubtedly a major deterrent, casting a shadow of insecurity over ambitious young women who, as one witness observed, 'wish to approach their work seriously, with a view to making it a real career and to rising high'. It was little wonder that such promising candidates chose to 'reject a service which imposes upon them either the abandonment of their career or celibacy'.[40] The other chief turn-off was the reservation of so many posts in the higher grades for men. Male candidates, it was pointed out, could compete for jobs in both home departments and the overseas services, whilst women were formally excluded from the latter and, as it had been revealed, from many posts in Whitehall, too. With such slim chances of success, many played for safety by opting for more conventional career paths for women graduates, such as teaching or secretarial work. The principal of Bedford College told the commissioners that 'the majority of University women are anxious to earn their living as soon as possible after they graduate', and therefore could not afford to devote themselves to months of intensive preparation for the administrative class exam when openings for women were so thin on the ground.[41] The Association of Headmistresses amplified the point: 'Parents expect a girl, if she is going to University, to have a definite aim in front of her, and to see her way through; whereas they are very often prepared for a little more uncertainty and a further period of education in the case of boys.'[42] With so many obstacles strewn across her path, it seemed to Ray Strachey 'inconceivable that a sensible young woman would go into the Civil Service at the present time'.[43]

The question of posts in the Diplomatic and Consular Services was raised against the backdrop of these mounting frustrations over the wider impediments to women's employment and progression. Having bided their time since the end of the war, the women's societies appearing before the commission now demanded immediate action to repeal the regulations barring women from jobs abroad. The National Union of Societies for Equal Citizenship declared itself 'unable to visualise any cause other than custom and prejudice' for the 'wholesale exclusion' of one half of the population from overseas service.[44] The Council of Women Civil Servants echoed the sentiment, remarking that it could not 'be to the public advantage that the State should be without the services of women for this type of work, more particularly when they have demonstrated their interest and competence in it'.[45]

Interestingly, the most memorable statements to be made on the subject came, however, not from feminist quarters, but from two heavyweight male officials from rival corners of Whitehall. Limbering up for the Foreign Office was its chief clerk, Charles Hubert Montgomery, a veteran of the pre-war diplomatic establishment. Sir Hubert had left his father's 500-acre estate in County Tyrone back in 1900 to join the Foreign Office as a clerk and spent all but one of his subsequent years of service in London, commuting in from a six-bedroomed mansion in leafy Sevenoaks. He spoke before Tomlin with the authority of one steeped in Foreign Office tradition and vastly experienced in the selection of men of the 'right type' to represent Britain abroad. What this task boiled down to, Montgomery told the commissioners, was spotting those with 'personality'. A few exceptional women might, it was true, possess this elusive but much-prized quality, but they could never, in practice, put it to effective use.[46]

Here Sir Hubert laid out a number of arguments which were to become crucial to the Foreign Office's defence of the status quo over the next fifteen years. The first hinged on the supposed backwardness of the societies to which female diplomats might be sent. 'What we feel generally,' he explained, 'is that in the matter of the employment of women [this] country is, in practice if not in theory, a good deal ahead of most other countries. What one can do in this country one cannot necessarily do in others.' Consular posts, he suggested, were especially unsuitable, with many based at insalubrious ports where officers had 'to deal with sailors who are not always quite sober, and who come into the offices of the Consul with various grievances, and if they are not met they are very apt to become violent and abusive'. Bigoted foreigners and drunken sailors thus seriously limited women's efficiency, ensuring that 'the field in which they might be used is very small'. A final argument rested on women's problematic marital status. 'Spinsters', as Sir Hubert described them, would struggle with the 'semi-official' business conducted between men 'over tête-à-tête meals and in clubs', whilst married women would fare even worse, forced to 'trail their husbands round from post to post'. Barred from gainful employment and unlikely to excel in the traditional spousal duties, these poor-excuses-for-men would soon become a menace to the smooth functioning of the mission. 'You mean,' Lord Tomlin interjected, 'the unfortunate Ambassadress would have a husband about the house all day?' Yes, agreed Sir Hubert, 'that puts the thing in a nutshell'. Women could best serve their country by doing as they always had, by performing 'supplementary' work as gracious host-esses, or uncomplaining typists, and leaving the serious business of diplomacy to the men. Sir Hubert rounded off his testimony by assuring the commissioners that he and his colleagues were not 'in any sense the natural enemy of women in these things'. Their objec-tions, he insisted, were practical and rooted in common sense. It seemed inconceivable that any reasonable person, contemplating the world as it existed today – rather than in some hypothetical feminist future – could possibly disagree.

This assumption, if allowed to stand unchallenged, would

probably have laid the matter to rest for some time. But Sir Hubert had not counted on the provocative intervention before the committee of Sir Warren Fisher, the brilliant and egocentric permanent secretary to the Treasury and head of the Civil Service. The very antithesis of the bowler-hatted bureaucrat, Fisher's career had begun inauspiciously at the Board of Inland Revenue in 1903 (he scraped through the exam, coming a mediocre fifteenth). It quickly flourished thereafter, as his natural flair for administration and fearless self-belief attracted the attention of his superiors, including the then Chancellor of the Exchequer, David Lloyd George, who put him to work in 1912 on the implementation of the Liberals' flagship National Health Insurance legislation. Made Head of the Civil Service in 1919, before his fortieth birthday, Fisher advised subsequent prime ministers on senior appointments and the conferring of honours, a remit which, controversially, extended to the Diplomatic Service. As an enemy of 'departmentalism' and crusader for greater esprit de corps and 'cooperative sense' across Whitehall, Fisher had little regard for the traditions of splendid isolation which had allowed the Foreign Office to run its own affairs more or less undisturbed for decades. Fisher's chairmanship of an enquiry into currency speculation by Foreign Office clerks in 1928 only aggravated these tensions, meaning that by the time he appeared before Tomlin in December 1929, refreshed from a long holiday in the United States, few expected Fisher to give his diplomatic colleagues an easy ride.[47]

Wholly unexpected, however, was his forceful denunciation of Sir Hubert's position on women diplomats. Asked, initially, for his general views on women's employment across the Civil Service, Fisher's forthright response set the tone for what was to follow. 'There is still a good deal of prejudice,' he told the commissioners,

and that prejudice is based on fear . . . it is quite premature yet for anybody even to try to prophesy or put any limit on what women may do in the future . . . If I had to hazard a guess, I should say that, when they have got the experience in a generation or so, they would give the men a jolly good run for their money.

Warming to his theme, Fisher turned to the question of the Diplomatic and Consular Services, upon which he was similarly insistent: 'To bring down a guillotine and to say that it is impossible for women to do this work is, to my mind, absolute nonsense.' Certainly there were posts where it might be impolitic to send a woman, and certainly such restrictions might create a minor inconvenience for personnel officers responsible for postings, 'but anything new is an inconvenience . . . It is not as though you are going to have a whole regiment of women unloaded on the Diplomatic Service at one go . . . I should not agree to disregard the principle for fear that this inconvenience might arise in 100 years' time.' Fisher reprimanded Sir Hubert for conjuring lurid images 'which made your hair curl' of well-bred Englishwomen accosted by oriental seamen in seedy ports, and declared that he took altogether 'too gloomy a view . . . I see no reason why a diplomat should not be a woman in the countries where it is customary to regard women with civility and courtesy'. Fisher recommended introducing women into the Diplomatic Service gradually, sending them to the most promising posts in the first instance and thus doing 'pioneer work on the part of this country'. When pressed on the problem of favouritism, the Head of the Civil Service replied: 'I do not look at it that way. If it were the case, which I do not think it is, it is a very small compensation for having kept women down for century after century.'[48]

When it reported in July 1931, the Tomlin Commission did not endorse Fisher's proposals, but nor did it let the Foreign Office entirely off the hook. The question of women's admission to the Diplomatic and Consular Services, the commissioners declared, raised 'issues of high policy' which required further consideration; the government, they concluded, 'should again examine the position at an early date'.[49] This cautious recommendation failed to fling the doors of the Foreign Office open to women, but it left them, at least, very slightly ajar. Along with the abolition of sex segregation in the Post Office and government inspectorates, and the opening of administrative posts in the Dominions Office to women, the report contained some good news for feminists.

Naturally, it was not enough: there were still the thorny issues of equal pay and the marriage bar to reckon with, together with continuing reservations of numerous supervisory posts and all higher-grade posts in the defence departments. Yet the promise of a proper enquiry into the opening of diplomatic careers to women was cause for modest celebration. Here was an opportunity to put together an unanswerable case, building on and embellishing the arguments that the Head of the Civil Service, no less, had presented before the commission.

Over at the Foreign Office, no one was celebrating. Sir Hubert's failure to put the matter to rest was a grave disappointment. In the short term it was decided that the best course of action in response to Tomlin's recommendation was to procrastinate for as long as possible, a bureaucratic art form in which Foreign Office chiefs proved highly skilled. Thus it was not until September 1933, more than two years after the commission's report had been published, that Charles Howard Smith wrote to Robert Vansittart, the permanent secretary, advising that the appointment of an 'ad hoc' committee to consider women's eligibility for the Diplomatic and Consular Services could no longer be delayed. 'It is to my mind useless for us to trot out once again the arguments developed by Sir Hubert Montgomery before the Royal Commission,' he opined:

> and it is necessary for us to have further ammunition of a kind which will convince not only the Civil Servants who are to form this <u>ad hoc</u> Committee but the Cabinet and the general public, if there is a strong movement in favour of admitting women, that their employment in our services at the present moment would not be conducive to the public interest.[50]

Here Howard Smith announced his plan to gauge opinion amongst serving heads of mission; the enquiry would be framed in wholly neutral terms, but its intent would be anything but. 'I anticipate that there are certain countries where H.M. Representative could truthfully say that women could be employed,' he told Vansittart, but I cannot help feeling that in the vast majority of cases [he] would advise that their employment would not be practicable or desirable. IF, when the <u>ad</u> <u>hoc</u> Committee is set up, the Foreign Office representative is able to communicate to his colleagues the letter and replies from all H.M. Representatives, and if the vast majority take the view that women should not be employed, this would sure go some way to influence the Committee, because we shall have the views of the men on the spot in each case.[51]

The circular letter was sent on 27 September and in less than a fortnight responses from Britain's ambassadors began to stream in. Howard Smith was vindicated. Nearly all testified to the inadvisability of posting women diplomats overseas; the exceptions could be counted on the fingers of one hand and were easily dismissed.

The next step was to appoint the members of the committee. Thanks to the vague wording of Tomlin's recommendation, it was possible to limit them to officials and to hold the committee's proceedings in private. Better still, there was no obligation to publish its findings. Last-minute efforts by women's societies to force the Foreign Office to reconsider these arrangements were in vain. They had to content themselves with the announcement that two women civil servants would sit on the committee: Muriel Ritson, an assistant secretary in the Scottish Department for Health; and Hilda Martindale, one of the earliest women factory inspectors and now Director of Women's Establishments at the Treasury. This, at least, was welcome news. Martindale, in particular, was a known champion of employment opportunities for women in the Civil Service and it could be reasonably assumed that both she and Ritson would give the women's societies a fair hearing. The rest of the committee, however, looked less promising. Alongside Howard Smith sat Sir Ronald Graham, freshly retired from a career which had began as unpaid attaché in 1892 and ended with the ambassadorship to Rome, who seemed an unlikely ally; ditto both Thomas Dunlop, representing the Consular Service, and Sir Roderick Meiklejohn, a Civil Service commissioner who was on record telling the Tomlin Commission in 1929 that he supported women's continued exclusion. As an outsider, Sir James Rae of the Treasury was potentially a more open mind. In fact, Rae lobbied hard for the women's societies to be permitted to present evidence, telling Howard Smith that it would otherwise appear that 'the matter had been settled already'. (In response, Howard Smith graciously agreed to 'let the ladies talk'.[52])

Then finally there was the chairman, Sir Claud Schuster, long-standing permanent secretary in the Lord Chancellor's Office, known for his quick intellect and no-nonsense style and a veteran of government committees. As for his position on the question of women diplomats, Schuster's evidence before Tomlin three years earlier had sent mixed signals. He referred to the 'greater diligence' displayed by many of the women employed in his own department and described two recent female appointees as 'head and shoulders' above the men who had applied for the same positions. Yet Schuster also argued forcefully in favour of the marriage bar, expressed strong unease on the question of equal pay, and made some extremely dubious remarks about women's higher absence rates due to sickness and their propensity to 'break down' under pressures of work.[53]

Moreover, Schuster's instinctive sympathy for the Foreign Office position was indicated at an early stage by his willingness to connive in the selection of material from the ambassadors' letters to be submitted as evidence to the committee. Perusing all fifty-one replies to Howard Smith's missive, Schuster suggested that those containing the most rabidly misogynistic or laughably Victorian observations be held back. They advanced arguments, he remarked, which 'seem to me untenable and, therefore, damaging to the case which they represent'.[54] As a result, the committee was deprived of the considered views of Sir Joseph Addison, writing from Prague, who confessed he would rather die than see 'England with 400 MPs, 15 Cabinet Ministers, 10 High Court Judges, 6 Permanent-Undersecretaries and 8 Ambassadors, all of the female sex and running the country on the famous "intuition" lines'. Nor were they treated to the enlightening insights of Sir William Tyrrell, ambassador to Paris, who believed it impossible for women to associate with male politicians or journalists 'without the gravest harm to their reputation', or to 'go about the streets of Paris in the small hours of the morning unchaperoned'. It would, Tyrrell added, be equally unwise to send a female officer to meet a visiting dignitary at the railway station, for 'most men would resent a woman looking after their luggage'. ('A small point,' Sir William conceded, but 'not altogether unimportant.'[55])

On Schuster's advice, these and other similarly unhelpful contributions were kept out of sight of his fellow committee members. Woman-haters and old fogeys were not the best advertisement for the virtues of the masculine status quo. To be certain of victory, the battle to defend the Foreign Office from feminine interlopers would need to be fought with faultless discipline and deadly precision. The preparations were complete. Howard Smith was ready to take the fight to the enemy.

Women of Exceptional Gifts

The Inter-Departmental Committee on the Admission of Women to the Diplomatic and Consular Services (to give it its official title) finally opened for business in February 1934, summoning as its first witness the American-born MP and socialite, Nancy Astor. If Schuster and his colleagues were hoping for a relaxed and relatively undemanding inaugural session, they were to be sorely disappointed. Famed for her general outspokenness and tenacious heckling in the House of Commons, Astor did not hold back, making hard work for the clerk to whom the unenviable task of recording the committee's proceedings had fallen. The Foreign Office, she snapped, had 'not budged a yard since before the war. It still has not taken into its head the position of women, not only in this country but in other countries.' The government, Astor went on, needed to get its act together and wake up to the vast pool of female talent sitting under its very nose. 'We are using women in a sort of subterranean way all over but there are not enough personalities,' she complained. 'There are not enough people who, as the Americans say, can "put it across" in the world.' If ever Britain needed her women, it was now, at this delicate moment in international affairs, when the global economy was gripped by crisis and authoritarian dictatorships were on the march across Europe. 'The world is in such a rocking reeling state,' Astor reflected gravely, 'that I myself being in politics see that it is blindness to shut your eyes to the work a good trained woman could do.' Such a highly qualified female, she continued, offered certain advantages: she would be 'less easily taken in' by the silver-tongued flattery of foreign officials, and she would set her womanly intuition to work for the interests of the British state. In short, it was unforgivable folly to continue denying women the opportunity to serve their nation overseas.[1]

As one of Britain's most prominent female politicians, Astor was, in many respects, an ideal candidate to fire the opening round of the battle for the Foreign Office. Virginian-born, wealthy and well connected, she first entered London's high society in 1904 as a glamorous divorcee, and wasted little time in finding a new husband, marrying Waldorf, son of millionaire William Waldorf Astor, two years later. Astor became mistress of Cliveden, the magnificent country house purchased by Waldorf's family in 1893, where she built her reputation as a political hostess whose witty repartee was as sparkling as the jewels which habitually decorated her slender neck. It was her father-in-law's death in 1919, and Waldorf's subsequent elevation to the House of Lords, which secured Nancy Astor's place in the history books as the first woman to enter Parliament, where she represented Plymouth Sutton, the seat her husband had held for nearly a decade. Initially, she had few feminist credentials to her name, having given the women's suffrage movement a noticeably wide berth before the war. Nevertheless, Astor became a vocal advocate of women's employment rights in the 1920s and a useful parliamentary ally for former suffragists, whose sights were now set on dismantling all remaining barriers to women's full and equal participation in British public life.

Astor's remarks to the committee spoke to these wider aspirations, but they also betrayed the eccentricities for which the Member for Plymouth was notorious. There was her lifelong devotion to temperance, an emotive cause for Victorian Liberals, but one whose resonance by the 1920s was fading fast; then there was her sudden conversion to Christian Science following an illness in early 1914, a spiritual awakening she fervently commended to Joseph Stalin (without success) and to Philip Kerr, later Britain's ambassador in Washington, whose rather more enthusiastic response had tragic consequences (he died in post in December 1940 from a uraemic infection after refusing medical treatment on religious grounds). Finally, there was Astor's fanatical anti-Catholicism, which stemmed from her strict southern Protestant upbringing. This spilled out in her testimony before the committee, who were regaled with stories of dastardly plotting by Spain, Italy, France and 'the Jesuits' at the League of Nations, and warned of Catholicism's sinister influence within the British Foreign Office (operating, ironically enough, in female form, through the presence of foreign-born wives). Neither claim was likely to have added much ballast to Astor's demand for women's admission to the Diplomatic Service.

Popish conspiracies aside, however, Astor's bracing performance got the committee's proceedings off to a lively start and set out lines of argument which subsequent witnesses would rehearse, elaborate and extend. First, there was the simple case of justice: fairness alone surely dictated that women should be given an equal opportunity to try their hand at diplomacy. Then there was the case for capitalising on women's 'special' qualities: Astor pointed to 'intuition' and immunity to flattery as uniquely feminine traits which would serve the female diplomat well (unlike Ambassador Addison, Astor saw 'intuition' as a positive rather than negative attribute); many more would be listed and duly noted before the committee's hearings were out. Finally, there was the compelling evidence of women's past and current deeds on the international stage; witness after witness vividly recalled the achievements of this or that exceptional female, whose courage, intellect and character proved beyond doubt that women had what it took to represent British interests overseas. Argument upon argument tumbled forth as Astor made way for a long queue of impassioned campaigners, cool-headed civil servants and no-nonsense heads of women's colleges. Listening from his seat at the committee table, Howard Smith might have felt a momentary chill as he realised how carefully his foes had been stockpiling ammunition of their own, which they were now ready to deploy.

———

Edith Lyttelton was one exceptional female with whose exemplary career Schuster and his colleagues were to become intimately acquainted.

In her late sixties and something of a *grande dame* when she addressed
the committee on 1 March, Lyttelton could draw on wisdom accumulated over a lifetime of public service. Like Astor, her story began with
a propitious marriage. Alfred Lyttelton, whom Edith wed in 1892, was
the eighth son of a baron, nephew to the Liberal Prime Minister
William Gladstone, and a famous amateur athlete and cricketer to
boot. Following his election to Parliament as Liberal Unionist member
for Leamington Spa, the quick-witted Edith sank her energies into
advancing Alfred's career, but eschewed, as an admiring profile put it
some years later, spousal devotion 'of the cocoa and comforter kind' in
favour of 'an equal partnership in work and life'.[2] Alfred's rising star
shone brightly on Edith, too. She accompanied him to South Africa in
1900 to investigate monopolies in the Transvaal, returning to London
as a lifelong devotee of the British Empire, and her lively interest and
mature judgement on all matters imperial proved a valuable asset when
Alfred was promoted to Colonial Secretary three years later.

Blessed with an agreeable and accommodating husband, Edith was
at liberty to pursue her literary ambitions – she wrote no fewer than
seven plays, one novel, several biographies and a number of works on
spiritual themes – and to take up pet causes, from women's suffrage to
the plight of the sweated labourer. Yet it was Alfred's sudden death in
1913 that launched Edith's second career as a public servant, the career
which would prove of such interest to the Schuster Committee twenty
years later. Had Alfred lived, it is inconceivable that Edith's services
would have been sought by the Ministry of Agriculture in 1917, when
she took charge of the Women's Land Army, chivvying on its quarter
of a million members to dig up the British countryside so that the
nation might be fed. It is equally unlikely that Edith would have been
invited to serve in the 1920s as vice-chair of the government's Waste
Reclamation Trade Board, or as a member of its committee of enquiry
on the protection of women and girls in Malaya. And there can be little
doubt that it was Edith Lyttelton's status as a politically savvy widow of
significant means that enabled her to leave British shores to pursue all
manner of interesting opportunities overseas. These included touring
the United States with Nancy Astor in 1922 as one half of a two-woman

lecturing team. It included lengthy travels in China and Japan as well as an extraordinary voyage to Delhi in 1931 in the company of Indian delegates returning from the first of the famous 'Round Table' conferences convened to determine India's political future. Edith, in fact, almost missed the boat, losing her porter and luggage at Boulogne and making the train to Marseilles with only seconds to spare ('Phew!' she wrote to her daughter-in-law back in England, 'I tipped everybody double and treble and flung myself into the train'). Once safely on the ship, she swiftly set about quizzing the delegates on the prospects for a new Indian constitution, carefully recording her own impressions of the mood on board and predictions for the future. These turned out to be eerily prescient. 'There never was such an opportunity for India to be united and try to work the new Constitution,' Edith wrote; 'But I have a feeling it won't be established without a long exhausting struggle and civil war of some kind.'[3]

Edith Lyttelton's gifts as a shrewd observer of colonial affairs thus did not desert her after Alfred's death. Yet it was her endeavours at the League of Nations, where she represented the British Empire at the annual Assembly in Geneva on no fewer than five occasions, which proved to be of greatest interest to the committee. Lyttelton, like others flushed with the heady idealism of the immediate post-war years, had high hopes for this new experiment in international cooperation. She dramatised its mission to preserve world peace in a specially penned League-themed pageant and, with Astor, talked up its achievements during their transatlantic lecture tour in a bid to persuade the USA to join (sadly, without success). When the call came to accompany the British Empire delegation to the League's General Assembly of 1923, Edith accepted without hesitation. She was a 'substitute-delegate' only, ranking below her full-delegate colleagues James Rennell Rodd and Lord Halifax, but nonetheless succeeded in making her mark.

On arriving in Geneva in early September, Edith found the city buzzing with nervous speculation as to the League's next move following Italy's sudden invasion of Corfu only days before. Despite this febrile atmosphere, she decided to stick to plan and speak on a subject close to her heart: the education of children for peace. 'I will tell you a secret,' Edith confided in a familiar tone to the assembled rows of suited and bespectacled delegates: 'If all the women combined all over the world to teach the children to hate war, and if they fostered the ideals of brotherhood, there would not be any war. If women chose to combine they could disarm the world.'[4] It was the first of many speeches delivered by Lyttelton on behalf of Britain and her empire. Watching her perform at the Assembly's Fifth Committee from the press gallery, the feminist writer Vera Brittain was impressed. 'Dame Edith Lyttelton, with her pale intent face and resolute manner,' she wrote, 'seems remarkably typical of her country in her clear effective speeches and her quiet persistence in proposing resolutions.'[5]

Brittain made a further observation: all the women from across the member state delegations appeared to have been appointed to this particular committee, whose remit covered assorted questions of a social or humanitarian nature, 'a sort of rag-bag of miseries and forlorn hopes' in the words of Helena Swanwick, who took Lyttelton's place as substitute-delegate the following year.[6] The pattern persisted at subsequent Assemblies, with Britain's female delegates (in step with those of other nationalities) despatched to the Fifth Committee, which quickly came to be regarded as women's natural home at the League, a place where feminine empathy and humanitarian instinct could flow freely and wash away the ills of the world. Contemplating the committee's typical agenda, Swanwick remarked ruefully: 'A woman, it appeared, was assumed to be well informed about Opium, Refugees, Protection of Children, Relief after Earthquakes, Prison Reform, Municipal Co-operation, Alcoholism and Traffic in Women.'[7] (Swanwick did, as it so happened, know a little about the last of these, but as for the rest was as ignorant as her fellow male delegates.)

This invidious typecasting of women as international social-workers-cum-saints presented Lyttelton and Britain's other female delegates with a dilemma. It was irritating to be sidelined with questions deemed of a 'feminine' nature and kept away from the problems of security and disarmament – what most saw as the 'real' business of the League. In her evidence to the committee, Lyttelton took pains to describe the 'purely diplomatic work' that she had carried out quite outside the Fifth Committee's womanly remit and on identical terms to her male colleagues. 'I have been sent on private Conferences,' she remarked, 'I have been used to try and get certain people to agree to courses.' On one occasion she was sent to negotiate a specific point with the French representatives and returned triumphant; the question, she explained, 'is not whether I did it well or ill, but the fact of being a woman was, I think, of no disability at all. I do not think it ever entered into the question in any way whatever.' To reinforce the point, Lyttelton produced a statement signed by seven of Britain's female League delegates which solemnly attested to the 'integral part' they had played in 'the whole policy and conduct of the British Delegation'.[8] Irene Wall, a principal at the Home Office who had represented Britain on a number of League subcommittees, offered further testimony on this subject: 'I myself have had to resort to the very practices of cafés and meals and little private consultations, and almost the forming of cliques for our point of view' – exactly, in fact, as Wall pointed out, the kind of 'semi-official' business that Sir Hubert Montgomery 'suggested we should not be able to do'.[9]

On the other hand, those problems which women were believed so eminently qualified to solve could hardly be ignored. *Someone* needed to speak up for the world's trafficked women, abused children and starving refugees, and if not the League's female delegates, then who? And perhaps the famous 'Geneva atmosphere' – which caused statesmen momentarily to forget their selfish national interests and think instead of the common good – would drag those 'feminine' issues out of the sidelines and into the centre stage of international politics. Lyttelton, for her part, certainly believed it possible. She seized upon the opium trade and 'white slavery' (as prostitution was then euphemistically termed) as evils which international cooperation could combat far more effectively than disparate national endeavours.

This view was shared by Rachel Crowdy, chief of the Social Questions Section and the highest-ranking woman in the League Secretariat. Another exceptional female much cited by witnesses before the Schuster Committee, Crowdy first made her name in the hellhole of war-torn northern France, where she arrived in October 1914 with a freshly trained unit of nurses just in time to witness the horrifying human loss of the first Battle of Ypres. Galvanised by the experience of tending the broken bodies of 30,000 men with fewer than two dozen staff, Crowdy soon acquired a reputation as a formidable administrator, setting up rest stations, ambulance depots, hospitals and hostels all along the Western Front. She was recruited to the League in 1919 and became an instant magnet for the women's societies swarming into Geneva bearing petitions, pamphlets and prospectuses aloft. Crowdy used what influence she possessed to divert Secretariat resources towards their favoured causes, and won a victory in 1923 with the appointment of a special commission to establish once and for all the true scale and nature of the notorious global trade in women. Feminists had been publicising for decades the plight of vulnerable young females of all nationalities, tricked or coerced into prostitution, whether it be in state-licensed establishments in continental Europe, military bases and trading posts in the colonies, or brothels throughout the Middle and Far East.[10] Yet coordinated action amongst governments had been lacking, with each nation state enforcing (or failing to enforce) its own laws and regulations in the manner it saw fit. The League Commission successfully challenged this status quo. By sending fearless investigators 'right down into the underworld' to watch the traffickers at work preying on their victims, it was able to produce a hard-hitting report whose unsentimental cataloguing of facts and figures revealed the terrifying human cost of this vile trade.[11] It sold out in weeks, generating press headlines across the world and stirring up public opinion, which at last turned against those governments under whose neglectful eye these exploitative practices had been permitted to persist for decades.

It was the opportunity to tackle such evils on a global scale that undoubtedly drew so many British women towards Geneva during the golden era of the League. A permanent, paid post like Crowdy's was the ultimate prize. Thanks to the propitious intervention by feminists at the Paris Peace Conference, the League's founding charter included a clause which provided for men and women to be equally eligible for all jobs in the Secretariat. Better still, there were no restrictions on the employment of married women, and the League and its sister body, the

International Labour Organisation (ILO), were amongst the tiny band of progressive employers providing paid maternity leave to female employees between the wars. Such enlightened employment practices were undoubtedly appreciated by the Secretariat's all-female army of typists, and by the smaller but far from insignificant group of women employed as translators, interpreters, researchers and clerks.[12] Life in the senior ranks, by contrast, was lonely. Crowdy had for company the League's chief librarian, the American Florence Wilson, until the latter was forced out in 1926 to make way, ostensibly at least, for a German man (Germany having recently joined the League), and fellow Briton Sophy Sanger, a leading figure in the women's trade union movement who headed the Labour Legislation Section in the ILO's Research Division until 1924.[13]

As appointments were carefully divvied up according to nationality, openings for British women – even assuming they could fight off the male competition – were far too scarce to meet the demand from ambitious female undergraduates pestering their tutors for advice on international careers. The response they received was usually discouraging. As representatives of the women's colleges at Oxford and Cambridge told the committee, it had to be, for there was little to be gained from encouraging girls to nurse professional aspirations which in nine cases out of ten would be met by bitter disappointment. The mistress of Girton College, Miss Wodehouse, remarked that a job at the League of Nations was a 'very common desire', but her girls were clear-eyed about 'how few opportunities there are and how almost hopeless it is, to get a post at Geneva'. It was the same story for school-leavers, as Miss Addison-Phillips, the outgoing headmistress of Clifton High School, testified: every year, she explained, at least two or three girls declared their burning ambition to 'take up work connected with the questions dealt with by the League of Nations, and it is very galling for me to have to tell them that only voluntary work in that direction is open to them'.[14]

This oversupply of talent was further evidence, witnesses before the committee argued, of the injustice of denying able young women a career in diplomacy. Women will jump at any chance to serve, Edith

Lyttelton declared, just as she and her fellow League delegates had jumped at the chance to enter the bustle and whirl of Geneva during the annual Assembly, when the whole world seemed to descend upon the city's conference halls, committee rooms and hotel lobbies. 'To receive, even for a few weeks,' Helena Swanwick observed in her memoirs years later, 'only such Foreign Office papers as are distributed to delegates, gave me an insight that probably thousands of men get daily and a bare dozen women ever get. Women,' she continued, 'outside the closed doors, have to guess, to infer, to put two and two together, to reconstruct imaginatively what men are told by obsequious secretaries and industrious officials, or hear in conference or through dispatches.'[15] For Swanwick, the League provided a rare glimpse into a world of masculine political privilege, a fleeting moment in which she felt what it was to be on the inside looking out. Few British women tasted such power between the wars.

Beryl Power might have counted herself amongst those few in 1934, if she had lifted her head from the piles of papers, reports and drafts strewn across her desk in order to entertain such a self-indulgent thought. Altogether less glamorous a figure than his celebrated older sister, the historian and broadcaster, Eileen, Beryl Power had embarked twenty years earlier on a career in His Majesty's Inspectorate, enforcing the provisions of the Trade Boards Acts of 1909 and 1918 for the Ministry of Labour. Fascinated by the conditions under which her fellow man (or, in Power's case, woman: lady inspectors were generally only permitted to investigate employers of *female* labour) sweated and toiled to earn a crust, she had to swallow her disappointment in 1920 when the ministry refused to release her to take up a fellowship in the USA, where she planned to study the effect of minimum wage legislation. Six years later, another prestigious fellowship presented itself, and this time Power packed her notebooks and pencils and crossed the ocean to commence an extensive study of the labour conditions of women and children. A year later she was back in London and riding high on the copious praise heaped upon the reports she had compiled during the trip for her superiors at the ministry.

It was undoubtedly the combination of Power's hardiness as a traveller and the skill of her drafting pen that pushed her name to the top of the list when the government was contemplating which 'English lady' to appoint to its Royal Commission on Labour in India in early 1929. Prompted by spiralling unrest in the jewel in Britain's imperial crown, this enquiry aimed to restore industrial harmony by discovering the genuine ills of the Indian worker and recommending methods of redress. It presented Power with a rare opportunity to influence government policy at a critical juncture in Anglo-Indian relations. Yet like Lyttelton and her fellow League delegates, Power was appointed specifically to fill the one seat on the commission reserved for a woman, whose occupant, it was assumed, would deal with the womanly aspects of the enquiry, leaving the remainder of the business in the capable hands of her male colleagues. This was certainly the assumption of the commission's chairman, John Whitley, a former Speaker of the House of Commons, who, on hearing of her appointment, told the India Office that he would invite Power to dine with him and his wife so that she could get started on 'some of the preparatory work regarding women & children'.[16] Once on the road with her ten fellow commissioners, Power was expected to be the chief point of contact with the 'Lady Assessors' nominated by each major province to supply additional feminine expertise as and when required (this scheme was something of an afterthought, hastily pushed through in response to the tenacious lobbying of feminists who were dismayed at the under-representation of women – especially Indian women – on the commission). In Burma, Power was accosted by pressmen and casual bystanders jostling to snap her posing with one such Lady Assessor, Mrs Luce, as she arrived on the quay at Rangoon.

In fact, Power exceeded her feminine brief almost from the start. Utilising her expert knowledge of labour relations – which extended far beyond those subjects which might be filed under 'women' – she prodded, probed, questioned and queried alongside her male colleagues and across the full remit of the enquiry. Whitley recognised this in Colombo, where he asked her to serve as chief questioner on the complex work-ings of the minimum wage ordnance for Indian plantation labour, prompting one of the British officials billed to give evidence to exclaim in rather schoolboy fashion: 'I have heard about Miss Power. Now I must pull my socks up!' All the same, as the token female member, Power stood at a distance from the masculine world inhabited by the employer and trade unionist members of the commission, and perhaps even further from that of the Indian representatives. She was particu-larly annoyed to find herself bracketed with the assorted womenfolk making up the spousal entourage. In Ceylon, Power found the gover-nor's wife 'a trifle insipid' with no conversation, while in Burma she was dismayed to find that of the fifty-odd wives frequenting the European Club, only a few 'ever went trekking into the hills among the many interesting hill people, though it is perfectly easy to do and of great interest'. When her fellow commissioner, Alexander Murray, announced that the 'ladies' were not to venture out alone in Delhi after reports of bombs being thrown at Europeans in the street, Power replied peremp-torily: 'My dear Sir Alexander, as far as I'm aware I am the one woman in our party who cannot be "forbidden" to go where she chooses, and I prefer to retain my freedom.'[17]

Good company was not wholly lacking amongst the Colonial Service wives. In Rangoon, Power found an 'intelligent wife' who whisked her off in a car to buy silks and gongs at the famous bazaar, whilst in Ceylon she befriended the Arabic-speaking Mrs Bourdillon, 'a wife after my heart', who had known Gertrude Bell in Iraq. Curious to hear more about this legendary figure from someone with first-hand knowledge of her, Power learned from Mrs Bourdillon that Bell was 'a brilliant linguist, a beautiful dresser and hostess, and a clever politician', and that King Faisal's regard for her was 'tremendous'. 'My feminist soul warms at the thought,' Power wrote, little knowing how fervently Bell's name would be invoked before Schuster's Committee four years later, 'when we hear so much of the impossibility of having the consular and diplomatic services opened to women'.[18]

Perhaps Power looked to Bell's celebrated White Paper on Iraq for inspiration when she finally sat down in December 1930 to do battle with the minutes of evidence amassed over the commission's mind-numbing tally of 128 public sessions at which a total of 837 witnesses had been examined. Ensconced at her desk in the 'two huge barracks of rooms' assigned to her at the Old Viceregal Lodge in Delhi, Power drafted furiously all morning and edited her fellow commissioners' papers until tea time, at which point she set down her pen and ventured outside for a spot of badminton, tennis or quoits under the cloudless blue skies. When the light began to fade and the temperature dropped sharply, Power repaired to her rooms for a hot bath and change of clothes and another hour of drafting by the fire before dinner. On many an evening she crept back to her desk, greeting the bundles of papers like old friends, and worked late into the cold Indian night. This dedication won her warm praise from Whitley, who later described Power as 'a delightful colleague' who had 'pulled her full weight with any man amongst us'. He urged Margaret Bondfield, Secretary of State at Power's home department, the Ministry of Labour, to look out for this talented administrator. Power's contribution to the commission's work, Whitley noted, 'will have increased greatly her value as a public servant'.[19]

Power's exceptional 'knowledge and gifts' had, in fact, already been noted by the Anglo-Persian Oil Company, which invited her to tour the Persian oilfields after the Royal Commission's work had ended, with a view to studying the welfare arrangements in place for the company's large and diverse workforce. Power arrived in Abadan in April 1931 and spent a month observing workers, conferring with managers, remonstrating with policemen and learning along the way how to dismember a chicken by hand and smoke bad Persian cigarettes. Power extended her stay in the region in order to visit Palestine, curious to see, as she later wrote, 'all I could of Jewish and Arab industries, and those few factories where the two races worked together'.[20] After that it was back to London, but Power was soon off again on her travels, sent by the Ministry of Labour to the Soviet Union in October 1932 to investigate factory conditions. There was no doubt she was the right woman for the job. News of her work for the Royal Commission had spread as far as Moscow and secured her lengthy interviews with high-ranking officials at the Commissariat of Labour and the Central Council of Trade Unions.[21] Power would later add China and Thailand to her list of countries visited during the course of a long career in public service.

————

Power was exactly the kind of female public servant – expert, dedicated, uncomplaining – whose accomplishments witnesses before the committee were anxious to showcase. The Council of Women Civil Servants hired a researcher to spend weeks compiling biographies of other 'pioneer' women, whilst the University of London Appointments Board raided its alumni records for suitable names. Many were to be found engaged, like Beryl Power, in endeavours of one kind or another within Britain's colonial empire. There was Gladys Broughton, who had advised the Government of India on the employment of women and children in factories and mines in the early 1920s; Irene Lowe, who held the post of Deputy Directress of Public Instruction in Madras; and Gladys Plummer, Lady Superintendent in Southern Nigeria since 1931, carrying out duties which, as the board's memo explained, 'necessitate journeying hundreds of miles with a native chauffeur and camping out in districts where she is the only white person'.[22] The Medical Women's Federation pointed to the impressive record of women doctors ministering to the sick in the furthest-flung outposts of Empire, whilst other witnesses spoke of hardy female settlers running farms single-handedly on the South African veld, lady archaeologists directing teams of male labour on digs in Palestine, and courageous missionaries in rural China. Unsurprisingly, Gertrude Bell's name was referenced repeatedly by witnesses. Her tireless service to the state was ample proof, they argued, that women, when given the chance, were capable of safeguarding the interests of Britain as well as any man, even in the notoriously patriarchal societies of the Middle East. As one women's society put it:

> There exists among women, as among men, a proportion of individuals
> with exceptional gifts which qualify them for exceptional posts, and we

feel that the State by depriving itself of the power of appointing such a woman as the late Miss Gertrude Bell to service overseas is neglecting one of its sources of strength.[23]

The recounting of exemplary lives did not stop there. The Cambridge University Women's Appointments Board proudly informed the committee that two recent graduates had won posts at the Union Cold Storage Company in South America, one based in Brazil and the other in Argentina. Meanwhile the British Federation of University Women described the work of female buyers sent overseas by the John Lewis Partnership to source new products for its expanding chain of department stores. One spent six months in Poland scouting for promising suppliers, whilst another followed the Silk Road into India in search of carpets, ending up bargaining with traders at the mouth of the Khyber Pass. Closer to home in Europe, the Council of Women Civil Servants chose to dwell at some length on the impressive curriculum vitae of Dame Adelaide Livingstone, which included a stint at The Hague in 1917 conducting talks with enemy belligerents concerning the treatment of British prisoners of war. The American-born Livingstone was entrusted two years later with the sombre mission of touring the devastated regions of Belgium and France to collect what scraps of information could be found on the thousands of British and Commonwealth troops reported as missing in the War Office's ledgers. Livingstone's service to the glorious dead continued in 1920 when she took up the post of assistant director of Graves, Registration and Enquiries, spending much of her time in delicate negotiations with German authorities in Berlin, and overseeing the work of a sizeable team of army officers.[24]

Having extolled the accomplishments of these and other doughty women, the council's witnesses unveiled their secret weapon, who just happened to be one of their own number: Alix Kilroy. Kilroy had entered the Home Civil Service in 1925, the first year in which women were eligible to sit the exam for the administrative grade, which she did bare-legged in a cotton dress due to the blisteringly hot August weather – a get-up which shocked the Civil Service commissioners when Kilroy appeared before them for the final viva. On her preference form, the twenty-three-year-old Kilroy picked the Colonial Office as her first choice – 'because it seemed like the next best thing to the Foreign Office which I should have liked of all things' – and the Home Office as her second, but was posted to her third, the Board of Trade.[25] (As she later realised, she stood no chance of being taken on by the Colonial Office for the same reason as the Foreign Office: their unwillingness to post women officers abroad.) This turned out to be serendipitous, for it was the Board of Trade which assumed responsibility for negotiating tariff agreements with Britain's major trading partners following the abandonment of free trade in 1931, in the wake of the global economic crisis. And so Kilroy, still elated by her recent promotion to principal (she was the first woman to achieve such rank in the Department), found herself in late 1932 seated around a table in a grand meeting room overlooking Parliament Square with members of the Swedish trade delegation.

In most other countries, this work would have been carried out by the foreign ministry, a point which the council's witnesses strived to ensure would not be lost on the committee. Kilroy became, as she wrote in her memoirs, 'the Council's Exhibit "A"', living proof that women could be trusted with diplomatic work, including that of a highly technical character. She kept her cool as Schuster grilled her on the particulars of the Swedish negotiations: did Kilroy have direct contact with the delegates? (Yes.) Did she meet with them alone or with her male superiors? (Both.) Did she ever meet them outside the Board of Trade? (Certainly, at their official apartments at the Carlton Hotel, and socially.) Were they reluctant to deal with a woman instead of a man? 'To begin with,' Kilroy answered carefully,

> before my official position had been explained to them, there was a certain amount of confusion because I was regarded as the Private Secretary of my Chief, but once they had gathered what my official position was I had no difficulty at all, and they did not seem to have any hesitation in coming to me.[26]

The fact that Kilroy had discharged the duties of a diplomat in all but name, the council concluded, exposed the absurdity of the Foreign Office's position.

It was made equally absurd in the council's view by the fact that other countries were already posting women to embassies overseas. Here, predictably, the precedent set by the USA took centre stage. Nancy Astor even went so far as to furnish the committee with a personal letter from Ruth Bryan Owen, the US minister in Denmark, who avowed emphatically that femininity was no disability in the discharging of her diplomatic duties: 'Neither in my contacts with the officials of the Danish Government and my colleagues in the Corps Diplomatique nor in my association with the members of the Mission and the legation staff have I felt handicapped at any time by the fact that I am a woman.'[27] (She was unaware, of course, of the more sceptical views of the British ambassador in Copenhagen, which had already been shared with the committee.) Other instances in which women diplomats had been sent abroad were cited from Norway, Finland, Hungary, Turkey, Uruguay and Spain.[28] Some of the countries listed were – at least as British feminists rather chauvinistically saw it – unlikely pioneers, like Chile, which, witnesses reported, had posted a female vice-consul to New York, another to Glasgow and a third to the Chilean legation in London.[29] The underlying motive in citing such examples was clear: how could a great nation like Britain, with its advanced civilisation, stand by and watch far lesser countries blaze a trail in the professional employment of women? The representatives from the National Council of Women declared themselves unable to believe that British women were 'any less highly qualified in character, education or experience than women of other nationalities, who have successfully represented their countries in diplomatic positions'. Or, as another feminist society had mischievously remarked before Tomlin a few years earlier, 'we dare to hope that what Chile thinks today, Great Britain may think tomorrow'.[*30]

* Although Chilean women did not have the vote until after the Second World War, there were in fact growing numbers of women active in public and professional life, including international politics. The poet Gabriela Mistral, for instance, represented

The witnesses who appeared before the committee in 1934 arguing for diplomatic careers to be opened to women chose their weapons carefully, but, as we shall presently see, not every shot fired hit its target. Drawing lessons from the proven deeds of great women might have appeared a sound strategy, and one which would appeal to the empirically minded Civil Service bureaucrat. Yet it was a risky tactic, as Howard Smith and his associates were only too ready to exploit any weakness or shortcoming that could discredit these purportedly exemplary lives. Many of the female foreign diplomats wheeled out in good faith by the women's societies fell quickly and fell hard at the hands of the Foreign Office's own selected witnesses.

On a deeper level, the advocates of equality in the Diplomatic Service were troubled by a basic tension between the claim that sex was no disability and therefore should be disregarded, and the belief that sex was a positive asset, a source of feminine qualities and perspectives lacking in an exclusively male corps and thus a powerful justification for the appointment of women. The Council of Women Civil Servants was the most cautious in arguing the second line; it downplayed the 'special contribution point', insisting instead that the trappings of office rendered the occupant's sex obsolete. 'Once you have the authority of your Government behind you,' Miss Ford told the committee, 'you become an official. You are no longer one sex or the other.'[31] St Joan's Social and Political Alliance, a body of Roman Catholic feminists, similarly chose to argue that sex made no difference to an individual's suitability for diplomatic work: 'the gifts of tact and courtesy, of understanding and of making social contacts which go to make the perfect diplomat are not the exclusive possession of men,' they argued, 'and in barring all women irrespective of qualification the State

---

Latin America on the League of Nations' Institute for Intellectual Cooperation in the 1920s, and later served as a consul for Chile, as did the writer Marta Brunet. Furthermore, unlike most European countries, Chilean women were not forced to forfeit their nationality upon marriage. See Corinne Pernet, 'Chilean Feminists, the International Women's Movement, and Suffrage, 1915 to 1950', *Pacific Historical Review*, 69 (2000), pp. 663–88.

is undoubtedly barring some who possess diplomatic gifts of a very high order.'

Other witnesses, by contrast, were happy to expound upon the 'natural' differences between the sexes and how these might be pressed into the service of Britain's national interests. The Quaker Ruth Fry articulated this most clearly when giving evidence on her humanitarian relief work in central and eastern Europe over the previous decade. 'The relationship of nations to each other are very complicated,' she remarked, 'and we feel that in these subtle human relationships we gain enormously by having the two points of view, the men and the women, together, that we get a synthesis of ideas which results in something much more complete and much more substantial than if it is only men or women.'[32] Representatives from the Association of Headmistresses agreed: 'more fruitful work is done in the world,' they argued, 'by men and women working in conjunction than by either working separately, owing to the differentiated but complementary endowment of the two sexes.'[33]

Other witnesses fudged, demanding no distinction of sex whilst at the same time extolling the uniquely feminine virtues to which the female diplomat could lay claim. Foremost amongst these was the affinity she would invariably feel with women's movements overseas, whose part 'in the development of civilisation', as one former suffrage society put it, was 'speedily increasing all over the world'.[34] Any Foreign Office serious about understanding modern conditions, Edith Lyttelton suggested, ought to be intimately acquainted with what women were 'thinking and feeling', an impossible task for an embassy or legation composed entirely of men.[35] Similarly, it was only a woman who, in the National Council of Women's view, could deal effectively with the female traveller who got herself into difficulties abroad, perhaps falling sick or even – heaven forfend – passing away whilst on holiday. Such things happened, the council's representatives remarked, and His Majesty's Consul was not always equipped to offer advice in a suitably sympathetic fashion, as correspondence from angry travellers in their possession testified. Nor, they further argued, was he well placed to spot commercial opportunities in overseas markets for British goods aimed at the female consumer: the John Lewis Partnership understood the value of womanly business acumen – why not the British Consular Service? On these grounds, a number of witnesses endorsed the appointment of specialist women attachés in selected posts as an interim measure should the committee fail to accept the case for full equality with immediate effect. Akin to the naval or military attachés routinely posted to embassies, they would exist, as Lyttelton explained, 'for the sole purpose of gathering and understanding what it is the women in enfranchised countries especially are thinking and doing'.[36]

Other witnesses rejected this proposal on the grounds that it boxed women into a separate, specialist career track and risked delaying their admission to the mainstream Diplomatic Service. Ray Strachey suggested an alternative compromise which revived the solution floated by Warren Fisher back in 1929, involving the posting of female diplomats on an experimental basis to countries where women's status was already high. Strachey even came prepared with a shortlist of potential destinations: France was possible, as was Romania, but Nazi Germany, Fascist Italy and other authoritarian states in central and eastern Europe were probably no-gos; Turkey got the green light from Strachey, along with Egypt and Liberia, but Iraq, Persia, Saudi Arabia and Ethiopia were ruled out. China and Siam appeared on the list, but not Japan or Afghanistan. South America, Strachey argued, was a perfectly workable posting for a female diplomat in those countries that had already extended the franchise to women. All told, the list of approved destinations numbered thirty-one, more than enough to get started, Strachey insisted, especially if women were initially sent to fill the less visible, junior posts.[37]

The Council of Women Civil Servants, however, took issue with this strategy, arguing that the general status of women in any given country was no indication of how a female diplomat would fare, 'because when she arrives they must know she either speaks on instructions from the Government or has been given freedom to act'. Misogynists or not, 'they have got to pay attention to her'.[38] The National Association of Women Civil Servants went even further, suggesting (in a markedly orientalist tone) that Britain would be doing humanity a great service by posting women diplomats to countries where, through century-old prejudices and lack of education the backward position of native races and, in particular, the position of native women, are a disgrace to modern civilisation. It is submitted that the very fact that an educated and trained woman was the acknowledged representative of the British Government would have an incalculable influence on the development of backward races.[39]

The women's societies were, then, agreed on the principle of women's admission to the Diplomatic and Consular Services on equal terms with men, but divided on the details. Some backed compromise, willing to entertain small experimental measures which would nudge open the doors of the Foreign Office inch by inch until eventually women could pass through shoulder to shoulder with men. Others were impatient, demanding nothing less than full and immediate access. Yet such differences concerning tactics were ultimately irrelevant, for their opponents, it would soon transpire, had no intention of making even the slightest concession to women's claims on the diplomatic profession. For Foreign Office chiefs, there could be no place for women in the service, either as career diplomats or specialist attachés, and no amount of talking up the exploits of Edith Lyttelton in Geneva or Beryl Power in India would convince them otherwise. For all her eccentricities and fanciful theories about Catholic plots, there was one point on which Astor was absolutely right: the Foreign Office *had not* budged a yard since the war. It certainly was not about to lose ground now.

6

Foiled!

Sir Robert Vansittart was no ordinary diplomat. From his early triumph in 1902 when he came top in the diplomatic exam, to his appointment as permanent secretary twenty-eight years later following an accelerated advance up the ranks, the Old Etonian radiated brilliance. Portraits from the early 1930s depict a coolly composed public servant at the peak of his powers, a handsome man with penetrating eyes, high cheek-bones and dark slicked-back hair beneath which lurked a fertile, literary mind. Starting with his very first posting to Paris, 'Van' (as he was habitually known) sustained a parallel career as a published poet, dramatist and novelist, a highly unconventional path for a senior offi-cial to follow in the mid-twentieth century Civil Service; Rebecca West described him as 'the last Renaissance man'.[1] This creative flair initially cemented Vansittart's reputation within the Foreign Office as an excep-tional intellect and original thinker, although these qualities would in the later 1930s contribute to his fall from favour, when his fiercely held anti-appeasement views set him at odds with the Prime Minister, Neville Chamberlain, and most of the Cabinet.[2]

In 1934, however, Vansittart's position on the employment of women as diplomats was nothing if not orthodox. He laid it out in an eight-page memo addressed to the Schuster Committee at the end of January, just under a month before the first witnesses took the stand. As befitted the head of the Foreign Office, the tone was authoritative and the message uncompromising. Admitting women, he believed, 'would be a mistake'. Those who advocated it failed to appreciate just what was involved in representing the Crown and its interests overseas, where a diplomat's usefulness depended 'upon the contacts which they can make with all classes of the population of the country where they are serving'. Women were inevitably disadvantaged in this regard. Echoing Sir Hubert Montgomery, Vansittart pointed the finger of blame not at women themselves, but at Johnny foreigner: 'he is not ready for the experiment. It is surely a false argument to say that, because we treat women as equal to men in this country, an Englishwoman abroad will be so treated by foreigners. She will not.' The memo listed some of the countries to which, as permanent secretary, Vansittart felt he 'could not honestly agree to their being posted', and pointed out the inequity this would produce for male officers lumped with a disproportionate share of the less coveted posts: 'The women may not foresee this,' he wrote, somewhat condescendingly, 'but the fact remains that this is what would happen.' Vansittart then turned briefly to the intolerable plight of any man unfortunate enough to find himself married to a female diplomat ('his position in diplomatic society would be embarrassing') before concluding with a sombre warning as to the likely effects upon Britain's standing in the eyes of the world. Admitting women to the Service would 'incontestably affect the prestige of His Majesty's Government abroad and the respect which the opinions and influence of His Majesty's Government at present command in international relations'. Britain's highest-ranking diplomat had spoken.[3]

Coming from the top, these views obviously carried weight. But to clinch the case against women diplomats, Charles Howard Smith needed to demonstrate that the permanent secretary's position was widely shared across the Diplomatic Service, including its consular arm. If he could find some presentable and articulate ladies willing to endorse the arguments contained in Vansittart's memo, even better. All this Howard Smith achieved. He assembled a formidable line-up of witnesses who piled objection onto objection, covering a gamut which ran from the mundane but unavoidable administrative complications of employing female officers, to the lurid spectre of sexual impropriety besmirching the British government's good name. The advocates of women's admission to the Diplomatic Service might have been good, but their opponents, it turned out, were better.

———

Naturally, the opinion of the 'man on the spot' was given a thorough airing during the committee's hearings. As well as perusing a selection of ambassadors' letters drawn from Howard Smith's personal arsenal, the committee heard evidence direct from the mouths of a number of serving diplomatic and consular officers. These were not selected at random – far from it. The first big Foreign Office beast to take the floor was Sir Henry Chilton, ambassador in Buenos Aires, who appeared on 16 March at the special request of Howard Smith. After several weeks of forcefully argued and unexpectedly well-informed testimony from the women's societies, the assistant under-secretary clearly felt it was time to call in reinforcements. His fear, as he explained privately to Chilton, was that the evidence heard thus far had been too theoretical in nature, 'and since on theoretical grounds it may be easy to justify the admission of women, it is becoming clear that we must stress the practical objections'.4 With its culture of machismo, Howard Smith reasoned, a Latin American country like Argentina would supply plenty of the latter, and Chilton could draw for further firepower on his earlier experiences of similarly woman-unfriendly postings, including Brazil and the Vatican.

Chilton did not disappoint. He spoke at length of the low status of women in Argentine society, a fact which in his view made it utterly impossible for any female officer to operate effectively outside the confines of the chancery. Yes, he confirmed in response to a question from Hilda Martindale (one of the two women on the committee), there *was* an active women's suffrage movement of sorts in Argentina, but no one took it very seriously in political circles, and it could hardly be described as holding great significance for Anglo-Argentine relations. There was certainly no pressing need for the addition of a woman on his staff to make contact with this marginal section of local opinion. Then there was the climate to consider: the lady typists at the embassy in Buenos Aires, Sir Henry testified, did not stand the heat very well and looked, in his words, 'pretty washed out' by the end of the summer.[5]

After Chilton came Ralph Stevenson, the Foreign Office's thirty-nine-year-old assistant Advisor on League of Nations Affairs. He was chosen, presumably, because his relative youth meant that charges of old fogey-ism would not stick, whilst his current brief would allow him to speak authoritatively on the supposedly enlightened practices of the League of Nations, of which the women's societies had made so much. In fact, Stevenson argued more expansively than that. Yes, he remarked, a woman diplomat might thrive at the League thanks to the famous 'Geneva spirit', but that spirit did not exist everywhere. From Stevenson's experience, it certainly did not exist in Berlin or Bulgaria, and it was wholly missing from The Hague, where diplomatic business was completed at clubs and golf courses to which women were not admitted, or at shooting parties and business dinners to which they were not invited. Were Britain to send a 'girl secretary' to its mission at The Hague, Stevenson warned, Dutch officials would 'probably look upon it as rather a bad joke'. Her colleagues in the embassy, meanwhile, would be aghast at the idea of sharing an office with a member of the opposite sex. 'The introduction of a girl into a Chancery,' Stevenson observed, 'unless she was quite exceptional, would be a very disturbing factor and quite possibly impair the efficiency of the Chancery machine.'[6]

There followed a collection of testimonies, both written and oral, from officials employed in, or closely connected to, Britain's various consular services. Again, this surfeit of evidence on the duties of consuls was not coincidental. Howard Smith firmly believed that the most compelling arguments against the admission of women would cluster around the rugged figure of the consular officer, who frequently resided in unpleasant, out-of-the-way places, with only mutinous sailors and unsavoury locals for company. Again, his allies did not let him down. The committee were regaled with typical scenarios from the life of a consul in which it was plainly obvious that strong, manly qualities were required: when revolution broke out, for instance, or natural disaster struck, and British subjects looked to His Majesty's Consul to keep them safe and 'in good heart'; or at times of war, when His Majesty's

Consul might be called upon to monitor movements of shipping or issue orders to the masters of merchant vessels; or, more routinely, when His Majesty's Consul was obliged to arbitrate disputes, pull rowdy sailors out of brothels, or investigate matters which would make any respectable lady blush, including alleged instances of 'homosexual crime' at sea. David Scott, head of the Foreign Office's Consular Department, thought that no female officer could discharge these functions without inviting comment and provoking rumour.[7]

These risks were even greater when it came to the practicalities of posting and housing consular officers. Harold Swan, consul-general in the Belgian Congo, pointed out that it was 'neither customary nor politic' for a white woman to live alone in a tropical climate, as was standard for many male consuls, meaning that female officers would be effectively exempt from the unhealthiest and least popular posts. Nor, in Swan's view, could two unmarried officers of the opposite sex work side by side in larger consulates in all seemliness, for the job required 'a mutual confidence and camaraderie which can hardly exist between male and female consuls at the same post without giving rise to appearances, real or fancied, which would lessen their utility and make their position ambiguous, at least, in the eyes of the surrounding population of the place'. There was the added cost and inconvenience, too, of providing separate accommodation for a female officer who, for decency's sake, could not be expected to share a house with her male colleagues.[8]

Howard Smith was delighted with all this grumbling and excessive dwelling upon difficulties. He congratulated Alexander Hutcheon, author of a detailed memo on consular duties which was passed on to Schuster and his colleagues, for producing 'precisely what we wanted . . . we have every hope that it will convince the committee that consular work is beyond the powers of a woman'.[9] Howard Smith similarly thanked Edward Crowe of the Department for Overseas Trade for his written submission, which he described as 'a most useful addition to our artillery'. It will, he added bullishly, 'certainly contribute to the demolition of the feminists' castles in the air'.[10]

Howard Smith had other reasons to feel confident. Not only had he presented a united front in favour of the status quo amongst Foreign Office witnesses, he had also found some obliging ladies whose testimonies would do further damage to his opponents' case whilst remaining entirely free – as Howard Smith put it – 'of any imputation of masculine prejudice'.[11] The first of these agreeable females was Lady Granville, a diplomatic wife of long experience. Born Nina Baring, she was the daughter of a diplomat, the niece of Lord Cromer (Britain's famous consul-general in Egypt), and wife of the 3rd Earl of Granville, whom she had accompanied to postings in Berlin, The Hague, Paris, Athens, Copenhagen and finally Brussels, where she was now ambassadress. These many years of service convinced her, she told the committee, that the time was not yet ripe for women diplomats. Most foreign governments would not tolerate them, and only the most exceptional woman would succeed in winning the confidence of her fellow officers. 'If she were a woman who is admirable in every way and just the right looking woman,' Lady Granville explained, 'not too beautiful and not too ugly, she might be able to hold her own but I do not see it.' Women, she argued, could serve their country far better by supplying wifely support, as Lady Granville had done for her husband for over three decades. This was not to disparage her own sex: 'I have a very good opinion of myself,' she told the committee; 'I have quite a decent brain, and I have certainly got knowledge of the world from having done nothing else all my life . . . but I should not have thought at any moment of my life that I was capable of doing what my husband was doing.'[12]

Spousal admiration was the keynote of the testimony supplied by another diplomatic spouse, now widow, a Mrs V. MacDonell, who had followed her husband on his consular postings to Greece, Brazil, Romania and Mozambique. 'It was so astonishing the various odd things my husband seemed to have to do,' she remarked with feeling; 'I could not picture a woman doing it.' When pressed, the only instance Mrs MacDonell could recall in which a female consul might have been of use occurred in Rio de Janeiro, when her husband was asked to procure feeding bottles for a British woman who called at the consulate with her starving infant in a state of despair. The rest of his time was spent remonstrating with uncooperative sailors, investigating murders within the British community, or talking shop with the 'man-in-the-street'. A woman could survive only in 'a very civilised town', Mrs MacDonell thought, and these were few and far between in the 'little foreign countries' which made up the vast majority of consular postings.[13]

Lady Granville and Mrs MacDonell both appeared before the committee after being specially pre-approved by Howard Smith. The other ladies in question, two Members of Parliament and a retired clerical officer, seem to have volunteered rather than been put up to it, but nonetheless produced testimonies which muddied the waters in ways that were supremely helpful to the case for no change. Marjorie Graves, Conservative MP for Hackney South since 1931, had some direct experience of international affairs, having worked at the Foreign Office during the war, but was by no means convinced of the desirability of letting women into the Diplomatic Service on a permanent basis. Graves, the committee learned, thought that female officers could do well in the junior grades but lacked the gravitas necessary to represent Britain as ambassadors, and it would therefore be an injustice to admit women to a profession in which they could not hope to achieve the highest distinction. Better, Graves warned, not to admit them in the first place.[14] Much the same message was received from Mary Pickford, another Conservative MP, who also had some relevant experience to boast of, having served as advisor to British delegations at several International Labour conferences in Geneva, and on a government committee sent to India in 1932 to implement franchise reform. Pickford agreed that women should be eligible for postings on exactly the same basis as men, or not at all; but the number of countries off limits to any female officer due to local prejudice she felt made this all but impossible.[15]

Neither Graves nor Pickford was exactly renowned for impassioned advocacy of feminist causes. Graves even admitted, mid-evidence, that she had 'never wanted the vote', a rather extraordinary confession from an elected Member of Parliament. The duo belonged to the cadre of worthy but rather nondescript Conservative backbenchers swept in by the dramatic swing against Labour in 1931, at the height of the economic crisis. They were, as Molly Hamilton (one of the Labour MPs to be unseated) archly remarked, 'women of the OBE type; the sort of women who "did such good work in the war"'.[16] Graves and Pickford were thus never likely allies for the women's societies, but it was, nonetheless, pretty galling to hear female witnesses embellishing the arguments of their Foreign Office opponents.

Especially disappointing was the equivocal testimony of Margaret Yates, who had been temporarily employed as an archivist at the British legation in Havana between 1928 and 1930. On the face of it, the particulars of her case appeared to pose problems for Howard Smith and his associates. Not only was Yates's post previously held by a man, but, because of the tiny size of the legation staff, it entailed additional duties very similar to those discharged by a regular diplomatic officer. By her own admission, however, Yates had struggled to overcome the deeply entrenched male prejudices of Cuban society. She transacted no business outside the chancery, the committee learned, and, as a woman, found it impossible to take messages to the Cuban State Department as her male predecessor had done (although she admitted, after probing by Hilda Martindale, that she did not actually ever attempt to do so). Yates felt that she was accorded respect by her legation colleagues and by other members of the European diplomatic corps, but was shabbily treated by Cuban officials, whose minds were closed against women wielding professional authority. She made the odd useful contact through attendance at sporting events (one of the few areas of public life in Cuba in which women's participation was not frowned upon) and her ability to drive a car proved handy on occasion. But Yates did not, unfortunately, demolish any myths concerning women's lower threshold for unpleasant climates: she resigned her post in 1930 on doctor's orders after developing anaemia, apparently brought on by the tropical heat.[17]

This was troubling news for the women's societies, who had set such store by the precedents showcased in their pantheon of exemplary females. It soon transpired that nearly every case which they believed would stand as compelling evidence of women's capacity for diplomatic work was vulnerable to attack. Alix Kilroy, the Council of Women Civil Servants' 'Exhibit A' for her work on Board of Trade negotiations with Sweden, received a mixed report from the British minister in Stockholm, whose letter to Howard Smith was amongst those forwarded to the committee. Miss Kilroy, the minister thought, might serve 'with efficiency and distinction' in certain European postings and in Washington, 'but I should not like to see her at Istanbul, a Balkan post, anywhere in the Middle East . . . Africa and probably also in Latin America'.[18] It was especially irritating how many witnesses dismissed the significance of Gertrude Bell's work in Iraq by referring to her as an 'exceptional' woman; she was, as Edward Crowe wrote in his memo, a gifted maverick blessed with talents rarely found in either sex and it was therefore 'a delusion and a snare to introduce the name of that heroic figure into this administrative problem'.[19] Marjorie Graves similarly described Bell's position as 'anomalous', whilst Lady Granville, who spoke with the authority of one who had known her, remarked that she should not have liked to see Bell 'as ambassadress in Paris'.

Nor did the examples set by other nations pack the punch the women's societies were hoping for. Robert Vansittart got his objections in early when he warned the committee to be wary of 'any specious argument drawn from exceptional doings in the United States or Soviet Russia'. He was especially scathing towards the US 'experiment'; political appointees like Bryan Owen he abjured, whilst most of the women appointed to the mainstream service it appeared had not stayed the course, and of the two still serving one – Frances Willis – had admitted frankly to the British minister in Stockholm that her usefulness outside the chancery was 'diminished by some 100 per cent by the fact that she is not a man'. (Although the minister could not help adding his gratuitous observation that Willis was 'of the slightly masculine schoolmarm type'.[20])

Other claims made by the women's societies were discovered to be bogus when subjected to close scrutiny: Norway, Finland and Hungary did not currently admit women to their respective diplomatic services, Howard Smith's informants confirmed. Any posts occupied by women of those nationalities were therefore not diplomatic posts proper, but more likely to be temporary, specialist or subordinate in nature. Suggestions to the contrary were highly misleading.[21] The 'What Chile Thinks Today' line did not go down well for much the same reason. Howard Smith's meticulous researches revealed the questionable particulars of some of the supposedly trailblazing appointments cited by the women's societies. The female attaché at the Turkish Ministry of Foreign Affairs, it turned out, had quickly resigned after being rejected for an overseas posting; her Spanish equivalent was still in post but was similarly confined to her desk in the ministry in Madrid with no hope of seeing service abroad.[22]

After a strong start, then, the women's societies appeared to be losing ground, but they did not let these setbacks dent their resolve. They were certainly not prepared to allow Foreign Office arguments concerning women's alleged unsuitability for the less salubrious aspects of consular work to stand unchallenged. Not only did the record of lady missionaries, medics and archaeologists in all sorts of perilous and far-flung places render claims about women's physical frailty highly questionable, they argued, but the squeamishness on display regarding the doings of inebriated sailors was wholly misplaced. Ray Strachey saw no reason why a female consul should not investigate an outbreak of venereal disease on board a British ship, or visit the docks late at night, when occasion demanded it. If it was genuinely dangerous, she could take a bodyguard with her, paid out of her own salary if necessary. 'That is what I should do if I were in that position,' Strachey told the committee. 'I should carry a good stiff stick, and if that was not sufficient I should hire a guardian or a big dog to follow on my heels.'[23] Alix Kilroy was similarly unconvinced that a male consul would naturally subdue obstreperous seamen more readily than a female officer. 'I have a very definite view,' she remarked, 'which is supported by a good many of my friends, that women have rather a special technique for managing drunken men, which they have acquired by long years of experience at home.'[24]

The women's societies were also anxious to rebut the various statements made by their opponents on the thorny subject of marital status. Here the female diplomatic officer apparently could not win. If she were single, the Foreign Office objected to her on the grounds that a married man represented better value for money, coming as he did with a dutiful spouse in tow who could be called on at any time for hostessing and pastoral duties. This lack would be felt especially keenly at the higher levels of the Service, as the ambassador to Brazil, Sir William Seeds, observed in his letter to Howard Smith, which was passed on to the committee. 'A feme sole as Ambassadress in Rio de Janeiro,' Seeds judged, 'would do no more than fifty per cent of the work done by my wife and myself.'[25] On the other hand, married female officers appeared to be entirely out of the question, mainly due, as Vansittart had first remarked, to the untenable position of the diplomatic husband. If he found local employment in business or a profession, it would in all probability conflict with the interests of the embassy, but the layabout husband would be even more of a menace. Schuster put this point directly to Nancy Astor: 'Is our work,' he asked, 'likely to be done properly if we have an Englishman of no particular occupation hanging around in a foreign city over whom we have no control and yet he is attached to us through the somewhat close relationship of the wife?'[26] The implications were obvious. If women were admitted to the Service a marriage bar would have to be strictly enforced; and as women naturally craved marriage, the wastage of trained officers would be unacceptably high.

Unsurprisingly, given their record of strenuous opposition to marriage bars in the Home Civil Service, the women's societies took a rather different view. They lobbed back a number of countervailing arguments. In the first place, they suggested, the type of woman attracted to a serious career in public service would be unlikely to marry. As the principal of Lady Margaret Hall, Lynda Grier, noted, 'very often the women with the greatest amount of initiative are those who do not marry, though they have plenty of chances'.[27] Furthermore, even if a woman diplomat did marry, she could be trusted to arrange her private life in such a manner as to avoid any interference with her official duties. If this meant in practice periods of separation, then it was entirely down to the officer in question and her husband to decide whether or not to make that sacrifice. But in many cases this would not be necessary, as Ray Strachey pointed out, particularly if the husband 'carried his job with him in his head, such as a writer or musician or archaeologist'. There was even the possibility that the husband, another witness daringly suggested, 'might help his wife in her diplomatic work', rather than taking on paid employment elsewhere. ('If he is the right sort,' Nancy Astor added, and not a 'nincompoop'.[28]) In any case, the Council of Women Civil Servants warned, the Service should not go on assuming that every *male* diplomat's wife would be prepared to pay, pack and follow in perpetuity, especially if she had a career of her own in Britain.

These propositions evidently baffled the men on the committee, to whom the notion of a woman giving her professional ambitions priority over the duties she owed her husband appeared utterly alien. Howard Smith intervened in the Council of Women Civil Servants' evidence to clarify that he had in fact understood their argument correctly. 'Surely,' he asked in a tone of incredulity, 'it is more important for them to do their jobs as wives than to do their jobs in the Service?' To which Kilroy replied: 'It's for them to choose,' whilst her colleague added: 'Not necessarily more important, it is for the individual to decide that.'[29]

Interestingly, neither side dwelt at any length on the specific problems posed by motherhood as opposed to mere marriage, presumably because they saw the likeliest female candidates for the Diplomatic Service as hailing from those social classes in which resident nannies and boarding schools were the norm. Even wholly leisured wives in upper- or middle-class families were generally relieved of the lion's share of childcare duties via these two methods. The debate over the status of the married woman diplomat had, therefore, less to do with her absence from the nursery than the neglect of her social obligations to her husband. The dilemmas of balancing professional aspirations with family responsibilities were largely unknown to this generation, although they would loom large in the lives of female diplomats and diplomatic wives later in the century.

Witnesses from the women's societies did recognise, nonetheless, that some female officers would inevitably wish to resign if and when they married and devote themselves to homemaking. Yet even this eventuality, they maintained, was no argument against admitting women to the profession in the first place. In many instances, the female officer in question would be marrying a fellow diplomat, meaning that her knowledge and skills would not be lost to the Service, quite the contrary: what better training could there be for a diplomatic wife? The same might be said were she to marry a foreigner and settle in his country. In such cases, Strachey remarked, 'she will bring to the British colony an element which will be exceedingly useful to her successor, and in such cases we do not believe that her preliminary training will be wasted'.[30]

———————

After hearing evidence from over twenty-five witnesses, and receiving written submissions from another dozen or more, the committee retired at the beginning of May to consider its conclusions. No record of those deliberations appears to have been preserved, but the final report revealed that the eight members quickly divided into three rival camps. Standing firm behind the policy of 'no change' were the Foreign Office representatives Sir Ronald Graham, Thomas Dunlop and Charles Howard Smith, plus the Civil Service Commissioner Sir Roderick Meiklejohn. Arguing for women's immediate admission to the Diplomatic Service and a trial period of employment in the Consular Service with a view to full instatement in the near future were Hilda Martindale and Muriel Ritson. The remaining two members, Sir Claud Schuster and Sir James Rae of the Treasury, prevaricated; the Consular Service, they felt, was definitely off limits, but diplomatic posts were less clear cut. They plumped in the end for an 'experimental measure' involving a small number of female appointments, the results of which would determine whether or not women's full admission should proceed. All three camps were in consensus, however, on the question of married women's ineligibility. Martindale and Ritson almost certainly sympathised with feminist opponents of the marriage bar, but whilst it remained in force in the Home Civil Service, there seemed little point in pushing the issue in regard to the much more controversial matter of women's overseas employment.

The report, which contained multiple addenda setting out each rival camp's position in some detail, was completed by the end of July 1934 – and immediately shelved. This came as something of a surprise to the women's societies, who had eagerly anticipated its publication. They lost no time in firing off letters and prodding sympathetic MPs to table parliamentary questions demanding an explanation for the delay. After nearly a year of these nuisance enquiries, Howard Smith wrote to the Foreign Secretary, Sir Samuel Hoare, gently suggesting that he publish the report with a definitive government statement and have done with it, but Hoare protested that he had 'really neither time nor inclination' to take up the matter.[31] As a result, it was not until April 1936, almost two years after the committee had concluded its enquiries, that the report finally appeared. It came prefixed with a statement which revealed, predictably, that the government accepted the recommendations of the majority view: that is, the case for leaving things exactly as they were. It endorsed the Foreign Office's position on nearly every essential point: women's unsuitability for consular duties; the backwardness of foreign opinion regarding sex equality; and the insuperable difficulties thrown up by the diplomatic husband. The statement even went so far as to suggest that the government was doing women a favour by denying them access to a profession for which they were genuinely unsuited. In short, it concluded, 'the time has not yet arrived when women could be employed either in the Consular Service or in the Diplomatic Service with advantage to the State or with profit to women'.[32]

Howard Smith had won. All the carefully compiled evidence, exemplary case studies and appeals to plain justice had failed to convince the masculine political establishment that Britain's interests overseas were safe in female hands. The women's societies immediately registered their disappointment and dismay through letters to the press, whilst Dorothy Evans of the National Association of Women Civil Servants went on the record to accuse the Foreign Office of filling the committee with professional diplomats 'who took a biased view'.[33] Editorials in the liberal-leaning press shared their indignation. A leader in the *Manchester Guardian*, for instance, condemned the report: 'For the Government to use the few countries with a barbarous attitude to women as an excuse for a general bar is really not good enough.'[34] The rest of Fleet Street, however, instinctively sided with Howard Smith. *The Times* praised the government for having 'wisely decided to make no change' and noted the absence of any 'clamant demand' amongst women for entry into the Service.[35] A cartoon published in *Punch* probably summed up the frustrations of the women's societies best: it depicted a well-heeled woman with fashionably waved hair and dressed in elegant evening attire staring furiously at the tightly shut door of the Foreign Office. The caption said it all: 'Foiled!'

PART THREE

Lady Diplomatists at War

San Francisco, 1945

Another war draws to a close, and again the victors gather to create a new world order. The setting this time is not a blood-stained, bomb-ravaged European capital, but the sunlit coastal city of San Francisco, an orderly gridwork of wide streets and open spaces hugging the rolling hills in an easy intimacy. This gold-rush town was spared invasion, occupation and blitzkrieg, yet evidence that war rumbled on was unmistakeable as the delegates assembled under unusually cloudless April skies, some arriving by air, others disembarking from specially laid-on trains after a long journey through the snow-capped Rockies and the expansive pastures of northern California.

Since 1940, few states had done more to build President Roosevelt's famous 'Arsenal of Democracy', and few cities had been more dramatically reinvented as a result than San Francisco and its surrounding districts: with shipyards, factories and workshops sprouting up to form a mighty production line for the American war machine, and everywhere around them new migrant communities – African Americans, Mexicans, poor whites from the Dust Bowl south – laying down roots and transforming the cultural landscape of the place for ever. As gateway to the Pacific theatre of war, San Francisco became a garrison as well as boom town, the entire bay dotted with forts, observation posts, temporary barracks, military depots, cluttered wharves and bustling piers. More than a million and a half American servicemen passed beneath the city's iconic Golden Gate Bridge en route to face the Japanese foe; for many, there was no return.[1]

For all the urban tensions and human heartbreak which war visited upon San Francisco, the town retained its characteristic optimism, channelling the same lusty spirit that saved the city's soul after the infamous earthquake some forty years before. What better place to give fresh life to Europe's discredited internationalism than this New World citadel of hope? Writing the Charter of the United Nations, humanity's second attempt at institutionalising peace, was the task ahead of the delegates of fifty allied nations, who, as they had in Paris in 1919, streamed into the city's better hotels with their advisors, secretaries and bodyguards. The Americans occupied the Fairmount in upmarket Nob Hill, whilst the British took rooms at the neighbouring Mark Hopkins, home to the legendary penthouse bar where officers bound for the Pacific could be seen every night sharing tender farewells with their sweethearts. Twenty-seven delegations squeezed into the St Francis, down on Union Square, including France, China and the Soviet Union, fellow members of the elite group of great powers who were to have permanent seats on the Security Council of the new organisation. Other delegates were scattered across town, shuttling from their hotels every morning to the main conference venue at the grand Memorial Opera House on chartered buses, and finding their way in the evenings to whichever cocktail party, reception or dinner promised the most by way of gossip, decent booze or access to VIPs. It was nine weeks of work, play and more work, the daylight hours spent drafting a detailed blueprint for world peace in meeting rooms and at committee tables; the twilight ones spent sealing deals and furthering understandings in ballrooms and at dinner tables.

As in Paris, women were plentiful: as typists, secretaries, switchboard operators, interpreters, note-takers, bag-handlers and coffee-makers. It was the ladies of the American Women's Voluntary Service who kept the conference fed and watered, dishing up hot lunches and afternoon teas for a dollar a head to twelve hundred hungry delegates daily in the basement of the Opera House. Accompanying wives slid into plush velvet seats in the auditorium stalls to hear their husbands deliver speeches, and made gracious hostesses at the parties which every delegation was expected to throw on at least one occasion, the ritzier the

better. Sharp-suited female reporters jostled for position at press conferences and buttonholed delegates in corridors, whilst prim college girls
from Berkeley queued patiently for spaces in the public gallery.

But this time, in 1945, women came to San Francisco not merely to
sit at the feet of great men. They came also as delegates in their own
right. For the USA came Virginia Gildersleeve, dean of Barnard College
at Columbia University; for China, another academic, Dr Wu Yi-fang,
president of Ginling College; for Brazil, the biologist and politician,
Bertha Lutz; for Uruguay, the senator, Isabel P. de Vidal; for Canada,
another parliamentarian, Cora Casselman; and for the Dominican
Republic, the feminist Minerva Bernardino. Half a dozen or so more
were present as assistant delegates or advisors, including two British
ladies: the Labour MP Ellen Wilkinson and her Conservative colleague
Florence Horsbrugh, both junior ministers and the sole female members
of Churchill's coalition government. Vastly outnumbered by their
fellow male delegates, these women nonetheless made history when
four of their number stepped forward on 26 June to affix their signatures to the Charter of the United Nations, leaving incontrovertible
proof in silky black ink that women were present at the rebirth of the
world's best hope for securing peace, truth and justice for all.

Yet the exact significance of women's presence was contested from
the start. When asked about the novelty of her status as a female
delegate by assembled pressmen, the petite, flame-haired Wilkinson
snapped back that she and Horsbrugh were present 'as political figures
in our own right'. A momentous conference, such as this, she insisted,
needed 'people who can speak with authority', not token women.[2]
Gildersleeve sympathised with the sentiment. Her appointment to
the US delegation, she knew, was partly tokenistic, insofar as the
inclusion of a woman member had been urged by feminists and
seemed fitting given everything that American womanhood had done
in the war. But Gildersleeve, a veteran internationalist, had no intention of preserving a silence on all except 'feminine' affairs. 'I was
confident,' she recalled, 'that I could serve my sex as well as my country best by just being a good delegate.'[3] The temptation to allow
oneself to be shunted off by kindly male colleagues to the committees

dealing with 'social' questions, as had been the fate of practically every female delegate to the League of Nations, was, Gildersleeve observed, to be resisted at all costs.

Not all the women representatives in San Francisco, however, saw it that way. What was the point of having women delegates if they were not prepared to stand up for women? For feminist Bertha Lutz, the willingness of the British and US delegates to sit back and watch a new world order unfold without any special mention of women's rights was shocking beyond belief. Gildersleeve she judged 'an extreme conservative'; Horsbrugh, it would appear, 'thought feminism rather unladylike', and Wilkinson she downright disliked.⁴ (At an ill-tempered tea party, Lutz listened to the latter's confident assurances that, given she had now obtained the rank of privy councillor, nothing more was required of feminism in Britain, as women 'had arrived'. Lutz replied archly: 'I am afraid not. It only means that *you* have arrived.'⁵) These differences of outlook came to a head when Lutz – who was swiftly renamed *Lutzwaffe* by some (masculine) wits on the US delegation – proposed the establishment of a Sub-committee on the Status of Women to sit within the commission on Human Rights in the new UN structure. Gildersleeve led the opposition, arguing that 'women should be regarded as human beings as men were', and therefore needed no special treatment, a view later echoed by British feminist Margery Corbett Ashby. 'Do not let us women press for work in separate compartments,' Ashby wrote. 'If peace is indivisible, if economic prosperity is one and individual, fundamental human rights are so likewise.'⁶

In truth, it was not altogether surprising that the female delegates, who were divided by culture, history, nationality and political tradition, should also diverge over women's representation in the new internationalist edifice under construction in San Francisco. It would have been astonishing if they had done otherwise. It was striking, though, that the Anglo-American contingent of Gildersleeve, Wilkinson and Horsbrugh stood united in 1945 against what they saw as a form of special pleading on behalf of women. In both countries, women had fought and suffered alongside their menfolk in the battle to defeat Nazism. Now they demanded in return full recognition as equal citizens. In Britain, they were hammering at the door of the Foreign Office once again, but this time the old maternalism which had justified women's inclusion by reference to their 'special' qualities was now less conspicuous. A mere handful of women had been recruited to temporary diplomatic posts by the wartime state, which remained supremely sceptical of their capacity to safeguard British interests. Yet in discharging their duties, this small band of female envoys demonstrated a competence and professionalism which spoke for itself, and which would, when the question of women's place in the Diplomatic Service duly returned at the end of the Second World War, make it all but impossible for the Foreign Office to maintain that diplomacy was a job for men and men alone.

7

Woman Power

Rowena Vining had a good war. It started one day in early 1942, when Vining, then twenty years of age and newly registered for war work, caught a bus in central London, her destination unknown. As the smog-filled streets of the capital melted into open fields dotted with hedges and trees, Vining wondered what future had been chosen for her by the powers that be at the Ministry of Labour. Might it be spying for MI5? She knew several young women, daughters of British Army officers like herself, who had been recruited as agents for the wartime secret service, and the very thought of it was rather thrilling. Thank goodness she had thought twice about joining the Auxiliary Territorial Services back home in Northern Ireland. Given her tender years, she stood little hope of winning a commission and would in all likelihood have spent the war peeling potatoes.

As it was, a far more exciting prospect awaited Vining as the bus turned up a long, tree-lined avenue dissecting vast, undulating parkland. Through the window she caught glimpses of several rare species of deer – strange creatures, some with antlers as thick as tree branches, others with large flat ears shaped like oyster shells. All in all, Vining felt thoroughly bewildered as she disembarked from the bus, brushing the city dust from her clothes and gazing up at the imposing white-grey mansion which was to become her home for the next year. In 1942, Woburn Abbey, the ancestral seat of the Dukes of Bedford for nearly four centuries, housed the headquarters of the Political Warfare

Executive (PWE), a secret operation under the joint command of the Foreign Office, the Ministry of Information and the Ministry of Economic Warfare. Following Winston Churchill's belligerent call to 'set Europe ablaze', the PWE was created to wreak havoc amongst enemy and occupied countries through an audacious campaign of misinformation and subversive propaganda.[1] Vining's entry pass to this most clandestine of government agencies was her fluency in Italian, taught to her by a childhood governess whilst the family was posted in Malta. She could hardly have foreseen how, with seemingly every Italian in the country flung into an internment camp, these precious linguistic skills would uproot her from a comfortable life as an officer's daughter in Belfast and set her down in the very control centre of Britain's propaganda war.

Naturally, Vining began her career at Woburn Abbey as a small fish swimming amongst much higher forms of sea life. The PWE recruited a distinguished cast of characters to write its phoney radio broadcasts, dream up mischievous rumours and draft leaflets which would be dropped in their millions over occupied Europe. Noël Coward, Quentin Bell, E. H. Carr and Air Marshal Arthur 'Bomber' Harris all lent their considerable talents to the operation, and many other eminent personages of all nationalities passed through. The petite-framed Vining nearly ran into the hefty bulk of General de Gaulle on one occasion. An average day, however, was far less eventful, spent in the company of an ageing Maltese – the Italian Section's one other member of staff – and occupied upon the task of reading Italian newspapers brought in from Switzerland. Vining scoured the pages, writing short summaries of their contents in English, and sifting out items of possible significance. After a year or so of this monotonous, if absorbing, work, Vining spotted a story which would bring her keen eye and sharp intellect to the attention of her superiors. An early signal of what was to follow, it was the first passage to appear in a Fascist Party publication which explicitly and unmistakeably criticised Hitler, Italy's war ally. As Vining recalled with modesty, 'I think it probably got me to be noticed as somebody who could pick things out of interest.' It was just the beginning of a wartime adventure which would take her from rural

Bedfordshire to the kasbahs of Algiers and the POW camps of conflict-torn Indonesia.[2]

———————

Millions of young British women were mobilised, like Rowena Vining, to serve the British state at war, although for most their induction took place in far less mysterious circumstances. From March 1941, all women aged between nineteen and forty were compelled to register at a local labour exchange and, from December of that year, unmarried women aged twenty to thirty became liable for call-up. Such was the pressing need to keep the wheels of the war economy turning that in 1942 compulsion was extended to childless married women, whilst mothers with young children, although technically exempt from conscription, were encouraged to take up paid work (and around three-quarters of a million did so). The jobs they performed, both paid and unpaid, were extraordinarily varied. They dished out hot meals to exhausted civil defence workers, drove ambulances by moonlight through bombed-out streets, bolted and welded together fleets of aircraft in cavernous hangars, and transported millions of evacuees from inner cities to rural parts. More generally, they gave a human face to the stern, bureaucratic machine summoned into being by the pressures of war: a machine which registered workers, issued ration cards, found accommodation for the homeless, and helped those injured by bombing raids to claim compensation.

Now fully enfranchised, British women were better equipped in 1939 to impress upon the government the importance of full and speedy employment of the many and varied talents of the female half of the population – or what became known in wartime parlance as 'woman power'. A cross-party committee of female MPs forced a parliamentary debate on this topic in March 1941 and won a series of small victories thereafter: persuading the Ministry of Labour to establish an advisory group to consult on female recruitment to war industries, and forcing a rethink on the appointment of a panel wholly composed of men to investigate welfare conditions in the women's armed forces.[3] (Much chastened, the Cabinet appointed a new taskforce of five women and three men under female chairmanship.) Ministers were deluged with pamphlets, memoranda and firmly worded letters detailing the extent of feminine grievances and demanding their redress. In response, state-funded nurseries were established for working mothers, whilst employers were instructed to create part-time jobs so as to allow women to combine paid work with their second (unpaid) shift of housework and childcare in the home. Certain categories of workers – including female pilots, women medics in the armed forces, and some engineers – even succeeded in securing equal pay. Feminism's greatest wartime achievement, however, undoubtedly came in April 1943, when the House of Commons voted to equalise the rates of compensation paid to men and women injured through enemy action, most commonly during bombing raids. The outrage provoked by the policy of differen-tiated payouts was neatly summed up by the Labour MP, Edith Summerskill, who invited a government minister to explain 'why a woman's arm or leg is not of the same value as a man's?' – a question to which, for a government calling for 'equal sacrifice' from all its citi-zens, there could be no satisfactory answer.[4]

For all this, however, many frustrations remained. As in the previous war, women workers were generally employed on temporary contracts, which paid lower wages, and enjoyed little prospect of promotion and no pension entitlements. And as before, women were glaringly under-represented in decision-making circles. The two female ministers in the wartime coalition government, Ellen Wilkinson and Florence Horsbrugh, were both in junior posts dealing with domestic affairs, whilst Churchill's inner War Cabinet, where the most important exec-utive decisions were taken, was an entirely male affair. A handful of women sat as 'experts' on assorted advisory committees, but they would have found few female faces amongst the civil servants who prepared the papers and took minutes; in 1943, only thirteen women were employed above the level of principal (the lowest rung of the adminis-trative grade) across the whole of Whitehall.[5] The presence of permanent, senior female civil servants – however few in number – was, of course, an improvement on the picture during the previous war. Alix Kilroy, who had withstood the interrogations of the Schuster

Committee so effectively back in 1934, continued to thrive at the Board of Trade, reaching the grade of principal assistant secretary in 1942, when she was put in charge of a senior staff wholly male in composition. Back from her travels, Beryl Power was another powerful female personality in wartime Whitehall, overseeing feeding schemes for air-raid shelters at the Ministry of Food and later moving on to the Ministry of Supply to head its housing and welfare branch.

As in 1914–18, this small band of pioneering female administrators was vastly outnumbered by the army of women filling lower-level clerical posts, although by 1939 skirt-lengths were rather shorter than in the previous war, and hair was shingled or permed rather than piled into voluminous halos, Edwardian-style. This concentration of women workers in the lowest-paid jobs was as true of the Foreign Office as any other department. By the late 1930s, women clerks had become a familiar sight, a far cry from the days when Sophia Fulcher, the Foreign Office's sole lady typist, had to lurk inconspicuously in an attic room with only formidable-looking dossiers to talk to. In 1937, over eighty women were on the payroll as clerical officers or lower-grade clerical assistants, whilst the typing pool had swelled to more than a hundred. These numbers did not, in fact, rise dramatically after September 1939, but many women clerks already in post at the Foreign Office found themselves happily redeployed on to more interesting and varied work, either to cover for male colleagues on active service or to grapple with an expanding wartime workload. For example, the Chief Clerk's Department, which kept the Foreign Office's finances in order, employed just six women in 1937; this almost doubled to eleven in 1940, and then doubled again by the end of the war to twenty-two. Similarly, the female presence in the Librarian's Department crept up from five ladies in 1937 to sixteen in 1945. Cornelia Polak and Dorothy Denny, who both joined the Foreign Office as lowly clerical officers in the 1920s and would go on to have long post-war careers in the Diplomatic Service, were transferred to the hitherto wholly masculine Communications Department, where they ciphered and deciphered telegrams alongside ten other female colleagues.[6]

For some clerical officers, the war also offered wider opportunities for service abroad. The Foreign Office had become notably more relaxed about posting women to overseas missions in subordinate roles as typists, clerks and junior archivists, where there was no question of them performing anything but the most routine administrative work. By September 1939, there were around forty women employed in such posts in British embassies and legations, mostly in Europe or North America. After the declaration of war, many stayed put; others returned to London, and some were transferred elsewhere, in a few cases to less conventional – and altogether more exciting – posts in the Middle East. Frances Flanagan, for example, who had worked as a shorthand typist in the Bucharest legation since 1930, received orders to transfer to Baghdad in July 1941. Another long-serving typist, Kathleen Potts, moved from Belgrade to the Cairo embassy just a few months earlier, whilst Sybil Streater was seconded in the autumn of that year to the staff of the Minister of State in the Middle East, also based in Cairo. By 1945, there were female clerical officers in Moscow, Berne, Stockholm, Brussels, The Hague, Lisbon, Prague, Santiago, Rome, Washington and Constantinople, and the Foreign Office had even taken the unprecedented step of appointing three female proconsuls – in Jerez (Spain), Lisbon and New York – to perform the occasional duties of this honorary post, which included administering oaths and recording affidavits.

Despite this widening of horizons for women employed in the lower and middling ranks both in London and abroad, the war initially did little to unsettle the prevailing structure of masculine authority at the senior levels of the Service. In June 1942, there were only three women in higher-grade administrative posts, all on temporary contracts. Of these, Lady Cynthia Cheetham was probably the most familiar with the ways of the Foreign Office, being the second wife and widow of Britain's former minister to Copenhagen, Sir Milne Cheetham. (He divorced his first wife, the daughter of the Russian ambassador in Rome, following the revelation that she was having an illicit affair with his chancery colleague in Paris, an occupational hazard of embassy life.) Before her marriage, Lady Cynthia had worked for the Foreign Office in a clerical role, and she re-entered it in July 1941 in the Refugee Department, joined a few months later by a Miss J. Howard. Mrs E. C.

Parsons in the Prisoners of War Department brought the tally of female principals to three.[7]

This figure, however, was soon to rise, following an explicit statement from the Foreign Secretary, Anthony Eden, in January 1942 to the effect that women would not be barred from applying for temporary administrative grade posts, a statement which was coaxed out of him only after persistent lobbying from female MPs and against the backdrop of ever-increasing shortages of manpower.[8] Eden's words would have greater consequences than perhaps he realised at the time, for he was forced to concede in the same breath that he did not regard the Schuster Committee's deliberations of 1934 as 'the last word' on the question of women's permanent admission to the Diplomatic and Consular Services, and that he was willing to revisit the whole debate after the war. After some foot-dragging, Eden's decree regarding temporary appointments was put into force, and by the end of the war there were over thirty female officers employed in administrative grade posts across sixteen different departments, turning what had been exclusively male staffs into strikingly mixed companies.[9] Foreign Office chiefs remained clear, nonetheless, in their own minds that throwing open temporary posts in London as an emergency wartime measure should not be allowed to prejudice the issue when – and it was now 'when' rather than 'if' – the wider question of women's longer-term future in the Service returned.[10]

This deep-seated concern to avoid queering the pitch against the masculine status quo meant that, whilst willing to tolerate women in London, officials were reluctant to send them to responsible posts abroad in case they made too conspicuous a success of their work. The number of women who managed to secure diplomatic (as opposed to clerical or secretarial) posts overseas was tiny, and in most cases their appointments – rather like those of Phillpotts and Bell twenty-five years earlier – occurred more through accident than design. Freya Stark and the Persian specialist Nancy Lambton were made temporary attachés in Baghdad and Tehran respectively. Canadian-born Mary McGeachy was bestowed with formal diplomatic status in Washington, whilst the journalist and historian Elizabeth Wiskemann was employed as an assistant press attaché at the legation in Bern, Switzerland. A few more were appointed towards the end of the war: Muriel Lamb as a third secretary in Oslo, Miss Hastings as an acting vice-consul in New York, and former Bletchley codebreaker Grace Thornton as press attaché in Copenhagen. In all cases, their official status was ambiguous. Only Lambton's name appeared in the *Foreign Office List*, the annual directory of all personnel employed in London and abroad. Yet, in time, these women's war service would provide exactly the kind of evidence of female ability and achievement that Foreign Office chiefs were so desperate to suppress.

So too would that of the high-ranking women employed in the overseas sections of the Ministry of Information (MOI), which worked closely with the Foreign Office to target propaganda and publicity at allies and neutrals abroad. The MOI would prove, in fact, something of a blind spot for opponents of women diplomats, for a number of talented female recruits found their way into the warren of offices at Senate House, the brutal modernist tower in London's Bloomsbury which housed the ministry's headquarters, and thence to various locations overseas. Freya Stark was initially recruited by the MOI in London as an Arab expert, a job which provided the launch pad for her colourful wartime career in Cairo and Baghdad. Less celebrated, but highly respected by her peers, Enid McLeod was recruited to the MOI's French Section at the beginning of the war, having previously worked for the foreign affairs think tank Chatham House, and rose to become its head in June 1943. Shortly after joining, McLeod was entrusted with a delicate mission to Paris to explain the section's work to a sceptical British ambassador and his staff, who had been notably underwhelmed by the visit of her then (male) boss a few months earlier.[11] Other notable MOI women included Elizabeth Monroe, a former employee of the League of Nations Secretariat, who headed the Middle East Division; and Molly Hamilton, the journalist and former Labour MP, who joined the American Division in May 1944. Hamilton's task, as she later put it, was to supply British representatives in the USA with 'all the material that could help to keep Anglo-American relations sweet', a job for which Hamilton was well equipped, having toured the continent extensively in 1942 in her former guise as a Ministry of Reconstruction official, talking up government plans for post-war social reform.[12]

In short, after a slow start woman power was on the march – abroad as well as at home. One consolation for Foreign Office chiefs who feared the consequences of this feminine advance was that the efforts of women like Rowena Vining in the wartime secret intelligence services would remain, at least in the short term, exactly that: secret. Freya Stark might write articles for *The Times*; news of Mary McGeachy's appointment might be splashed across the British and US press; Molly Hamilton might give public lectures and appear on the BBC *Brains Trust*; but in the post-war debates over women's suitability for diplomatic careers, the clandestine activities of the young women recruited to the PWE, to the cipher school at Bletchley Park, or to the Special Operations Executive (SOE) hardly featured, for understandable reasons. It was only later that the courageous deeds of the fifty or so female SOE agents dropped into occupied France became widely known, through films like *Now It Can Be Told* (1944–46), featuring agent Jacqueline Nearne; *Odette* (1950), based on the real life of French-born agent Odette Sansom; or *Carve Her Name with Pride* (1958), a film which paid tribute to the young widow Violette Szabo, shot dead by the Nazis at Ravensbrück.[13] Indeed, well into the twenty-first century, historians are still uncovering the daring exploits of these extraordinary patriots.

Rowena Vining's story has never been previously told, even though few can rival it as an eyewitness account of some of the war's most dramatic twists and turns. One day in spring 1943, when she had been working at Woburn Abbey for just over a year, Vining received word that she was to join a new mission in Algiers, the exact purpose of which was undisclosed but which she guessed (correctly) would have something to do with a planned invasion of Italy. She set sail for North Africa on an ocean liner packed with British and American soldiers and equipped, as the odd little man in charge of the civilian passengers informed her unapologetically, with lifeboats sufficient only for the fighting troops on board. Much to the disgust of her British colleagues, and greatly adding to the tedium of the voyage, not a drop of alcohol was to be found on the ship, the Americans having insisted on an entirely 'dry' crossing. Arriving in Algiers stone cold sober, Vining hunted for suitable lodgings and found a large flat on the edge of the bustling kasbah, which she shared with a couple of pleasant French-Canadian girls. Once settled in, it was time for work. Vining's day job was to read captured Italian mail for the purposes of gauging enemy morale, although she also worked in the Allied broadcasting station. It was there one day in July that Vining found herself, along with the rest of the staff, locked in the building in anticipation of General Eisenhower's formal announcement of the invasion of Sicily. This weighty utterance lost some of its solemnity when one of the technicians played the recording backwards, reducing the General vocally to something resembling Donald Duck. Thankfully the glitch was resolved in time for the broadcast proper.

As the Allied forces advanced up the Italian peninsula, Vining was transferred first to the port town of Bari, with its handsome Norman castle, and then on to Naples, just in time for the dramatic eruption of Mount Vesuvius in March 1944, which rained hot ash down upon aircraft stationed at the US airfield outside neighbouring Pompeii. As the Allied campaign made progress, Vining was sent to record the mood of crowds attending the 'Blood Miracle' of St Januarius in Naples' main cathedral: if the blood liquidated, as it usually did, it augured well. If not, Vining recalled,

> it means there's going to be a disaster. By this time the allied forces were moving on Rome and word had got around that if he didn't liquidate this year that Rome would be destroyed. So I was told to go off and join the crowd and see if he did, and he did, thank goodness!

Vining soon had the opportunity of inspecting for herself the state of the ancient imperial capital, as she sped through battlefields and smoking villages on the back of a lorry towards Rome. She was astonished to find the place largely untouched, 'a golden city' only lightly scathed by Allied bombing raids, which had ceased in August 1943 following negotiations between President Roosevelt and the Pope. It was the start of another fascinating year for Vining, still engaged on propaganda work, but now in the company of some of the most distinguished intellectuals and artists, including the celebrated philosopher Benedetto Croce, surrealist painter Giorgio de Chirico, novelist Alberto Moravia and his wife, writer Elsa Morante.

Vining continued to impress her superiors, leading to her selection for yet another new mission in July 1945, this time under the auspices of Lord Mountbatten's South East Asia Command in the Pacific, where battle was still raging with the Japanese. The idea, in Vining's words, was to follow 'the – we hoped – conquering armies, and take over radio stations and establish newspapers and the sort of thing we'd been doing [in Italy]'. She was given five days' leave in England, where she heard the news that atomic bombs had fallen on Hiroshima and Nagasaki, and then boarded an aeroplane ('which was then quite a thing') for Ceylon, the seat of the headquarters of the South East Asia Command. There, Vining was told that the focus of her work was to be the Dutch East Indies, a historic European colony now in the process of being dismantled piece by piece. When the Japanese finally surrendered at the beginning of September, Indonesian nationalists immediately declared a state of independence, and in so doing opened a new and bloody chapter of revolutionary conflict which would only reach its conclusion with the Netherlands' official recognition of Indonesian sovereignty in 1949. When Vining arrived four years earlier, this post-colonial struggle was just beginning. The Dutch she encountered in Ceylon resented her presence (they were 'absolutely furious, they wouldn't speak to me. They thought it was their country'). In Jakarta, where she was transferred a month or two later, Vining grasped the true depth of nationalist feeling. There she arrived to find Indonesians slaughtering Dutch prisoners of war recently released by the Japanese, a scene of chaos which prompted the British to send in Gurkhas to provide protection and restore some semblance of order. By befriending a couple of friendly translators and talking to the

English-speaking Indonesians with whom she came into contact, Vining soon realised that the colonial order of the old Dutch East Indies would never be restored, 'but it took the Dutch quite some years to accept that'.

By now, Rowena Vining was quite transformed from the wide-eyed, twenty-year-old officer's daughter who had visited her local labour exchange looking for work in December 1941. The war had taken her on a journey far from home across continents and conflict zones, throwing her into the company of Frenchmen, Italians, Americans, Algerians, Dutch and Indonesians, and testing her capacity for mental and physical endurance to the limit. At Woburn Abbey, Vining had been entrusted with work of a secret and often highly delicate nature, and her intellectual aptitude and resilient character subsequently earned her a front-row seat at some of the most dramatic episodes of the war. With these experiences under her belt, it was not surprising that the Foreign Office was unwilling to release Vining at the end of her service in Indonesia, and she was offered a job in the Public Relations Department in London, dealing with British policy towards South East Asia. Vining would remain a public servant for the rest of her working life.

It has become fashionable for historians to pour scorn on the popular narrative of British women's wartime lives. In its most simplistic guise, this typically characterises 1939–45 as years of emancipation which transformed millions of bored, downtrodden housewives into liberated, empowered breadwinners. It is certainly true that for many – perhaps for most – British women, the war was not a march out of the shadows of dreary domesticity into the sunlit uplands of paid work, but a time of material deprivation, of anxiety about husbands and sons in active service, and of hard, exhausting and unrelenting labour both inside and outside the home. Paid employment might have given some women their own independent income for the first time, but, unlike male earners, they were expected at the same time to bear the full burden of household drudgery and childcare, which more than filled whatever hours of leisure they were allowed by their employers.[14]

This rather bleak corrective does not, however, represent the experience of all. For young women like Vining, whose jobs transported them from home front to fighting front, the war could have a transformative effect. Before her call-up, Vining's most likely future was matrimony and a life of full-time housewifery. That is what her education had prepared her for. Up to the age of eleven, she learned to read and write and perform elementary arithmetic from a series of dull governesses. This was followed by a spell at a boarding school which, as Vining remembered it, 'would have fitted into Jane Austen's time!' There she was taught 'ladylike things' such as ballroom dancing and elocution, but not hockey ('because it might damage your legs') and not ballet ('because it would damage your feet'). Vining had to plead with her parents to allow her to sit an exam for the School Certificate, which they eventually agreed to. But university or a profession were very remote prospects. Vining's Italian lessons in Malta were intended to extend her menu of feminine accomplishments and, by implication, to increase her marital currency; they were certainly not intended to lead to a career. 'Everybody,' Vining recalled (by which she meant every girl of her particular social class), 'was expected to marry.' In short, the war changed Vining's life irrevocably. Although her lack of formal education would later hold her back from rising to the very highest ranks of the Diplomatic Service, Vining's wartime adventures were decisive in securing her access to a masculine world whose borders, only a few years earlier, had been so stringently policed against female intruders.

Vining's story, like those untold stories of the female clerks and typists employed at home and away by the wartime Foreign Office, would not be recounted during subsequent debates over women in diplomacy, but would instead be swept up into the general tributes to British 'woman power' that were seemingly on everyone's lips by VE Day. Proponents of women's admission to the Diplomatic Service hoped that the nation's gratitude to nameless women such as Rowena Vining would make it nigh on impossible for the Foreign Office to dismiss their claims yet again. But as well as invoking the steady patriotism of British womanhood at large, feminists would, as they had before, point to the exemplary deeds of outstanding individuals in foreign lands, including women formally recruited by the government for wartime service overseas. The number of these temporary women diplomats was small, but not so small that they could be loftily dismissed, like Gertrude Bell, as 'exceptional' cases.

Two Attachés

Freya Stark

On 2 September 1939, one day before Britain formally declared war on Germany, Freya Stark described the mood in London to her old friend Herbert Young:

> Last night London looked like a dead city – all the houses dark, a drizzle descending, and the streets very empty as everyone stayed as stationary as possible so as to make the evacuation easier. I bought: (1) a gas mask, (2) a little bag for one's toilet things to take with me to the basement, (3) a winter suit, and (4) French face powder which I may never see again for the next five years. I shan't go down to anything lower than the sitting rooms where there are divans that one can go on sleeping on.[1]

Stark's meticulous preparations for life in the soon-to-be Blitzed capital were, as it transpired, unnecessary. Before very long she had secured employment as a 'South Arab expert' on a salary of £600 a year in the Ministry of Information's Mid-Eastern Division, which 'bivouacked' in a corner of the famous Locarno Room at the Foreign Office 'rather like Beduin among the ruins of some lost civilisation'.[2] After only a few weeks of amiable discussion and cups of tea with colleagues around a long trestle table, Stark received an invitation from the ministry's man in Yemen, Stewart Perowne, to join him in the work of selling the Allied cause to the peoples of Arabia. Readily accepting, Stark set about packing her face powder and bidding farewell to her beloved collection of expensive hats. Before setting sail for Aden, the British protectorate on the southern tip of Arabia, she found time for an intimate tête-à-tête with Malcolm MacDonald, Secretary of State for the Colonies, and was delighted to find him interested in her 'pet plan' for creating a democratic, pro-Western Middle East, a 'strong Arabia, as united as we can make her', as she put it to Sydney Cockerell, another long-time confidant. Exhilarated at the thought of the task ahead, Stark boarded a ship at Folkestone. 'It will be useful to have all things so truly laid that we can build a good post-war world out there,' she wrote. 'It is nice to be *building* in these days of destruction.'³

The journey which had taken the forty-six-year-old Stark from an unconventional childhood in Italy and early fascination with the cultures of the Middle East to war service for Britain in the heart of Arabia, was an eventful one. Stark was born in 1893 into an artistic but impecunious household. Both parents were of a bohemian bent: her father, Robert, had studied and taught fine art on and off in Italy and London for some years, and her mother, Flora, was the daughter of a English painter based in Florence, who also happened to be Robert's uncle – making the couple first cousins. It was not a harmonious match and the pair spent long periods of time apart, with Freya and her younger sister Vera living out of a packing trunk much of the year. In 1903, when Freya was ten years old, Flora Stark abruptly removed her daughters to the town of Dronero, where, unbeknownst to her husband, she had entered into business with a young Italian count who owned a rug factory there. This rather eccentric move changed Freya's life for ever. Her character was profoundly shaped by her mother's casual neglect and overriding preoccupation with both the factory and her business partner, Mario di Roascio, with whom Flora Stark had an intimate but apparently platonic relationship. Flora's new career as a businesswoman was also indirectly responsible for the traumatic incident which occurred two years later and left Freya with physical and mental scars from which she would never fully recover. During a visit to the factory, Freya's long hair was accidentally sucked into the whirring machinery. Without thinking to switch off the power, Mario grabbed the hysterical twelve-year-old and pulled her out, ripping off half her scalp and right ear in the process. This action left a terrible wound which eventually healed following a hasty skin graft and months of recuperation, although Freya was left with a disfiguring scar which she did her best to conceal in subsequent years with strategically placed hair-pieces and ribbons.[4]

Freya escaped this unhappy domestic atmosphere and the site of her childhood trauma in 1911, when she persuaded her father to pay for tuition at Bedford College, one of the women-only colleges of the University of London. The First World War brought to an end this period of relative liberation, during which Freya drank deeply at the fount of learning, attending inspiring lectures, taking tea with distin-guished professors, and making the acquaintance of intellectuals, artists and politicians whose conversation sparkled with a brilliance quite unlike anything that she had known in Dronero. Initially Freya returned to Italy to train as a nurse in Bologna, but a disastrous love affair with a young doctor followed by a bout of illness saw her back in London by August 1916. There she typed lists of the missing for the Canadian Red Cross ('such sad work'), subsequently found a secretarial job at the British Museum ('copying at 30/- a week, what one may call sweated labour!') and eventually secured employment at the War Office in the postal censorship division.[5] Despite receiving praise for her effi-ciency, Freya disliked the long hours – she had only one weekend off in every six – and found the work exhausting. Pleasant colleagues could not compensate for the discomfort of sitting in an underheated room all day. 'The W[ar] O[ffice] insists on all windows being open,' she reported in a letter to Flora, 'and as there has been fog, snow, and all sorts of weather lately, it wasn't at all pleasant and probably the regula-tion was made in August!'[6] By March 1917, Freya had handed in her notice and started a training placement at a small civilian hospital in Hornsey, just north of London. By October she was back in Italy, serv-ing in a British ambulance unit close to the front.

After the excitement of the war years, there followed for Freya a dispiriting period of what felt like suspended motion. She was dogged by poor health, family problems and precarious finances, all overlaid by a niggling and increasingly distressing feeling that life was passing her by. The sudden death of her sister in 1926 was a turning point. Vera had married Mario, Flora's business partner, back in 1913 when she was just eighteen, and had thereafter lived a wretched existence, enduring several miscarriages, losing one child to typhoid, and never escaping her mother's controlling presence. Freya knew she had to act if she was ever to strike out on her own, and in November 1927, aged thirty-four, she caught a cargo ship for Beirut in French-controlled Lebanon with a plan to master that notoriously fiendish language, Arabic.

It was the beginning of a new life and a passionate love affair with the East. Freya was dazzled by the beauty of the desert, the splendour of the Bedouin people, and the richness of the civilisation that she found as she travelled on to Damascus and then out to the countryside where rough scrubland met an ocean of sand. With her friend, Venetia Buddicom, Freya dreamt up a daring plan to venture into the Jebel Druze, a mountainous region which had been under the rule of French martial law since local uprisings broke out two years previously. Accompanied by their guide, Najm, the two women left Damascus at dawn on donkeys, passing through villages and relying on the hospitality of their inhabitants for food and shelter each night. Through a mix of audacious effrontery and feminine coquetry (a formula she would come to rely on again and again), Freya succeeded in persuading the officers of a French garrison to let them pass further into Druze territory, where they met and conversed with holy men and chieftains on various subjects, from devil worship to the French League of Nations mandate. Back in Italy, via Basra, Jerusalem and Cairo, Freya penned an article on the shortcomings of French rule in Syria. ('The French are not going to like it much,' she wrote to her father.[7]) To her delight, the article was accepted by *Cornhill Magazine* and appeared in November 1928, not under Freya's name but her chosen Arabic pseudonym, Tharaya, a female name which referenced the Pleiades (or Seven Sisters), a cluster of seven stars often compared to a necklace in both Arabic and Persian culture.[8]

With her first publication under her belt, Freya was eager to plan her next odyssey. She chose for her subject the Assassins, a murderous eleventh- and twelfth-century Islamic sect whose fortress castles lay in ruins somewhere in the treacherous embrace of the Persian mountains. She set off from Baghdad in April 1930, equipped with a few rudimentary maps, and trekked with three guides into the interior, carefully writing up her observations of geological and archaeological landmarks along the way. She returned the following year, anxious to make further discoveries about the bloody history of the Assassins which might be deemed worthy of publication in *The Geographical Journal*, the organ of the prestigious Royal Geographical Society. A debilitating bout of malaria prevented Freya from making it to the summit of Takht-i-Sulaiman, the second-highest peak in Persia, but she did valuable work in the valleys below and trekked on into the western region of Luristan, where she corrected government maps and captured the kaleidoscopic sounds and sights of the landscape and its peoples in her notebooks.

Returning to Baghdad and staying there until March 1933, Freya Stark became a familiar and even rather admired figure in British colonial and diplomatic circles. Writing in the *Baghdad Times*, and sending exclusive stories on British military action in Iraq to London, her fame was growing. She travelled to London in June 1933 to receive the Back Memorial Prize at a grand ceremony at the Royal Geographical Society, after which the invitations poured in. The plucky female explorer was highly sought after for dinners and receptions; the BBC asked her to broadcast a talk; *Who's Who* requested biographical details for her entry in the latest edition; publishers lined up to offer book contracts; and the Royal Asiatic Society provided her with a platform for her first public lecture, which she delivered in the autumn before a packed auditorium. Publishing glory followed. *The Valley of the Assassins* hit the bookshelves in May 1934 and was met with universal critical acclaim. Stark followed up two years later with *The Southern Gates of Arabia*, an account of the epic journey along the ancient incense route in Yemen which she embarked upon in January 1935. Her final trip before the war was again to Yemen, this time to the remote Hadhramaut region, where she led an archaeological expedition with two other pioneer women explorers, Gertrude Caton Thompson and Elinor

Gardner. The impetuous, ill-disciplined Stark clashed with her more methodically minded companions almost immediately, but the resulting publications, a book of photographs and a travelogue entitled *A Winter in Arabia*, were more popular than ever.

With her intimate knowledge of the Arab lands, acquired at source through extensive travels, Freya Stark found herself endlessly – and inevitably – compared to Gertrude Bell, who had died the year before Freya first set sail for the Middle East. Dismayed by the idea of living in another woman's shadow, Stark remained infuriated by these comparisons throughout her life. Yet she could hardly blame others for making them: the similarities were unmistakeable. Both women immersed themselves in the alluringly unfamiliar cultures of Arabia, studying the languages, history and beliefs of its peoples. Both found initial fame through their pens, publishing lively accounts of their journeys and discoveries in the region; and both were recognised as genuine experts in the field by the masculine authorities of the Royal Geographical Society. Both women were also sharp dressers, although Stark was perhaps more eccentric, purchasing flamboyant hats and, during the London season of 1938–9, appearing in company with Himyar, a lizard she had befriended on her second trip to Yemen, draped around her neck. Of course there were differences, too. Bell was born into a wealthy and well-connected family and benefited from a privileged education at a top London day school, followed by Oxford. Stark had a disrupted upbringing in Italy involving very little formal schooling of any kind. Bell was tall, elegant and self-assured. Stark was five foot one, slim in her youth but increasingly stout thereafter, and remained deeply insecure about her looks, even after cosmetic surgery in 1934 greatly improved the appearance of her childhood scars.

But perhaps more importantly, what Bell and Stark both learned to do was to seek out and cultivate powerful male allies. Like Bell before her, Stark encountered dozens of British officials in the course of her travels, to whom she handed over updated maps and details of what she had seen and heard in hard-to-reach territories. This intelligence was invariably rewarded by favours and advice. In Baghdad, she became a particularly avid admirer of Captain Vyvyan Holt, Bell's replacement as Oriental Secretary, from whom she learnt much of the nuances of British policy in Iraq, and who in turn came to hold the diminutive female explorer in high esteem. In Yemen, she eventually earned the respect of the British resident advisor, Harold Ingrams, after a shaky start. She had enraged him in 1937 by wilfully refusing to board a plane which Ingrams had arranged to fly at great expense into the Hadhramaut to transport a bedridden Stark to hospital in Aden. The praise which she lavished upon Ingrams and his wife, Doreen, in an account of the journey penned for *The Times* did much to restore his goodwill.⁹ By contrast, Stark hit it off from the start with Ingrams's dashing junior officer, Stewart Perowne, who had greeted the troupe of lady archaeologists upon their arrival in Aden and was later much amused by Stark's deeply unflattering accounts of the haughty manners of Caton Thompson and Gardner during the expedition.

It was Perowne who, in the autumn of 1939, urged Stark to pack her bags for Aden, where the race was on to win hearts and minds for the Allied cause – or, at the very least, to persuade Yemen to embrace neutrality and shun the Axis powers. Mussolini, who did not officially declare Italy's entry to the war until June 1940, had his eye on the region as the ideal location from which to launch air strikes on neighbouring British and French Somaliland. Enemy agents were, therefore, thick on the ground, spreading 'the worst sort of Italian unpleasantness', as Stark described it in a letter to the Foreign Secretary, Lord Halifax.¹⁰ As an assistant information officer, her initial task – once she had settled into her rented rooms overlooking Aden's bustling harbour, which was now crowded with the thick iron bodies of British warships – was to reiterate and amplify the case against Germany to the Yemeni people by writing pamphlets, newspaper articles and rousing radio broadcasts, all in faultless Arabic, of course. 'There is not a moment's boredom,' she told her mother in January 1940, 'our office is like a variety show, such a peculiar mixture of people come in and out.'¹¹

The following month saw her back on the road, travelling north into territory controlled by Yemen's aged but formidable imam, a wily old man who was only too aware of the strategic significance of his lands to both Allied and Axis powers. Stark's mission, as she put it, was 'to sit there, rectify rumours, and alter the atmosphere as much as one can from the standpoint of feminine insignificance, which has its compensations'.[12] The latter were in evidence at a Yemeni checkpoint, where Stark turned on the charm, sweet-talking the customs officials into believing that the film projector hidden in her luggage was in fact a portable commode. She then continued to the ancient walled city of Sana'a, where the imam kept his court. Stark knew she was unlikely to win an audience with the spiritual leader himself ('as women are beneath him'), so instead began to work on the Foreign Minister's wife, whom she had soon persuaded to host a film-show for the ladies of the royal harem.[13] The flickering images of heroic British servicemen in combat, interspersed with idyllic scenes of the English countryside, enthralled her audience, and Stark's little projector was in high demand over the next six weeks. Curiously enough, the most popular film by far, as she relayed in a letter to Perowne, was *Ordinary Life in Edinburgh*: 'they adore it – just people walking up and down Princes Street!'[14]

By keeping her eyes and ears open, befriending local notables like Sana'a's governor ('a cheerful old boy, voluminous in white silk dressing-gown embroidered with yellow flowers'), and delicately steering casual conversations into useful directions, Stark was able to report back to her superiors at the end of March with details of the size and location of arsenals and garrisons, estimated numbers of battle-ready Yemeni troops, and the scope and scale of Italian influence.[15] When Italy began bombing Aden a few months later, following Mussolini's declaration of war, she took to lying out on her balcony at night, where she watched the 'terrible beauty' of the shellfire bathing the city in blinding white light.[16] Through 'womanly persisting', she helped to summon into existence a volunteer Arab police reserve to protect the blitzed city from looters, and argued forcefully for the appointment of Arabic-speaking female wardens with authority to enter harems during raids ('they might be blazing from top to toe,' she told Cockerell, 'and a man could not go in').[17] In July, Stark was called upon to interrogate

Italian prisoners from a captured submarine and translate various operational papers discovered on board. These turned out to contain the
imminent movements of two other enemy craft – vital intelligence
which allowed the Royal Navy to despatch its own destroyers in a little
over an hour to launch a surprise attack. She later watched the torpe-
doed Italian ships 'burning on the outskirts of Aden' from her rooms,
her bosom swelling with patriotic pride.[18]

Freya Stark's wartime adventures, however, were only just beginning. Soon she was in Cairo – 'the keystone of our Middle Eastern
arch' – on a salary now doubled to £1,200.[19] Winning the trust and
confidence of further male allies, including the British ambassador, Sir
Miles Lampson, and the commander-in-chief, General Sir Archibald
Wavell, she found herself charged with a thrilling new venture: the
fomenting of pro-British sympathy across the region through the creation of a secret society, to be known as the Ikhwan al-Hurriyah, or
Brotherhood of Freedom. In the short term, this network of Arab politicians, officials, business and professional men, tribal chiefs and
spiritual leaders was to serve as a vehicle for anti-Nazi propaganda. In
the long term, it was to lay the foundations for a secular, democratic
order in the Middle East post-war, one which was, naturally, sympathetic to British commercial interests in the region. Stark began sowing
the seeds in Cairo by hosting regular tea parties, lectures and discussion
groups, to which she invited a carefully selected mix of Egyptian and
British guests, later adding a weekly bulletin and growing the
Brotherhood to over five hundred members by the end of February
1941. A year later, membership stood at an impressive 6,000.

She revelled in the 'gaiety and glitter' of Cairo in wartime. Stark
confided to one friend in August 1940 that she had 'dined out twenty-
five nights out of four weeks and am rather a wreck'.[20] Many of these
evenings were spent in the luxurious environs of the British embassy,
where guests retired after dinner to lounge on chaise longues in the
garden, which stretched down to the Nile's edge. Others were whiled
away in the company of Wavell, who enjoyed Stark's witty conversation
and ability to recite English poetry (a talent which he shared), and was
most amused by her collection of outlandish hats. She surpassed even

Gilbert Scott's classical Italianate palace, *c.*1880, where all new entrants to the Foreign Office and Diplomatic Corps spent their first weeks.

The Old Diplomacy: Otto von Bismarck, the German Chancellor, commissioned court artist Anton von Werner to capture the scene at the final session of the Congress of Berlin in 1878.

Above, foreign diplomats alongside the leaders of London society flocked to Lady Palmerston's lavish soirées in the mid-nineteenth century.

Charles Hardinge with his wife, Winifred, and family photographed in 1910. Winifred's social graces and royal connections proved useful to Hardinge as he climbed the diplomatic career ladder.

A diplomatic partnership: Lord Dufferin pictured in 1885 with his wife, the energetic and fun-loving Hariot, who founded the Countess of Dufferin Fund to provide medical care to poor Indian women.

As Ambassadress in Rome during the First World War, Lilias Rennell Rodd channelled her artistic and creative energies towards the deepening of ties with Britain's wartime ally.

William Orpen, *The Signing of Peace in the Hall of Mirrors* (1919): Women were among the spectators but not the signatories to the Treaty of Versailles, which was concluded in Paris in June 1919.

Orientalist Gertrude Bell (*standing, first row, second from left*), was the only woman included in the discussions of British policy in Mesopotamia (Iraq) held in Cairo in January 1921.

Bell in Cairo with fellow Orientalist T. E. Lawrence, whom she thought 'exceedingly intelligent' when they first met on an archaeological dig ten years earlier.

Alexandra Kollontai, Soviet Ambassador to Sweden, pictured at her desk in 1934. Kollontai's name would be frequently mentioned during debates over women's suitability for diplomatic careers.

Dame Edith Lyttelton pointed to her service as British delegate to the General Assembly of the League of Nations in Geneva to argue for women's admission to the Diplomatic Service.

Nancy Astor MP, the first woman to sit in the House of Commons, spoke forcibly in favour of female diplomats at the committee convened by the Foreign Office in 1934.

'To say it is impossible for women to do this work is absolute nonsense.' The words of Warren Fisher (*left*), Head of the Civil Service. Claud Schuster (*centre*), who chaired the 1934 committee, and Robert Vansittart (*right*), Permanent Secretary at the Foreign Office, disagreed.

Punch captured the frustrations of feminists in 1936 when the government announced that women would continue to be ineligible for posts in the Diplomatic and Consular Services.

The renowned traveller Freya Stark, in Yemeni dress, in 1944. Stark's wartime vision was of a 'strong Arabia, as united as we can make her'.

Herbert Olivier's portrait of a youthful Freya Stark. She always wore her hair low over her right ear to conceal a disfiguring scar from a horrific childhood accident.

Persian scholar Nancy Lambton, press attaché at the British Legation in Tehran, accompanying her Ambassador, Reader Bullard (*right*), as he presents his credentials to the Shah in December 1939.

Lambton with her chancery colleagues in Tehran. On formal occasions, Lambton wore academic robes as no protocols existed concerning official dress for female diplomats.

INSTITUTE OF ELECTRICAL ENGINEERING

Caroline Haslett speaking to the press on her return from the United States in 1941. Her visit was funded by the Ministry of Information as part of a wider campaign to persuade the Americans to join the war.

NATIONAL ARCHIVES OF CANADA

MARY EVANS / © YEVONDE PORTRAIT ARCHIVE

Canadian-born Mary McGeachy, the first woman to be given formal diplomatic status by the British government, at her desk in the Washington Embassy in 1942.

'An ambassador of British women': Winifred Cullis, head of the women's section at British Information Services in New York, which sought to promote and explain Britain's war aims to a sceptical American public.

Florence Horsbrugh MP (*left*), one of two women included in Britain's delegation to the San Francisco conference which created the United Nations in June 1945, pictured next to the Canadian delegate, Cora T. Casselman.

The US delegation, including sole female delegate Virginia Gildersleeve (*front row, second from right*), sign the UN Charter. As 'assistants' rather than full delegates, neither Horsbrugh nor her colleague, Ellen Wilkinson MP, signed for Britain.

'Is the Foreign Service of such a special nature that it denies the fundamental principle that men and women are equal in the Civil Service?' Ernest Gowers, chair of the committee which recommended women's admission to diplomatic careers in 1946.

Autumn 1956: Mary Moore seated behind British ambassador, Sir Pierson Dixon, in the UN Security Council, when Soviet tanks were rolling into Budapest and the Suez crisis was about to break.

Anne Warburton, Britain's first woman ambassador, in her official residence in Denmark. She told the press: 'a husband would be useful, but I suspect that a bachelor ambassador would miss a wife more.'

SOMERVILLE COLLEGE, UNIVERSITY OF OXFORD

PRIVATE COLLECTION

Georgina Butler, a fast-stream high-flyer, pictured in 1970 with colleagues in the garden of the British Embassy in Paris. Soon after, Butler became engaged and was forced to resign due to the marriage bar.

Delegates to the United Nations Conference on the Status of Women, held in Mexico City in 1975.

The Mexico gathering was the first international conference dedicated to discussion of women's issues, although delegates clashed over how those issues should be defined.

Lady Mary Henderson with husband, Nicholas, on his appointment as Ambassador to Washington in 1979. She told young Diplomatic Service wives that the embassy workforce was akin to 'an old-fashioned family'.

Morning Prayers: The Permanent Secretary's daily conference with senior officials in the early 1990s – an all-male gathering, despite women's increasing representation at the Foreign Office.

Pauline Neville-Jones (*left*), Britain's highest-ranking female diplomat, looks on as statesmen sign the Dayton Peace Accord in November 1995, which brought over three years of violent conflict in the Balkans to an end.

Our woman in Lebanon: British Ambassador Frances Guy meets with Grand Ayatollah Mohammed Hussein Fadlallah in November 2008.

her own record for eccentricity in July 1941, when she wrote to her mother with news of a new millinery acquisition: a hat 'like a cart-wheel, pale blue, with the hours and dials of a clock on top in pink braid'.[21] But Stark worked as well as played, running her office from the dining table in her flat, and driving from committee to committee all day long in her little blue car ('said to be one of the chief menaces to the general safety of Egypt').[22] She travelled to Alexandria and Luxor to start the Brotherhood there, organising sections for Egyptian women as well as men. 'It is of course the greatest mistake,' she informed Walter Monckton, head of propaganda in Cairo, 'to think that ladies in harems do not run the worlds they live in just as any woman does anywhere!'[23]

By the autumn of 1941, Stark was in Baghdad, nurturing into existence an Iraqi branch of the Brotherhood, a job which rewarded her with a temporary diplomatic post. Stark was no stranger to the British embassy in Baghdad, having spent a month besieged inside its walls during the dramatic coup d'état staged by pro-German Iraqi generals in the city in April 1941. This episode presented a glorious portrait of British resilience and resolve under fire. Sandbags, barbed wire and a fleet of motor cars ringed the main gates of the compound for defence, but the embassy's gardeners kept the lawn watered and its flowers in bloom throughout the crisis, whilst the stoical ambassador, Sir Kinahan Cornwallis, could be seen dining in his habitual manner, the table replete with the usual blue-and-gold china, silver plate and freshly cut flowers. The evenings, Stark recalled, were pleasant and convivial, when, ignoring stray sniper fire,

> the camp strolled out, or played clock-golf, or sat in friendly circles on the grass till the moment came for the bar to open on a long wooden table under trees, and people brought their glasses and drank their small allowance of beer or whiskey, sufficient (perforce) for the day.[24]

Despite having no electricity, no telephone lines and a temperamental water supply, the 366 inhabitants of the British compound – which included a multicultural mix of Iraqi, Indian, Armenian and Yugoslav servants and clerical staff – were kept entertained with open-air lectures, concerts, film shows and gymnastics, plus a daily bulletin of news gleaned from the one wireless which had not been confiscated by the military rebels. This daily spectacle of bodies sprawled higgledy-piggledy on the immaculate lawns, Stark noted, made the embassy gardens rather resemble 'those of a country house when opened to the public'.[25]

Stark herself slept during the siege on a plain mattress on one of the embassy's many terraces, where she could look out across the Tigris to the opposite shore (not that it was an especially scenic view, appearing 'like some rather drab Canaletto whose varnish has altered with time'[26]). She struck up a friendship of sorts with the policemen who patrolled the river, and took charge of the welfare of the *cawasses* or servants, ensuring their morale was sustained with adequate food and plentiful cigarettes. She also procured face powder, soap and other feminine accoutrements for the embassy's nineteen female residents, of which there were but two British women, Stark and Mrs Pott, the consul's wife – the other diplomatic womenfolk having been evacuated when the coup first broke. All in all, it was an exhilarating drama in which to have played a part, and Stark made the most of it. She penned a three-part series of articles for *The Times* entitled 'In Iraq during the Crisis', and devoted much space in her post-war autobiography to the siege, which drew to a close at the end of May with the arrival of the British Army and the restoration of the Iraqi royal family and government.

The alliances and confidences Stark forged during those warm evenings on the embassy lawns were renewed and repaid upon her return in the autumn. Adrian Bishop, a brilliantly witty and erudite intelligence officer, was a constant companion during the siege, and a most amiable colleague thereafter. Her relationship with Sir Kinahan, whom she had first met during those brief weeks camped out in the Locarno Room, was greatly strengthened during the siege by shared breakfasts, teas and dinners in the residence, which helped to relieve the strains and uncertainties of that eventful May. It was Cornwallis who had insisted on Freya's transfer from Cairo to Baghdad, and formalised her status at the embassy, where she worked again under Perowne, now posted to Iraq as director of publicity.

As in Egypt, Stark set about growing the Brotherhood of Freedom through her tried and tested methods of constant conversation and personal contact. 'The whole of my work was talk,' she recalled, 'and it sometimes seemed endless: men in long gowns would be sitting in a row waiting for me before breakfast, and it went on all day with only a break for the sacred hour or two of the afternoon.'[27] Progress was slower than in Cairo, however, for anti-British and pro-Nazi sentiment was strong in Iraq, and Stark struggled to persuade her listeners that an Allied victory would create the most propitious conditions for a strong and united post-war state. She remained convinced of the profound importance of the Brotherhood to Britain, both as a 'band of friendly democrats', and a 'powerful instrument' for the long-term prosperity and stability of the region.[28] Yet despite intensive committee work and travels into Kurdistan and to Mosul in the north, she had established just fourteen branches with 150 members by the summer of 1942. When she resigned her post a year later in order to complete a lecture tour in the United States for the Ministry of Information, Stark had recruited 7,000 Iraqis to the Brotherhood, a vast improvement but still some way off the target she had set herself of 10,000, which in itself equalled only about one per cent of the male population.

Through all of this, what difference did Freya Stark's femininity make? Her presence as a woman on the payroll of the British administration in the Middle East was not quite as unusual as Bell's had been during the First World War. Stark had several female colleagues, both in Cairo and Baghdad. Indeed, the day-to-day running of the Brotherhood of Freedom was largely left in female hands until 1943. In Egypt, she supervised the work of two assistants: Pamela Hore-Ruthven, the young wife of a British officer posted in the Western Desert, and Lulie Abu'l Huda, an Oxford-educated princess of Turkish ancestry. In Baghdad, she had Peggy Drower, the daughter of an old friend, working under her, alongside Barbara Graham, another young Englishwoman who also became Stark's lodger. Stark was, however, the only female endowed with substantial professional authority, and one of only two women – the other was Nancy Lambton – honoured with diplomatic rank in the region.

She revelled in her exceptional status and in the personal connections she enjoyed with powerful men. 'I have now come to have some real influence out here on politics,' Stark told her mother in September 1942, 'more perhaps than any other woman.'[29] At times, this self-belief gave Stark the confidence to fight her corner over her pay (she threatened to resign when a reduction was proposed on the grounds of 'sex differentiation') and entitlements. In Cairo she pushed her superiors hard for higher-standard accommodation, fuming to Cockerell that 'every political officer gets more salary than I do, house, entertainment allowance – and it is *far* easier at the moment to get political officers than Arabistic women'.[30] Although insisting to her grave that she was *not* a feminist, Stark could recognise sexism when she saw it – as in the unpleasant treatment meted out to her by Perowne and Ingrams in summer 1940 when news broke of her transfer and promotion to Cairo. 'What does not go down of course,' she complained to Cockerell, 'is that a mere female *should* be able to go off and get £1,200 a year for the asking and both Stewart and Harold have been at ludicrous pains to miss no chance of telling me that merit, mere merit, has nothing to do with it: just pure accident.'[31]

Later in life, Stark demonstrated considerable ego by writing no fewer than four volumes of autobiography and publishing – at her own expense – eight volumes of collected letters. Contemporaries recalled a wilful, often demanding woman who could at times be excessively self-regarding. Yet human beings are complex creatures, and deeply rooted in Freya Stark's character was another side – that of the unhappy little girl in Dronero who was left to make her way in the world without beauty, money or education. Those early experiences planted in Stark an eternal ambivalence about her abilities and professional success. This insecurity frequently manifested itself in illness or nervous collapse, with Stark taking to her bed when the pressure to perform overwhelmed her. Speaking in public was 'agony'; the thought of it filled her 'with a feeling only comparable to drowning'.[32] She repeatedly implored her superiors to entrust the Brotherhood work to a more qualified male. 'If the thing does develop,' she wrote to Rushbrook Williams, her chief in London, shortly before leaving Aden in August 1940,

> it might become very important, and I very much hope that then the *direction* might be taken out of my hands. I rather hate being at the head of things and only do so when I see my pet dreams about to die for want of support.[33]

Just over six months later, she wrote to Stewart Perowne in the same vein: 'My little show is growing and it is beginning to be agreed that a Man ought to take it over.'[34] And in March 1941 she wrote again, this time expressing the hope that Perowne might find his own way to Cairo to take the helm: 'It would be fun working with you again. I much prefer a feminine subordination to the running of anything myself and feel very much overweighted here – and the bigger it gets the more it frightens me.'[35]

Some of this fawning self-deprecation – 'you can't think how I shall appreciate being a mere harim again and having you to do the real work!' she wrote on returning from her mission in the Yemeni interior in March 1940 – was undoubtedly the product of Stark's complicated feelings for Perowne, with whom she would later make a disastrous marriage (he was a closet homosexual).[36] Some of it may have resulted from her shrewd observation of the vulnerability of the flattered male ego, and of the subtle influence that the woman who feigns ignorance or naivety in male company can exert. (As she had earlier noted, feminine insignificance had its compensations.) But much of her ambivalent relationship with power stemmed from Stark's own deep-seated insecurities – about her appearance, her intellect, her social status, and her financial means. Pushing fifty and growing plump, she often felt threatened by younger, more attractive women, and this occasionally surfaced in high-handed behaviour towards her female assistants, to whom she delegated such menial tasks as packing up her trunks and dealing with trivial domestic chores.

This imperiousness sometimes threatened her relationships with men, too. Having grown up in relative poverty, Stark became a genius at maximising her income, exploiting her entitlements to housing, travel and entertainment allowances to a degree which some – particularly those who had never had to worry about money – found distasteful. In the spring of 1943, she badly overstepped the line. Having spent two pleasant weeks in Delhi as the guest of Sir Archibald Wavell, by then Viceroy of India, Stark decided to buy a motor car for the return journey to Baghdad, with the intention of selling it at her destination at a handsome profit. Although it was her own money at stake, she relied on Wavell's good offices to acquire a permit in order to get round the rules forbidding the export of private motor vehicles from India. The permit was issued on the understanding that Stark would be reimbursed for her expenditure in Baghdad and would hand her vehicle over to the embassy's official car pool. Stopping off along the route in Tehran, however, she chose instead to sell the car on the black market for £5,000 – five times the price she had paid for it. Worse still, she engaged the assistance of a chauffeur from the British legation in the hunt for a buyer, an embarrassing fact which found its way to the minister, Sir Reader Bullard, who was furious and made it quietly known that Miss Stark would no longer be welcome under his roof.[37]

The story was circulated widely in diplomatic circles and did Stark's reputation much damage – although Stark herself never really grasped why her actions had caused such a scandal; she romped through them breezily in her autobiography. It is quite possible that the episode helped to put paid to any hopes she might have nursed of a longer-term career in government service. She confided in Cockerell in May 1943 that, 'if I were asked to go on in diplomatic [sic] I should think of it with great interest', and on several later occasions shared with friends her dreams of retiring to a sleepy vice-consulate 'in some little town by the river or sea shore'.[38] It was not to be. After her American tour, Stark busied herself with new writing projects and a spell in India inspecting philanthropic initiatives for Lady Wavell, before finally returning to Italy following the Allied victory in summer 1945. Having reclaimed the house that she had acquired in Asolo, not far from Venice, back in the 1920s, she found herself again in the employment of the Ministry of Information with a temporary assignment to organise 'reading centres' throughout the British Zone. The purpose of the scheme, which was launched under Foreign Office auspices, was to feed Italians – intellectually starved by years of Fascist dictatorship and now in danger of turning to communism for nourishment – with a healthy democratic diet of British newspapers and periodicals. Reporting to the embassy in Rome, Stark motored around northern Italy in her government-sponsored car visiting these fragile schools for democracy for nearly a year, until the British Council took over the scheme. Her contract was at that point terminated and she never worked for the British state again.

Freya Stark's post-war career settled instead back into the literary groove that had first brought her success in the 1930s. She wrote her autobiography and a dozen other books, straddling the genres of travelogue, history and philosophy, and helped to build her own legend through press interviews and appearances on *Woman's Hour* and *Desert Island Discs*. As a writer, traveller and literary personality, Freya Stark shone, but as a diplomat she was a mixed success. Her linguistic skills, regional knowledge and instinctive feel for propaganda (what she preferred to call 'persuasion') were without doubt Stark's strongest suit. She could not have cultivated so many allies within civil and military officialdom had she not demonstrated an ability to put the British case across to thousands of Egyptians and Iraqis with flair and conviction – and in the Brotherhood of Freedom (which survived in Egypt until 1952) she produced real results. Less helpful to Stark's cause, however, was her imperiousness over subordinates (especially female ones), her willingness to take advantage of others' kindness (especially where it saved her personal expense), and her tendency to respond to high-pressure situations with physical and nervous collapse.

Would a man with similar personality quirks have fared any differently? It is impossible to tell, although quite apart from any considerations of sex, any man with the same unconventional upbringing and limited formal education as Freya Stark would have struggled to enter the top ranks of the British Diplomatic Service before 1945. Like Gertrude Bell, Stark was a unique character from whose experience it would be dangerous to generalise too widely. Nonetheless, unlike Bell, Stark was not quite alone as a female diplomat in the Middle East. Across the desert in Tehran was Britain's other lady attaché – a twenty-eight-year-old Persian scholar, Ann Katherine Swynford Lambton, known from childhood as Nancy.

Nancy Lambton

Reader Bullard, the British minister in Iran, was evidently fond of his young female press attaché. She accompanied him to church on Sundays, lunched regularly at his residence, and proved a willing companion on visits to the local cinema where Hollywood films cut and dubbed into Persian regularly played. Bullard took her on one occasion to see *Little Women*, starring Katharine Hepburn, having discovered to his delight that Miss Lambton, like himself, had been 'brought up on the book'.[39] The solicitous chief instructed that steaming coffee be sent down to Lambton's office every morning during the winter and, with fatherly magnanimity, forgave her occasional absences of mind – like the day she forgot he had invited her for lunch with a group of ambassadors. Shortly after his arrival in December 1939, Bullard insisted that Lambton be included in the party which accompanied him to the Marble Palace, where he presented his diplomatic credentials to the Shah, the ruler of Iran, and much later, after the war, wrote appreciatively to her offering his thanks 'for overworking for six years for the public good and for taking so much trouble with a people that doesn't deserve it'.[40]

Lambton, in return, developed a soft spot for her old chief, whom she suspected was lonely, with his wife and five children thousands of miles away in England. He was 'a shrewd old bird', she thought, good-natured, kind, and always entertaining with his blunt appraisals of people for whom he had no time, like the lady visitor who, in Bullard's withering description, was 'interested in birds and flowers and doesn't get up till 10 in the morning'. (Lambton noted that her own rather less leisurely habits stood her in good stead, 'for the Min. has rather a bee in his bonnet about getting up early!') The more she observed Bullard in action, the more Lambton's admiration for his qualities as a diplomat grew. 'As things approach and look worse,' she remarked to her aunt in May 1941, 'he gets in better and better form!'[41] Looking back, many years later, she paid tribute to his 'tremendous strength of character' and 'unflagging capacity for work', and described her time working under him during the war as 'a great and unforgettable privilege'.[42]

Despite the strength of their mutual appreciation, Bullard was not, as it happened, responsible for first recruiting Lambton to the Tehran legation.* That was the work of his predecessor, Sir Horace Seymour, who ran into Lambton one afternoon in late August 1939 (she had been playing tennis) and proposed in passing that she join his press and publicity section in the event of war. Lambton was delighted and agreed to meet Seymour again the next day to discuss details. She visited the legation once more on 1 September ('look at some papers, write a short note & return to town' she recorded in her diary), and again on the fourth, the day after Neville Chamberlain formally declared Britain to be at war with Germany.[43] From that date, Lambton became a full-time employee of the British state, bestowed with the formal title of press attaché, or 'P.A.' for short, and in possession of her own desk in the corner of the chancery, which was quickly buried under mountains of files. ('It's not good,' she confided in her aunt: 'I tidy it from time to time but in vain for by the next day it's just as full again.'[44])

Femininity notwithstanding, Lambton was an obvious candidate for temporary wartime employment on Seymour's team. Born in 1912 in Newmarket, she was the eldest daughter of one of Britain's leading racehorse trainers, granddaughter of the 2nd Earl of Durham, and a niece of Viscount Cecil, the Conservative politician and son of the former Prime Minister Lord Salisbury. As a teenager, Lambton read T. E. Lawrence's *Revolt in the Desert* (the forerunner of his bestselling *Seven Pillars of Wisdom*) and was entranced by the evocative portrait of the Arab world which she found within its pages. Encouraged by the renowned orientalist Denison Ross, Lambton defied her mother's scepticism towards the education of daughters and enrolled, aged

* It was upgraded to embassy status in February 1944.

eighteen, at the School of Oriental Studies in London on a two-year certificate course, from whence she eventually emerged with a full bachelors degree in Persian in 1935. Fascinated by her chosen subject, Lambton embarked immediately on a doctorate which, with the help of a prestigious travelling scholarship, enabled her to spend over a year in Tehran and the surrounding provinces discovering the land and its people. Her doctoral thesis on eleventh- and twelfth-century Seljuk institutions successfully submitted, Lambton returned to Iran in July 1939 to continue her studies, and it was shortly afterwards that she came to the attention of Sir Horace as a potential recruit.[45]

Despite her impressive academic credentials, the young woman who stood before the British minister on that airless August afternoon was no dry, bookish scholar. Her network of Persian friends and acquaintances was extensive, whilst her grasp of Iran's contemporary problems was astute. During her doctoral studies Lambton had found time to teach history in a girls' high school, travel deep into rural areas to record local dialects, and carry out a detailed study of the traditional craft guilds which were still common in Iran's slowly modernising economy. As this menu of activity suggests, Lambton was physically tough. A childhood spent in her father's stables had made her a keen and talented horsewoman; tall and sturdily built, she would later drag her colleagues for treks through the massive Elborz mountain range outside Tehran, play football with street children, and ride her bicycle to the office nearly every day.

In short, Lambton's mix of formal expertise, practical experience and physical robustness meant she was better placed than anyone to take on the duties of press attaché to the British legation in autumn 1939. Her work, as she described it to her friend Violet Rhodes (niece of the famous imperialist Cecil) consisted 'largely in reading newspapers, supplying material to the press, making reports on public opinion as reflected in the press and elsewhere, establishing contact with as many people as possible and so on – the latter you will observe is a task to which there is no end'.[46] This last reflection was no exaggeration. Like Stark, Lambton spent many hours of her day making personal calls or receiving visitors, gradually accumulating a network of contacts

which stretched from press correspondents and Western diplomats to
local businessmen, schoolteachers and politicians. At first, her work
was largely confined to Tehran, but before long Lambton was spending
weeks at a time away from the city, meeting up with British officials
from Cairo and Baghdad to compare notes, and usually dropping in on
consuls and their wives in lesser outposts dotted along the route. Her
first journey to Baghdad did not start well: soon after setting out
Lambton realised that she had hired possibly the worst driver in Tehran,
who developed hiccups from the moment they left the city and did not
shake them off until they stopped later that night. She enjoyed a more
comfortable ride on the Trans-Iranian railway in January 1941, and in
early 1944 had the privilege of flying in the relative luxury of an Anglo-
Iranian Oil Company plane to Abadan, the major base for British oil
interests in the region.

When Nancy Lambton joined the legation staff in autumn 1939,
Iran's political and military significance for Britain's struggle against
Hitler was yet to be fully determined. Reza Shah had ruled for nearly
twenty years and maintained an uneasy position of neutrality,
although his sympathies were suspected to lie with the Axis powers.
Much of Lambton's time was taken up with closely monitoring and
actively countering the pro-Nazi propaganda flowing daily from
Radio Berlin and imported German newspapers and from the whis-
pering campaigns of German agents active in Iran, many of whom
were posing as legitimate businessmen or tourists. It was difficult to
know exactly how many of these were at large – Lambton estimated
there were at least eight hundred in Tehran alone – but whatever their
numerical strength, their activities certainly appeared to be producing results. 'German propaganda here,' Lambton wrote to her uncle,
Robert Cecil, in January 1941, 'has to date rather made mincemeat of
us instead of the other way round!'[47] Especially worrying were the
German engineers and contractors employed in factories, broadcasting stations and on the railways – where, as Bullard noted in August,
the potential for sabotage was enormous. The Shah, however,

continued to ignore British demands for the immediate deportation of these presumed enemy partisans.[48]

By the late summer of 1941, a sequence of events had changed this picture dramatically. First, there was Hitler's attempted invasion of Russia in late June, an act which pushed Stalin into the arms of Churchill and intensified British fears of a German advance through the Caucasus combined with a coup staged by Nazis already inside Iran. The Führer's plan did not work out. The Red Army prevented a German breakthrough and on 25 August joined the British in a coordinated invasion of Iran, which was met with little or no resistance by the Shah's troops. Many of the ruler's supposedly devoted officers simply abandoned their posts and fled. Fearing Tehran was about to be stormed, Reza Shah did much the same thing three weeks later, leaving the throne to his son, Muhammad Reza, and exiting the country on a British ship bound for Mauritius. 'Now, perhaps, things are moving a bit,' Lambton wrote excitedly to Rhodes, 'and everyone is prepared to enter into intrigues!'[49] The immediate impact of this dramatic episode for Bullard's staff in Tehran, however, was irksome rather than thrilling, as hundreds of anxious civilians descended upon the legation seeking sanctuary. On arriving at 7 a.m. on the morning of the Allied invasion, Lambton found in the chancery 'a seething mob of British subjects, allies and our Indian brothers', who 'infested one's office, mostly with trivial and unreasonable requests', and were finally despatched to the legation garden, where they remained for more than a week.[50] Yet for all the inconvenience of accommodating these unwelcome visitors ('the result was very bad for the Temper!' she confided in Rhodes), Lambton was evidently pleased to see the back of Reza Shah. She had herself worked to bring about this eventuality in the run-up to the invasion, supplying damning evidence of his corruption and greed to the recently established Persian Service of the BBC, whose daily broadcasts from London Lambton believed to have been decisive in finally ousting the autocratic ruler.[51]

Most ordinary Persians shared Lambton's relief at hearing of the Shah's political demise, but for Bullard and his team the Allied occupation did nothing to simplify their diplomatic mission in Iran. Reza

Shah had first seized power in 1921 through a military coup backed by the British, who judged that this Cossack commander of obscure origins would serve as a useful bulwark against Bolshevik ambitions in a region of prime strategic importance both for Britain's oil interests and her trading routes to India. As a purported 'moderniser', the Shah brought about limited improvements to Iran's urban and transport infrastructure, curbed the traditional power of the clerics and abolished the veil for women. But these reforms, although welcomed by some, came at the price of political freedom. Critics of the regime were quickly silenced, sometimes brutally, and many of the Shah's flagship policies, like the costly Trans-Iranian railway which opened after a decade of construction in 1937, were pushed through with no regard to the views of those whose taxes went to pay for them. Iran's road network, by contrast, used by a far larger proportion of the population, was allowed to languish in the most rudimentary state well into the 1950s.[52] This flawed regime was tolerated by the British until 1941 because it seemed to offer stability. When this was no longer the case, the British turned against their former ally, decrying his mendacity and cruelty, only later to grant the deposed Shah asylum in Canada with full access to the healthy sums accumulated in numerous overseas bank accounts at the expense of his people. It was under British protection that Reza Shah made the first leg of his journey to South Africa, and it was only the aggravation of a long-standing – and, as it would transpire, fatal – heart complaint which prevented him from reaching his destination. He died in Johannesburg in July 1944.

These uncomfortable facts made Britain's position in Iran a delicate one, exacerbated by food shortages and economic dislocation amongst the local populace, plus the worrying machinations of the Soviets in the outlying provinces of Azerbaijan and Kurdistan, where separatist sentiment was on the rise. As a result, Lambton's workload at the legation steadily increased. Noting with approval how she was 'always branching out in fresh activities', Bullard provided her with an assistant, a secretary and several typists, although the speedy departure of the former and the constant ailments of the latter meant that she was still working flat out most days.[53] 'Instead of having only 2 people's work to do,' she moaned to her aunt in December, 'I now have three and a telegram came in a day or two ago, the gist of which is that I shall have four people's work to do!'[54] Tehran had, by this time, become a regular stop for important personages, placing even greater pressures on Bullard and his team. Oliver Lyttelton, Churchill's Minister of State in the Middle East (and son of Dame Edith, who argued so forcefully for women diplomats in 1934), paid a visit in February 1942 and Lambton was called in to translate at the press conference that followed. Her interpreting skills were further put to the test when a group of British MPs passed through in March 1945 on a goodwill tour to Russia. At a gathering hosted at her house, she was forced to 'translate two simultaneous conversations for them while trying (but failing) to listen to a third conversation in French', and later at a press conference sat through an inordinately long preamble to a speech by one of the MPs. 'He turned to me,' Lambton related to Rhodes, 'and said "Now translate that and then I will come to the point," so I said "Let's come to the point first, and then I'll translate", to the delight of all his colleagues.'[55]

Sadly, a rare bout of ill health meant that Lambton was not present during the famous meeting of the 'Big Three' (as Churchill, Stalin and Roosevelt became known) in Tehran in November 1943, where agreement was reached on the opening up of a second front against Hitler. The conference proceedings took place at the neighbouring Soviet embassy, with most of the negotiations on the British side carried out by the Prime Minister and his chiefs of staff rather than by members of the legation. But Bullard was responsible for housing Churchill and, more importantly, hosting his sixty-ninth birthday party in the Victorian dining room of the legation (after it had been swept by Soviet secret police). Even if she had not been on leave in England, Lambton would undoubtedly have been deemed too junior to warrant an invitation to this jovial gathering. Had she been, she would probably have earned the doubtful honour of clinking glasses with a high-spirited Stalin, who reportedly worked his way round the room with every toast. In fact, the only woman present that evening was Churchill's daughter, Sarah, a photo-intelligence officer at top-secret RAF Medmenham in Buckinghamshire whom the Prime Minister decided to bring along for company.[56] Even she, however, played no part in the proper business of the conference, which remained – like the other great wartime gatherings of the Allied leaders at Cairo, Moscow and Yalta – a wholly male affair.

Like Stark, Nancy Lambton was the only woman in the British legation entrusted with work deemed to be of a 'responsible' nature. Indeed, at the time of her appointment she was the *only* female employee in the chancery, although the workforce subsequently expanded to include a sizeable team of lady typists and secretaries, including the wife of a British aircraft mechanic who called on Lambton to offer her services *pro bono*. 'She's quite nice and very willing but frightfully slow and not very bright,' she wrote to her aunt and uncle: 'However when she offered to come she said she thought propaganda was very important, which was quite the right spirit!'[57] By the end of 1944, one of the big houses within the legation compound had been converted into a hostel to accommodate the chancery's nine female employees (Bullard mischievously called them 'the Nine Nuns'[58]), the city's hotels and boarding houses having been judged unsuitable for English ladies.

Naturally, Lambton was not included in this appellation, but – again, like Stark – rather seemed to revel in her exceptional status as a lady attaché with diplomatic rank. She recounted several times to family and friends an amusing account of her first (and only) audience with the Shah in December 1939, when the whole chancery staff accompanied Reader Bullard to present his credentials. Protocol ruled that full diplomatic uniform be worn on such occasions, but for the reception of a female diplomat, no precedent existed. What should Miss Lambton wear? After some discussion, it was decided that she should don a long black academic gown, hastily assembled by the counsellor's wife from fabric bought at the bazaar, and a hood borrowed from someone at the American College: 'it was rather a good solution', Lambton initially thought, 'at least as far as comfort went'. The party crammed into a fleet of cars and processed slowly through the streets, saluted along the way by policemen and even a few passers-by ('I expect they did not know who we were!'). A guard of honour playing 'God Save the King' ('quite recognisably') greeted Bullard and his staff at the palace, and they were quickly shown into an antechamber by the Iranian chef de protocol ('who looks rather like a codfish'). Bullard was taken in first to see the Shah, accompanied by the Iranian Prime Minister, whose job it was to introduce each officer one by one in order of seniority. Lambton was last in, and took up the story in a letter to Violet Rhodes:

> When the man in front of me began to walk forward and I moved in through a door, resplendent in robes (!), Majesty pointed and said 'Who's this, who is this?' The P.M. began to explain who the secretary in front of me was, and Majesty interrupted and said, 'No, no not that one. That behind!' Where upon the P.M. began to explain and Majesty said I had a judge's cap on (which had I think rather shaken him). P.M. explained it was academic dress and I was a doctor of philosophy and knew Persian well, and tried his best to make M speak to me but he wouldn't, and was, I fear, rather shaken by the whole affair![59]

Lambton found the whole episode highly entertaining, as suggested by the grin on her face in the photograph which captured the scene as she processed in to see the Shah. She did not take umbrage at the ruler's refusal to talk to her. Lambton thought, in fact, that it was 'a little unfair that he hadn't been warned in advance he would be confronted by a woman, for it's never happened to him before'. She was wholly aware that many Persian men found the spectacle of an unmarried, professional woman both unnatural and disturbing, but she usually brushed off their hostile reactions with bravado. On the road to Abadan in January 1941, Lambton was stopped by a policeman who demanded to know, 'Whose burden are you?' – meaning, as she explained in a letter to Rhodes,

> whose wife are you, using the Arabic word for wife which means a burden. I replied no one's so he, thinking I hadn't understood, repeated

his question using the Persian word for wife which is the same as the word for woman. This time I said I'm not a wife (which might also mean I'm not a woman), with a look of astonishment in his face he said 'Are you a man, then?' at which there were hoots of laughter from the chauffeur and his boy, to the discomfiture of the poor policeman, who then tried to get out of it by asking (as a rhetorical question) whether it was a bad thing to be married.[60]

On her travels, Lambton was often mistaken for a lady doctor or missionary, or the wife of a British official or oilman, none of which bothered her in the least. She was equally at ease in the company of her predominantly male contacts in Tehran. As for her legation colleagues, Lambton developed several amiable relationships, affectionately dubbing her two regular walking companions 'long legs' and 'short legs' on account of their vastly contrasting levels of physical stamina. She retained, nonetheless, a certain detachment from the world inhabited by the gentlemen of the Foreign Office, whose personal animosities and petty slights amused and exasperated her in equal measure. 'This place is at times almost like a detective book,' she wrote in July 1940, 'and not a very nice one at that.' 'How I loathe my office at times!' she complained a year later.[61] The nicknames her colleagues gave each other she thought absurd (one man was known as 'pinkers' or pink elephant, 'because he looks just like one') whilst their capacity for interference during her absences was infuriating: 'A certain matter I've been working up for months has been nearly wrecked,' she fumed to Rhodes in November 1940. 'Some ass butting in instead of doing nothing till I returned as I had said.'[62] The consuls were the worst when it came to misplaced self-importance. Lambton told the story of one officer in Alwaz who had ostentatiously hung an enormous Union Jack on the wall behind his desk, 'to impress, I suppose, those who came to call on H.M.'s Representative'. She added, 'Living in out of the way places perhaps tends to make one lose a sense of proportion.'[63] As for the wider diplomatic corps of Tehran, Lambton found them dull company and described them derogatorily in her letters as 'd.d.', which stood for dithering diplomats. Every week there was some 'ghastly' dinner or 'awful' lunch at one or another legation, and the pleasure which her *chers collègues* appeared to take in late-night bridge-playing she found unfathomable.

Much of this critical detachment stemmed from Lambton's status as a professional outsider rather than as a woman per se, although a few casual comments suggested otherwise, such as the faintly school-marmish note struck in her likening of the chancery to a 'kindergarten', or her confession that her colleagues' '"old school tie'ishness" makes one sick'.[64] On the whole, however, if Lambton felt she never truly belonged to the British Diplomatic Service, this was due more to her self-image as a serious scholar than to any sense of inferiority on grounds of sex. She was grateful to have a job 'in which I can make use to some extent of my specialised knowledge (such as it is)', aware perhaps that many similarly educated and capable women back in Britain were not so fortunate.[65] But for Lambton, the task of producing propaganda was no substitute for the 'peace and quiet of a life spent doing research work', and she never seriously considered a post-war career in diplomacy. 'How nice it will be to go back to normal pursuits again one day,' she wrote to her aunt in August 1941, 'instead of telling people what they ought to think (or what you think they ought to think which isn't quite the same thing) and other equally vain occupations!'[66]

In this respect, Lambton was a very different character from Freya Stark. The two had met a decade earlier in Britain, when Lambton appealed to the renowned traveller for help in persuading her parents to allow their daughter to travel to Iran for the first time.[67] They met again on a few occasions when Stark visited Tehran during the war, but the two women were never bosom friends. Lambton suffered none of Stark's insecurities when it came to social status and professional esteem, owing no doubt to the more fortuitous circumstances of Lambton's birth and her formal education. She never seemed to question her own intellect or abilities or feel the need, like Stark, to flatter male egos in order to smooth her path. Nor was Lambton in the least bit vain about her appearance. She was a handsome woman with striking features, but seldom put on make-up, wore her dark hair in a plain, somewhat unruly bob, and favoured sensible shoes and unexciting skirt suits – which she rarely replaced. Bullard even had to take her aside one day and explain in the nicest possible way that she needed a new wardrobe. 'It is such a bother,' she wrote to Rhodes after this somewhat awkward conversation, 'and I have enough to do as it is and little or no spare time – however I suppose it will have to be done.'[68] Unlike Stark, who longed for matrimony, attracting the opposite sex did not appear to rank high on Lambton's list of priorities. She remained a spinster throughout her life and her personal papers tell of no significant love affairs, either before or after her six years as an attaché in Tehran.

Of Nancy Lambton's private life we know, in fact, very little. Unlike Stark, she wrote no autobiography and in later years was never one for lengthy personal reminiscences. Whilst Freya Stark remains a household name due to her prolific writings and broadcasts, Nancy Lambton's is far less known outside academia, to which she returned in the autumn of 1945 when she took up a lectureship at the School of Oriental and African Studies (SOAS) in London. There she stayed until retirement in 1979. In the longer term, however, Lambton's influence within Foreign Office circles was arguably much greater – and more contentious – than that of her more celebrated counterpart. Stark was an occasional guest at British embassies in the post-war Middle East and a colourful personality known, by reputation at least, to most Foreign Office Arabists. Lambton's published works, by contrast, became standard texts for young men preparing for a posting to Iran or Afghanistan, and Lambton herself taught dozens of diplomatic officers who were sent to SOAS to learn Persian (and not every student survived Lambton's famously exacting tutelage and stiff exams).[69]

Even more importantly, Lambton's advice was directly sought by officials dealing with post-war policy towards Iran, most controversially during the run-up to the CIA-orchestrated coup of 1953 which removed the fiercely nationalist Prime Minister, Mohammad Mussadiq, from power. One distinguished historian describes Lambton as a key 'architect' of the plan to overthrow Mussadiq. She painted a portrait of the leader as fanatically anti-British and impossible to negotiate with, which quickly became Foreign Office orthodoxy in the early 1950s. Even though Lambton was not directly privy to the discussions which subsequently determined British policy, so respected was she as an interpreter of Iranian politics that officials cited her authority on count-less occasions and acted on her suggestion to employ Robin Zaehner, a former SOE officer turned Oxford don who had worked as Lambton's deputy in Tehran, for purposes of fomenting anti-Mussadiq sentiment on the ground in Iran (a mission in which, as it transpired, he was not wholly successful).[70]

Lambton's hand in urging British support for the 1953 coup – which, indirectly at least, helped to bring about the Islamic revolution of 1979 – remains a point of contention to this day, a subject on which she maintained a discreet silence even to those who knew her best. The true extent and significance of her involvement will probably never be known. What is clear, however, is that Lambton was one of the few women (perhaps the *only* woman) to have any real, substantive input into British policy in the post-war Middle East. Had either Stark or Lambton made a serious stab at joining the Diplomatic Service once the bar to women had been lifted in 1946, both would have been frus-trated and perplexed to find that the region they knew and loved so well had been designated a no-go area for female diplomats. It was deeply ironic that the wartime record of these two lady attachés would help to clinch the general argument for women's permanent admission to the diplomatic profession, but do nothing to convince the men in power that a woman diplomat could serve her country with distinction in the Arab world.

9

Ambassadors of British Women

Around lunchtime on 6 November 1941, a plump and rather drearily dressed Englishwoman rose to address the assembled press corps of New York. The setting was a conference suite in the opulent Hotel Roosevelt, which, with its Tiffany chandeliers, grand wall murals and prime location on Madison Avenue, offered a stark contrast to the portrait of austerity and universal self-sacrifice painted by the visitor from overseas. All her fellow countrywomen were doing their utmost to defeat Hitler, she assured her listeners, 'from serving maid to the duchess's daughter', whilst class distinction, that British disease that Americans detested so wholeheartedly, had virtually disappeared. The British people were pulling together like never before, and none more so than the nation's women, whose lives, as she told an exclusively female audience at the equally luxurious Hotel Biltmore a week later, had been turned upside down since September 1939. The war, she said, had meant 'a complete readjustment of our outlook and a complete reshuffling of all the old accepted values'. In such a world, she told her listeners, who included some of America's most powerful women, there could be 'only one sure thing – the hand of friendship'. Her mission was to grasp this hand of friendship on behalf of all British women and to 'tell the women of America how much this friendship means to us at the moment'.[1]

So who was this middle-aged spinster, so eager to boost Britain's cause to her neighbour across the Atlantic? In 1941, Caroline Haslett was a

familiar and respected figure in British public life. An engineer by training, Haslett was best known as a champion of women's admission to this
most masculine of professions and an evangelist for the use of labour-
saving technologies in the home to ease the housewife's burden. From
September 1940 she served as advisor to the Ministry of Labour with
special responsibility for the recruitment and training of women, a
subject which she discussed at length with industrialists and government
officials during her US tour. It was through her connections to the British
arm of the International Federation of Business and Professional Women
that Haslett officially crossed the Atlantic in November 1941, but it was
the Ministry of Information – the department which, alongside the
Foreign Office, was responsible for promoting Britain's war aims abroad
– which obligingly picked up the tab, as it did for so many British visitors
to America, including a significant number of women from various walks
of public and professional life.[2]

Such women, alongside the handful who found longer-term employment in Washington or New York, contributed to the forging of the
wartime alliance between Britain and the USA. As lecturers, publicists
and temporary diplomats, they proved that the 'special relationship'
which drew these two English-speaking nations into common cause,
was not a solely male achievement. Nonetheless, it was striking that
these women were selected to perform an unmistakeably *public* form of
diplomacy which focused primarily on winning hearts and minds,
rather than the more conventional diplomatic work of influencing
power-brokers in government. More often than not, the specific target
was *female* hearts and minds, to which it was assumed women like
Caroline Haslett – with her vision of transatlantic sisterhood – were
uniquely qualified to speak. In this respect, the women sent to the USA
to court Britain's wartime ally breached only the outer defences of the
masculine diplomatic establishment, leaving its inner sanctum largely
intact, at least for the time being.

─────────

When Professor Winifred Cullis arrived in New York in September
1941 to report for duty, she could hardly have wished for a

more stylish address: 30 Rockefeller Plaza was a landmark in early twentieth-century architecture, an elegant art deco finger pointing to the heavens. The centrepiece of philanthropist John D. Rockefeller's 'city within a city', the Rock, as it was commonly known, was home to the Radio Corporation of America, the headquarters of broadcasting station NBC, the ritzy Rainbow Room restaurant, and a roof-top observation deck from which visitors could enjoy stunning panoramas stretching over Manhattan and the slow-moving waters of the Hudson to the city's outer districts on the far horizon. Cullis's destination, however, as she passed through the lobby and into an elevator (the fastest she had ever experienced), was none of these iconic places. Stepping out at the fifty-second floor, Cullis tapped lightly on a door marked 'British Information Services' and entered. Here she would work for the next two years.

Cullis's new employer (known as 'BIS' for short) was quite unlike any conventional embassy or consulate. Its origins were found in the innocuously titled British Library of Information, a Foreign Office agency established in New York back in 1920 to provide authoritative facts and figures on all things British – from the workings of Parliament to the length of a cricket pitch – to any inquisitive journalist or college student who came a-calling. Although in theory limited to providing factual information on request, the library was intended to serve the wider political purpose of projecting Britain and the British way of life to Americans in a favourable light. It was a modest and exploratory venture in what political scientists now term 'soft power' and historians call 'cultural diplomacy', a subtle (and sometimes not-so-subtle) form of statecraft which would become a familiar feature of the ideological battles of the Cold War. When Britain went to war in September 1939, this art of persuasion through overseas publicity was still very much in its infancy, a problem which the establishment of a Ministry of Information in London was designed, at least in part, to rectify. The USA presented a particularly challenging case: here was an emergent superpower, capitalist and democratic, and tied to Britain through a shared history and tongue, but wedded to an isolationist mind-set which abjured any foreign entanglements that might result in American youths being summoned to their deaths on European soil, as they had in 1917. Foreign Office and MOI chiefs knew that something more sophisticated than the old Library of Information was now required. If Britain was to persuade the USA to join the war, a professional machine would have to be assembled, capable of producing publicity of the highest order which could subtly undermine – without openly antagonising – isolationists in Congress and beyond.[3]

This was far from a simple task. There was no shortage of Republican senators or newspapermen simply itching to expose the supposed ulterior motives of America's former colonial master. Britain's intention in fighting the war, they argued, was the preservation of class privilege at home and imperial dominion abroad; America, the land of the free, should have nothing to do with it. Central to this isolationist message was the – dubious but nonetheless powerful – claim that devious British propaganda had lured the US into the First World War with disastrous results. Any activity which carried the merest hint of sponsorship from the British government was therefore potentially suspect. This meant that BIS was initially forced to proceed with exceeding caution, until Japan's attack on Pearl Harbor in December 1941 triggered America's entry into the war and allowed British publicists to breathe a little more freely. From that date onwards, the challenge became one of managing this powerful new ally so as to extract maximum support – moral and material – for Britain's prosecution of the war in Europe.

These ends BIS pursued in a style which owed little to the long-established traditions of British diplomacy. The personnel recruited to run the main New York operation were certainly not typical Diplomatic Service material. Although answerable in theory to career-diplomat chiefs in Washington, the moving spirits of the outfit were men like the historian John Wheeler-Bennett, who sneeringly described the British Library of Information, BIS's predecessor institution, as having 'a sort of "Sleepy Hollow" existence with a decreasing prestige and a diminishing clientele'. Another was Aubrey Morgan, the well-connected son of a Cardiff businessman who had handily married in succession *both* daughters of the American diplomat Dwight W. Morrow; and another, Isaiah Berlin, the Latvian-born Jewish philosopher who, as Freya Stark remembered, always led one 'into the most beguiling by-paths of conversation and makes one late for meals (but it is worth it)'.[4]

These colourful characters were running the show that Winifred Cullis joined in autumn 1941, at a point when British efforts to bring America into the war were reaching crescendo. BIS's staff had swelled to more than two hundred by this stage, each busily answering enquiries, handling the press, organising lecture tours, putting together travelling exhibitions on patriotic themes and licking, stamping and despatching more than 260,000 items of mail each month. Cullis was appointed on a salary of $412 to head a brand new section dedicated to the building of goodwill amongst women's organisations, whose power over American public opinion BIS chiefs had only very belatedly woken up to. Cullis became the highest-paid woman by some margin, BIS's sizeable female staff occupying for the main part subordinate roles as typists, secretaries or assistants. Miss M. E. Herrington was the only other section head, appointed on a much lower salary of $180 to counter untruths circulating in the US press about the British Empire in India. She was later joined by Hilda Beal, 'an indefatigable educationalist', as one colleague described her, who kept BIS in touch with the schools; by Barbara Hayes, who became head of the Speakers Section in February 1942; and by a young Cambridge graduate called Joan Burbidge, who would, after the war, be amongst the first women to join the Diplomatic Service on a permanent basis.[5] There was also the dynamic – and unpaid – presence of Constance ('Con') Morgan, Aubrey's wife, overseeing a team of writers in her husband's Survey Section, which became locally known as the 'Clip Club' due to the sea of newspaper clippings in which its staff appeared always to be swimming.

Cullis, however, was the only officer charged with a special remit to court female public opinion, a mission for which she was admirably qualified. An elegant, white-haired spinster of sixty-six, Cullis had impressive form in overseas public speaking. Back in 1918 she had visited Malta and Gibraltar under the auspices of the National Council for Combating Venereal Disease, and during the 1930s lectured in Canada, Australia and India on her personal passion: education for healthy living.[6] After retiring from her chair in physiology at the London School of Medicine in 1939, she embarked immediately upon a three-and-a-half-month goodwill tour on behalf of the British government, a trip which took her to Japan, Shanghai, Hong Kong, the Dutch East Indies, Singapore and Malaya and was subsequently extended to include Canada and the United States.

With further transatlantic connections through the International Federation of University Women and the English-Speaking Union, Cullis was an ideal candidate to lead this new branch of BIS activity – and she did not fail to deliver. Supplied with a weekly cable from London packed with news of British women's heroic activities on the home front, Cullis and her trusty assistant Marjorie Walters planned a punishing schedule of talks, meetings and press conferences in locations across the United States. By June 1942, Cullis had travelled almost 30,000 miles, spoken in seventy different cities, and given countless radio interviews and broadcasts along the way. In press releases she described herself as 'an ambassador of British women', sent by her government to 'answer enquiries about the organisation and work of British women for their country in war-time'.[7] This broad theme Cullis dressed up in various guises, her talks ranging from 'Food in War-Time' and 'How England has Trained Her Women', to 'A Child in the War' and 'The Woman Power of Democracy'. New Yorkers were the first to see women's work on the British home front on the big screen at a documentary film show which Cullis masterminded in January 1942, well timed to capture the feverish and expectant mood of the weeks immediately following the Pearl Harbor attacks. The *New York Times* applauded the images of Women's Voluntary Services volunteers and uniformed auxiliary workers for their authenticity and ordinariness: 'There are no glamourised movie actresses; the heroines are one hundred, one thousand, one million women, all with the fear of war in their faces and parts in the same plot – defeating Hitler.'[8] Cullis also impressed the numerous audiences she addressed during her travels with her public-speaking skills. These included the New York City League of Women Voters, the Camden County Branch of the American Association of University Women, the Newport County Women's

Republican Club – and others too numerous to name. Walters carefully preserved the thank-you letters these organisations sent to her chief, pulling out choice remarks for her report for MOI bosses in London, including one rather pleasing description of Cullis as a 'woman Churchill'.[9]

It is impossible to measure the full effect of Cullis's campaign as an ambassador of British women, dealing as she was – as, in fact, was BIS *in toto* – with moods, impressions and images in the mind's eye of the American public. But there could be no doubt that in targeting women's organisations she was doing valuable work. Americans, to quote Wheeler-Bennett, were 'ear-hungry people' and none more so than women.[10] Freya Stark was struck by this fact during her lecture tour for the MOI in 1943–4, when she encountered dozens of attentive female audiences, including fifty doughty ladies of the Foreign Policy Association. 'Of course what is astonishing,' she recorded in a letter home, 'is that there should be so many females interested in foreign policy enough to lunch out on it.' In Washington, Stark met one of the organisers of the national women's club movement, who, by virtue of her post, 'thereby wields an instrument of incalculable and terrifying capacities'.[11] Stark was further impressed by the number of female power-brokers she encountered in press and political circles; she met big names like Dorothy Thompson of the *New York Herald Tribune*, whom she liked ('she was fun: when she starts talking she looks round for an audience as if it were a missing handbag'), and Republican congresswoman Clare Boothe Luce, whom she did not ('She interrupted so often that at last I protested and said I must be allowed a "say"'[12]). By January 1944, Stark was writing to the MOI and Foreign Office with her impressions of 'how more efficient, adventurous and alive the women are than the men in this country', although she also found something 'quite unendurable' about certain aspects of American feminine efficiency, so different from the more forgiving British kind.[13]

Unlike Cullis's work, Freya Stark's mission to the USA was not exclusively focused on female public opinion. As an advocate of British policy in the Middle East, she conversed with State Department officials, senators and Rotarians just as often as she did with over-efficient female journalists. Yet Stark's gender undoubtedly heightened the interest with which female opinion-formers received this short, bird-like visitor from Britain, who seemed to know so much about the Arab world. By mid-1941 the MOI, Foreign Office and BIS had finally grasped the potential value of public diplomacy delivered with a feminine touch. Not only was Cullis's appointment confirmed around that time, but a whole series of lecture tours to the USA involving female speakers was mooted and approved, with more following in subsequent years. Alongside Caroline Haslett, the veteran trade unionist Margaret Bondfield and Labour MP Jennie Lee both toured in 1941. They were joined by Molly Hamilton from the Ministry of Reconstruction, then by the veteran suffragist Kathleen Courtney in 1942, and by Freya Stark in 1943, whilst others on the wartime lecture circuit included the junior minister Florence Horsbrugh, Conservative MP Irene Ward, Anglican lay preacher Maude Royden and businesswoman Ethel Wood. Not all these visitors necessarily saw themselves, like Cullis, as ambassadors of British women per se. The socialists Bondfield and Lee had little time for such sex distinctions and addressed mixed audiences of trade unionists, although Lee's trip was arranged under the auspices of the Women's Trade Union Congress and she managed to find time to talk to a few women's clubs before heading home – details unlikely to be found on the itinerary of a male speaker.[14] In general, however, MOI chiefs assumed that female lecturers would hold a special appeal to female audiences and could speak authoritatively on matters which specially concerned those audiences – and, on the whole, they assumed right.

Caroline Haslett certainly had no doubts as to her target market when she arrived in New York on 5 November 1941 as the guest of the International Federation of Business and Professional Women. As Haslett told her distinguished female audience at the Biltmore, she came at the instigation of the women of England, with instructions to 'take the hand of friendship' that their sisters across the ocean had extended with such generosity and warmth, and to tell America something of the extraordinary transformation now taking place in British women's lives. Like Cullis, in her speeches and press conferences Haslett vividly described the astonishing range of jobs now being filled by women of all classes, taking care to pick out the most arresting and unusual examples – the female bus conductors, milk-women, dust-women, post-women and bricklayers – confident they would make a good story in the newspapers.[15] Haslett further endeared herself to America by gushing sentimentally on the radio about the wonders of orange juice and Christmas lights, and subtly reminding her listeners in the process of the material privations being nobly borne by Britons. She offered warm thanks for the gifts sent across the Atlantic by American women, from shiny new mobile canteens to bundles of clothes for families made homeless by the Blitz. She spoke with awe of the glories of high-speed air travel and the modern home appliances and air conditioning that she had discovered during her trip. Haslett was soon swamped with invitations to at-homes, teas and dinners and all manner of platforms were put at her disposal, from the Society for the Advancement of Management to the Detroit Women's Business Club. After the attack on Pearl Harbor brought America into the war – which took place almost exactly midway through her trip – Haslett's expertise as a government advisor on the training and recruitment of women in industry was in high demand. She lunched with officials from the Departments of War and Labor, visited aircraft factories and attended employers' conferences, from which she came to the surpris-ing conclusion that 'the general view held in American industry about woman power is astonishingly old fashioned!'[16]

The MOI was sufficiently pleased with Haslett's performance to approve a return visit in the summer of 1944. As before, the trip was ostensibly at the invitation of the Canadian and US Federations of Business and Professional Women's Clubs, but Haslett packed into her six-week stay dozens of additional engagements. She made radio broad-casts, met the editors of *Harper's Bazaar*, *Vogue* and *Cosmopolitan*, and had private interviews with Frances Perkins, the Secretary of Labor, and with Mayor LaGuardia of New York. She addressed private gatherings on the subject of the social welfare reforms mooted in William Beveridge's much discussed report and post-war economic planning, visited the International Labour Office in Montreal, and also found time for a quick trip to Knoxville, Tennessee, to inspect the work of the Tennessee Valley Authority, a pioneering state-owned corporation created a decade earlier under the auspices of Roosevelt's New Deal. Two and a half years into the wartime alliance, Americans were even more welcoming towards the forty-something spinster from England. Haslett's utter lack of glamour (she was fond of dowdy polka-dot dresses and unfashionably peaked hats) only enhanced her sincerity and authenticity when she spoke movingly of the stoical endurance of Londoners, now being pounded by German flying bombs. She was greatly admired in the press for her appearance at a glitzy dinner at the Waldorf Astoria wearing a simple 'make-do-and-mend' frock which had been produced under the strict rationing regulations in force in Britain. Haslett was amused by the piece in the *Washington Post* which described her as 'the ruddy-faced Englishwoman with no make-up', but was pleased to see that the potent symbolism of her plain attire amidst a riot of evening gowns and tiaras had not gone un-noted.[17]

Haslett's two missions to America as an envoy for British women were unanimously agreed to have been a great success. The chairman of the Tennessee Valley Authority wrote to Sir Stafford Cripps, then Minister of Aircraft Production, to pronounce Caroline Haslett 'one of England's ablest people', whilst the secretary of the US Federation of Business and Professional Women thanked Haslett profusely, remarking that 'your ambassadorship has been of great value to the Canadian Federation, and to our Federation, and you have again left behind you a host of loyal friends – loyal not only to you, but loyal to Great Britain, and our Allies'.[18] What undoubtedly enhanced Haslett's appeal to the latter was her staunch advocacy of women's employment rights, an issue dear to the Federation's heart. Haslett, after all, was a self-avowed feminist and forceful proponent of 'woman power', having spent much of her career battling for better training and employment opportunities for women in some of the most male-dominated occupations in industry. Her patriotism was never in doubt: Haslett loyally avoided dwelling on controversial topics, such as equal pay, during her US tours. But she was no stooge dutifully parroting the government line. She used every platform to talk up the ways in which the war had revealed untapped talents amongst the female workforce and to argue for 'a new social and economic order' which would allow women to take their rightful place next to men as equal workers and colleagues.[19] Strikingly, Haslett did not forget the British housewife, whose unpaid labour she regarded as every bit as valuable as that of the woman who worked outside the home. 'She must have her electrical washing machine, her washing up machine,' Haslett insisted, and homes equipped with 'all the best that science can give'.[20]

Perhaps most uncomfortably for the Foreign Office, Haslett also advocated the greater use of women in the settling of great world affairs through international diplomacy. In a widely publicised speech in Winnipeg in 1944, she insisted that 'women must play an important part at the peace table', noting how even with conflict still raging, the contours of the post-war world order were already being shaped – at Bretton Woods and other weighty conferences, and through institutions such as the United Nations Relief and Rehabilitation Administration and its nascent Educational Organisation (which would later become UNESCO).[21] Where, Haslett demanded, were the women? Too many, she believed, were stuck in secondary, subordinate roles, chained to typewriters and hanging on the words of their male superiors. Throwing every nation's diplomatic service open to both sexes, Haslett argued, was a crucial step towards rectifying this sorry situation and unleashing the world's woman power for peacemaking. Haslett would argue this case again in late 1945 before the committee reluctantly convened by Foreign Office chiefs to reconsider the question of women's admission to the Diplomatic Service – as promised by Anthony Eden three years earlier. Haslett's testimony would demonstrate just how much damage women's wartime record in America and elsewhere had done to the case for preserving the masculine status quo – more even than German V-weapons had been able to effect on her house in London whilst she was away: it had suffered an indirect hit and lost several ceilings, but, like the spirit of the resilient nation that Haslett had so skilfully channelled during her US tour, remained standing.

Haslett, Cullis and the other British women sent across the Atlantic to spread goodwill were publicists rather than diplomats, but in wartime America distinctions between the two became increasingly obsolete. Haslett got to know the inside of the Washington embassy, together with the consulates in Chicago and Detroit, extremely well in the course of her two tours, and developed some friendly contacts within the British diplomatic corps. Ernest Owen, a consul in Detroit, was so taken with Haslett when he met her in 1941 that he subsequently wrote with his daughter's address in England and asked Haslett to pay a visit: 'she would love to see someone who had so recently seen her "old Dad"'.[22] On her second tour, Haslett formed an equally warm friendship with Alan Judson and Betty McCall, a young married couple both working at the Washington embassy, who invited her to join them for a weekend in their log cabin on the Maryland coast. On her return to London, Haslett provided Judson with a useful introduction to Waldorf and Nancy Astor, whom Judson hoped would agree to entertain a delegation of US congressmen shortly due to arrive in Britain on a fact-finding visit (they did).[23] But Haslett's closest contact in Washington was not, in fact, any permanent male officer of the British Diplomatic Service, but instead a temporarily employed Canadian-born woman of Scottish descent with fair skin and copper-blonde hair who went by the name of Mary Craig McGeachy.

Six years younger than Haslett, McGeachy – who signed her letters as 'Craig' – had spent her childhood and youth in small-town Ontario before entering the University of Toronto and training to be a teacher. This rather modest and unimaginative trajectory jumped onto a much more adventurous track in 1927, when McGeachy relocated to Geneva to edit a trilingual student magazine, a job she readily abandoned when an opportunity to work in the Information Section of the League of Nations Secretariat came her way the following year. For the next twelve years, McGeachy lived and breathed international cooperation. 'There was no separation of work and life,' she wrote; 'Every waking moment went to the League.'[24] It was a good time to be young, single and engaged in building what seemed like a new world. But mixed into McGeachy's idealism was a professional ambition which listened and learned and seized every opportunity to gain practical experience – whether of drafting memos, translating articles, lecturing to summer schools or liaising with the countless international organisations which based themselves in Geneva for the purpose of lobbying the League. She became a fixer, conciliator and consummate networker, a self-assured and independent woman utterly committed to her work.

With the approach of war, and the future of her cherished League in doubt, McGeachy's thoughts turned to the contribution that she, an international civil servant with over a decade's experience under her belt, might usefully make to the struggle against Hitler, which Canada loyally joined in step with Britain in September 1939. She briefly considered and then dismissed teaching the history of international institutions to undergraduates in Montreal, and at Christmas discussed the possibility of British government work with friends in London, who promised to put out feelers on her behalf. This eventually paid off. In August 1940, whilst driving the families of League employees stranded in Geneva through France to the safety of neutral Portugal, McGeachy received a telegram containing an offer of employment in the public relations section of the Ministry of Economic Warfare. The Ministry had been created at the beginning of the war for the purpose of paralysing Germany's economy by attacking her supply lines and trading links, thus (in theory at least) forcing an early surrender. The centrepiece of the economic warfare strategy, as in the First World War, was the blockade. Enforced by the Royal Navy, it was designed to prevent imports headed for Germany from reaching their destination, and to stop enemy exports getting out. For this to work, the cooper-ation of the USA, a mighty global trading power, was crucial. But there was a problem. Isolationist opinion had latched onto the British block-ade, presenting it to the American people as a cruel, inhumane policy which punished innocent civilians in occupied countries, including children. Naturally, the British government saw it differently: the blockade, ministers argued, was intended to bring a speedy end to the war, thus liberating the oppressed peoples of enemy and occupied

Europe from the Nazi yoke as well as minimising battlefield slaughter. The sum of human suffering would be much greater, they reasoned, if Germany's capacity to wage war was left unchecked. In the long term, the moral calculus clearly fell in favour of the blockade. But the challenge was how best to explain this to the American people.

This predicament provided McGeachy with her first opportunity. Towards the end of 1940, instructions came to pack her bags for Washington, where she would begin a campaign of publicity designed to hammer home the case for the British blockade to American public opinion. McGeachy's selection for this task was in part a stroke of luck. The obvious candidate was David Bowes-Lyon, the brother of the Queen and McGeachy's boss. But he was considered insufficiently plebeian to appeal to America's democratic instincts by the British ambassador, Lord Lothian, which left the way clear for McGeachy. Her public-speaking experience, North American roots and personal contacts with American internationalists through the League made McGeachy a safe pair of hands. It is also possible that Lothian, a lifelong advocate of closer union between the English-speaking peoples of the white dominions, liked the idea of appointing a Canadian, whose presence would remind Americans of the strong familial bond shared by the Commonwealth nations. Whatever the deciding factor, at the beginning of 1941 McGeachy quit London and set sail across the Atlantic to join the British campaign against continued American neutrality.

At the time of McGeachy's arrival in Washington, the British embassy had stood for more than a decade in its leafy grounds at 3100 Massachusetts Avenue, a handsome red-brick manor designed by Edwin Lutyens in Queen Anne style. The ambassador was now Lord Halifax, who replaced Lothian following the latter's sudden death in December 1940. A Conservative peer and member of Churchill's War Cabinet, Edward Frederick Lindley Wood, 3rd Viscount and 1st Earl of Halifax, was another political appointee and an aristocrat and ex-appeaser to boot. His appointment was initially looked on with dismay both in London and Washington. How could this old landed gent, publicly identified as one of the 'Guilty Men' of pre-war foreign policy, possibly persuade the Americans to join Britain in her democratic struggle against the dictators? As it turned out, Halifax overcame some early gaffes (which included leaving a hot dog uneaten on his seat at a baseball game in Chicago) and grew into his role, forming warm relations with President Roosevelt and his advisors and developing a genuine rapport with ordinary Americans.[25]

In this he was assisted by a surfeit of British diplomatic talent. The Washington chancery was staffed by career officers like Sir Ronald Campbell, Derek Hoyer Millar, William Hayter and Roger Makins who would all go on to glittering careers, and brilliant amateurs like the lawyer John Foster and Oxford don Isaiah Berlin, who was transferred from BIS in New York in early 1942 to draft the ambassador's weekly political despatch. The embassy workforce multiplied several times over between 1939 and 1945, with sections created or expanded to deal with everything from public relations and Allied food supply to intelligence sharing and post-war planning. Besides Foreign Office staff, there were military, naval and air attachés, plus dozens of officers seconded – like McGeachy – from government departments in London, turning the Washington embassy into what Berlin described as 'a short-lived microcosm of Whitehall', with all the personal enmities, inter-departmental warfare and bureaucratic log jam which that label implied.[26]

Into this engorged administration McGeachy, aged thirty-nine, arrived at the end of 1940 'quite alone', Lothian's untimely demise having robbed her of a chief whom she had hoped would ease her entry onto the Washington political scene. Never one to play the helpless damsel, however, McGeachy immediately secured for herself a charming little house in Georgetown, a fashionably grubby district a mile or so from the embassy, from which she walked briskly every morning to her office, clearing her head for the day to come. She was given a small, bare room in the annexe, the three-storey wooden structure containing hundreds of poky cubbyholes which had been hastily bolted on to the back of the embassy to accommodate the temporary wartime sections.

This 'ramshackle barrack', as Berlin recalled, had an atmosphere of 'agreeable informality' which contrasted with the stuffier atmosphere infecting the permanent staff inside the chancery. As a newcomer with scant knowledge of the British Diplomatic Service, McGeachy appreciated the company of these fellow government outsiders; as a woman entrusted with responsible work, by contrast, she was very much on her own. The embassy was full of girl typists and lady assistants, plus the ever-present wives, but there were few women wielding significant authority or equipped with serious administrative experience like McGeachy. Most of those falling into the latter bracket were, in any case, merely passing through, like Lucy Sutherland, the historian and later principal of Lady Margaret Hall, Oxford, who made McGeachy's acquaintance in Washington during a long visit on behalf of the Board of Trade, where she was a temporary assistant secretary.[27] McGeachy also got to know Caroline Haslett during the latter's first lecture tour, making all the arrangements for Haslett's speaking engagements in Washington and putting her up in her spare room in Georgetown. The two women hit it off immediately and maintained a warm regular correspondence after Haslett's return to Britain.

McGeachy's colleagues in the public relations section were, by contrast, all male, working initially under the ineffectual Sir Gerald Campbell, a career consul, and later for the more robust, pipe-smoking Harold Butler, whom McGeachy knew from Geneva where he had served as Director of the International Labour Organisation. McGeachy enjoyed a relatively free hand in organising her own work. She travelled extensively to spread the word about the British blockade, visiting BIS colleagues in New York every month and venturing much further afield to address audiences in the south and mid-west of the country. In the first half of 1941, McGeachy gave talks to branches of the Council on Foreign Relations in Chicago and New York, to the Economics Club and Co-operative Forum of Washington, to the School of National Civilian Defense at Westbury, Long Island, and to student societies at the universities of Harvard and Bryn Mawr, as well as meeting with editors and journalists of leading daily newspapers and representatives of the Federal Council of Churches. 'Every invitation of this kind,' she reported in August, 'results in contacts which provide us with useful ways of communicating information at our disposal and the view held generally by the Ministry of Economic Warfare, to some section of the American public.'[28] In these talks, McGeachy ranged beyond the narrow subject of the blockade, attempting to build up a broader picture in her listeners' minds of the evils of Nazism, and spelling out the terrible consequences of allowing Germany to triumph in Europe. She also sought to counter the ubiquitous stereotypes of the British circulating in America: of a backward-looking, class-ridden society ruled by horse-riding squires and populated by forelock-tugging workers. As Haslett was to do in her speech at the Biltmore Dinner in New York, McGeachy emphasised the courage and bravery of all classes of Briton on the home front, and pointed to the ways in which social distinctions were falling away in the face of common danger and government demands for equal sacrifice.

Haslett and McGeachy also shared the instinct that women would respond especially enthusiastically to this kind of approach. When Haslett arrived in New York in the autumn of 1941, she discovered that McGeachy had already taken the temperature of female public opinion, having attended the biennial conferences of the American Association of University Women, the League of Women Voters and the Federation of Business and Professional Women, as well as having met privately with representatives of the Women's Trade Union League, the YWCA and National Women's Democratic Club (amongst many others). McGeachy knew all the key women in the federal government, like Mary Anderson, Chief of the Women's Bureau at the Department of Labor, and was able to get Haslett in to see the officials who could benefit most from her expertise, including the Secretary of Labor, Frances Perkins. McGeachy secured Haslett invitations to all the department's major conferences and carefully briefed her on the chief personalities and policies in play. Haslett was lost in admiration: 'She knew the people whom I ought to see and was already aware of the kind of information they would be wanting from me.'[29]

McGeachy's efforts to cultivate female opinion were entirely at her own initiative, starting as she did at least six months before Cullis arrived in New York to establish her Women's Section at the British Information Services. Indeed, it seems likely that McGeachy's success as an outrider into this territory influenced the decision to place publicity targeted at women on a permanent footing. Back in Geneva, McGeachy had observed just how much a well-organised female lobby could achieve in shifting issues onto institutional agendas, and American women's organisations were, if anything, even more tenacious in passing resolutions, issuing press releases, writing to senators and congressmen and generally getting their voices heard. McGeachy developed a two-pronged approach towards the winning over of these powerful bodies of strong-minded females. At their public meetings she talked up the achievements of British women in civil defence and the war industries, and waxed more generally about social conditions on the home front – all in order 'to create the kind of atmosphere in which one could carry on later discussions in private on our problem in the war – viz., the blockade of foodstuffs'.[30] Her ultimate goal was to argue so convincingly that female opinion-formers would themselves become evangelists for the British point of view. McGeachy scored a major success in this respect in the summer of 1942, when she arranged for the *Washington Post* reporter Agnes Meyer to tour Britain in order to see for herself the scale and scope of civilian mobilisation. The result was a six-part series of articles containing vivid portraits of the British at war, which was distributed by the Associated Press across America. This kind of invisible hand was exactly what the British publicity machine aimed to achieve: pro-British propaganda delivered by Americans to Americans.

If Mary McGeachy became a familiar figure amongst women's organisations during the course of 1941, it was in the autumn of the following year that she achieved wider fame. Newspapers on both sides of the Atlantic reported in October 1942 that the British government had appointed its first woman diplomat – or, more precisely, had taken the unprecedented step of bestowing upon a woman the privileges of official diplomatic status. Up to that point, McGeachy remained a temporary employee of the Ministry of Economic Warfare on second-ment to Washington, without the special immunities (against prosecution, for example, and local taxation) that diplomats tradition-ally enjoyed. *The Times* described her new appointment as 'recognition of the invaluable work which Miss McGeachy has done for the British cause in wartime', and added, 'Men doing similar, or less important, work for British wartime missions in Washington, have been given diplomatic status; and at last the question was faced whether it should be withheld from Miss McGeachy simply because she was a woman.'[31]

A few months later, the *New York Times* ran a prominent feature entitled 'Britain's First Woman Diplomat', which included a large photograph of McGeachy seated in an authoritative pose at her desk, dressed in a plain but well-cut black suit with a string of pearls around her neck and an elegant brooch pinned to her lapel. In line with earlier press coverage, the article dwelt upon the wider significance for women of McGeachy's professional breakthrough, describing her as 'the first of her sex to crack a once exclusively male field'.[32] But in truth, the bureaucratic logic behind her altered status was rather more mundane. The Foreign Secretary, Anthony Eden, wrote to the Conservative MP Irene Ward to explain that McGeachy's promotion was the result of a higher-level decision to give her boss, Harold Butler, official diplomatic rank, and a subsequent move to extend this privilege to all those working under him. Upon reviewing the case, there seemed no reason not to include McGeachy in what was essen-tially an administrative re-labelling exercise. Eden was, moreover, careful to point out that McGeachy did not as a result become a fully fledged member of the Diplomatic Service. Far from it; her post remained wholly temporary, McGeachy being herself informed in no uncertain terms by the Foreign Office that she could make 'no claim to further advancement in the Diplomatic Service'.[33]

McGeachy's position thus remained as ambiguous as those of Freya Stark in Baghdad and of Nancy Lambton in Tehran. Unlike the latter, McGeachy's name never appeared in the official *Foreign Office List*. Nonetheless, McGeachy would stand as a formidable witness before the Foreign Office committee convened in late 1945 to reconsider the question of women in diplomacy. There were very few chinks in her professional armour. Always a private person, she lacked perhaps the warmth and likeability of Caroline Haslett. In her early forties, she had not yet acquired the *grande dame* status of Winifred Cullis. But McGeachy's professionalism was widely endorsed by colleagues, and few could fault her strategy when it came to selling the blockade policy to the Americans. McGeachy's manner was direct but relaxed. She spoke to the point with quiet authority, wasting no time 'on adrenalin or non-essentials' and rarely allowed herself to get flustered. When speaking to the press, McGeachy was modest and self-effacing. She insisted to Elizabeth Valentine, who interviewed her for the *New York Times*, that her promotion to the rank of first secretary was less a reflection of her own ability than it was 'a way of honouring British women for the part they have been playing in the war'. As to her supposed efficiency in the office, McGeachy was equally downbeat: 'they say I am efficient . . . if I am, it is because I loathe office work and want to get it out of the way as quickly as possible'.

This apparent lack of ego undoubtedly smoothed McGeachy's path in her dealings with male colleagues. Valentine described her subject as

> totally non-competitive and objective in her attitude towards men and work. She has not the kind of personality that puts men on the defensive – on the contrary, co-workers and dinner partners alike are inclined to purr – and if there is any modern phrase Miss McGeachy dislikes it is the term 'career woman'.[34]

It is certainly true that McGeachy was not a feminist in the sense of publicly espousing causes. But she suffered from no feelings of female inferiority and rarely deferred to male authority on matters with which she believed herself best placed to deal. As her biographer has shown, McGeachy's sharp mind was constantly in motion, devising new initiatives or schemes which she did not hesitate to present to her superiors in London. When Isaiah Berlin learnt that McGeachy had, without prior consultation, approached his contact at the MOI to float the idea of a lecture tour in neutral Sweden, his instinct was to do anything but purr. McGeachy, he wrote in response, was a 'minx' who never ceased 'from fulfilling her peculiar nature', and a 'bare-faced equestrienne' in search of 'fresh fields over which to gallop'. Patronising and misogynistic Berlin's language was for sure, but there lurked underneath it an unmistakeable note of admiration for McGeachy's tenacity and pluck: 'that Miss McGeachy!' he added: 'What a woman! . . . I must say I hand it to her . . .'[35]

Mary McGeachy was undoubtedly a fine ambassador for British women in wartime America. It is tempting to speculate how her career in the post-war Diplomatic Service might have unfolded, had she pursued that path. By late 1943, however, McGeachy was angling for a high-ranking job in a new international agency, the United Nations Relief and Rehabilitation Administration (UNRRA), and in 1944 was appointed its Director of Welfare, the only woman to hold an executive position. McGeachy then took the bold step of getting married to the handsome Viennese-born banker Erwin Schuller, whom she had met in London in 1942. As Mrs Schuller, there could be no possibility of further employment in the British Diplomatic Service, even had she actively desired it. As it turned out, McGeachy's UNRRA job came to an end in 1946, after which she retired from paid employment, adopted two children and devoted her later years to the International Council of Women, an umbrella body for women's organisations across the world. But if her diplomatic career was brief, it was without question distinguished, and McGeachy could be satisfied with the knowledge that she had played her part in cementing the Anglo-American alliance. Freya Stark's experience was rather different.

———

A ruptured appendix almost halted Freya Stark's American adventure before it had even begun. Within four days of boarding a troopship destined for Halifax in the autumn of 1943, she had retreated to her bunk, watching the Atlantic howling by 'in its usual gruesome hurry' through her porthole from beneath a pile of blankets.[36] Her condition worsening, she was stretchered off the ship as soon as it dropped anchor and operated upon. Despite the seriousness of her condition, and to the wonder of her surgeons, Stark was miraculously on her feet a fortnight later, and by the third week of November was happily installed in a plush apartment belonging to a friend of a friend in uptown New York, ready to begin her official work on behalf of the MOI. Her mission was to counter the influence of the powerful Zionist lobby – which had recently stepped up its activities in the US – by explaining and defending British policy in the Middle East.

At the heart of this policy stood Palestine, which Britain had held in trust as a League of Nations mandate since the First World War, and its political future continued to provoke profound and often violent clashes between Arabs and Jews, both inside the territory and beyond. Back in 1939, Neville Chamberlain's National Government had produced a White Paper which abandoned any plans for partition and proposed instead the creation of an independent state with a government in which both communities would be represented in accordance with their respective population size. What caused controversy, however, were the temporary restrictions which the White Paper placed upon Jewish immigration (which were enforced against the backdrop of growing persecution of Jewry in central and Eastern Europe), and the clause which stipulated that any immigration beyond 1944 could take place only with the consent of the Arab majority. For Zionists, who regarded Palestine as the Jewish national home, this was an intolerable injustice. But for many in the British government, and especially those colonial officials who were operating on the ground in Cairo and Baghdad, appeasing Arab opinion on the question of Palestine was regarded as vitally necessary if the war was to be won and Britain's strategic interests in the region preserved. Moreover, many British officials, Stark included, saw genuine force in the Arab case against unrestricted Jewish immigration over which non-Jewish inhabitants could have no control.

The White Paper remained the basis of the British position in autumn 1943, when Stark arrived in New York to begin the tour which was to so impress on her the power and efficiency of American womanhood. She knew she had to tread carefully. The Palestine question

divided opinion. State Department officials and American businessmen with oil interests in Saudi Arabia were inclined to support the
British line, but sympathy for the Zionist case was strong, especially as
reports of the scale of Nazi atrocities against the Jews in Europe grew
ever graver in nature. Moreover, many Americans viewed the White
Paper policy through the prism of Britain's wider imperialist ambitions, and listened with scepticism to the rhetoric of colonial
'trusteeship' which professed to lay the way for eventual self-govern-
ment. The British Empire was a major fault-line running through
wartime Anglo-American understanding. America was, of course,
itself a former British colony whose nationhood was founded in the
late eighteenth century on a defiant declaration of independence.
Everything in their history and republican tradition bred in the
American people a deep-seated aversion to the doctrines of imperialism (US policy in Mexico and its treatment of indigenous peoples and
African Americans notwithstanding), and for many the war marked a
welcome final reckoning for Britain's historic global imperium.
Support for nationalist aspirations in India ran high amongst promi-
nent political figures, leading to much resentment on the part of
British ministers, who felt that vocal American senators like the
Republican Wendell Willkie knew little about the intricacies of Indian
politics and would do better to keep their mouths shut. Although
conscious of the political chaos which might follow over-hasty action,
President Roosevelt left Churchill with no illusions as to his own feelings on the eventual future of Britain's colonial subjects.
Self-determination, he believed, was the destiny and right of all peoples
throughout history, and Roosevelt used America's considerable political and economic muscle in the great Allied conferences which marked
the later stages of the war to bring this eventuality closer.[37]

This was the complex weather system of opinion that Freya Stark
advanced into as she proceeded from New York to Washington,
Boston, Chicago and California, with a final stop over the frontier in
Canada. She delivered numerous public addresses (preceded by the
usual agonies), but devoted much of her time and energy to private
meetings with influential individuals, including the leaders of Jewish

opinion, both Zionist and, as Stark described them, 'moderate'. Her
early efforts to talk up British imperialism as an enlightened civilising
force made few converts: 'until they [the Americans] get rid of the
Empire complex,' she wrote to Elizabeth Monroe at the MOI back in
London, 'and think of us as a Commonwealth, no question which
attaches to that concept can find its level . . . nothing makes one so
unpopular as the showing of Great Britain in a liberal light; they change
the subject instantly, like shutting down a lid.'[38] By mid-December,
Stark was feeling increasingly despondent for her mission ('I can't think
why I have been sent here,' she complained to Stewart Perowne; 'I have
no mass appeal'), and was thoroughly fed up of hearing Winston
Churchill's scathing remarks on the White Paper – which he had made
in May 1939 when in opposition – quoted back at her at every possible
opportunity: 'I hate to criticise where I so much admire, but if it were
the Archangel Gabriel I should feel this as a sabotaging of one's own
side. Either the White Paper is our policy or it isn't.'[39] Much as she was
dazzled by the wealth and dynamism of American society, Stark was
further discouraged by the soullessness and materialism of its culture.
The USA, she thought, was ruled by a 'business morality' which was
leading its people down the road of standardisation, and which she
could not help comparing to the spiritualism and rich variety of her
beloved Middle East.[40]

Despite this unpromising start, Stark persevered with her campaign
of persuasion and by the New Year thought she detected a subtle change
in fortunes. 'I have got a reduction of *our* line of argument down to a
few basic principles, and got agreement on it,' she wrote to Sydney
Cockerell, 'and have got into touch and had some little effect on the
State Department of our part of the world . . . and today a man from
our Ministry in New York said "Thank God for your coming" – so I
feel it may not after all be such a fearful waste of public money.'[41]
(Stark's concern for the British taxpayer did not, however, extend to
economising on her own wardrobe: she wrote haughtily to Monroe
with details of the 'two months' salary' she had personally expended on
clothes after the MOI refused to provide a dress allowance for her
tour.[42]) Stark would have been pleased to learn that the Washington

embassy concurred with this evaluation of her usefulness. Lord Halifax told the Foreign Secretary that her visit had been 'of great value and assistance', and she won an extended tribute from the embassy's press officer, Michael Wright:

> I cannot speak too highly of the work she has done here. Her talks have been good and her handling of personal contacts admirable. She has seen a great deal of those in the Sate Department and the War Department who are responsible for taking decisions, and I would judge her influence to have been considerable . . . She has been equally good with journalists.[43]

Nonetheless, in the longer term, Stark's mission was destined to fail. The policy contained in the White Paper on Palestine was overtaken by events in the final year of the war, when Zionist leaders abandoned their efforts to place pressure on Britain indirectly through her US ally, and sought instead to mobilise direct American support (chiefly, money) whilst at the same time fomenting armed resistance to British rule on the ground. President Truman, who succeeded Roosevelt after the latter's death in April 1945, was notably sympathetic to Zionist claims that Palestine was the only acceptable asylum for displaced Jews in Europe. Moreover, Truman abjured what he saw as Britain's inhumane indifference to the plight of a people whose systematic extermination by the Nazis was now in no doubt following the gruesome discoveries made in the concentration camps liberated by Allied troops in spring 1945.* The British government, however, did not make this same moral connection between the Palestine issue and the victims of Nazism, glossing over – as indeed did much of the British press at the time – the specifically racial dimension to the atrocities uncovered and confirmed by the scenes at Belsen, Dachau and the other liberated

---

* The Soviet army had reached the extermination camp at Auschwitz in early 1945, but the greatest impact on Western public opinion came in April, when newsreels began broadcasting to domestic audiences the shocking images of human suffering from the concentration camps liberated by British and US troops, including Buchenwald, Belsen and Dachau.

camps.[44] Instead, the government, now led by Labour's Clement Attlee following the general election of July, continued to search frantically for a Palestinian solution which would satisfy both Jews and Arabs and avoid any need for a costly show of military force. By February 1947, and against a backdrop of continuing tensions and growing lawlessness, ministers ran out of ideas. Britain referred Palestine's political future to the United Nations, and in September declared its intention to give up the mandate entirely and evacuate the territory. The UN voted for partition; the British troops departed, and on 14 May 1948, David Ben-Gurion declared the creation of the State of Israel. The USA was amongst the first to recognise its sovereignty.

As persuasive and experienced a propagandist as she was, Freya Stark could not overturn in a six-month lecture tour the ideological stumbling block of Empire which threatened the wartime 'special relationship'. Stark's contribution to the forging of the transatlantic alliance was ultimately inauspicious. Other women sent by Britain to America between 1939 and 1945 had a smoother path. When it came to convincing Americans of the courage of the British people and the dire consequences of a Nazi victory for democracy everywhere, Winifred Cullis, Caroline Haslett and Mary McGeachy played their part with distinction. They were only small cogs in an enormous publicity machine created to sell Britain's war aims to an isolationist superpower; yet as women, they made an invaluable contribution to this campaign of persuasion by issuing a special appeal to female public opinion, a formidable entity whose goodwill would form a central pillar of Anglo-American friendship, both during the war and after it.

Nonetheless, these ambassadors of British women were few in number and their public diplomacy, useful though it was, did not earn them seats at the table where statesmen and generals determined high policy. They were not aboard the USS *Augusta* where Churchill and Roosevelt drew up the Atlantic Charter in August 1941, a document which helped to shape the fate of the post-war world. Nor were they privy to negotiations at Casablanca, Tehran or any of the other great wartime conferences where Allied chiefs hammered out grand strategy over maps in smoke-filled rooms. At its highest levels, Anglo-American diplomacy remained a closed world. Yet by admitting even a handful of women to its outer limits, the British state made a final breach of diplomacy's masculine defences ever more likely.

Equally Eligible

When the Foreign Office convened its long-awaited committee to reconsider the question of women diplomats in autumn 1945, amongst the first pieces of evidence it received was a lengthy and unsolicited memorandum from a career consul in Geneva by the name of John Price. Had they been granted access to this document and the fine sentiments contained within it, those societies who campaigned so doggedly for women's rights in the years before the war might have wondered where John Price had been all their lives. 'During the whole of my 18 years' service,' he began,

> I have been consistently in favour of the employment of women both in diplomatic and consular posts and have used every available chance to give expression to these views and to promote women, as far as it lay in my power, to such posts of authority as might be open to them already . . . Women are discreet, reliable and intelligent and a woman's instinctive or even emotional approach to the problems of a strange country or foreigners, or again of British subjects in need of help, is sometimes more practical than a man's logical and analytical approach.'

In Price's experience, women were more 'tolerant of routine duties, and more exact in their discharge of them', and regarded their employment 'with a seriousness which is very valuable'. He had known many female clerical officers in his time who were 'more efficient than the male vice-consuls under whom they nominally serve', and yet were 'condemned permanently to the status of clerks'. The old 'drunken sailor' argument against female consuls Price thought absurd, not only because dealing with intoxicated seamen took up an 'infinitesimal proportion' of a consul's time, but because 'anyone familiar with service canteens knows that women handle drunkards quite as well as men could do it'. Likewise, women were men's equals when it came to 'unhealthy climates', and in many cases fared better, perhaps, Price speculated, 'because they drank less'.

Much of this reprised themes from the evidence heard by the Schuster Committee back in 1934. But there were two important differences. First, John Price was no hardened feminist but a long-standing member of the Service. He had joined as a consular officer in the late 1920s and based his observations not on personal experience of 'exceptional' posts like Washington or Moscow or Stockholm, where it was generally agreed that a woman diplomat might just possibly be of use, but on places like China, Nepal and Tunis, hardly at the top of the list of 'woman-friendly' posts.[1] The second difference was, put simply, the war. Price reminded the committee of the patriotic and selfless service rendered by British women in their nation's hour of need. 'It seems almost an insult,' he argued, 'in view of what women of this country have done for us during the last few years, that they should not be thought worthy of sharing the honour of representing it abroad.' How, he demanded to know, at the end of a war fought to defend freedom and democracy against oppression and tyranny, could the government continue to deny women justice? Pandering to the bigotry of misogynistic foreign officials would no longer wash:

> Surely the equality of women is a principle admitted in British life and one of which we have no reason to be ashamed. To deprive them of opportunities in an important public service because of the prejudices of less advanced nations seems no more justifiable than, for instance, refusing to employ any Jews or any negroes in positions of trust because the Germans do not like the former and the Americans do not like the latter.[2]

Price chose his examples advisedly. Invoking anti-Semitism in the wake of the Holocaust was obviously intended to provoke an emotive response, while the reference to African Americans was almost as poignant, his fellow countrymen having witnessed first-hand the shocking racism dealt out to black GIs stationed in Britain by their white comrades.*

John Price – whose middle name, rather appropriately, was Playfair – could not have written such a memorandum in 1934, not simply because he was back then a junior officer of only a few years' service, but because the wider social and political momentum required to break the masculine monopoly at the Foreign Office simply did not exist. By September 1945, it was in place. Historians have become notably sceptical, of late, towards old established narratives which depict the Second World War as a transformative moment in British history. Continuity, they argue, rather than change, characterised much of the post-war landscape in which the British people remade their civilian lives.[3] Yet there can be little doubt that the war created a new world for British diplomats, not only in the grim geopolitical realities of the Cold War after 1948 and the rise of multi-lateral institutions like the United Nations and NATO, but also much closer to home, in the look and feel of the Diplomatic Service itself. The permanent admission of women to its ranks, which the committee recommended after four months of deliberations, was integral to this remaking of British diplomatic culture – although its full effect would take many years to be felt.

If Anthony Eden, the Foreign Secretary, imagined that he would be quietly allowed to forget the pledge he had made in January 1942 concerning the future employment of women, he could not have been more wrong. The women's societies certainly saw to that. They continued to harass the Foreign Office for the remainder of the war with queries about the numbers of women employed in temporary

* This was before Commonwealth immigration would allow the prejudices of the British people to find full expression in the 1950s and '60s.

administrative grade posts and demands for clarification as to exactly
which jobs were now open to both sexes. A firm commitment to reconsider the question of women's long-term status as diplomats was, naturally,
most welcome, but feminists were soon pushing Eden for more. The
Council of Women Civil Servants queried whether another committee
was really necessary, given that 'the issue is at bottom a plain and simple
one of women's right to equal citizenship and service'.⁴ They hoped to
bounce Eden into making a decision before the end of the war, rather
than dragging it out. Normal recruitment into the Diplomatic and
Consular Services had been suspended, and the number of vacancies
waiting to be filled once peace returned would be considerable. It was
unfair, they argued, to deprive qualified female candidates of their chance
because of bureaucratic delay. Even the Civil Service commissioners, who
were responsible for administrative-grade recruitment across Whitehall,
saw the justice of this case. One of their number, Percy Waterfield, wrote
to the Foreign Office in February 1945 for an update on its intentions
regarding women's admission, noting that 'it would be unfortunate, I
think, if it were announced after a substantial proportion of the
Reconstruction vacancies had already been filled'.⁵

This wish was not to be granted. Although Churchill's Cabinet
approved the appointment of a new committee in March, it did not
meet for another six months, delayed initially by procrastination at the
Foreign Office and then by the intervening general election of July.
Labour's new Foreign Secretary, Ernest Bevin, immediately gave the
green light to the committee but it was still not until September, more
than four months after VE Day, that it was in a position to begin its
proceedings. One reason for the delay was the ponderous discussions
over who should sit on it. Eden had earlier stipulated that the committee's members should not be confined to the Civil Service, conscious
perhaps of earlier accusations that the Schuster Committee had been a
stitch-up. This time, there was no shadowy figure like Charles Howard
Smith stockpiling ammunition behind the scenes (he died in 1942), but
there was still plenty of debate over names to fill the two seats earmarked
for 'outsiders'. David Scott, the former head of the Consular
Department who had argued against change in 1934, canvassed Sir Alan

Barlow at the Treasury for ideas in March. Barlow responded with a string of names, recommending Lady Reading, who had organised the Women's Voluntary Services during the war and was the wife of a former Foreign Secretary, as one whose 'first instinct may be slightly against admission of women', but whom he felt was 'capable of making up her mind without prejudice on the evidence which she hears'. He warned against the economist Barbara Wootton, left-leaning journalist Barbara Ward and the Liberal Lady Simon, 'because they are almost certainly strongly biased in favour of admission', and later added Lady Nunburnholme of the National Council of Women to the list of approved candidates on the grounds that 'she is not a rabid feminist'.[6] The Home Secretary, Herbert Morrison, added his two penn'orth, suggesting to Eden that Lady Rhondda of the Six Point Group be included, conceding that she was a feminist, 'but not irrationally so'.[7]

The change of government and uncertainty over the identity of the committee's chairman led to further delay, but by mid-August the final line-up had been settled. Thomas Dunlop, a former inspector general of Consular Establishments, and Guy Locock, chief of the Federation of British Industry, were unpromising prospects from a feminist perspective, both having voted against women's admission in 1934. The four female members, by contrast, were unknown quantities, chosen, presumably, because they did not hold strong views either way. They included Dorothy Elliot, a trade unionist, Ethel Strudwick, the high mistress of St Paul's Girls School, Lady Limerick of the British Red Cross, and Joyce Yencken, a diplomatic wife of long standing. Even if none of the four were 'rabid' feminists, it was still better odds than in 1934, when the two female committee members had been outnumbered by hostile males. Moreover, the chairman, Sir Ernest Gowers, a retired civil servant who had spent a busy war organising Civil Defence in London, was a more sympathetic character than Claud Schuster. Gowers was known for his courteous manner, ability to enjoy a good joke, and crusading belief in the merits of plain English.[*] This last

---

[*] In 1948 Gowers wrote a short book, *Plain Words: a Guide to the Use of English*, which became a primer for entrants to the Civil Service.

quality was evident at a preliminary meeting of the committee, when Gowers intervened to correct Locock's interpretation of their remit. In Locock's view, the investigation hinged on the question: 'Did women have ability suited to the Foreign Service?' No, countered Gowers. The issue at stake was, rather: 'Is the Foreign Service of such a special nature that it denies the fundamental principle accepted by Parliament that men and women are equal in the Civil Service?'[8]

If Gowers's apparent lack of bias set him apart from Schuster's rather more partisan chairmanship of 1934, proponents of women's admission had two further factors on their side. In the first place, the new Labour government was already essentially convinced of women's suitability for diplomatic careers. Although the party had shown precious little interest in the matter before the war, by 1942, Ernest Bevin was sufficiently struck by the absurdity of the Foreign Office's intransigence that he wrote to Eden to advise admitting women on the spot. Spinning it out via a post-war committee would be a mistake, Bevin argued: 'Go right out and accept terms of equality, purely on the basis of ability, it would be far better.'[9] Eden demurred, but by early 1945 even he appeared to accept that Bevin had correctly judged the way the wind was blowing. 'It has been represented to me,' he wrote in a memo to the Cabinet in March, 'that any committee examining the question, either now or after the war, is bound to recommend the admission of women to the Foreign Service.' Eden was still opposed to making an instant decision, feeling that 'it would be undesirable to take such a step without first reinforcing ourselves by the recommendations of an impartial committee'.[10] But the expected outcome of the process – a recommendation in favour of women's admission – was nonetheless clear.

The women's societies, naturally, knew nothing of these confidential exchanges, but were only too aware of the second factor in play: the belated return of a broader reforming impetus at the Foreign Office. The limited reorganisation of 1919–20 had done little to silence critics of the Diplomatic Service. They continued to decry the hopelessly frag-mented structure of Britain's overseas representation and the narrow social pool from which its personnel was drawn. The unavoidable halt to recruitment effected by the war created a natural pause for reflection on these unresolved issues, which in turn led to Eden announcing in 1941 his intention to introduce a wide-ranging reform programme at the end of the war, the details of which were set out in a White Paper published two years later. This pithy document offered a clear indication of the likely direction of travel. 'The conditions which the Diplomatic Service originally grew up to meet no longer exist unchanged in modern international affairs,' it observed; the 'modern diplomat' now needed to master an entirely new set of problems – concerning economics, finance, social conditions and labour movements – with which international relations were today 'inextricably interwoven'. Reform was urgently required to: 're-equip the Foreign Service to meet modern conditions and to create a Service which . . . shall be better able not merely to represent the interests of the nation as a whole, but also to deal with the whole range of international affairs, political, social and economic'.

The White Paper set out an ambitious programme: the Diplomatic and Consular Services would at last be amalgamated into a single, integrated body to be known as the Foreign Service. The antiquated system in which candidates privately financed several years of language tuition would be replaced by state-sponsored training so as to permit the entry of candidates 'from any social sphere', whilst additional living allowances would further eliminate the need for private means in order to get ahead. 'Equality of opportunity for all' would be the name of the game, with none of the old prejudices against men who had come up through the consular route, and no more easy rides for officers who underperformed.[11]

Most significantly of all, hidden away at the end of the White Paper was a short paragraph on the question of women's eligibility. This was non-committal, simply restating Eden's promise to convene a committee to reconsider the position. But its inclusion in a document which in all other respects explicitly acknowledged past failures to recruit from all sections of British society would have consequences. As Eden's ministerial colleague, Richard Law, acknowledged when presenting the White Paper to the House of Commons, there was 'a certain lack of logic in proposals which, intending to make the Foreign Service more representative of the people of the country as a whole, yet debar rather more than half of the people of the country from entering the Service'.[12]

———————

All the same, if the prospects looked hopeful for women's future in the diplomatic profession, there remained no shortage of critics prepared to defend the masculine status quo just as vociferously as they had in 1934. If anything, they were now *more* outspoken in their opposition because they sensed the tide finally turning against them. The most high profile of these critics was MP and former diplomat Harold Nicolson, who used one of his regular columns in the *Spectator* in 1942 to explain in elegant detail exactly why women as a sex were collectively unsuited to diplomatic work. The ideal diplomat, in Nicolson's words, was 'impartial, imperturbable and a trifle inhuman. These,' he asserted, 'are not feminine qualities; they are male qualities.'[13] Nicolson aired this argument again during a debate in the Commons, in which he questioned, as Ambassador Joseph Addison had back in 1933, the desirability of so-called womanly 'intuition'. 'The special virtues of women,' he remarked,

> are singularly ill-adapted to diplomatic life. These virtues, I should say, were, first, intuition and, secondly, sympathy. Intuition is absolutely fatal in diplomacy. It tempts people to jump to conclusions. Sympathy is equally fatal because it leads people to identify themselves with causes or personalities with which or whom they feel sympathy. That is fatal to that very balanced attitude which it is the business of the Diplomatic Service to preserve.[14]

Many senior members of the Foreign Office evidently agreed with this assessment of women's intellectual and emotional infirmities. David Scott reprised Nicolson's views in his evidence to the committee in November 1945: 'Women,' he argued, 'were only too apt to espouse causes, and would be even if fully trained in the Foreign Service. It was a matter of their very nature.'[15] Further indictments of female 'nature' came from the evidence of Permanent Secretary Alexander Cadogan, who reflected on the female employees he had observed in Geneva (presumably in the League Secretariat) during his time as head of the League of Nations section at the Foreign Office: 'where women were in charge of officers,' Cadogan recalled, 'a certain amount of bickering and personal strife was apparent. It was possible that the women in question, having won their places by dint of hard struggle, were probably of the "prima donna" variety.'[16] This, he implied, boded ill for the British Foreign Service, which would invariably attract the same highly strung feminine type.

In truth, these dubious claims concerning temperamental differences between the sexes did the Foreign Office case no favours. They were readily dismissed by Gowers as matters which lay firmly in the ground of 'conjecture'. Charles Howard Smith, had he been around, would undoubtedly have weeded out this kind of speculative nonsense (even if he personally agreed with it), as he had in 1934, advising his colleagues to stick instead to objections of a less anecdotal nature for which evidence could be readily supplied. As it was, there were still plenty of witnesses willing to restate two of the key arguments which had proved so powerful before the Schuster Committee: namely, the backwardness of foreign opinion and the intractable problem of married women's mobility. According to several Foreign Office witnesses, foreigners remained as uncivilised as ever in their attitudes towards women. George Kitson, a long-serving officer in the China Consular Service, attested to the parochialism of Chinese officials outside the largest cities, who, if confronted with a female diplomat, would 'either be inclined to give way too much in their embarrassment or be overbearing. Women,' he felt, 'would cut little ice with officials or residents who felt ill at ease.' His colleague, Sir Humphrey Prideaux-Brune, was even more emphatic in his belief that the Chinese were not 'prepared for the innovation' of women diplomats.[17]

It was a similar story for the Middle East. No fewer than seven heads of mission from this region appeared in person before the committee to register their opposition. Sir Maurice Peterson, ambassador to Turkey, spoke for the group when he insisted that 'women just could not "put it across"' in Middle Eastern countries, including the more 'advanced' ones like Egypt or indeed Turkey. Nancy Lambton and Freya Stark were, he argued – like Gertrude Bell before them – exceptions, and in any case had not held posts of any real significance. Had they done so, there was no knowing what the consequences might have been. Despite his personal regard for Lambton, Reader Bullard wholeheartedly endorsed this verdict. As a minister rather than advisor, Gertrude Bell would have 'aroused horror', he remarked, 'and the same applied to Miss Lambton'. Peterson made the further observation that all three ladies in question had already established their reputations by the time they were appointed, and with certain individuals, 'sex objection was often overridden by exceptional ability'. He added: 'Freya Stark, for example, was very popular' (a remark which Bullard presumably listened to tight-lipped, remembering how she had brazenly sold an official car on the black market in Tehran right under his nose).[18]

Several businessmen also reasserted the case against posting women to Latin America, still, as they saw it, a land of hot-blooded males. Sir William McCallum, president of the British Chamber of Commerce in Buenos Aires, believed that the appointment of a female diplomatic officer could result in nothing but embarrassment for the British state, and ditto Sir Montague Eddy, a railway magnate in Argentina, who felt that even a limited experiment would be too risky to British business interests in the region. Nor did Sir Montague, the minutes noted, 'approve of "forcing" British ideas on foreign countries through the medium of our women'.[19] This point was made more broadly by Ivone Kirkpatrick, a future permanent secretary. The Foreign Service's job, he remarked, was 'to "cater for a client", not impose British views abroad', a view further echoed by Scott, who, in words reminiscent of Sir Hubert Montgomery back in 1929, told the committee:

It is not for us to try to promote enlightened ideals abroad by sending women officials to countries where these ideas do not exist, for to do so would be at the cost of the national interest in a field – the field of foreign relations and trade – where we cannot afford to take risks.[20]

The antis' case thus remained essentially unaltered: even if public opinion had moved on in many places, there were still large swathes of the world where female diplomats would not be welcome, and reserving for them the cushiest posts in Europe and North America would be a gross injustice to their male colleagues.

The other major argument reprised from 1934 was the problem of married women. This remained as insurmountable as ever in Foreign Office eyes, and even those sympathetic to the idea of spinsters in the Service drew the line at admitting women who came with husbands in tow. Drawing on her experience as spouse of an ex-Foreign Secretary and viceroy, Lady Reading (who, having been passed over as a candidate for the committee, was invited instead to appear as a witness) was adamant on the need for a strict marriage bar: 'A husband consort would feel neglected,' she argued, 'and would injure his wife's reputation.'[21] Likewise, Ina Strong, who had posted many female typists and clerks overseas in her capacity as staff officer at the wartime Foreign Office, favoured resignation on marriage. 'She pointed to the difficulty of performing two jobs at once,' the minutes read: 'one in the home and one in the office, and of carrying a man around to different posts.'[22] Even John Price, right-thinking champion of women's equality, reluctantly conceded that a marriage bar was probably inevitable, as 'it would no doubt be unsuitable to have a husband as a sort of dependent on a woman diplomat'.

These objections Gowers and his colleagues found far more convincing than arguments of the 'when in Rome' variety. One could debate forever exactly which countries might or might not accept unmarried female diplomats, but there was much greater agreement on the inadvisability of posting a married woman overseas. Naturally, this consensus did not include the women's societies, who continued to plead for employers to stay out of the domestic affairs of their female employees. Hilda Martindale made an appearance to restate the case she had made for women's admission back in 1934 and added that, in her view, the question of employment after marriage 'might well be left to the good sense of women themselves'.[23] The representatives of the Woman Power Committee concurred with this verdict, whilst the

Council of Women Civil Servants stated their opposition to the marriage bar in even starker terms, describing it as an 'unwarrantable interference in the private life of the citizen'. They went on:

> We have never been able to understand why the husband should present
> a greater problem than the wife, when the husband chooses to follow his
> wife and we consider that changing social customs and the speeding up
> of communications make the problem much less difficult than would
> appear at first sight or than has been the case in the past . . . in any case
> the problem is one which concerns, we suggest, only those two people.[24]

The Gowers Committee, as we shall see, was not moved by this argument. The principle that married women were unfit for diplomatic life proved axiomatic – and would remain so for another twenty-five years.

———

Nonetheless, on the prior question of whether women should be admitted to the Service at all, the women's societies and their supporters could sense victory round the corner. Nancy Astor was not invited to give evidence again (probably much to the relief of the clerk responsible for taking the minutes), but she brought up the question of women with her usual tenacity during the Commons debate on the 1943 White Paper, berating the government for being 'completely out of touch with the country' and the Foreign Office for failing to fall in 'with the spirit of the times'. She exhorted her parliamentary colleagues to 'think of what women have done in this war' and to ask themselves,

> is it really fair and just . . . that they should at this moment deny to
> women their chance of rebuilding the new world after the war? Women
> will have the most tremendous work to do, not only in Europe, but all
> over the world. The democracies have to give a lead to the rest of the
> women of the world.

Astor being Astor could not resist having another pop at Catholicism, attributing past foreign policy failures to (at least in part) the unhealthy influence of the 'Latin point of view' in the higher echelons of the Foreign Office.[25] But if this sectarian fanaticism once again rather detracted from the gravity with which her wider remarks were received, Astor's Commons performance rehearsed an important theme which would be taken up by the women's societies before Gowers. The long memorandum submitted by the Council of Women Civil Servants made the same powerful link between their claims upon the diplomatic profession and women's wider wartime patriotism. 'Women are citizens equally with men,' it argued, 'and, during the war, have proved their willingness and ability to share in every national responsibility. To deny their entry to the Foreign Service is to deny them one of their rights as citizens.' The committee, the council insisted, could only be justified in excluding women if it could conclusively prove that their presence would be positively harmful. Echoing John Price's words, the memo continued:

> On any other ground their exclusion in a fully democratic State is an outrage. Public opinion would be outraged by a proposal that Jews or Roman Catholics or boys from State schools should not be eligible for the Foreign Service. It should be, and in our view large sections of it are, equally outraged that women, who have played so big a part in forming and defending our democracy, are not eligible too.

Caroline Haslett, whose work for the Ministry of Information in America had been so widely admired, developed the same line in her evidence, telling the committee that 'the story of British women's achievements in the war had gone around the world . . . and therefore no one would be surprised if we appointed women to our Foreign Service'. In fact, she said, going further, foreigners would be 'astonished if we did not use our women in peace-time as we had used them during the war'.[26]

Others dwelt upon the precedent which the overseas service of women like Stark, Lambton and McGeachy had set, alongside the sterling work performed by dozens of women employed in responsible posts by the Foreign Office and Ministry of Information in London.

Some of the most compelling evidence came direct from the mouths or pens of these individuals. Freya Stark was unable to travel to London, but sent a letter instead which was circulated to all committee members. In it she refuted claims that women could not operate effectively in Arab countries. 'On the contrary,' Stark wrote, 'in countries where women are still, even if not veiled, inclined to be rather secluded, a man cannot possibly have as intimate a knowledge of the country as is open to a woman if she tries.' Nancy Lambton,* she added, was received in Tehran 'as a perfectly natural phenomenon by Arabs and Persians'.[27]

Mary McGeachy (or Mrs Schuller, as she was by September 1945) found time to appear before the committee in person, and left them in no doubt as to her own position on the question of careers for women in diplomacy. Her appointment as a first secretary in Washington in 1942, McGeachy remarked, 'had been greeted by the Americans as a mark of our progression, even as a sign of the breakdown of feudal conditions' both in Britain and in her native Canada. Diplomatic officers ought 'to reflect almost every aspect of their own national life in their work abroad', whilst a female officer, she argued, had the added advantage of being of interest to women's organisations, through whom she could subsequently work to improve understanding of British culture and society, just as McGeachy had herself done in America.[28]

The committee also heard from Muriel Lamb, who had been working as a temporary third secretary in Oslo since June where, they were informed, she found herself treated with complete respect and equality by Norwegian officials. Other wartime appointees singled out for praise in the testimonies of witnesses included Miss Hastings, who was described as an 'outstanding young lady Vice-Consul' by her boss, Francis Evans, Britain's consul-general in New York; Miss Headley of the Cultural Relations Department of the Foreign Office, who was, in her chief's view, 'one of the ablest Civil Servants he had ever known . . . quite up to the standard of any man . . . with a good brain and a

* It is unclear as to why Nancy Lambton did not appear before the committee. One might have expected her to have received an invitation, given that she had returned from Tehran to London by this time, but there is no record in the archive of any correspondence between Lambton and the committee.

detached attitude'; and Elizabeth Monroe and Enid McLeod, both of whom, according to the MOI witness, demonstrated 'a considerable flair for dealing with foreigners, political sense, knowledge of world affairs, understanding of publicity methods and technique and administrative ability'.[29] Surveying the full complement of female talent employed by the British wartime state, the representatives from Cambridge University Women's Appointments Board declared it 'absurd' that such women 'should be thought capable of holding responsible posts under the strenuous conditions of war time and yet incapable of filling them in peace time'.[30]

This was far more potent stuff than the exemplary deeds of female missionaries and League of Nations delegates, or the exceptional cases of a Gertrude Bell or Alexandra Kollontai, upon whom proponents of reform had relied back in 1934 for evidence of women's potential for diplomatic work. Then, witnesses extrapolated from these quasi-diplomatic roles or isolated examples; now, in 1945, they had concrete, indisputable proof. Women had been appointed to diplomatic posts and the world had not stopped turning. The war had transformed the hypothetical risks taken so seriously by the Schuster Committee into groundless speculations. It was for this reason that arguments based on women's so-called 'special' expertise, which had featured so prominently in the evidence of the women's societies a decade earlier, were now notable for their absence. Sensing a shift in the balance of power in their favour, witnesses were adamant that nothing less than full admission to the mainstream career service would satisfy. It was telling that it was their *opponents* who now suggested the creation of specialist posts dealing with 'women's affairs' as a compromise measure. Feminists had asked for this in 1934 as a means of inching open a tightly closed door; defenders of the status quo now raised it as a possibility in the hope that it would delay the inevitable.

Final confirmation of this reversal in fortunes came from the representatives of the Admiralty and the British shipping industry. A decade earlier, much of the case against female consuls had rested on the assumption that no woman could possibly command authority over the captains of merchant vessels and their frequently obstreperous

crews. Yet this, as witnesses acknowledged, was exactly where officers
in the Women's Royal Naval Service had succeeded during the war.
Mr H. V. Markham of the Admiralty observed that some two thousand Wrens (as WRNS members were known) had been posted
overseas, with nearly two hundred entrusted with duties – such as
inspecting ships and issuing routeing orders – that would ordinarily
fall to a consular or naval control service officer. 'No report is known
to have been received of any Masters of Ships objecting to being
interviewed by women Officers in respect of any of the above duties,'
Markham noted, 'and these Officers are believed to have proved
themselves equally efficient as men from the technical point of view
in spite of the handicap of not having served afloat.'[31] Mr Kendall,
representing the Chamber of Shipping, was less guarded in his praise
for the Wrens. His members had been 'seriously impressed' by their
work, 'particularly by their ability to administrate and to handle situations firmly and quickly'. Some ship owners, Kendall added, 'were
"violently" in favour of women officers'.[32]

There was little doubt as to where all this was leading Gowers and his
colleagues. By early January 1946, the committee was ready to deliberate, and the minutes reveal that the chief issue at stake was not *whether*
women should be admitted to the Foreign Service, but on exactly what
terms their admission should take place.[33] Just as Eden had suspected,
and in spite of the last-ditch efforts of men like Cadogan and Scott to
preserve the status quo, the weight of the evidence pointed ineluctably
to women's inclusion in the new-look Foreign Service. The report
which Gowers handed over to Bevin in February briskly dismissed
claims concerning the alleged physical and emotional frailties of the
female sex, and pooh-poohed the contention that women officers
would cause the smooth machinery of the all-male chancery to malfunc-
tion. Women's war record put paid to that old-fashioned line of
reasoning. 'That arguments of this sort should no longer be used is
natural enough,' Gowers remarked,

now that men and women have worked together during the war in the closest association in so many fields of action. Any dismay that might have been felt ten years ago by an Ambassador on being told to admit a young woman into his team could hardly have exceeded that which would have been felt by the average Battery Commander on hearing that he was to take women into his gun teams; yet this was done with success in many anti-aircraft batteries.[34]

The report also noted how the spectacle of women's war work had vanquished what stood in 1934 as 'the strongest bastion of the strongest case against their admission – their supposed natural unsuitability for consular duties'. The change of opinion on this matter, Gowers remarked, had been 'profound', and, in his view meant there was only one argument of substance against the immediate admission of women outstanding: would the prejudices of foreign officials and businessmen limit women's efficiency and usefulness? Here, as before, Gowers took an upbeat view. Foreign Office witnesses, he felt, displayed a 'natural tendency to exaggerate' the difficulties and they overlooked the fact that only women with exceptional ability and true grit would stand any chance of getting through the rigorous recruitment process. The temporary appointments of women like Stark, Lambton and McGeachy proved admirably what a suitably qualified woman could do. Any wrinkles which might appear would soon be ironed out, and in any case could not be of such a magnitude as to justify the Foreign Office's continuing exemption from the principle of a 'fair field and no favour' which governed the rest of the Civil Service. Finally, there was the wider government reform agenda to consider, and Gowers described himself as much persuaded by the argument that 'a New Model Foreign Service of the sort described in the White Paper . . . must necessarily be an imperfect instrument for the purposes claimed for it unless it includes women in its ranks, carefully chosen and trained, and working as members of a team'. The crucial sentence finally came on page eleven, paragraph forty-five: 'We therefore recommend that women should be equally eligible with men for admission to the Foreign Service.'

The phrase 'equally eligible' was, however, misleading, as two restrictions on women's employment were discussed and agreed. The first was that a marriage bar should be enforced; the second, that a quota should apply limiting the proportion of female candidates recruited in any given year to ten per cent, so as to ensure women did not enter 'in embarrassing numbers', as Gowers put it in the report. The cap on numbers, as it transpired, proved obsolete, as at no time was it found necessary to enforce it, and the policy was quietly dropped in 1963. The marriage bar was another matter altogether. It had been temporarily suspended in the Home Civil Service during the war and, with labour in high demand for post-war reconstruction, few expected to see it return. The introduction of a marriage bar in the Foreign Service was therefore viewed by feminists as a highly retrograde step when Bevin announced his intention to accept the committee's recommendations in full in March 1946. One women's society wrote to him describing the policy as 'wholly unworthy of a Party which had given a pledge of equality of treatment for men and women', and another pointed out that such sex discrimination was in direct conflict with the provisions of the Charter of the United Nations.[35]

All the same, the women's societies could not help but rejoice in the larger victory which had come after nearly two decades of dedicated campaigning. Women could now compete for places in the administrative grade of the Foreign Service. They could become fully fledged diplomats, not temporaries or 'advisors' of uncertain status. These were facts. The opportunity had finally been granted. Now all that was left was to see what women would do with it.

PART FOUR

Equal Colleagues?

Mexico City, 1975

Nearly every member of Britain's ten-strong delegation to the United Nations Conference for International Women's Year fell ill for at least part of their stay in Mexico City. Some were laid low by the altitude of the place, a massive mountain metropolis nestled in a valley perched high on the rocky plateaus of central Mexico. Others caught unpleasant stomach bugs or developed debilitating colds, brought on, no doubt, by long hours seated in stuffy committee rooms or trapped in taxis imbibing the fumes of Mexico City's notoriously slow-moving traffic. The weather did not help. Although the days usually started fine, rain clouds moved in with sinister intent by afternoon to release heavy downpours, making the air thick with humidity and the streets perilous for any pedestrian without an umbrella or stout pair of waterproof boots.

Even without these material discomforts, Mexico City would have still appeared to most casual onlookers as a curious choice of venue for the world's first intergovernmental conference on the status of women. The Latin American republic was not exactly a global leader in the advancement of the female sex. It was, as one British delegate put it, a 'land of machismo', where millions of women lived in dire poverty, trapped by illiteracy, repeated childbearing and errant husbands.[1] Yet in other respects, the Mexican capital's dramatic geographical location and sprawling cityscape of modern skyscrapers, domed cathedrals, colonial-era townhouses and teeming slums provided a perfect setting for the stormy meeting of global north and south, capitalist West and communist East, which took place over two weeks in June 1975.

This truly was a conference like no other. Of the 133 national delegations, no fewer than 113 were led by women, some of them international celebrities, such as Soviet cosmonaut Valentina Tereshkova, or First Lady of the Philippines Imelda Marcos, or Princess Ashraf, twin sister of the Iranian Shah. Television cameras captured the scene at the opening ceremony held in an enormous indoor arena constructed for the Olympic Games of 1968, panning across rows and rows of trouser suits, dresses, kimonos and saris, zooming in on heads covered and uncovered and faces bearing every complexion from the palest shades of pink to the richest and darkest brown. Five miles across town at the National Medical Centre, some six thousand activists crowded into the 'Tribune', an alternative, unofficial conference organised by women's NGOs, where the stiff protocol and diplomatic language of the UN were swapped for free-flowing panel debates, impassioned speeches and an exhibition hall festooned with posters advocating everything from abortion rights and the ordination of women priests, to nuclear disarmament and world peace. Here prominent figures from the US feminist movement like Gloria Steinem and Betty Friedan mingled with Mexican lesbians and Cuban revolutionaries, pitting Western notions of 'liberation' and 'autonomy' against developing nations' demands for economic justice and bread.[2]

Despite this historic and heady atmosphere, the experience of the British delegation was not a happy one. The nominal leader of the delegation, junior Home Office minister Shirley Summerskill, barely had time to notice the altitude or suffocating smog, flying in to deliver her opening plenary address and then promptly flying out again. The deputy leader, Labour MP Millie Miller, however, was present for the entire fortnight and grew increasingly despondent as each day passed. First, there was the excruciatingly slow pace of business in the main plenary sessions, which began with the recitation of lengthy and largely banal messages of goodwill from various heads of states, followed by the leisurely reading out in turn of each delegation's opening statement (all 133 of them). After a week of sitting through this barrage of ponderous oratory, Miller fled the conference hall and joined her colleagues on the First Committee, which had been tasked with drafting the main conference document, the World Plan of Action. Here, thankfully, speeches were limited to five minutes, but even with this self-denying ordinance in place, there was not the remotest chance of debating all 894 amendments on the table, and the committee was forced to adopt the plan with alterations to only the introduction and first chapter agreed.

Although hardly an ideal method of working, this procedural log jam did at least minimise the damage inflicted to the document by delegates determined to press what Miller saw as inflammatory, tendentious and utterly irrelevant ideological agendas. She was genuinely shocked by the extent to which delegates from Asia, Africa and South America were prepared to play 'politics' with women's rights, using every available opportunity to decry 'foreign domination' of developing economies, to lambast 'imperialism, colonialism, racism and apartheid', and to press for the addition of 'Zionism' to this list of global evils – a thinly veiled attack on Israel, whose lead representative was met with a staged walkout when she rose to deliver her plenary speech.[3] Miller reluctantly stuck to her instructions from London to 'steer a middle course' and 'maintain a low profile' on these and other controversies, dutifully abstaining on objectionable resolutions and studiously avoiding making any suggestion that the Western model was the best possible route to women's rights.[4]

Miller's colleagues on the delegation did not lighten her ordeal. The two Foreign Office diplomats – both men – who had flown down from Britain's Mission to the UN in New York were smooth operators but had a tendency to act without consulting her, as did Janet Cockcroft, British representative on the UN's Committee on the Status of Women where the idea for the conference had originated. Miller was not impressed by the two officials from the Overseas Development Ministry, especially the highly strung young man who, as even his boss in London later admitted, was 'apt to expose some not fully controlled enthusiasms'.[5] The two ladies from Gibraltar and St Kitts, who had been tagged on as an afterthought, were charming but ineffectual, whilst the press officer, a young woman supplied by the Central Office of Information, was well meaning but had been instructed without Miller's knowledge to hold back from sending press notices to the UK on the assumption that British newspapers would not be interested. Miller had more time though for Kay Carmichael, a Scottish academic and advisor to the Prime Minister, who largely shared Miller's views on the shambolic organisation of the delegation and lost no time in expressing them fully and frankly to Downing Street after their return.

In truth, the Foreign Office was not an avid enthusiast for International Women's Year. It had taken a dim view of UN efforts to advance the 'status of women' for decades, mainly because this amorphous topic seemed only to invite self-satisfied Soviet trumpeting of the alleged freedoms of women under communism, or hectoring by developing nations of former colonial powers like Britain, whom they held as solely responsible for the problems of non-Western women. The fact that, by 1975, women were moving into the senior ranks of the British Diplomatic Service – the first woman ambassador would be appointed the following year – made little difference to the half-hearted manner in which the Foreign Office prepared for the Mexico conference. There were still very few female diplomats around with real policy influence, but even those who had advanced beyond the junior ranks did not judge it their special responsibility to speak up for 'women's' rights. Tessa Solesby, an officer of twenty years' standing who helped to prepare the delegation's steering brief from her desk in London, did not noticeably stray from the government's official line, which held International Women's Year to be of marginal importance to Britain's long-term foreign policy interests. In response to its proposed continuation into an entire Decade for Women, Solesby cited 'our traditional dislike of such ideas', whilst of a mooted new UN Centre for Women's Affairs, she wrote, 'we are not entirely convinced that this gap needs filling, at least as a matter of high priority'.[6]

The writer and ex-diplomat Harold Nicolson, who had opposed women's admission to diplomacy in the 1940s on the grounds that they were 'apt to espouse causes', could not have been more wrong. By the time of the Mexico conference, there were plenty of feminists in Britain loudly berating the government for its lukewarm approach to combating sexism and prejudice on a global scale, but precious few of them were to be found inside the Foreign Office. In the decades following their entry to the diplomatic profession, women slowly broke down the existing male monopoly and, through a combination of talent and hard work, proved what female diplomats could do when given the chance. Yet they did not, as some feminists had predicted they would, work collectively to bring questions of particular interest to women into the purview of British foreign policy. Millie Miller noted archly that it was male delegates who pushed most aggressively for discussion of 'political' controversies at Mexico City, a tactic which she believed was deliberately deployed to prevent female delegates from holding a serious debate about women's social, political and economic rights. John Macrae, one of the two male diplomats on the British delegation, did not, however, agree. 'I did not leave Mexico City in a deep state of depression at the outcome,' he wrote to his superiors in London. 'The world is a very large and complicated place and the aspirations of women in different parts of it differ to a marked degree.'[7] It was a sentiment with which most of Britain's pioneering women diplomats would have wholeheartedly concurred.

Pioneers

On the morning of 1 October 1951, a nervous twenty-two-year-old arrived at the Foreign Office to begin her career in diplomacy. Upon arrival she was directed up an imposing staircase to the second floor and ushered into an enormous high-ceilinged room with large windows overlooking the central courtyard. Six men in dark suits with stiff collars were seated around two blocks of tables, some talking into telephones, others engrossed in large piles of buff-coloured files. They did not look up until the personnel officer who had accompanied the fresh-faced recruit cleared his throat and announced, 'Miss Galbraith, this is Southeast Asia Department. Gentlemen, this is Miss Galbraith. She will be in charge of Indonesia and Nepal.' After that, he was gone, leaving the newcomer in some uncertainty as to what she should do next. Fortunately, one of the men waved her over to a vacant desk next to his and in a friendly manner handed her a pile of telegrams to read. This was Reginald Hibbert, a future ambassador to Paris, who became Mary Galbraith's guide and protector in those early days and weeks. With no proper training to speak of, she relied on 'kind, kind Reg' to apprise her of the most rudimentary facts, from the name of the room that she was sitting in (it was the 'Third Room' of the department, where all the juniors worked), to the rule which decreed that telegrams be written on white paper, and memos on blue. Even to Reg, however, she dared not admit that she had only the shakiest notion of *where* Indonesia was. After a day or two of bluffing, she slinked over to an atlas lying open on one of the tables near the fireplace, but was dismayed to find that it was out of date, showing only the old Dutch East Indies ('of which I had equally never heard'). It was several weeks before Galbraith successfully located the country on whose affairs she was purported to be the Foreign Office expert.

She soon found her feet, however, with the help of Reg and the other Third Room chaps, most of whom were a good ten years her senior with military service under their belts and wives and children at home. By the end of her first year, she had discovered a great deal more about Indonesia than its position on the map and had become equally knowl-edgeable about Nepal, a brief which involved the rather intimidating task of joining a company of grey-haired generals on the War Office's Gurkha Recruitment Board. Soon she was penning memoranda and drafting speeches for ministers with ease, so much so that it was with some trepidation that two years later Galbraith received news of her first overseas posting: to Budapest. It was not a destination much coveted amongst Foreign Service cadets. Conditions behind the Iron Curtain were known to be tough and Western diplomats were severely restricted in the contacts they could have with ordinary Hungarians. But it was, nonetheless, regarded as a suitable place for a woman, partly because Foreign Office chiefs were keen that female officers should get their fair share of 'hardship' posts to appease their male colleagues; and partly because young single men sent to Eastern Europe had an unfor-tunate propensity to get caught in honeytraps engineered by the secret police. As Galbraith recalled, young single Englishwomen, by contrast, were thought to be 'a) so unattractive, and b) so well brought up, that they wouldn't get caught in honeytraps – which was on the whole true, as far as I know!'

In fact, she ended up enjoying her two years in Budapest immensely, where she lived in a little flat in the old town amidst bombed-out build-ings and piles of rubble yet to be cleared almost a decade after the war's end. Outside her window stood a handsome pair of chestnut trees, and beyond those there unfolded a beautiful vista over the ramparts encir-cling the city. Despite the general air of austerity, Galbraith was not unduly deprived of her creature comforts, looked after as she was by a maid, Ada, who, as was perfectly standard practice at the time, simultaneously spied on her for the communist state. 'I didn't mind at all,' Galbraith remarked, 'because I knew she was doing it and I never said anything to her that could have been damaging – not only damaging to me but damaging to her to know. This was very much the way it worked.' Social life, however, was largely non-existent, and she fled the dreary company of the diplomatic corps whenever she could for high-spirited weekends in Vienna with friends from England.

Galbraith left Budapest a few months before the popular uprising of autumn 1956 (which was hastily halted by Soviet tanks), but arrived at her next posting, the British Mission to the United Nations in New York, just as the political powder keg of the Suez crisis was about to explode. Revelations that Anthony Eden – by now Prime Minister – had connived with the French and Israeli governments to create a pretext for invasion following Nasser's nationalisation of the Suez Canal had shocked public opinion both at home and abroad. The British, as a result, were deeply unpopular at the United Nations, whose authority they had so flagrantly flouted. Those early months, she remembered, 'were frightful. No-one knew what was going on. The Foreign Secretary, with all his party of people, secretaries, the press, all arrived, and out-numbered the delegation itself. It was chaotic, that first session [of the Assembly].' To add to the pressure, when protests broke out on the streets back in Budapest in October, Galbraith was ordered to prepare a speech for the British delegate to deliver to one of the UN's high-level committees. 'Because I'd been there I was the obvious person to deal with it, and I had no idea what to do . . . It was really a very unhappy time.'

All the same, work was never dull. As one of just five political officers in the mission, she sat behind Britain's ambassador during all the major sessions of the Security Council, and got to know most of her opposite numbers in the other delegations through the frenetic rush of meetings, briefings and receptions. Those intense six weeks when the Suez affair was at its height were the hardest of her working life. She was in almost constant communication with London, rushing off telegrams at all hours of the day, drafting speeches and briefs in response to every twist and turn of events, and getting very little sleep throughout. Eventually the dust settled on the Suez crisis and the pace of work slackened, allowing Galbraith to settle into a more manageable routine, which she kept up for another three years, finally leaving New York in 1959 for a series of desk jobs back at the Foreign Office. The moment to be posted overseas came again in 1963. Her superiors decided that Moscow was the place, and she was duly packed off for a crash course in Russian with an émigré Jew in the basement of Carlton House Terrace. But it was not to be. A month before she was due to depart, Galbraith wrote to the ambassador to inform him regretfully that she would be unable to take up her post, as she was getting married to Tony Moore, a British diplomat whom she had first met in New York. In keeping with Diplomatic Service Regulation No. 5 on Marriage, she was therefore tendering her resignation, which the ambassador accepted without question. After twelve years, matrimony brought the diplomatic career of Mary Galbraith (now Mary Moore) to an abrupt end.[1]

Mary Galbraith was a pioneer, one of the first generation of young women to win a place in the reorganised Foreign Service during the immediate post-war years. No fewer than seventeen female officers were directly recruited to Branch A (as the elite administrative grade was now known) between 1946 and 1951, representing a tiny fraction of the total intake over that period, but offering nevertheless an early indication of the Foreign Office's willingness to appoint talented young women. Ernest Bevin's announcement in March 1946 was followed by a flurry of activity at the Civil Service Commission, which rushed out a press notice inviting female candidates to apply for the Foreign Service exam taking place that summer.[2] Perhaps because of the short notice or relative lack of publicity, the commission was not exactly overrun with takers in that first year. For one reason or another, the handful of high-ranking women who had made their mark in temporary wartime posts were not contenders. Freya Stark and Nancy Lambton returned to their former careers as writers and scholars, whilst Mary McGeachy was by now married and retired from the UN Relief

and Rehabilitation Administration (UNRRA), the body to which Beryl
Power was seconded at the end of the war and with whom she served in
China,* then teetering on the brink of communist revolution. Enid
McLeod, by contrast, who headed the French Section at the Ministry
of Information, *had* made a bid for a diplomatic career earlier in 1945,
after being recommended for permanent government employment by
her boss. She was called to interview and asked which department she
would prefer. McLeod's instant answer – 'the Foreign Office' – rather
ruffled the 'large and imposing body of men' comprising the interview
panel, who were forced to explain apologetically that women were as
yet ineligible for the Foreign Service. There was also the rather delicate
matter of McLeod's 'seniority' (she was forty-eight), which, as she later
paraphrased, 'would present difficulties, owing to my lack of training
in their ways'. Having thoroughly enjoyed this spectacle of discombobulated bureaucrats, McLeod let them off the hook, revealing that
she had, in fact, received an offer of employment from the British
Council (an arm's-length cultural agency of the Foreign Office), 'and
of course they instantly begged me to take it'.[3] This McLeod did,
becoming, in 1954, representative in Paris – the first woman to hold
such a high-ranking British Council post overseas.[†]

As McLeod's experience revealed, what Civil Service chiefs really
wanted, at least in the immediate post-war period, were younger
women who would enter the reformed Foreign Service alongside the
demobilised officers now being recruited in droves, and who could be
trained up from scratch. Now that the battle was ended and women
were in, the Foreign Office was anxious to attract only the

* Power was appointed initially as a consultant on administrative and welfare policies
but later became the ILO's advisor to the Chinese Ministry of Social Affairs. She subsequently worked for the UN's Economic Commission for Asia and the Far East (ECAFE),
based in Bangkok, before retiring in 1951.
† The British Council was created in 1934 in the light of increasingly aggressive cultural
propaganda activities by Nazi Germany and Fascist Italy. Women were not recruited to
overseas posts for many decades. Anne Stoddart applied for the council's general overseas service in 1960 and recalls being told openly at the interview that the Council
preferred to recruit young men. She was eventually offered a post, but Stoddart decided
to join the Diplomatic Service instead.

highest-calibre females. David Scott, who had defended the masculine status quo to the bitter end, wrote to the Civil Service Commission in August 1946 expressing his hope that 'the first woman candidate who got in should be an outstandingly good specimen and thoroughly British in every way'.[4] Miss Monica Milne, a young woman who had impressed at the Ministry of Economic Warfare, was deemed to fit the bill. She became the first female Branch A appointee, starting work in autumn 1946, and was joined within a year by three others: Cicely Ludlam, Caroline Petrie and Grace Rolleston. A further trio followed in 1948: Margaret Anstee, Patricia Hutchinson and Jennifer Turner.

Over the next two decades, around forty more women were recruited via the annual open competition, although that figure was swelled over the years by the entry to Branch A of a handful of mainly older women via alternative routes. This included the American-born Barbara Salt, who had served with SOE in Tangier during the war and subsequently as a Foreign Office temporary before winning a permanent post in 1949 at the age of forty-five.[5] It also included Gillian Brown, a temporary in the Research Department who successfully passed the Senior Branch exam in 1951, and Kathleen Graham, a senior clerical officer who would eventually be promoted into Branch A in 1955 aged fifty-one, becoming the highest-ranking woman in the Foreign Service. One final feminine presence in the Senior Branch was supplied by women recruited by MI6 to spy for Britain overseas, who usually operated under the cover of a diplomatic title. The most respected female intelligence officer of the post-war period was undoubtedly Daphne Park – later known as 'Queen of Spies' – who was posted to Moscow in 1954 as a 'second secretary', and held further diplomatic posts in Zambia, the Congo, Vietnam and Mongolia. After retiring from the Service in 1979, Park became principal of Somerville College, Oxford, and in 1990 took up a seat in the House of Lords as Baroness Park of Monmouth.*

---

* In April 2013, Lord Lea revealed that shortly before her death in March 2010, Park told him that she had 'organised' the abduction and murder in 1961 of the Congolese Prime Minister Patrice Lumumba, who was suspected of pro-Soviet sympathies. Some former officials have expressed doubts about the claim, although it seems possible that British intelligence knew about the planned assassination. With the MI6 files closed, the true

Even with these additions to the regular annual intake of fresh graduates, women never made up more than two per cent of Branch A
personnel throughout the post-war period. There were typically five
male candidates for every woman who came forward for the annual
exam, and the success rate amongst men was higher, in some years
dramatically so: male candidates were twice as likely to pass muster in
1959 and 1960, and between 1952 and 1954, and again between 1956 and
1958, not a single female candidate was deemed to have met the grade.[6]
Women's numerical strength in the Service was further eroded by wastage due to the invidious operations of the marriage bar; by 1954, at least
seven of the eighteen women recruited to Branch A had resigned for
this reason. Others evidently did not even bother to apply, drawn
instead to careers in the Home Civil Service, where women were
(slightly) more plentiful in the higher grades and were not forced to
choose between having a husband and having a career.[*]

There were, nonetheless, exceptional young women like Mary
Moore who refused to be deterred, either by the Foreign Office's
shabby treatment of married women or by its long history of masculine
exclusivity. These pioneers fought for and won their place in the post-
war Diplomatic Service, in the process opening up to women a
profession which had been jealously guarded by its male practitioners
for so long.

———————

Joan Burbidge did not nurse dreams of a career in diplomacy when she
came down from Oxford with a respectable second-class degree in
History in mid-1941. Her future, she hoped, lay in academia, where she
could indulge her love of all things medieval which had been inspired

---

extent of British involvement will not be known for many years. See Gordon Corera,
'MI6 and the Death of Patrice Lumumba', 2 April 2013, http://www.bbc.co.uk/news/
world-africa-22006446

[*] Women were still badly under-represented in the higher grades of the Home Civil
Service, but there were two female permanent secretaries in this period: Evelyn Sharp,
who headed the Ministry of Housing and Local Government from 1955 to 1966, and
Mary Smieton, permanent secretary at the Ministry of Education from 1959 to 1963.

during her undergraduate years at St Hilda's, one of Oxford's four women's colleges. Like many young people, however, Burbidge was forced to put long-term plans on hold for the duration of the war and instead find something useful to do. It did not take her long to secure a job at the Ministry of Information in London, where she spent her days working under Mary Agnes Hamilton (a 'remarkable woman') in the American Section, and her nights either in a shabby bedsit in Chelsea or sheltering in the nearest underground station during air raids. Within a year, Burbidge was sent to New York to join the British Information Services as a lecturer specialising in education policy and, by the end of the war, had transferred to the Washington embassy, where she covered the educational attaché's desk.

It was therefore by luck rather than design that, still only twenty-five years of age, Burbidge found herself plunged into the world of wartime diplomacy, but it was such a thrilling ride that she did not want it to end. Her job took her all over the US, giving talks to colleges and student societies on the great changes afoot in the British schooling system as a result of R. A. Butler's famous Education Act.* In Washington, she rented a lovely flat with bay windows overlooking the bustling Dupont Circle, and acquired her first car – a second-hand LaSalle convertible coupé – and a nice boyfriend from the Norwegian embassy who took her to parties. Burbidge evidently impressed her superiors, as they kept her on after a permanent (male) replacement was found for the educational attaché post, and strongly encouraged her to try her hand at the Foreign Service exam, now open to both sexes. She took their advice and returned to England to take the exam, which she aced, coming top for the Home Civil Service and second for the Foreign Service. After her Washington adventure, there was no question as to which Joan would choose. In the autumn of 1948 she started her Foreign Office career in the Third Room of the European Economic Department. Like Moore, however, it was a career cut short

* The Education Act (1944), which was strongly associated with the Conservative minister R. A. Butler, introduced a tripartite system of secondary schooling (comprising grammar, secondary technical and secondary modern schools) and raised the school leaving age to fifteen.

– in Burbidge's case, after only two years – by the marriage bar.[7]

Joan Burbidge tumbled almost accidentally into diplomacy, drawn by the promise of travel and adventure rather than any burning professional ambition. In this she was not atypical. As an undergraduate at Cambridge during the war, Margaret Anstee had liked the idea of a job which would enable her to see the world, but took the exam more or less 'as a joke', having already started work on a doctoral thesis with an academic career in mind.[8] Mary Moore was, similarly, rather surprised to find herself working at the Foreign Office. She had spent much of her spare time as an undergraduate at Oxford in amateur theatricals, forming vague hopes for some post-university career in the theatre, or, failing that, in journalism, given that writing was another of her great pleasures. It was through the influence of tutors at her college, Lady Margaret Hall, and more precisely of the principal, Lucy Sutherland (who had been seconded to the Washington embassy during the war), that the thought of applying to the Foreign Office entered Moore's mind. There was a feeling in college, she recalled, that the Foreign Service was 'the "New Frontier", the current feminist hurdle. Very few women were known to have got in, and therefore it was very important that women should get in. So the College was very keen.' This stiffened Moore's resolve to give it a try – that, combined with the absurd advice she'd received from the university's women's careers advisor to the effect that she should get an office job with Metal Box, a large firm which manufactured metal boxes: not a terribly tantalising prospect.

Other female recruits to the post-war Service received similarly uninspiring careers advice. Even as late as the 1960s, women graduates were faced with a dismal range of options when it came to paid employment. Teaching was by far the commonest route, absorbing perhaps as many as two-thirds of all female graduates.[9] Anne Stoddart, who joined in 1960, was told by her advisor at Oxford to train for primary school teaching, whilst Margaret Rothwell, who entered a year later, was advised to consider becoming a librarian or hospital almoner ('which didn't actually appeal').[10] Pauline – later Baroness – Neville-Jones, who joined in 1963, had originally set her heart on a career in private industry, but soon found that the opportunities were 'strictly limited and that if you wanted to go into a big corporate as a woman, they'd shove you into personnel as it was then known'.[11] Her contemporary, Veronica Sutherland, initially enrolled on a secretarial course because she did not know what else to do with her degree from Westfield College other than *not* to teach; she subsequently wrote a Master's thesis on the German playwright Brecht and would in all likelihood have drifted into academia had she not, in the intervening period, passed the Foreign Service exam on her second attempt.[12]

Doubtless many of the young men who tried for the Foreign Office in these years did so, like their female peers, after periods of indecision, or kept other professional possibilities in mind. But in post-war Britain, those possibilities were dramatically richer for men. There were still whole swathes of professional life – law, accountancy, big business, politics, journalism – where women were woefully under-represented. In part this was a reflection of the skewed composition of Britain's undergraduate population, which in 1945 was three-quarters male, a ratio that hardly shifted before the mid-1960s and only reached parity some twenty years after that.[13] Pre-war attitudes, which held that educating girls beyond school age was a waste of time and money, died hard. The first female recruits to the Foreign Service were, therefore, relatively unusual (and lucky) in having parents willing to see their daughters aspire to higher education, and – unless generous scholarships were forthcoming – prepared to foot all or part of the bill.[14] A far more typical story was that of Patricia Lever, who joined the Foreign Office in the Secretarial Branch, having left school at eighteen after sitting her A-levels. Going to university, she recalled, was not really discussed, either by her parents (neither of whom had been), or by the teachers at her small girls' Catholic grammar school in Battersea. 'There was no expectation that a girl would go to university,' Lever remarked. 'In fact, with my family background it would have been a bit odd; it would have been seen as a bit self-indulgent for me to go to university rather than going and earning money when money was quite short.' Lever would eventually rise through the ranks to become a first secretary in the late 1990s, but her lack of a university degree put Branch A wholly beyond her reach as a young woman.[15]

All the same, the privileged minority of women for whom going to university *was* a realistic ambition did not compete with men on a level playing field. They were systematically disadvantaged in relation to the ancient universities of Oxford and Cambridge, which supplied some ninety per cent of Foreign Office recruits in the 1950s, because of the limited number of places available to them at the women's colleges. Before the men's colleges were opened up to both sexes in the 1970s and '80s, it was much harder for a bright eighteen-year-old girl to get into one of the two elite universities which prepared their male peers so admirably for high-flying careers in public service. And this had consequences: between 1952 and 1963, candidates from Oxbridge had a one in twelve chance of passing the Foreign Service exam, compared to a one in sixty-nine chance for University of London graduates (where female candidates were over-represented), and a one in seventy-seven chance for graduates from everywhere else.[16] Added to this, the old school tie was strong, with over eighty per cent of new entrants boasting a public-school education – a fact which rather dashed the lofty ideals of the 1943 White Paper, with its talk of throwing the service open to candidates from 'any social sphere'. This public-school–Oxbridge nexus, alongside the marriage bar, probably goes a long way in explaining why far fewer women put themselves forward for the Foreign Office exam, and why so few got in.

Of course, women had their own elite schools and colleges too. A newspaper profile of the twelve women serving in Branch A in 1955 noted that no fewer than four were alumni of Roedean, the prestigious girls' boarding school on the south coast dating back to the late nineteenth century.[17] Right into the 1960s, the majority of female entrants were privately educated like their male counterparts, with most, again like their male peers, hailing from middle-class, professional families. By the mid-1950s there was in operation, if not exactly an 'old girls' network', a set of school and university-based connections upon which those in the know could draw. Oxford provided the hub: at least twenty of the women recruited to Branch A between 1946 and 1965 had been educated at one of Oxford's women's colleges, with Somerville alone supplying ten of their number.[18] Juliet Campbell, Margaret Rothwell and Pauline Neville-Jones were, like Mary Moore, beneficiaries of Lucy Sutherland's regime at Lady Margaret Hall, whilst over at Joan Burbidge's alma mater, St Hilda's, Catherine Hughes was told by her tutors after passing the exam in 1955 to write to Moore for advice, including tips on what to wear ('she sent me back a very long letter all about long gloves'[19]). Moore also served as something of a role model for Rothwell, who knew all about her success because their fathers were both medieval historians and close acquaintances.[20] In London, Veronica Sutherland was inspired – at least in part – to try for the Foreign Service by the example of two women from Westfield College, who had entered a few years earlier.[21]

Naturally, there were exceptions to these tales of middle-class networking. Margaret Anstee was the first in her family to go to university, and she had to win multiple scholarships in order to get there: one to attend the local grammar school, another to pay for sixth form, and another to secure a place at Newnham College, Cambridge to read modern languages. She might have taken comfort from the fact that the permanent secretary at the time, Sir William Strang, was himself a grammar-school boy (and non-Oxbridge to boot); but it was not until the 1960s that the post-war expansion of grammar-school places made serious inroads into the public-school monopoly within the Foreign Office, and it took even longer for the stranglehold of Oxbridge to loosen its grip.[22]

Catherine Hughes could hardly open the heavy oak doors at Burlington House when she was called in to face the Final Selection Board for the Foreign Service in 1955. Evidently not designed with twenty-one-year-old women of slight build in mind, their immense weight destroyed any mental equilibrium that Hughes might have summoned up ahead of the interview which would determine her future. She had negotiated the earlier hurdles without too much difficulty: first the qualifying exam which whittled hundreds of hopeful candidates down to a few dozen, and then the famous 'house party' test, which put the remaining contenders through two and a half days of group exercises under close observation by officials and psychologists. Her final trial at Burlington House, the seat of the Civil Service Commission, lasted about an hour and passed in something of a blur. Hughes remembered sitting before a 'great panel of people, and you didn't know who any of them were', and then being asked questions 'about things going on at the time and whether one would enjoy living in different climates'. When it was over Hughes rose to wrestle once more with the mighty doors and left the room utterly clueless as to whether she'd passed or not – 'they gave me no indication of that at all'. She need not have worried. The news soon arrived that she was in, and on 30 August 1955, Hughes reported for duty at the Foreign Office with her fellow A-streamers: two women and eleven men all told.

Catherine Hughes's experience would be familiar to any of the hundreds of university graduates who applied to join Branch A of the Foreign Service in the post-war decades. Mary Moore took the initial qualifying exam four years earlier and remembered her amazement at learning that she had scraped through: 'there was a maths paper, and I couldn't do one single question! I've never been able to do maths.' A decade later, Veronica Sutherland was even more astonished by how well she had done in the qualifying tests: 'I think I was about fourth or fifth out of the whole lot. Quite extraordinary, I don't know how I managed that but I did.' The next stage, the house party – or, to give it its proper title, the Civil Service Selection Board (abbreviated to CSSB and almost universally referred to as the 'Sisby') – was more varied if no less gruelling. Until 1950, this two-day process took place in a stately home in Stoke D'Abernon, a picturesque village about twenty miles outside London, following a model established during the war to select commissioned officers for the armed forces. The purpose of the scheme, in which candidates chaired pretend committees and devised policies for fictitious British territories, was to identify talent beyond that show-cased in the written exam, and to evaluate how well these future public servants might respond to 'real-world' problems.[23] Known as 'Method II' to distinguish it from the older format of university-style exams followed by an interview, the new model was originally adopted across the Civil Service to cater for those undergraduates who had been prevented from completing their degrees by the advent of war. It was subsequently judged so successful as a 'creaming process' for spotting outstanding ability that it was decided to retain Method II as one means of recruitment to the Home Civil Service fast stream, whilst in the case of the Foreign Service, it became the exclusive route into Branch A until 1957.[24]

Despite this general consensus within Whitehall as to the merits of Method II, for the public outside the 'house party' acquired a certain mystique during its early years of operation. Rumours circulated about sinister 'personality' tests, whilst the press gleefully printed stories about candidates being rejected because they drank too much at dinner or used the wrong set of cutlery. In an effort to silence these accusations, the Civil Service Commissioners invited journalists to observe the 'Sisby' in action at Stoke D'Abernon in May 1948. This largely had the desired effect. The correspondent from *The Times* concluded that the tests were a fair and effective method for judging ability and conceded that, unlike written exams, there was no obvious means by which candidates could 'cram' for the impromptu group discussions and simulated committee meetings.[25] The memories of those who went through the process, however, suggest that earlier caricatures of the Sisby were not wholly fanciful. Joan Burbidge found the weekend at Stoke D'Abernon sufficiently full of intrigue to use it as a setting for one of the detective novels that she wrote in her spare time. Similarly Margaret Anstee recalled how the purpose of the test – at least in part – was 'to more or less prove that you could drink three martinis before dinner and still be coherent and able to administer a colony after-wards . . . They were looking at your social graces as well as your intellectual ability.'

Much of the air of mystery surrounding the house party was lost in 1950, when ongoing criticism from press and Parliament of the high running costs resulted in its being reconfigured along non-residential lines and transferred to the less glamorous setting of a dingy office suite on Savile Row in London. Those who spent two days in these inauspicious surroundings being put through their paces remember the experience as tough but hugely stimulating and, at times, great fun.

Veronica Sutherland was given a file of papers concerning the budget of a fictitious town council and recalls advising it be spent on the construction of a new car park: 'I can't think why on earth,' she later reminisced, 'I should think that a car park would be the best idea!' Anne Warburton, who attended the Sisby a few years earlier in 1957, was initially unsettled by the probing nature of the tests, which forced candidates to be 'very self-critical and self-analytical', but soon warmed up and by the final round table she was in her element: 'At the end we had to say which of us we would nominate to go on a holiday with, to work with, to have as a colleague in a crisis . . . I thought it was a very good thing.'[26] Having their every word scrutinised by the Civil Service assessors – including during a one-to-one interview with a professional psychologist – did not particularly faze these female candidates. Sutherland was bold enough to ask the psychologist directly how he could possibly tell whether she was answering his questions truthfully (to which he confessed that he probably could not). Mary Moore was secretly rather pleased with how her group conspired against the assessors during the committee meeting exercise, by agreeing amongst themselves that they would each take a turn in leading the discussion, and hence each have a chance to shine. 'Four out of the six of us of that group got in, so it did work,' she recalled. 'It was a thoroughly dishonest way of proceeding!'

Others members of the first generation of women diplomats remember a similar mood of pleasant camaraderie amongst candidates at the Sisby, and absolutely no discrimination on grounds of sex on the part of the assessors. The next stage, the Final Selection Board interview, by contrast, was far less congenial in mood and potentially more intimidating for women. Here the candidate was outnumbered by the (mostly male) members of the panel by at least six or seven to one, whilst the immense oval table behind which these interrogators were seated in a long row, combined with the cavernous ceilings and grand furnishings of Burlington House, were sufficient to unnerve even the coolest-headed young graduate. In most respects the interview board made no distinction between male and female candidates, who were generally grilled for an hour or two on their motives for applying to the Foreign Service and asked to expand on the various interests they had noted down on their application form. But towards the end of this lengthy ordeal, female candidates were fired a final question which no man was ever required to answer. The exact form of words varied, but it essentially boiled down to this: what will you do if you want to get married? Mary Moore, who already knew about the marriage bar, gave, as she put it, 'the obvious correct answer: "Yes, I think it's a great pity, but I'm not going to allow that to put me off going into a career I very much want to enter."' Twenty years later, Sarah Squire was faced with the same question, but unlike Moore, she was wholly unprepared for it. Squire was astonished to learn of the existence of this regulation (and well she might be: it was 1971 after all). 'I knew nothing about this at all,' Squire recalled. 'I was just rather affronted and surprised and said "That's a completely hypothetical question, the sort of thing one meets when one comes to it" . . . I wasn't sure what answer one could give.'[27]

In fact, most female Branch A recruits offered some variation on the responses of Moore and Squire when confronted with the intractable fact of the marriage bar. These women were, at the time of the interview, young, ambitious, highly educated and in most cases romantically unattached. In an era in which it was unusual for women to pursue full-time professional careers after marriage and motherhood, what alternative answer might they have given? Certainly not those supplied by interwar feminists, who belonged to a now bygone era in which middle-class women looked to servants and full-time nannies to shoulder the bulk of housework and childcare. Even those who abjured this blatantly discriminatory practice – Anstee thought the marriage bar 'exceedingly frustrating and unfair' – were unlikely to regard the Final Selection Board at Burlington House as the appropriate venue in which to voice their complaints. Later, by the early 1970s, the mood across the Service was beginning to change, but for the immediate post-war generation, pragmatism seemed the best policy. Margaret Rothwell regarded the marriage bar as 'something that one would confront if it happened', whilst Anne Stoddart thought that in the event of getting married she could always transfer to the Home Civil Service and not

give up work (which is exactly what some of her contemporaries did –
although not Stoddart, who remained unmarried).

In truth, most members of this generation did not bristle instinctively at the thought of resignation for matrimonial purposes. Juliet
Campbell freely confessed that her values were highly conventional:
'Certainly as a young-ish woman I took it for granted that I'd get
married and have a family, and that I would at that stage leave the
Foreign Service.' Campbell was acutely conscious of her privileged
position as a female graduate who had won a much coveted post in a
prestigious arm of government, but she did not assume that, as a
woman, she should be entitled to pursue both motherhood *and* a
career. Some female graduates, by the 1950s, were beginning to contemplate taking up part-time employment once their children were at
school, but opportunities to do so in professional occupations were
scarce, which was why teaching was so popular, and the concept of
'dual career' families was practically unheard of.[28] In any case, long-
term planning was not on Campbell's mind. The marriage bar thus
'wasn't for me as much of a deterrent as you might possibly think,
because I regarded the Foreign Office as something that would be great
for however long I did it; a tremendous adventure in a sense – to see
what I could do and see how far I could get.'[29] Mary Moore felt much
the same way about the regulation:

> I didn't let it worry me. I think I was really not thinking. By the time it
> got to about five years ahead, heaven knows how I would feel about
> things or who I would meet . . . Honestly, it would be absurd to pretend
> I weighed up the advantages or disadvantages. I didn't. I ignored it.

The building on King Charles Street that Mary Moore reported to on
her first day at the Foreign Office was, by the early 1950s, feeling and
showing its age. The grand exterior was blackened with soot and
disfigured by bird excrement and inside many of the haphazard
wartime arrangements were still in place. The Locarno Room
remained divvied up into offices separated by makeshift walls, the

iconic Durbar Court was filled with ugly wooden huts, and every room and passageway seemed to contain odd pieces of furniture or long-abandoned boxes brimming with dusty books and files. The original scale and lavish detail of Sir Gilbert Scott's classical palazzo still could not fail to impress, of course, but if new cadets (of either sex) were expecting their physical surroundings to mirror the personal glory they felt at having secured one of the few places in the Senior Branch of the Foreign Service, they were to be seriously disappointed. Everywhere was evidence of neglect, from the peeling paint on the walls, dim lighting and creaking lifts to the malfunctioning lavatories and woefully inadequate heating system. For her first post in 1948, Margaret Anstee was sent to work in the South American Department, based in a bitterly cold room with high ceilings and an open fire which needed constant stoking throughout the day by an aged messenger. A decade later Anne Warburton found herself employed in the Economic Relations Department, where she shared with one other man a cramped space in the Locarno Room sectioned off by sacking walls. Margaret Rothwell did not fare much better, given a desk in the tiny office shared by four men and ten telephones which masqueraded as the Third Room of the Northern Department.

Throughout the post-war decades, the size of the diplomatic work-force massively outgrew its historic accommodation, initially as a result of the short-term recruitment drive during the reconstruction period, and later as a corollary of the merger between the Foreign Office and the Commonwealth Office (which was itself an amalgam of the old Colonial Office and the Commonwealth Relations Office). From 1968, the new Foreign and Commonwealth Office (or FCO) assumed responsibility for Britain's former and remaining colonies, in addition to bilateral relations with sovereign states and new multilateral organisations such as the United Nations and the European Economic Community, which Britain eventually joined in 1973. This meant that, even once the old India Office had departed following Indian independence, Scott's Victorian edifice was full to bursting. Some post-war recruits were immediately despatched elsewhere, like Rowena Vining, whose first permanent job at the Foreign Office was in a department based at Carlton House Terrace, or Katherine Smith, who joined Branch B* as a graduate in 1965 and spent her first days in the Passport Office on Petty France near St James's Park. The problems of accommodating Britain's diplomatic workforce at home dragged on into the 1970s, when one observer likened the Foreign Office to 'a stately home whose occupants have long been fighting a losing battle against death duties and general dilapidations'.³⁰ They were not finally resolved until the expensive refurbishments implemented by Margaret Thatcher's Foreign Secretary, Geoffrey Howe, in the 1980s.³¹

Nonetheless, leaking radiators and broken lifts did not prevent members of the Foreign Office from creating cosy pockets of camaraderie within the departments, much as they had in earlier decades. For an organisation which outsiders associated with stuffiness and snobbery, and in which it was still not uncommon to see a bowler hat, striped trousers or frock coat, social relations were remarkably laid-back. Just as the late-Victorian Foreign Office was in the vanguard for dropping the 'Mr' in forms of address, so was its post-war incarnation ahead of the curve in deploying forenames as a matter of course, even between lowly third secretaries and department heads.† Anstee remembered the mood in the Third Room of the South American Department in the late 1940s as 'all rather friendly'. There were plenty of pranks, such as the occasion on which Anstee and another third secretary gate-crashed the Paraguayan ambassador's cocktail party at the Ritz after purloining an invitation from the desk of a senior colleague on leave. The atmosphere in the Northern Department in the early 1960s was similarly congenial as Margaret Rothwell recalled it. She rubbed along easily enough with her fellow third secretaries, including a young chap 'who ambled in about 11 o'clock in the morning, rang his stock-broker

---

* Branch B, roughly equivalent to the executive grade in the Home Civil Service, was a rung below the prestigious Branch A and its personnel tended to carry out the more routine administrative work, including much consular work.
† As late as 1977, this informality struck the twenty-two-year-old Sherard Cowper-Coles as 'revolutionary' (see *Ever the Diplomat: Confessions of a Foreign Office Mandarin*, London, 2012, p. 4).

and spent the next half hour dealing with his investments'. Nor had the rhythms of work changed so radically from earlier in the century, although the hours were longer – usually 9 or 9.30 a.m. till about 7 p.m. – and the technology used for communications had moved on. In most departments the day began with the unlocking of padlocked safes, the opening of files, a thorough sifting of telegrams which had come in overnight, and a wrestle with the metal cylinders into which papers were stuffed and whizzed across the building courtesy of a network of tubes powered by compressed air.[32]

The post-war pioneers found their male contemporaries to be, on the whole, helpful and supportive colleagues who were perfectly willing to work alongside women on an equal footing. This was especially true of those who had served with women in the armed forces during the war, or who had close female friends at school or university. Rodric Braithwaite, who joined in 1955 in the same cohort as Catherine Hughes and would later serve as ambassador to Moscow, had attended Bedales, a mixed independent school of a progressive stripe, followed by a stretch of military service and then a degree in French and Russian at Cambridge, where he had a wide circle of women friends. As a result, he felt it was 'fairly normal to have women around'.[33] Margaret Anstee certainly felt well treated by her male colleagues, who selflessly insisted she take the desk closest to the fire in their chilly Third Room, and with whom she enjoyed good-natured banter and mutual chaffing, such as the bet that she could not come into the office in a different outfit every day for thirty days in a row: with some late nights and the help of her trusty sewing machine, Anstee won. Veronica Sutherland was similarly delighted with the welcome she received in the German Room in 1965. Her colleagues, she recalled, 'were perfect gentlemen who treated me great courtesy. It was very nice. I enjoyed myself hugely.'

One can question, of course, how far this kind of chivalrous attention signified true acceptance of women as equals, rather than simply good manners on the part of these (largely) public-schooled men. Far less ambiguous, by contrast, was the hostile reaction of some – by no means all – of the older veterans of the Foreign Office to the invasion of their club. Nearly every member of the pioneer generation of women diplomats had a run-in with at least one member of this recidivist group, whose prejudices occupied a spectrum which stretched, as Anstee later described it, from a 'pained paternalism' to 'outright hostility and disdain'.[34] Anstee was aware of both extremes, having heard second-hand of her colleague Caroline Petrie's treatment at the hands of the eccentric vice-marshal of the diplomatic corps, the legendary Marcus Cheke (who was known to write memos with a quill pen in one hand and a long cigarette holder in the other). Petrie, the story went, had drafted a note which required Cheke's approval. He called her in and asked in a voice dripping with disbelief: 'Did *you* write this?' Petrie replied: 'Yes!' to which Cheke said, with scarcely less incredulity, 'What, *all* of it?'[35] Cheke did, at least, acknowledge the quality of Petrie's work, unlike one of Anstee's chiefs, an old Etonian who gave Anstee very short shrift when she presented him with a policy document requiring his clearance. 'He was very disagreeable, almost sneering,' she recalled.

Unfortunately, such incidents were not isolated. Mary Moore encountered a senior colleague in London who 'really couldn't be doing with having women about at all . . . He was just beastly to me from the word go.' Real unpleasantness of this kind was thankfully rare, but Moore later became aware of a 'sort of layer of people at Head of Department level who thought it was absolutely incredible having women in at all – that it was really just a nuisance and there was no point in hiding the fact that they thought that'. Her ambassador and his deputy in New York belonged to this category: 'they did their best to be polite,' Moore recalled,

> but they couldn't actually hide the fact that I was really rather an embarrassment and they didn't quite know how to use me . . . they didn't see me as any kind of addition to the team. It was quite clear that I knew nothing about, understood nothing about politics or how things worked in Whitehall or anything, and I certainly had no idea. So I was more a liability I think to [the Ambassador] and certainly to the number 2; he

was a very distinguished man but he just found me quite impossible to deal with.

When Margaret Rothwell joined in the early 1960s, this kind of defensive disregard of junior female officers had not gone away. Her first chief in the Northern Department, she remembered, 'couldn't cope with women . . . didn't approve, didn't like them, [thought] they were a waste of space . . . he clearly regarded me as expendable and not worth paying much attention to'. His attitude, Rothwell added, 'wasn't hostile, it was just complete incapacity to cope. He was a nice enough man, competent . . . Just didn't know what to do with a woman in the service.'

Accustomed to running an exclusively male team with women present only as clerks or wives, many men of this pre-war generation were utterly thrown by the arrival of a female diplomat in their department or embassy. These feelings were probably strongest abroad, where diplomatic communities were still tightly knit and the representational character of the work meant great store was set by formal protocol and time-honoured tradition. Integrating a young female officer into a world which had revolved around a masculine model of professionalism for so many decades must have often seemed more trouble than it was worth. Some heads of mission took the easy way out and simply told the personnel department in London that women would not be welcome in their chanceries. Juliet Campbell was certain that she had been turned down for overseas jobs during her early years in the Service, whilst as late as 1976 Margaret Rothwell's posting as first secretary to Helsinki was repeatedly delayed by a sceptical ambassador who complained that a female officer would be unable to transact business in the sauna, where elite Finnish males met daily.

Where efforts to block postings failed, ambassadors could still make life uncomfortable for women. Katherine Smith endured a series of slights from her chief in Moscow, where she was posted in the late 1960s. An ambassador 'in the traditional style', on one occasion he prevented Smith from accompanying the Bishop of Fulham on an official visit to the Foreign Relations Department of the Moscow

Patriarchate, the seat of the Russian Orthodox Church, even though the visit fell unambiguously under her brief, which was to look after religious affairs. A male officer was sent instead, a decision which 'at the time', Smith recalled, 'really did rankle'.[36] The same ambassador excluded Smith from the embassy's annual Queen's birthday party, where, according to tradition, all Branch A and Branch B officers would be on duty to welcome the largely Russian guests and usher them through to the reception. There was no question that this decision to exclude Smith was made on grounds of sex, as her Russian (which she had studied at university) was much better than that of several male officers who did receive invitations. Smith decided, however, to take it 'on the chin' and not make a fuss, as doing so was likely to achieve very little. Rothwell made much the same calculation in Helsinki, where the ambassador finally agreed to her posting on the express condition that she take on the running of the Diplomatic Service Wives Association, a job traditionally carried out by the wife of the head of chancery, the post Rothwell was filling. Even though it was inconceivable that such a demand would have been made of an unmarried male officer, Rothwell chose magnanimity over aggravation and concurred with his demands (which, on arrival, she discovered extended to working as his unofficial chauffeur on a regular basis). This probably worked out for the best, as it was in all other respects an attractive posting, and one which Rothwell was keen to take up.

Some ambassadors were never troubled by unwanted female cadets, for, despite the Foreign Office's willingness to send young women beyond the Iron Curtain to Eastern Europe and even to Russia, there were many further flung posts which were considered out of bounds. In accordance with the line maintained by witnesses before the Gowers Committee in 1945 (and despite the wartime precedents of Freya Stark and Nancy Lambton), British missions in Arab countries remained destinations earmarked for male officers alone. The belief that female diplomats 'could not as yet make a full contribution in a Moslem country', as one personnel chief put it in 1956, due to the low status of women in those societies, remained axiomatic.[37] This rule did not apply to women occupying lowlier roles as clerks or secretaries, who did not carry out 'representational' work involving professional contact with members of the host countries in question. Nor did it preclude the ad hoc appointment of female officers with specialised briefs focused on 'women's affairs'. Between 1946 and 1948, for instance, a Mrs E. Pemberton was employed in the British legation in Beirut as assistant information officer with instructions 'to spread British publicity among the women of Syria and Lebanon'. This post was revived in 1961 by Elizabeth Waller, a Branch B recruit who described her efforts to cultivate Arab female opinion as an exercise in the 'projection of Britain' which would supply a '"positive" answer to anti-Western influences'.[38]

Waller was based in the misleadingly named Information Research Department (IRD), a semi-clandestine unit created at the beginning of the Cold War to counter Soviet propagandist activity overseas. There she would have encountered Ann Elwell, a glamorous ex-MI5 officer who, as the IRD's Middle East Section Head, offered further evidence of the Foreign Office's apparent inconsistency in its attitude towards posting women to this region, not to mention its policy towards married women: Elwell had a husband and four small children.[39] The explanation, presumably, was that neither Waller nor Elwell were engaged in mainstream political or representative work of the kind carried out by 'proper' diplomats, and therefore neither had access to the Foreign Office's rigorous Arabic training programme – Arabic being one of the core 'hard' languages which could determine an officer's long-term career trajectory. Wives were permitted to join their husbands in classes at the Middle East Centre for Arabic Studies (MECAS) at Shemlan, a village nestled amongst apple orchards and olive groves in the mountains high above Beirut.[40] Female officers, by contrast, were denied this privilege and, as a consequence, could wave goodbye to any possibility of joining the 'camel corps' – the Arabist specialists who would spend large chunks of their careers in this fascinating and strategically important region.

The Foreign Office was similarly reluctant to train female recruits in other 'hard' languages, including Japanese and Chinese. In this case it was not so much because of 'backward' attitudes towards women in these countries (although that was a factor), but because of the possibility that, having spent a year or more in full-time study, these recruits would get married and resign, and hence the Foreign Office's precious investment would be lost. (The fact that it was the organisation's own regulation on marriage which made this eventuality a certainty was not much dwelt upon in official circles.) Female candidates were largely ignorant of this policy – if indeed it can be described as such – before entering the Service. Unlike the marriage bar, which was written into the Diplomatic Service regulations, women's limited access to language training was not explicitly set out or justified in any official document; it was simply accepted practice. As Rothwell put it: 'I don't think it was stated openly, it just didn't happen.' When Veronica Sutherland joined, she hoped her job would take her to Asia and India – 'what seemed to be exotic places' – and was bitterly disappointed to discover that the chances of acquiring the languages that might secure one of these longed-for postings were slim. 'There'd been a woman shortly before me,' she recalled, 'who had joined in Branch B. She'd been put on Thai language training and promptly got married, so they were not prepared to risk another woman at that stage.'[41] By the time Sarah Squire joined in 1971, these restrictions on access to training were less readily enforced, but there was still a lingering assumption that women represented a poor investment. Squire recalled being told by a contemporary after taking a language aptitude test during her first week: 'Well you won't be doing a hard language because you won't be with us for very long.'

The post-war Foreign Office did not know quite what to make of the first generation of pioneer women diplomats. On the one hand, these female recruits were forced to resign on marriage, were disadvantaged vis-à-vis language training and overseas postings, and often found themselves blocked or berated by sexist chiefs. On the other hand, many male diplomats treated their female colleagues with great kindness and, where ambassadors and departmental heads took an enlightened view, women were entrusted with absorbing and stimulating work without any distinction of sex. The enforcement of both the marriage bar and the ten per cent cap on annual recruitment kept the numbers of women in the Senior Branch very low, meaning that there was never any real possibility of a serious 'backlash' against these newcomers, either from young men who might feel that their own career prospects were under threat, or from veterans who had not the faintest clue how to manage a junior female officer.[42]

Indeed, because of this fact, many members of the pioneer generation discovered that they had a kind of scarcity value. In a sea of dark suits, the female third secretary in a red blouse or green skirt was infinitely more memorable than her male counterpart. As Pauline Neville-Jones recalled: 'In the end there was nobody who didn't know me and nobody who didn't know my name . . . if you were any good, of course, then you got known and it got known and so you did stand out in the crowd, there's no doubt about that.' In some overseas postings, foreign officials appeared positively to relish the opportunity to deal with a young woman rather than a man. Mary Moore remembered the male delegates at the UN who 'visibly cheered up when you turned up', whilst in Washington in the late 1960s, Rothwell similarly found her femininity to be a definite advantage: 'men being men, they'd much rather have a fairly personable female coming in to call on them than just any old little Third Secretary male. So doors did open to you, which you milked to the maximum, if you had any sense!'

Naturally there existed foreigners who, as Foreign Office witnesses had predicted back in the 1930s, were dismissive or high-handed when asked to do business with a 'girl' secretary. But at least as numerous, if not more so, were officials and informants who seemed almost more inclined to let their guard down and talk openly. Rowena Vining, who served during her time as a Branch B officer in Pakistan, Australia, Austria and Italy, discovered this to be the case. 'I think people were not afraid of me,' she reflected. 'I certainly found it fairly easy to get under the skin of the country or the people I was dealing with because people would talk to me and I think probably they talked to me more freely than they would to a man.'[43] Likewise, Anne Stoddart found it useful to affect an unthreatening, feminine demeanour during a tour of Britain's remaining possessions in the Caribbean in the late 1970s at a time of political unrest. The elderly male premiers who ran these small island nations, she recalled, 'liked the idea of a young, white woman from London coming and being suitably impressed . . . And I was allowed to go and see things that other people hadn't been because they'd had rows with men in London.'

These instances seemed to substantiate feminist claims about women's capacity to bring a different – and equally valuable – perspective to bear on diplomatic work. Members of the pioneer generation, however, rarely saw themselves in these terms. They were too young to remember the struggle for women's suffrage or the campaigns of the interwar years, but too old to be formed socially and politically by second-wave feminism, which in the 1970s would force a radical rethinking of the sexual politics of the workplace (as of so much else). These post-war recruits were not later unaffected by the new doctrines of sexual equality, but when it came to personal values and general outlook on the world, they were indisputably products of an era in which terms like 'sisterhood' or 'liberation' were as yet unknown. For these young women, being a diplomat was simply a matter of getting on with the job of representing British interests abroad and deploying whatever skills or qualities they had at their disposal to do that effectively. Reflecting excessively on the pros and cons of being a woman was just not their style. As Anne Warburton recalled, her minority status was 'not something which I've spent time worrying about. It just seemed to me so natural that women should be there, that I should be there and I was a woman. I certainly didn't spend my time saying, "Is this going wrong because . . . ?"'

That said, no Branch A woman could entirely ignore or escape the novelty of her femininity. She was faced with it every time a male official mistook her for a typist, every time her male colleagues disappeared off to the Travellers Club for lunch, and every time she found herself retiring with the ladies at the end of an official dinner whilst the menfolk remained behind for brandy and cigars. To the outside world, the woman diplomat remained an exceptional and intriguing figure. Press coverage of the doings of the pioneer generation inevitably dwelt on their youth and appearance and usually featured somewhat gratuitous photographs under snappy headlines like 'Diplomat Joan is for Bermuda' – a reference to Caroline Petrie's inclusion in the British delegation to an international summit being held on the island in 1953 (Caroline was her middle name). In fact, this story appeared in several papers. The *Daily Express* noted that thirty-one-year-old Petrie was the only female official to be accompanying the Prime Minister, Winston Churchill, on his long flight to Bermuda, whilst the *Daily Mirror* went into greater detail, informing readers that 'green-eyed' Petrie lived in Putney and was packing a swimsuit in the hope that she might find time 'for a dip in the warm Caribbean'.[44] The Atticus column in the *Sunday Times* also reported the government's decision to introduce 'a beautiful girl on the British side of the table at Bermuda', noting that the 'extremely attractive' Miss Petrie had caught the eye of US President Eisenhower, who apparently devoted most of one conference session to executing a pencil sketch of her: 'and it is rumoured that the drawing was put carefully away in his wallet'.[45]

A less frivolous and much longer piece by the journalist Elizabeth Adams appeared in the *Evening Standard* two years later. Rather than detailing eye colour and hairstyles, Adams reflected on the longer-term career prospects for the twelve women then serving in Branch A. Was Kathleen Graham's promotion to the post of deputy consul-general in New York, she asked, 'the start of jobs for the girls?' Answering her own question, Adams thought not. She noted how few women were putting themselves forward for the Foreign Service and left her readers in no doubt as to the reason why:

> It is the little matter of the marriage bar. For a female diplomat the path to the altar – even with a Briton – leads automatically straight through to the exit door from the service. I admit that a woman might find it difficult to run a husband in Surbiton in sweet accord with a career in Washington – and would have to resign her career on marriage anyway. But at least that would be her free choice . . . At least she should not be at the mercy of an arbitrary condemnation to spinsterhood if she wishes to prosper in her chosen career.[46]

The feature ended with a glance forward to the future. 'Prospects for the gallant 12 are, perhaps, fairly bright,' Adams noted, 'so long as they keep their third finger, left hand, suitably naked and deprived.' But, she asked, 'is Britain to insist that forever she is to be served by a negligible number of diplomatic spinsters?' By challenging the marriage bar as early as 1955, Adams showed herself to be ahead of opinion, amongst Foreign Office chiefs certainly, but even amongst the pioneer women diplomats themselves, who largely accepted that they would need to choose between husband and career and had no right to demand both. A decade and a half later, however, the sentiment expressed in Adams's piece could no longer be dismissed as feminist fantasy. Profound changes were afoot in the wider society, and they were changes which left the Foreign Office at grave risk of looking absurdly anachronistic in its attitudes towards married women.

Diplomatic Women's Lib

Women's Liberation reached the Foreign Office in February 1973. It came in the form of a handwritten letter, forwarded from the Home Office, from a Ms G. E. Sorenson of Pimlico, which demanded to know exactly what the Secretary of State had meant by his recent reference in Parliament to the government's opposition to all 'unwarranted discrimination' on grounds of sex. 'I wonder if you could find out for me,' Ms Sorenson asked,

> what HMG regards as 'warranted discrimination' and whether this includes refusing to let women drive buses, and drink in certain pubs, or stand in El Vino's,* or keep their job at the Foreign Office once they marry, or fill in their own tax or building society forms. To be honest, I always thought that all forms of discrimination on grounds of sex was unwarranted.[1]

The civil servant who passed the letter on did so with a request for advice as to how he should answer the specific complaint about the Diplomatic Service marriage bar. If Ms Sorenson had written even a year earlier, Foreign Office officials would have found themselves in a

---

* El Vino's, a long-established wine bar on London's Fleet Street and familiar haunt for journalists, enforced a rule which forbade women from standing at the bar. The proprietors were forced to end this practice following a court ruling in 1982 which found it to be incompatible with the Sex Discrimination Act (1975).

rather uncomfortable spot. As it happened, by February 1973, they were able to inform the Home Office that the regulation concerning marriage was on the verge of being dropped, leaving married women officers subject only to 'the same mobility requirements as all members of the Diplomatic Service'.[2] Sure enough, a month or two later, this pledge was formally announced and thus a hugely damaging and objectionable practice which had imperilled the careers of dozens of women, and deterred countless others from applying to the Service in the first place, was at last consigned to the past.

The abandonment of the marriage bar naturally marked a major turning point for women in the Diplomatic Service.[*] It was no coincidence that it occurred in the early 1970s, just three years after the first National Conference on Women's Liberation and the passage of the Equal Pay Act, and only two years before the landmark Sex Discrimination Act of 1975 would outlaw sexist practices in the workplace, training and education. It was an era in which thousands of feminist activists – like Ms Sorenson of Pimlico – told with righteous fury the ugly truth about sexism in British society, from the objectification of women's bodies in the media to the harrowing experiences of battered wives behind closed doors. The most apparently mundane details of women's lives, such as who made the tea or whether one should wear trousers to work, now became subject to radical feminist analysis. The personal was political, meaning that no institution, be it the nuclear family or the mighty machinery of central government, could escape the critical scrutiny of the new sexual politics.

The Foreign Office was certainly not insulated from this sea change in attitudes, and yet even if, by the late 1960s and '70s, it could no longer be described as a creaking bastion of traditionalism, nor could it be said to be exactly leading the charge for sex equality. Much of the

* The Foreign Service was renamed the 'Diplomatic Service' in 1965 following the publication of the Plowden report, which recommended the creation of a unified service encompassing the Foreign Service, Commonwealth Service and Trade Commission Service, together with the merger of the Foreign Office and Commonwealth Relations Office in London. The Foreign and Commonwealth Office (FCO) came into being in 1968.

pressure for action on this front came from beyond its own marble precincts: from ministers and Parliament, from press and public opinion, and from the political advances being made by women worldwide. Female diplomats naturally played a part in forcing the Foreign Office to recognise that women's aspirations had changed, especially in relation to balancing professional ambitions with marriage and motherhood. Yet many disliked the 'militant' tone of second-wave feminism and continued to adopt the individualistic outlook of the post-war pioneer generation – even when faced by instances of blatant sexism, which, unsurprisingly, did not disappear from the Diplomatic Service overnight. If Women's Liberation called for revolution, female diplomats preferred evolution. Given the culture and history of the institution to which they belonged, this was probably a wise choice, but it came at the cost of what might have been a much speedier advance in women's status within the Diplomatic Service.

Katherine Smith was one of the final victims claimed by the Foreign Office's marriage bar. A Sussex graduate and fluent Russian-speaker, Smith joined Branch B in 1965 and was posted three years later to Moscow, where she fell in love with Roland Smith, a high-flying Branch A cadet. When he proposed, Smith knew she had a tough decision to make. She had learned of the marriage bar on her very first day at the Foreign Office, when a jolly man from personnel handed her a red ring-binder containing the standard regulations of service, saying as he did so, 'Of course if you were to marry, the Secretary of State would require your resignation.' Smith was taken aback by this news, but, like most other new female recruits who were young and unattached, decided not to worry about it until an occasion to do so presented itself. That moment occurred in 1970, when Roland's proposal coincided with the tantalising prospect of a new posting as information officer in Bonn which, as Smith later observed, 'would've been a nice job – a good one to have got at my stage'. After much thought and soul-searching, she sat down to write her letter of resignation. 'I never thought of challenging it,' she recalled. 'And I sometimes wonder whether . . . if I'd hung on or challenged it, something might have come of it.' As it happened, Smith was almost instantaneously hired back by the embassy to perform exactly the same job she had just resigned from, due to the sudden expulsion of her (male) replacement by the Soviet government. This brief period of being a working wife, however, quickly came to an end when Roland received his next posting to Brussels. Katherine accompanied him as a full-time spouse.[3]

It is possible that, had Smith argued her case with the personnel department in London, she would have been permitted to continue working for another year or two, but by no means certain. By the early 1970s, the marriage bar policy, considered so essential by the Gowers Committee at the end of the war, was becoming increasingly hard to justify to the outside world. For those journalists and critics who made a sport of berating the Foreign Office for its old-school-tie stuffiness, Diplomatic Service Regulation No. 5 on Marriage stood as the perfect symbol of antediluvian bureaucracy. Foreign Office chiefs vainly protested that amendments introduced in 1964 following Lord Plowden's wholesale review of Britain's overseas representation had watered down the policy considerably, allowing exceptions to be made. Yet this was cold comfort to the women's societies who had lobbied the review committee with demands for the marriage bar to be abolished in its entirety. In doing so, they recycled many familiar arguments from the 1930s about husbands with 'portable' careers, and asked why married women could not simply be subject to the same general rule governing the mobility of all employees, 'whereby any officer whose circumstances change in such a way as to prevent his serving wherever directed is required to resign'. Such a rule, they pointed out, covered any individual whose efficiency was seriously impaired by the intrusion of domestic responsibilities, without imposing blanket discrimination against all married women.[4]

Plowden's colleagues, who included several former (male) diplomats, remained unconvinced, with the sole exception of the Labour MP, Arthur Henderson, who protested that the marriage bar was unfair and pressed for its abolition. So insistent was Henderson that he even threatened to issue a minority report if at least some concession to his position was not agreed. The committee's final report, whilst concluding that there remained 'valid reasons for the existence of the "marriage bar"', therefore recommended a slight relaxation of its enforcement, allowing the Foreign Secretary to use his discretion in retaining the services of married women where circumstances allowed. The committee made it abundantly clear, however, that they did not expect these exceptions to be numerous: 'We doubt whether it will often happen that a woman will wish to remain in the Diplomatic Service after marriage. In most cases it will be her intention to settle down with her husband in this country or wherever he may be living.'[5]

The Foreign Office was unimpressed by the amendment, but none-theless felt that it was a concession it could live with. As one official remarked, 'the distinction between the old and suggested new regula-tion is a very fine one and an actual case is most unlikely to arise'.[6] The circular sent to all female officers in 1965 to inform them of the change was couched in notably discouraging terms. It warned that, whilst efforts would now be made to allow a woman to remain in service after marriage, there could be no guarantees. Moreover, she should be aware that no dependants' allowances would be payable in respect of any husband, and any requests for permanent service in London would be likely to affect her promotion prospects adversely.[7] These disincentives probably explain why no more than a handful of requests were received each year from women wishing to take advantage of the new arrange-ments. In the main they came from Branch B officers rather than high-flyers from Branch A, and the response they received was mixed, with some encouraged to transfer to the Home Civil Service, whilst others were begrudgingly allowed to stay on for a year or two, or offered lower-grade jobs on temporary contracts.* Either way, the picture did not exactly suggest that personnel officers were falling over themselves to help young women combine marriage with long-term careers.[8]

---

*An exception was Caroline Petrie who married Sir Maurice Bathurst QC in 1968 when she was in her late forties. She was permitted to retain her position, becoming head of the European Communities Information Unit in London and promoted to counsellor grade. She retired voluntarily, however, in 1972, when it became apparent that she would be unable to accept any overseas postings due to her husband's job. (See inter-view with Rosamund Huebener, 11 May 2000, British Diplomatic Oral History Project.)

The plain truth was that, even by the late 1960s, married women officers were still regarded as highly undesirable. One of the justifications for turning down requests for continued employment was that young married women, particularly if they wished to stay in London, would 'block' posts which fully mobile officers would find useful in their upward trajectory through the Service. This need to keep promotion routes unclogged was undoubtedly genuine (although half a dozen Branch B officers each year were hardly going to tip the balance one way or the other). The real objection against married women diplomats, however, ran deeper and was essentially unchanged from the interwar years. Put simply, it was the same old thorny problem of the diplomatic husband: what to do with him? A wife could be reasonably expected to devote herself to the full-time role of spousal helpmeet, but a husband could be expected to do no such thing. As the Plowden Committee put it, if he had a 'job of his own',

> this will normally preclude him from accompanying his wife on her postings abroad. If on the other hand, he is able to move from post to post with his wife, and few will in fact be able to do so, it is hard to see what contribution he can make to the work of the Service.[9]

Mary Moore testified to the existence of this intransigent mind-set amongst her senior colleagues, who found it utterly impossible to imagine a world in which female diplomats had husbands: 'I mean, how would you seat a husband at a dinner table? . . . They really, seriously found this just a no-no. They really couldn't see that you could deal with this problem of a married woman diplomat. It wasn't frivolous, it wasn't an excuse. It was a genuine problem to them.'[10]

It was still a genuine problem in 1969, when the Civil Service Commission pressed for clarification as to the position of female applicants for the Diplomatic Service exam who were already married. In response, one personnel officer conceded that there were 'a few categories of married women' who could probably meet the mobility requirements of the Service (namely, those legally separated from their husbands). But the general consensus was that married

women applicants should be actively discouraged. 'I can see no operational need at the present time to leave the door open even slightly
to the recruitment of married women,' scribbled one official in a
memo on the subject. His colleague agreed: 'From the operational
point of view married women with husbands can only be a drawback
& we should like to see the rules drawn as tightly as possible against
allowing them entry.'[11]

This attitude was reproduced in official recruitment literature
almost up to the moment that the marriage bar was officially scrapped.
A 1971 booklet aimed at undergraduates warned that women who
chose to marry might 'find it difficult to fulfil the obligations of overseas service and consequently be asked to resign', whilst a general
brochure on careers in diplomacy published the following year emphasised that the 'need for mobility may present special difficulties for a
married woman'. The overall picture painted of men and women's
respective roles in the Service was drawn in highly conventional and
sex-differentiated terms. Although the 1971 publication briefly profiled
a female Branch A officer, the 1972 booklet described the career trajectories of four 'typical younger members of the Service', which turned
out to include two male graduates, one in Branch A and the other in
Branch B, and two female school-leavers, one employed as a clerical
officer and the other as a secretary. In their profiles, the two men
talked about their intellectual interests, the nature of their work and
the challenges of learning a new language, and paid tribute to their
wives for providing invaluable support along the way. The women, by
contrast, gushed giddily about the thrills of travel and living away
from home and described busy social lives packed with parties and
visits by VIPs. 'For the girl who wants to travel, meet different people
and do different things,' the secretary reflected, 'I think there are few
more exciting jobs.' She then revealed that she would soon be resign-
ing to get married. The message for potential applicants could hardly
be clearer: men in the Service pursued serious long-term careers,
whereas women, by contrast, were only in it for a few years of fun
before settling down to life as wife and mother.[12]

Given this weight of opinion against the employment of married women, how on earth, then, was the Foreign Office finally persuaded to drop the marriage bar in 1973? Put simply, it was left with very little choice. By the early 1970s, it was clear that the introduction in Parliament of some form of legislation to outlaw sex discrimination was imminent. By clinging on to a policy of excluding married women, the Foreign Office was laying itself open to the very real possibility of future legal action. Added to this were pressures from inside government, which had finally decided that it was time to put its own house in order following the publication in autumn 1971 of a wide-ranging review of the position of women in the Home Civil Service. Chaired by Elizabeth Kemp-Jones, a senior (and married) official from the Department of Health and Social Security, the review was hailed by the press as a 'Women's Lib charter in Whitehall' for its attack on the sexist and discriminatory practices which kept women out of top jobs in government service.[13]

Although Kemp-Jones did not explicitly consider the Diplomatic Service in her final report, Foreign Office chiefs could not simply ignore her recommendations, which placed heavy emphasis on the need for flexible working practices designed to support women with family responsibilities. The Foreign Office was already badly out of step with home departments, which had employed married women since the Second World War and had a much stronger – albeit far from perfect – record of promoting women into the highest grades. To set its face against reform *yet again* risked placing the Service, as the chief clerk put it at a meeting of senior administrators in July 1972, at odds with 'the changing climate of opinion in the country'. It was therefore decided during that meeting – at which, incidentally, not a single female officer was present – that the marriage bar should now be dropped, although it would take nearly a year for the amended regulation to be finally signed off.[14]

This decision, significant though it was, did not create a new world for women in the Diplomatic Service. The official responsible for redrafting the marriage regulation remarked that merely changing the rules would not solve the practical difficulties of combining 'the domestic responsibilities of marriage with the mobility obligations of the Diplomatic Service'. In his view, it was reasonable to expect that most women would still 'resign on or shortly after marriage'.[15] This judgement was to be proved broadly correct. In 1973, the number of British males willing to trail across the world to support their wives' careers, or to shoulder the burden of childcare (a problem breezily dismissed before the war by feminists accustomed to full-time nannies and domestic help – both now well beyond the average middle-class income) was as yet infinitesimal. The tally of married women officers therefore remained low. In 1988, some fifteen years after the marriage bar was lifted, there were still only 284 married women across all grades of the Service.[16] It was telling that the Diplomatic Service Wives Association (DSWA), formed in 1960 to represent the interests of spouses, felt no urgent need to alter its name in recognition of the existence of diplomatic husbands until as late as 1991.

The group which appeared, on the face of it, most likely to benefit from the new policy consisted of those female officers who wed fellow diplomats and could now press for a joint posting, thus potentially enabling both spouses to continue their careers. The US, West German and Israeli foreign services were known to have made experiments in this direction, and Foreign Office chiefs were urged by staff representatives in London to do the same. Their response, however, was equivocal. Sophia Lambert, a London School of Economics graduate who joined the Senior Branch in the mid-sixties, caused some consternation in 1974 by drafting a comment for the staff newsletter which claimed that the administration had 'agreed to consider sympathetically the possibility of posting couples together'.[17] Nervous of being bounced into making a firm commitment to the principle of joint postings, the personnel department watered down the wording to 'on a case by case basis', conscious perhaps that there were many heads of mission who would never countenance having a husband and wife working together on their team. The objections varied from the dangers of 'pillow talk', to the inevitable messiness of workplace relations if and when marriages came off the rails. Then there was the loss of unpaid spousal labour to consider, as the female officer who, in earlier times, would have re-invented herself as a dutiful diplomatic wife after marriage, would now continue to work a full-time paid job. According to Rodric Braithwaite, who served as head of chancery in Brussels in the mid-1970s, the British ambassador there was 'furious' to discover that one of his younger male officers had a working wife, because 'he expected her to be around to do the entertaining'.[18]

In this particular instance, the wife in question had been posted not to the embassy where her husband worked but to the British mission to the European Economic Community (known as UKREP), which was also based in the Belgian capital.* To supporters of joint postings, major cities where Britain maintained multiple missions or large embassies seemed to offer the perfect solution to the 'pillow talk' problem: husbands and wives could live together whilst keeping their profes-sional lives relatively separate. However, this raised another – arguably more justified – objection: namely, that married diplomats would hoard the most prestigious posts such as Paris, Brussels, Washington or New York, whilst single officers might feel they were being relegated to smaller, less desirable ones simply because they were unmarried. This, Foreign Office chiefs were keen to avoid, and it was a combination of both resistance amongst heads of mission and fears of fuelling tensions between married and unmarried officers that progress in arranging joint postings proceeded only very slowly.[19]

Where joint postings were deemed impossible, the alternative option was Special Unpaid Leave (SUPL), which allowed an officer to accompany his or her spouse overseas for a period of up to five years without having to resign from the Service. The Foreign Office would undertake to match the officer in question to any suitable vacancy which might arise in the interim and make strenuous efforts to organise a joint posting once the five years had elapsed. On paper, it looked good, but in practice, SUPL did not solve all the problems

---

*The couple in question were Charlotte Rycroft and Nigel Wenban-Smith. They successfully negotiated another joint posting to the High Commission in Ottawa, Canada, between 1985 and 1989.

of the ambitious dual-career couple. Time spent on leave would not count towards 'seniority', meaning that promotion prospects were delayed, and there could be no guarantee of suitable jobs arising, either during or at the end of the five-year period. Nor was the policy gender neutral. In theory, leave could be taken by husbands *or* wives, but in reality the arrangement was designed almost exclusively with female officers in mind. Put bluntly, it was simply assumed that, in any given marriage – even one involving two equally high-flying Branch A officers – the wife would put her husband's career first and be the one to take SUPL, with all the consequences it might have for her own professional ambitions.

This is essentially what happened to Georgina Butler, who joined the Service fresh from university in the autumn of 1968. Initially, her prospects looked bright. Within just six months she was singled out by her bosses for a plum first posting to the Paris embassy, much to the envy of the two dozen or so other Branch A cadets recruited that year. By then, however, Butler had been swept off her feet by a fellow new recruit, Stephen Wright, who quickly proposed marriage before jumping on a plane to his first posting in Cuba. After some months of intense, long-distance courtship, Butler decided that she had to make up her mind. She knew about the marriage bar, but had not fully thought through the implications for her own career and future plans for a family. 'I suppose I'd always thought if I did get married that I'd work for a few years and maybe get to a few countries,' she later reflected; 'and then like my mother, I'd have the children and step aside for my husband who would go on and do his career.' In the short term, however, she was determined to keep working and, having submitted her official letter of resignation, managed to secure a 'semi-promise' of reinstatement from the personnel department in London. Sure enough, after a stint of working (unpaid) alongside her husband in the embassy in Havana, followed by some short-term contract work in London, Butler was fully reinstated in Branch A, with a desk in the South European Department. The marriage bar now lifted, Butler's career, it seemed, was back on track.

Soon, however, it was time to go overseas again. Naturally, Butler hoped for a joint posting, but here personnel proved far less accommodating. Her husband's posting – to British Information Services in New York – had already been arranged and Butler was told that no job was available for her, although she extracted a promise that the first suitable vacancy at Britain's Mission to the United Nations (UKMIS) – also in New York – would be hers. After a few months of kicking her heels on SUPL, Butler lost patience and got herself a job at the Press and Information Department of the UN Secretariat, where she was kept busy editing its enormous yearbook. Then, in 1977, two things happened. The Foreign Office came good on its offer of a proper post at UKMIS, and Butler discovered that she was pregnant. Had it been almost any other job, she would probably have found a way of making it work, but the one on offer involved long periods of travel to the UN's office in Geneva. With a new baby, it would be impossible. Moreover, maternity pay and leave arrangements were far better at the UN Secretariat. So she turned it down:

> And I felt bad about it because I felt that all the men who had said, 'You shouldn't let these wretched married women in,' were going to be proved right: you know, here they are, they're offering me this job and I say, 'No, sorry'. But it just didn't fit. Nowadays they'd be much more flexible about trying to find out how to accommodate you, but in those days it was: 'You're jolly lucky to be offered this plum job in the UN Mission.'

Butler remained on SUPL, juggling her work at the UN Secretariat with the demands of motherhood and giving birth to her second child, when, in 1979, her husband received word that he was to be posted to Brussels. Butler saw her chance to recover her diplomatic career: 'I said, "Right, now is the time we'll go together, a joint-posting, my five years is going to be up and I want a posting."' She was disappointed to discover, on arriving in the Belgian capital, that the Foreign Office 'had done zero' to find her a job, but after determined prodding they came up with a short-term post in UKREP, followed by a secondment to the European Commission. Butler enjoyed both posts, but was annoyed by the initial attitude of commission officials, who assumed that they 'were being fobbed off with somebody's wife'. When Stephen's posting came to an end in late 1984 and he was recalled to London, Butler had to face up to the fact that, for all the determination with which she had fought her way back into the Diplomatic Service, her career prospects had suffered badly from the choices she had made – or been forced to make. She was offered a job as deputy head in the Information Department, not a high-prestige job, but she felt that she could not really complain:

> I couldn't expect to go back into one of the frontline departments having sort of semi dropped out and having let them down in New York. I can remember those sorts of feelings going round in the back of my head, that I deserved a department that was less than front rank.

With her husband's star continuing to rise, Butler became increasingly pessimistic about her own chances of ever getting to the top. She had simply interrupted her career too many times, and when in 1988, Stephen was posted head of chancery in Delhi, a post where the services of a full-time spouse were still deemed highly desirable, she decided that it was the moment to retire gracefully. 'That's when I thought my career was over, other than being the spouse.'[20]

As it happened, Georgina Butler's career was not quite over. She worked again for a private company in Brussels and, after her marriage broke down in 1998, was reinstated and ended her Foreign Office career as ambassador to Costa Rica and Nicaragua. But what Butler's story reveals is just how difficult it was, even once the formal bar on marriage had been lifted, for women to balance family life with a successful career.

Sarah Squire's experience as a married female diplomat was not wholly dissimilar. When she and her husband went to the personnel department in 1976 to request a joint posting, they were told that one of them must be nominated as the 'lead career', with the other spouse fitting in if and where possible. As Squire's husband was twenty years her senior and had already secured a much-coveted job in Washington, there was no debate as to whose would be the 'lead career'. Even so, Squire was appalled to find herself, only five years out of university, idle and unemployed, and she watched the months on SUPL ticking by with increasing desperation: 'I just thought I was going to be out of the Foreign Office, out of my career, just going out with a whimper.'

Like Butler, Squire spent the following years alternating between stints on SUPL and periods back in work, giving birth to two babies and intermittently taking on the duties of a diplomatic wife. She was not overly impressed by the Foreign Office's efforts to organise joint postings. When her husband was appointed ambassador to Israel in 1984, Squire expected, as a fluent Hebrew speaker with relevant experience (she had served in Israel in 1972–5) to be in the running for a first secretary job in the embassy. It turned out, however, that the personnel department had not even read her file and, when she pressed them further, she was told that as the ambassador's wife she could hardly expect to be working. Two years later, Squire persuaded the Foreign Office to give her a first secretary post which had fallen vacant, but won her argument almost purely on the grounds of cost (it was far cheaper to employ her than send out a new officer and his family – an argument which, fortunately for Squire at least, had real force amidst the public-spending cuts of the 1980s).[21]

It was no coincidence that of the female diplomats who climbed highest in career terms in these decades, most remained unmarried. Not until 1987 was a married woman, Veronica Sutherland, appointed to an ambassadorship, closely followed by Juliet Campbell, but it was perhaps significant that both had married relatively late in life and were childless.[22] More generally, the numbers of women – married or single – rising up the ranks were conspicuously low and lagged well behind those of other government departments. In 1974, women made up about fourteen per cent of Branches A and B combined, with only six serving in the counsellor grade, traditionally the springboard for prestigious ambassadorial appointments.[23] Two years later, forty-eight-year-old Anne Warburton made that historic leap, becoming the first British woman to win an ambassadorship. To give credit to the

Foreign Office, Barbara Salt had received this honour back in 1962, when she was offered the post of ambassador to Israel, but serious illness intervened to prevent her from taking it up. The fact, however, that it was fourteen years before senior officials deemed any other woman worthy of this distinction did not say much for female diplomats' career prospects in the interim.* Once it had been decided, however, the Foreign Office made much fuss of Warburton's appointment, calling a press conference and inviting television cameras inside to film Britain's first female ambassador enjoying a cosy chat on the sofa with the permanent secretary, Sir Michael Palliser.[24] As Palliser later recalled, 'The Foreign Office were very keen for us to show that we were letting women into top jobs, and of course Anne did a very good job.'[25]

It was not coincidental that Warburton's destination was Denmark, the country which had welcomed Ruth Bryan Owen, the USA's first female chef de mission, back in 1934, and which was generally viewed, like its Scandinavian neighbours, to be in the feminist vanguard. Palliser recalled that Copenhagen was 'certainly chosen with the feeling that in Denmark a woman ambassador would be totally acceptable in the way that in Saudi Arabia she would not be', a sentiment with which Warburton herself was in full agreement: it was 'a posting where you could actually achieve something. There were no limits on what you could do because you were a woman . . . It was just taken for granted that a woman was able to do the job.'[26] Nor did the absence of a spouse apparently pose any insurmountable problems for the self-sufficient and energetic Warburton. One journalist who interviewed her in 1978 remarked on how admirably she appeared to be coping with 'a two-pronged life . . . doing the job of both husband and wife'. In response Warburton commented modestly: 'socially speaking, a husband would be useful, but I suspect that a bachelor ambassador would miss a wife more'.[27]

* Eleanor Emery became the first female head of mission (as distinct from ambassador) when she was appointed high commissioner to Botswana, a former British colony, in 1973.

For all Warburton's success as Britain's woman in Copenhagen, her appointment did not, however, settle the wider question of how far the Foreign Office was willing to go in sending women diplomats beyond what were considered 'safe' postings, which for the most part meant Europe and North America. Rather like Mary Moore's first job in Budapest in the 1950s, there remained certain posts which women were sent to fill as a matter of course, and which therefore acquired an identity – and arguably an inferior one – as a 'woman's post'. Sarah Squire was annoyed to find in 1972 that she was the third new female recruit in succession to have been posted to Tel Aviv as third secretary, a fact which she suspected meant that the job was viewed as 'slightly second rate' by Foreign Office authorities. She certainly did not find the political work especially scintillating: 'I was just sitting around, a spare wheel a lot of the time.'

Squire's posting was determined also by the fact that Israel was considered the only suitable destination for a female diplomat within the Middle East.* Although most restrictions on women's access to 'hard' language training were lifted around the same time as the marriage bar, female recruits were still refused the opportunity of learning Arabic in view, as one official put it, 'of the relevant countries' attitudes to women diplomats'.[28] Japanese remained off limits for the same reason, and staff representatives who queried this policy were smartly told that the Foreign Office had no choice but to 'take account of the fact that social attitudes remain in a number of countries which make it difficult for women to operate effectively in some jobs'.[29] Just how far this argument, which had been deployed back in the 1930s by opponents of women's admission to the diplomatic profession, was still justified in the 1970s is difficult to judge. The political status of women globally was in flux, and not just in societies with Western-style feminist movements. The previous decade had produced the world's first

* The first Branch A woman to be posted to Israel was Barbara Salt in 1957. She served as consul-general.

female heads of government – Sirimavo Bandaranaike in Sri Lanka, Indira Gandhi in India, and Golda Meir in Israel – whilst the emerging women's agenda at the United Nations, kick-started by the Conference for International Women's Year in Mexico City in 1975, provided a global platform for prominent women from the developing world, like Princess Ashraf of Iran and Jehan Sadat, the First Lady of Egypt.

The elevation of such elite females, many of whom belonged to powerful political dynasties, did not, of course, necessarily signify dramatic advances in the general lot of women in their respective countries, which in many cases remained characterised by poverty, frequent pregnancies and second-class citizenship status. Yet the growing visibility of women as political leaders, particularly in high-profile international venues like the United Nations, was impossible to ignore and became reflected in the ever-lengthening list of destinations for British female diplomats. Anne Stoddart speculated that the decision to appoint her head of chancery in Sri Lanka in 1974 was at least partly influenced by the presence of Prime Minister Bandaranaike, and she thought it likely that other foreign ministries had much the same idea. There were, she remembered, at least three women ambassadors in what was not at that time a terribly large diplomatic corps.[30] Similarly, the towering figure of Indira Gandhi made India an easy place for a woman diplomat to operate, at least in professional terms, as Veronica Sutherland discovered when she went there in 1975.[31] As Sutherland put it, 'Mrs Gandhi was the Prime Minister and if they could cope with Mrs Gandhi they could certainly cope with me.'[32] Slowly, in the course of the decade, other previously closed frontiers were opened to female diplomats, including countries formerly deemed suitable only for women filling subordinate roles as typists or clerks. British missions in Turkey, Japan and Argentina all saw Branch A women officers join their staffs, and in 1980 the Foreign Office took the step of appointing Patricia Hutchinson ambassador to Uruguay in South America, where one of her predecessors, Sir Geoffrey Jackson, had been kidnapped and held for eight months by guerrillas.[33] Hutchinson's own life came under threat when Britain went to war with Uruguay's neighbour, Argentina, over the Falkland Islands in 1982. During this intense period, security guards accompanied the ambassador at all times, even stationing themselves outside her bathroom door.[34] This was quite a departure from 'safe' Denmark where Anne Warburton had been posted only six years previously. China was finally added to the list of woman-friendly postings in 1983, when Claire Smith arrived in Beijing as a second secretary, having persuaded reluctant Foreign Office authorities to train her in Mandarin.

Arab states remained the hardest nut to crack. Veronica Sutherland had a stint in the personnel department in the mid-1970s and recalled that the question of posting women diplomats to these countries simply never arose. 'If a woman had come to me and said, "I really, really would like to go to a Middle Eastern post," I think I'd have thought about it, but nobody ever did. It was a tacit understanding that it just wasn't the best use of resources.' This consensus that Arab countries were out of bounds for women (except in subordinate roles or as wives) was, however, eventually challenged. Taken as a whole, women's political status in the Arab world undoubtedly lagged behind that of other regions, but there was considerable variation between countries. To take, for example, voting rights, Algeria, Tunisia and Egypt had granted equal suffrage back in the 1950s, whilst Jordan only did so in 1974 and Iraqi women would have to wait until 1980.[35] Similarly, there were important differences in levels of female literacy, access to higher education and representation in professions such as law, medicine and academia, making unqualified statements about how female diplomats would fare in 'Arab' societies open to challenge. When Margaret Rothwell became head of the Training Department in the early 1980s, she decided to confront head on the received wisdom about women's unsuitability for Arab posts. Rothwell started by identifying all the jobs in the Service in which knowledge of the Middle East and/or Arabic was desirable, and then asked the relevant ambassadors and departmental heads whether, in their view, those jobs could be performed satisfactorily by a woman. In an incredible seventy-five per cent of cases, the answer that came back was 'yes'. Even in Saudi Arabia, where women remained heavily secluded, it was felt that there were jobs for female officers, such as consular posts which dealt primarily with travellers and British businessmen. As a result of this survey, Arabic language training was finally opened up to female officers, whilst women graduates with degrees in Arabic could now join the Diplomatic Service confident that their linguistic skills would be put to good use. It would still be some time before any woman would hold a top post in an Arab country, but the basic principle had at least been conceded.[36]

Rothwell recalled her victory in 'opening the Middle East up to women' with some pleasure. Back in the early 1960s, she had shared digs with another female Branch A recruit who was, as Rothwell put it, 'Arabic mad', and who was therefore crestfallen to discover that, as a woman, she would have no opportunity to train in the language. Rothwell, who would have quite liked to learn Arabic herself, felt great satisfaction in settling this score on both their behalves twenty years later. Rothwell was, however, no 'feminist', at least not in the sense of wishing to pose a radical challenge to male authority along the lines advocated by the contemporary Women's Liberation Movement. In fact, very few of Britain's women diplomats openly identified themselves as 'feminists' in these years, despite the growing influence of Women's Lib. There were certain practical obstacles to doing so, such as the rules which restricted civil servants' political activities, and the expectation of regular overseas postings, which made it difficult to stay closely in touch with causes or campaigns at home. More importantly, though, there were philosophical objections. Although second-wave feminism drew followers from all walks of life, it would be fair to say that the intellectual type attracted by the prospect of representing the British Crown overseas was less likely than others to be stirred by radical doctrines of sexual revolution. The Diplomatic Service had never, even in its earlier history, demanded ideological conformity from its members, yet diplomats were, by definition, patriots and servants of the state, and those with deeply felt anti-establishment views did not generally flourish in the profession. For this reason, diplomacy was never likely to provide fertile soil for the cultivation of an ethos of feminist sisterhood. Britain's female diplomats did not follow their chosen career in order to smash glass ceilings, and never felt that, by virtue of stepping into a male-dominated profession, they were somehow striking a collective blow for all women within a larger, epic struggle against institutionalised patriarchy. Pauline Neville-Jones spoke for many of her generation when she later reflected: 'I never thought of myself as being somebody who somehow had to do this for women. I certainly wanted to do it for myself . . . What motivates you I think, well for me anyway, is a professional attitude to my job and a desire for personal achievement.'[37]

That said, the women of the British Diplomatic Service were not, of course, passive bystanders in the feminist battles of the 1970s. Although never 'a campaigner or one to make public alliances', Sarah Squire read the works of Germaine Greer, Betty Friedan and Simone de Beauvoir as a young woman and felt that their ideas about sexual equality 'went in at a profound level', perhaps explaining, at least in part, why Squire was so determined to stay in the Service and pursue her career after marriage and motherhood. Similarly, Sophia Lambert was, in her own words, 'a bit of a women's libber' who was happy to 'press the boundaries', which she did by wearing a trouser suit to work and insisting that women be permitted to use 'Ms' rather than 'Miss' in their passports. It was Lambert who pushed for many of the administrative reforms of the early 1970s in her capacity as secretary of the Diplomatic Service Association (DSA), the staff association representing Branch A officers. She pressed in 1973 for clarification on various matters affecting female officers, including married allowances, special unpaid leave, part-time employment options and reinstatement for women who had resigned before the marriage bar was lifted. Lambert's later comments on joint postings which so unsettled the personnel department were, as she eventually admitted, designed to nudge the administration into making more specific commitments to the principle of finding jobs for both spouses wherever possible. It was an issue, Lambert recalled, which 'I pushed forward because it was something one had to do. It was obviously unfair the way women were treated.'[38]

All the same, Lambert's interventions were hardly the work of a diehard revolutionary. Her offending draft for the DSA newsletter reads remarkably mildly. It notes approvingly the Foreign Office's willingness to act on the recommendations of the Kemp-Jones report and concludes by suggesting that 'women are now very fairly treated in the Service, and have little cause for complaint'. Lambert added a final sentence inviting anyone who felt she was 'not being militant enough in the cause of Diplomatic women's lib' to write to her with their grievances, but no great flood of replies followed.[39] As Lambert later reflected, 'women's issues' were not especially high on the DSA's agenda, and there was never any concerted demand from Branch A women for a dedicated officer or separate organisation to represent their views. Interestingly, this provided a striking contrast to the situation in the USA, where female Foreign Service officers (the equivalent of Britain's Branch A) had formed their own lobby, the Women's Action Organisation (WAO), in 1970 for exactly this purpose. Acting as 'initiator and watchdog on women's issues', the WAO fought over the next decade for improved gender ratios in recruitment, an end to discrimination against married women officers, better training opportunities (including language tuition), and more women on panels adjudicating on promotions. The WAO won concessions from the State Department on nearly all of these points, including the lifting of the marriage bar in 1971, and could point with satisfaction to a sharp rise in recruitment rates of women: the proportion of women amongst the annual intake of new officers jumped from a measly seven per cent during the 1960s to over twenty per cent.[40]

One might ask why American women diplomats were apparently so much more proactive than their British counterparts when it came to fighting sexism in the workplace. Discrimination against women did not appear to be especially worse on the other side of the Atlantic. Indeed, the US Foreign Service had opened its doors to women much earlier – in 1922 – and by 1962, the year that Barbara Salt was offered the ambassadorship to Israel, had already appointed no fewer than six female heads of mission.[41] Moreover, women diplomats in the US had better access to hard language training, with the first woman to learn Arabic, Winifred Weislogel, commencing her studies in 1962, some twenty years before the British Foreign Office would follow suit.

In other respects, however, the US Foreign Service was every bit as unwelcoming towards women. As in Britain, female officers were massively outnumbered by men, were expected as a matter of routine to resign on marriage, and were frequently passed over for top postings due to the sexist prejudices of heads of mission. Mary Olmstead, who joined the Foreign Service in 1945, recalled that during the early years of her career she was forced to accept jobs at a lower grade than those of her male peers and on one occasion was flatly turned down for a post that she dearly wanted in the Lebanon by a senior official who said that 'over his dead body would the Department send a woman to Beirut'.⁴² Alison Palmer's treatment was even more disgraceful. A graduate of Brown University, she first entered the Foreign Service as a secretary, but in 1958 sat and successfully passed the exam for the prestigious officer class. Her promotion, however, was delayed for almost a year by an obstructive boss, which rankled with Palmer who had watched male colleagues in identical situations given hearty pats on the back and warm send-offs. Worse was to come. After a posting in the Belgian Congo followed by a year's training in African Studies at Boston University, Palmer was rejected for *three* postings in a row, in Tanzania, Uganda and Ethiopia, by ambassadors who objected to being sent a woman (the third apparently wrote that 'the savages in Ethiopia would not be receptive to a woman, except maybe to her form').⁴³

Faced with such blatant discrimination, Palmer was torn: should she play it safe and simply accept a personnel or consular posting which would allow her to get on with her life, or should she fight back? Eventually, she chose to fight back, and in 1972 became the first woman to file a sex discrimination suit against the State Department. Her victory – her employers conceded that Palmer had been treated unfairly on grounds of sex and her career had been adversely affected – was only the beginning. As word spread of her legal challenge, Palmer began to receive dozens of messages from other women desperate to share their horror stories of sexism and prejudice at the hands of the State Department. Her case was self-evidently not an isolated one, and Palmer decided to use the funds from the settlement to prepare a larger, class-action suit alleging that sex discrimination at the Department was systematic and entrenched. The case, which involved more than five hundred women, dragged on for years, coming to trial only in 1985. The initial ruling was unfavourable, but was reversed by the Court of Appeals and eventually the State Department was found guilty of engaging in a wide range of discriminatory practices against women. The final ruling resulted in large payouts and compensatory promotions, but the very act of mounting a legal challenge had nudged the State Department into taking pre-emptive steps to address its own failings, including affirmative action measures and an explicit commitment in 1977, direct from the pen of Secretary of State, Cyrus Vance, to uphold 'Equal Employment Opportunity' in the Foreign Service and all of its activities.[44]

Divergent histories and different political traditions probably explain why women in the US Foreign Service took a bolder – and more litigious – tack than their British counterparts in demanding their rights in this period. The intense confrontation with questions of black civil rights and early adoption by the federal government of affirmative action programmes meant that debates about equal opportunities in the workplace were further advanced in the USA than in Britain by the early 1970s. The British Civil Service did at this time begin to acknowledge the existence of discrimination within its own ranks, but it was not until 1986 that the Foreign Office faced its own Alison Palmer case, involving a female officer of twenty years' service, who, like Palmer, was turned down for a posting explicitly on grounds of sex. Susan Rogerson had been offered the job of deputy high commissioner in Zambia, but very soon after accepting it learned that the posting was to be cancelled due to the objections of the head of mission. His reasoning was this: there was already a female diplomat employed in the political section of his chancery, and the addition of another would, in his view, compromise the embassy's efforts to promote British interests in what was widely acknowledged to be a 'male-dominated society'. In short, he wanted a man instead.

This was not, of course, the first time a head of mission had resisted the posting of a woman to his team. It was, however, the first time that a female officer had threatened to sue for discrimination in response. Even so, the case did not escalate into a full-blown and prolonged attack on ingrained sexism at the Foreign Office, as had occurred in the USA. Backed by the Equal Opportunities Commission (which had been created to enforce the provisions of the 1975 Sex Discrimination Act), Rogerson began legal proceedings in the autumn of 1986, but quickly dropped them when the Foreign Office admitted its error and offered her a post of equal seniority as consul-general in Perth, Western Australia. The episode generated some bad press in the short term, but it did not open the floodgates to a tidal wave of complaints of alleged sex discrimination from female employees.[45] Possibly this was because such incidents had, by the mid-1980s, genuinely become extremely rare. Certainly there appeared to be no general resistance to sending Branch A women to African posts, which the Foreign Office had done since the 1960s, when large numbers of former colonies won their independence. Yet it was also symptomatic of a longer-running tendency amongst British women diplomats to meet sexism with pragmatic forbearance rather than outspoken indignation.

Whether a more combative stance would have forced the Foreign Office to take bolder action on promoting women into top jobs, opening up language training, setting up joint postings, experimenting with part-time options and job shares, improving maternity-leave arrangements and childcare provision is difficult to say. These were reforms which would largely have to wait until the 1990s. The US Foreign Service certainly seemed more willing by the 1980s to appoint women diplomats to high-profile posts in Arab countries, although this might have been as much a reflection of America's political and military pre-eminence as it was a result of internal pressures from female employees. One senior State Department official said as much in the late 1970s when asked about the potential risks of sending a woman diplomat to a Muslim country: 'If the human being walking into the office represents the United States of America,' he replied, 'you bet your neck they'll deal with that person. And if she's a good person, they'll like it.'[46] Advocates of women's admission to the British Diplomatic Service had once made much the same argument, but they had done so at a time when such professions of faith in the nation's power and prestige were justified by the reality of Britain's vast imperial dominion and military and economic muscle. By the 1970s, decolonisation and economic strife at home had greatly reduced Britain's global standing and had cast her out of the premier league of international super-powers. If it required a certain degree of national self-confidence to send an unveiled white woman in to negotiate with an Arab dictator – as the USA did in 1989 when it appointed April Glaspie ambassador to Iraq – then this was a quantity with which the British Foreign Office was not exactly overflowing during these years.[47]

Quite apart from defending itself from radical feminists like Ms Sorenson, or dealing with the administrative headaches of arranging joint postings, the 1970s was a difficult period for the British Diplomatic Service. A series of reports, beginning with Plowden in 1964, continuing with Sir Val Duncan's 1969 review and ending with the controversial 1977 report of the Central Policy Review Staff, questioned nearly every aspect of – and nearly every penny spent on – Britain's overseas representation. Keen to placate a media determined to recycle old stereotypes of diplomats as profligate, public-school amateurs, governments from the mid-1960s onwards consistently demanded that the costs of diplomacy be reduced and that the Diplomatic Service embrace a more commercial mind-set focused on boosting British business interests abroad. The call for more economic expertise at the Foreign Office was nothing new, but Britain's relative economic decline in the post-war decades did have the effect of raising expectations of diplomats as salesmen for British exports – a recalibrating of priorities which suited some temperaments more than others. At the same time, the Service was adjusting itself to a new set of realities governing Britain's foreign policy: the loss of empire and the (albeit belated) turn towards Europe; the growth of 'summitry' and multilateral negotiations in which politicians, rather than trained diplomats, took the lead; and the gradual encroachment upon traditional Foreign Office turf by other Whitehall departments with rival expertise on questions of trade, debt, defence, environment, energy and international development. All these existential threats to the entrenched power and status of the Diplomatic Service had to be mastered and contained during this troublesome decade.[48]

Against this backdrop, it is perhaps unsurprising just how little interest Britain's female diplomats showed in the nascent international women's rights agenda drawn up at the Mexico City conference of 1975, and further elaborated over the subsequent UN Decade for Women. That sometimes unruly Mexico meeting, which was followed up by inter-governmental gatherings in Copenhagen (1980) and Nairobi (1985), undoubtedly helped to establish questions of women's equality as legitimate subject matter for international discussion and debate, and to promote women's political leadership on a global scale. Yet for the ambitious female diplomat in the British Foreign Office, the appearance on the international scene of this 'women's' agenda had little significance. There was no expectation that female officers should, by virtue of their femininity, declare a 'special' interest in and aptitude towards such matters. Most probably recognised that the route to career advancement was unlikely to lie in associating oneself with an emerging policy area whose relevance was judged both by ministers and senior officials as marginal at best. Evidence of this was supplied by the Foreign Office's response to the declaration by the United Nations of International Women's Year (IWY) in 1975, which, in addition to the lacklustre preparations for the Mexico City conference, took the form of a modest grant of £10,000 to the Women's National Commission, the umbrella body for women's Non-Governmental Organisations (NGOs) in the UK. This meagre sum reflected the view pithily expressed by the assistant under-secretary, Ronald Scrivener, to the permanent secretary in July 1974: 'I cannot say that I regard support of the International Women's Year as a priority aim of United Kingdom foreign policy.'[49] Scrivener was unlikely to have been speaking only for himself on this point.

In fact, Foreign Office chiefs regarded International Women's Year as more of a political menace than an opportunity to advance British interests. The idea for the IWY was known to have originated with Soviet representatives at the UN, with the result that many senior officials judged it deeply suspect from the beginning. Some even objected to the paltry grant earmarked for the Women's National Commission on the grounds that 'IWY was a Communist-inspired occasion' of which the United Kingdom ought to steer clear.[50] Foreign Office funds did, in the end, go towards supporting a number of IWY-related events, but officials remained vigilant against any possible Soviet machinations. Especially embarrassing in this respect was the bureaucratic mishap which resulted in Russian ex-cosmonaut Valentina Tereshkova being invited to a formal reception at Lancaster House at which members of the royal family were to be present. (Fortunately, Tereshkova declined the invitation, to much relief all round.[51])

This tendency to view the international women's agenda through Cold War-tinted spectacles had been evident several years earlier, when, in 1967, Elizabeth Waller, who had been previously engaged in publicity work amongst women in the Middle East, was appointed 'Women's Affairs Officer' for the entire Foreign Office. Based in the Information Research Department, Waller spent much of her time identifying and cultivating women's NGOs (what she termed 'good WINGOS') who could be relied upon as allies in the West's struggle against global communism, and it was in this capacity that she attended the 1975 Women's Conference in Mexico City as a member of the British delegation.[52] In this rather shadowy role, Waller had very little to do with any of the women recruited to Branch A. She regarded diplomatic wives as potentially of far greater use for purposes of propaganda amongst women of foreign nations.

This was an arrangement which most women diplomats – who were not keen to spend their time attending endless charity bazaars or coffee mornings – were more than happy to endorse. Yet just as the position of women officers in the Diplomatic Service was in flux during the radical decade of the 1970s, so too was the traditional role of wives. As the Foreign Office was soon to discover, it could no longer be safely assumed that diplomatic wives would offer unstinting loyalty and devoted service to husband and country. This would have serious consequences for the old model of the extended embassy 'family' which had stood at the heart of diplomatic communities for a century or more.

Still Married to the Job

Around 9.30 p.m. on Thursday, 18 December 1958, Thomas Bromley returned home to the large mansion in a leafy corner of Surrey where he lived with his wife, Diana, and two young sons, Martin, aged thirteen, and Stephen, aged ten. It had been another long day at the office and Thomas was looking forward to a good night's sleep before rousing himself and making the drive back to London the following morning. The last eight months had been a hard slog, working long hours on sensitive defence matters at the Cabinet Secretariat, where he was on secondment from the Foreign Office. It was a pity the boys would be in bed, Thomas thought, as he clicked opened the front door; they had returned home from boarding school only two days before for the Christmas holidays, and he had not yet had a chance to sit down with them and hear their news.

Nothing immediately seemed amiss as Thomas entered the hall, but his attention was quickly drawn to the odd sight of a child's cricket bat lying on the floor, apparently covered in blood. Had one of the boys had an accident? A rush of nauseating unease swept through Thomas's body as he moved further into the house and opened the drawing-room door. Inside he found his wife in a highly agitated state, dressed in wet, slightly bloodied clothes, and seated next to her were two elderly neighbours with anxious expressions on their faces. 'Where were the boys?' he demanded. They did not know. Now Thomas was frantic. He started moving through the house calling their names, but there was no answer. In one of the upstairs bathrooms, Thomas's worst fears were realised. The body of ten-year-old Stephen lay motionless in the bathroom, an ugly wound slashed open across his delicate young throat. Numbed with shock, Thomas continued his grisly search and eventually discovered the lifeless body of Martin in the garage. It was clad in blood-stained pyjamas and was stretched out on a makeshift bed next to the exhaust pipe of the family car.

Later police investigations established that at some time in the late afternoon or early evening of that same day, Diana Bromley had drugged her sons with barbiturates and carried them unconscious into the garage. There she had laid them on the floor, before backing the car into the garage and then kneeling down beside them, leaving the car engine running. When it became obvious that the billowing fumes were not having their desired effect, she strangled Martin with a cloth belt and took Stephen back into the house and drowned him in one of the upstairs bathrooms. She then slashed both boys' throats with a razor before turning the blade on herself. Having failed to kill herself by this method, Diana Bromley plunged into the lily pond around the back of the house, hoping for oblivion, but the shallow waters refused to take her to her death. It was shortly after this second suicide attempt that neighbours found her pacing the garden, hysterical and half-dead, and persuaded her to come inside. They enquired after the two boys, but, ominously, she gave no reply. Soon after, Thomas Bromley pulled into the drive and made his grim discovery. His wife was taken to hospital that night with a police escort and later charged with the murder of her sons. After another suicide attempt in prison which resulted in permanent brain damage, Diana Bromley was declared insane and unfit to face trial, and it was ordered by a judge at the Surrey Assizes that she be detained indefinitely at Her Majesty's pleasure.

Press reports do not reveal what became of this unfortunate woman after this date. Thomas Bromley continued his diplomatic career with high-profile ambassadorial postings to Algeria and Ethiopia, until retiring at the end of 1969. *The Times* reports that he quietly remarried in 1966.[1]

It will never be known what drove Diana Bromley to murder her two
sons on that fateful December day. Neighbours on the exclusive country estate where the family lived declared themselves dumbfounded by
the news. The Bromleys were 'so happy and united', one said, 'the
whole thing is inexplicable'.² From the outside it certainly might have
appeared that Diana Bromley led an enviable life. She lived in a beautiful house in an affluent Home Counties town, had two healthy and
high-spirited sons and a husband with a successful career in government service. Her own background was privileged; she was the daughter
of Sir John Pratt, a former Foreign Office under-secretary, and a niece
of the famous Hollywood actor William Pratt, better known by his
stage name, Boris Karloff. According to press reports, Diana had studied History at university and worked at the Foreign Office during the
war, where she met her future husband. They married in December
1944, and within a year Martin was born. There followed a series of
overseas and home postings for Thomas, another pregnancy, and then
in 1957 the family returned to England and moved into their mock-
Tudor mansion in Haslemere.

There was nothing especially unusual about this spousal career
trajectory; countless wives had followed it before, and Diana Bromley
was not unaccustomed to the peripatetic life, having herself grown up
the daughter of a diplomat. It could hardly be said that she had not
known what she was getting into when she married Thomas Bromley,
a rising star who had started his career in the Japan Consular Service
before winning more prestigious postings to Washington and Baghdad.
But there were, nevertheless, those who had grown increasingly
concerned about Diana's mental state – like Masha Williams, a fellow
diplomatic wife, who brought up her case informally with officials at a
Foreign Office Christmas party in 1957. The answer she received was
dismissive: wives should not be mollycoddled, she was told, and if they
could not 'take it', then their husbands were clearly in the wrong line
of work.³ Diana Bromley's mental problems might very well have
begun years earlier, but it seems significant that her final breakdown

occurred during a UK posting, when she was living an isolated, uneventful existence in her Surrey home, seeing her children only in the school holidays and sending her husband off to London every morning, from whence he would return late in the evening. It is tempting to diagnose Diana Bromley as suffering from a classic case of what Betty Friedan would, just a few years later, call 'the problem that has no name' in her feminist classic, *The Feminine Mystique*: a reference to the despair experienced by intelligent, college-educated women condemned by marriage and motherhood to a life of dreary home-making in identikit suburbs and provincial towns.[4]

The expectation that middle-class wives would sink their energies into housekeeping and childcare was, of course, nothing new, but by the post-war decades the ideal of motherhood as vocation was being pushed and pulled into unfamiliar territory by a barrage of contradictory forces. On the one hand, wifely submission was replaced by more egalitarian modes of 'companionate' marriage, whilst outside the home the confluence of labour shortages, smaller families and newly available part-time employment created opportunities for mothers of school-aged children to re-enter the workforce and earn an independent income. On the other hand, psychoanalytical notions of 'maternal deprivation' promulgated by experts like Donald Winnicott and John Bowlby popularised the belief that mothers were uniquely responsible for their children's mental welfare, thus injecting the old adage that a woman's place is in the home with a new psychic charge. The disappearance of servants from most middle-class homes, plus ever higher standards for domestic cleanliness and comfort, only added to the burdens of the post-war British housewife. It was perhaps little wonder that many women developed a habit for the little tablets willingly prescribed by the doctor to settle their 'nerves'.[5]

These developments affected diplomatic wives to different degrees. In some respects, their role had hardly changed at all since the days of Mary Fraser or Hariot Dufferin. Diplomatic missions overseas were still tightly knit communities which relied upon a feminine presence to protect the bonds of fellowship from wear and tear. As late as 1976, Lady Henderson, an ambassadress of long experience, described the embassy workforce as akin to 'rather an old-fashioned family', in which younger diplomats and their wives came under the domestic authority of the head of mission as they had a century before. Assisting the ambassador and his wife at an official function in the residence, Lady Henderson explained, 'really means doing what you would do if your parents gave a party'.[6] The social ambience was perhaps less glamorous than in the days of the old diplomacy, but the social duties which befell wives could be no less exacting and the hierarchies just as robust. Each wife slotted into a pecking order determined by her husband's grade, and she was expected to run his household, entertain his professional contacts and do her duty to the rest of the embassy family just as she had in times gone by. Sally James, the wife of a first secretary, wrote to her mother from Ceylon in 1967 describing how attendance at the wives' sewing group was more or less mandatory: 'I loathe it,' she complained, '[but] as I am on our Charity Committee, and one of the senior wives (don't laugh), I have to seem keen to encourage the junior ones.'[7]

In other ways, of course, the lot of the diplomatic wife had dramatically improved since the nineteenth century. Air travel eliminated those long, dangerous sea voyages to reach remote postings, and made regular family reunions during the school holidays infinitely more possible. Advances in medical care greatly reduced the risk of death or disease in those euphemistically named 'unhealthy' posts, whilst electricity and central heating removed some of the less congenial aspects of living abroad. These material advances were accompanied, however, by new physical and mental strains with which the middle-class wives of the 1950s were arguably less equipped to deal than their pre-war antecedents, who could take for granted that housework and childcare would largely be seen to by servants and full-time nannies. At the time of Diana Bromley's breakdown, moves were, in fact, already being made to address some of these problems. Masha Williams had returned to the UK with her family in 1956 at short notice following the outbreak of civil unrest at her husband's posting in soon-to-be-independent Tunisia. Flu-ridden herself and struggling with two small children struck down with whooping cough, Masha arrived in London with nowhere to live, no GP, no childcare and not a single offer of help from anyone at the Foreign Office. Soon her husband was posted overseas again as an inspector, which meant a long, gruelling tour of British missions, whilst Masha was left to battle on alone at home. Fortunately, she ran into three wives whose husbands were on similar inspectorate postings, and together they began to hatch a plan. 'We felt like conspirators as we compared notes over coffee and decided that the strain on us all was intolerable,' Williams later recalled. 'We agreed to meet informally and to sound out any other Foreign Service wives whom we happened to meet. All admitted they were living on their nerves but insisted that they spoke in confidence. They did not wish to be labelled grumblers.'[8]

This reluctance to rock the boat placed Williams in a tight spot when it came to presenting the Foreign Office with a carefully compiled memorandum detailing the major problems affecting wives and setting out suggested remedies. No one wanted to sign it. 'We were afraid of attracting unfavourable attention to ourselves and of spoiling our husbands' careers,' she remembered, 'and we worried about being labelled "bolshie", the most devastatingly effective way of silencing criticism.' Encouraged by a sympathetic doctor who had treated hundreds of Foreign Service personnel and their families, and with the further help of Osla Henniker-Major, wife of the then head of the personnel department, Williams finally threw off her inhibitions and delivered the memo in her own name towards the end of 1958. Magically, doors began to open once the Bromley murder case had been splashed across the front pages of the national press, and Williams and her fellow wives were quickly invited into the Foreign Office to discuss their grievances.

The outcome was the creation of the Foreign Service Wives Association, a voluntary organisation which aimed to offer a lifeline to women 'living on their nerves' both in the UK and abroad. Every wife of a service officer, of whatever grade, was automatically a member and received invitations to the association's regular tea parties and excursions in central London and its twice-yearly *Newsletter* (later *Magazine*), which contained practical information about allowances, boarding

schools and babysitting services, as well as entertaining articles penned
by wives posted overseas. In 1965 it was renamed the Diplomatic
Services Wives Association (DSWA) following the merger with the
Commonwealth Service, by which point the organisation had firmly
established itself with an office and paid secretary in Whitehall, regional
groups in London and the Home Counties, and local branches formed
or in embryo in dozens of missions abroad.

At last, diplomatic wives had a collective voice which could bend
the ear of the administration. An early indication of the seriousness
with which Foreign Office chiefs now regarded the welfare of wives
came in 1963, when representatives of the association were invited to
give evidence to the Plowden Committee, the high-powered (and all-
male) body appointed a year earlier to undertake a wholesale review
of Britain's overseas representation. Mrs Beckmann, Mrs Cope and
Mrs Wilson, together with four wives from their sister association at
the Commonwealth Relations Office (a body known affectionately as
'the Crows'), appeared on 13 May and put a range of proposals before
Lord Plowden and his colleagues. Top of the list were increased educational allowances for parents who had no choice but to send their
children to boarding schools during postings, and more generous
travel expenses for visits during the holidays. Next was help with
expensive rents for the temporary accommodation which families
were inevitably forced into on their return to the UK, and following
that came demands for improved medical facilities in post, more help
with recruiting reliable servants, and larger pensions for wives whose
husbands died in service.[9]

Although not all of these requests were granted, when the committee
published its report the following February there was ample evidence
that the message from wives had been received loud and clear. The role
of the diplomatic wife, Lord Plowden concluded, 'is important both
from a private and public point of view. A wife has to cope with the
special family problems inherent in a career of constant movement and
at the same time make a contribution with her husband to the work,
welfare and way of life of an overseas Mission.'[10] In recognition of this
fact, the report recommended that boarding-school allowances be

raised 'substantially'; that the Foreign Office pay for two annual return fares for children visiting their parents rather than just one; and that a more flexible approach to the cost of furnishing official residences be adopted across the board. The wives were delighted, particularly by the increased travel expenses, which were implemented almost immediately. Mrs Wilson told members at the AGM in May 1964 that families 'have had the thrill of an Easter holiday spent together, with the happy feeling that there are only three months to go till the children come out again at public expense'. The Plowden Report, she thought, was a landmark for 'the very generous recognition it gives to the part played by the wives'.[11]

Despite this growing assertiveness, the wish list which the association put before the Plowden Committee suggested that few wives were as yet seriously questioning the basic assumptions underpinning their role within the Diplomatic Service. The core business of the DSWA presupposed that their members did not have paid jobs and were primarily responsible for childcare, housekeeping and hostessing. Tea parties and outings took place on weekday mornings or afternoons, special courses were organised in cookery, upholstery and first aid, advice was imparted on such subjects as letting houses, finding schools and hiring nannies, and lists were compiled of members willing to visit wives in hospital or collect children from airports. Not all of this activity, it was true, necessarily had a domestic or pastoral flavour. Conscious of how little they knew about current affairs in their own country, hundreds of wives participated in fact-finding visits to national institutions such as the Houses of Parliament, the BBC Television Centre and the head office of Marks and Spencer, and toured schools, hospitals and new housing estates to witness British public policy in action. The DSWA also arranged public-speaking courses, pressed for wives to be included in Foreign Office briefings ahead of their husbands' postings, and demanded more access to language tuition, a request which was eventually granted in the early 1970s, when spouses became entitled to a hundred hours of private tuition at public expense.

Yet all this improving educational activity was ultimately pursued with a familiar and uncontroversial aim in mind: that of supporting husbands' careers and the work of the mission. When Fionn Morgan was interviewed for *Woman's Hour* in 1968 and quizzed about the role of the diplomatic wife, she offered a highly conventional reply: 'I think that the most important thing is to make a home for your husband and your children as soon as you can when you arrive in a foreign post,' she said: 'And then to entertain the people of the country, to make lots of friends and to further British interests by so doing.' Her fellow wife, Enid Venable, agreed that women who married diplomats had to be be prepared to meet the obligations of the role. 'It's a duty,' she insisted, 'it's part of the job. You don't do it from choice . . . The wife must do her share, entertaining for her husband, and she can be very very helpful making contacts for him and, for instance, joining local organisations and charities.'[12] A wife who knew about housing policy or trends in British industry, and who could talk to dinner-party guests in their own tongue, was undoubtedly a valuable asset to her country; but an unpaid asset whose status derived solely from her husband's occupation she remained.

Yet even as Morgan and Venable reaffirmed the traditional model of loyal spouse, others were beginning to contemplate this life of housewifery and hospitality with far less equanimity. An editorial in the *Newsletter* of spring 1969 took issue with the 'hat and gloves brigade' image of diplomatic wives peddled in the national media and appealed for contributions from members currently in paid employment, either in the UK or abroad.[13] With the proportion of married women with jobs steadily growing at home in Britain, the whole question of whether diplomatic wives could or should work became a pressing – and extraordinarily vexed – issue for the DSWA. It dominated much of the discussion at committee meetings and AGMs for the next decade and filled nearly every issue of the *Newsletter* with strongly worded letters and commentary from members, many of whom held wildly divergent views.

The Foreign Office, for its part, had no general policy on the matter, but left it to heads of mission to judge whether, in any given case, the employment of an officer's spouse might compromise British interests. Exactly how a wife taking a job might do this was not always clear, but an oft-cited problem was the waiving of her diplomatic immunity, which she held courtesy of her husband's official status, and which included exemption from paying taxes and protection from prosecution under local laws. Forfeiting a wife's immunity in order to enable her to work might, it was argued, lead to all sorts of legal disputes and bureaucratic entanglements, and many heads of mission were therefore reluctant to give their blessing. This was especially the case within the Soviet bloc and other countries where judicial systems were deemed to operate in a rather rough and ready manner, but it could affect Western posts too. Jill Wilson, a trained architect, ran up against this problem in Washington, where the US State Department insisted she waive her immunity if she wished to practise, whilst the British embassy insisted she keep it.[14]

As DSWA investigations subsequently discovered, there were further practical obstacles in the form of local restrictions against the employment of foreign nationals and the accreditation of professional qualifications. Many wives found it impossible to secure work permits, particularly in countries where unemployment was high, and the fact that Britain already allowed foreign spouses in London to work meant that the Foreign Office had little bargaining power when it came to negotiating reciprocal arrangements. For younger wives with university degrees or professional training under their belts, whose numbers were growing by the 1970s, these constraints were deeply frustrating. Many had started promising careers before marriage and were dismayed to discover how difficult it would be both to practise their professions overseas and, later on, to pick up the threads during home postings in the UK.

Those wives who *did* manage to secure paid work were, therefore, generally forced to take temporary or part-time jobs of relatively low status. A DSWA survey carried out at the end of 1975 revealed the proportion of working wives within the membership to be around twenty-two per cent, with well over half of these employed in the embassy, consulate or high commission to which their husbands had been posted.[15] For many wives, casual employment – albeit, as Bridget Cowper-Coles observed, on 'local and appalling rates' – within the Service seemed a good solution: it sidestepped the work permit and immunity problems, could be fitted in around domestic responsibilities and, for women like Katherine Smith or Georgina Butler, who had resigned from permanent posts, it allowed them to put to use their previous knowledge and experience.[16] One DSWA member in Washington noted in 1973 that there were eight or nine wives currently employed by the embassy, whilst another correspondent in Tripoli described how the secretarial staff of the chancery had been composed wholly of wives since August 1972, following mob attacks on the British embassy.[17] Alternatively, some wives picked up work at neighbouring Commonwealth embassies or international bodies such as the World Bank or the United Nations, whilst another popular choice was to teach English as a foreign language. Sally James, who had trained as an actress, was unusual in finding part-time work performing plays for the New Zealand Broadcasting Corporation during her husband's posting to Wellington, made possible by the High Commissioner's relaxed attitude towards working wives. James also earned a small income from painting portraits and selling batiks, whilst in Ankara she taught English to Turkish military officers and French at the British Embassy School. In Singapore she worked briefly for the British Council, making educational films to support the teaching of English in local schools, as well as offering private language tuition to Japanese bankers and their wives.

All the same, even if these kinds of jobs allowed wives to keep one foot in the labour market, they were no substitute for a proper career. The uncertainty regarding overseas postings made it difficult to stick at any profession when based at home in Britain, and employers were naturally reluctant to promote workers who were unlikely to stay for longer than two or three years, and might be called away at any time to follow their husbands. One wife who taught in a comprehensive school in London remarked in the *Newsletter* in 1977 that 'one cannot in all honesty go for the senior jobs and promotion, knowing all the time that in a year or two one will be off'.[18] A survey carried out five years later found that nearly half of all respondents had given up a career (as opposed to a 'job') in order to accompany their husbands overseas, and had been forced to adapt themselves to whatever employment was on offer: one barrister, it was reported, had retrained as a potter.[19] Responding to a subsequent DSWA enquiry, another wife confessed that she had even been tempted to lie to employers about her husband's profession so as not to damage her chances of promotion.[20]

Nevertheless, many wives remained determined to work, however unsatisfactory the job. Their reasons were various. Some worried about their future employability should they remain out of the labour market for too long, whilst others valued the additional income which even a poorly paid casual teaching post could supply. For most, however, work was a crucial source of self-respect and an escape route from social duties and domestic drudgery. Gillian Bryan applied for a post as a nursery teacher at a kindergarten in Bangkok because she had become 'bored with the "social" round of morning coffee and sewing for bazaars', and wanted to do 'something constructive which would not merely be a time-filler'. Similarly, the chancery wives in Tripoli agreed that their secretarial work had 'given us a feeling of involvement in the work of the embassy and an insight into the day-to-day problems of bilateral relations not normally obtained on the "coffee-party circuit"'.[21]

By the mid-1970s, this desire to be something more than 'just a wife and mother' was palpable amongst many DSWA members. Elizabeth Fawcett summed up what she saw as the key arguments in favour of working wives in a letter published in autumn 1974. Paid work, she remarked, protected a woman against future divorce or widowhood, provided her with a sense of independence and personal contentment and, moreover, broadened her knowledge of the local culture in ways which could be positively advantageous for British interests. 'Whereas a homebound wife's acquaintance,' Fawcett pointed out, 'may be limited to her husband's contacts and the frequenters of the diplomatic cocktail round, a working wife will often bring into the Mission's orbit a new and useful cross-section of the local working community.'[22] Jill

Pellew, a young Oxford graduate posted with her husband in Vietnam around the same time, certainly felt that her part-time teaching job at the University of Saigon was just as valuable – both to the Vietnamese people and to the British embassy – as any unpaid charity work she might have been doing, and had allowed her to develop useful contacts amongst her Vietnamese colleagues and students.[23]

Pellew was unnerved, however, by comments made by fellow embassy wives to the effect that she should give up any idea of working once her husband had moved up to first secretary rank, as she would then be expected to devote all her energies to supporting him in his official, representational duties. The belief that employment interfered with a wife's social obligations and was therefore undesirable was widely shared amongst many older members of the DSWA. Lady Henderson spoke for this section of opinion in 1976 when she told new service wives at a 'Going Abroad' course in London that employment was possible in the 'junior' ranks and only 'sometimes, but not often, in the senior ones'. She personally never regretted giving up her own job on marriage, as she found her new role 'working with and for one's husband' far more rewarding. 'Being the wife of a member of the Diplomatic Service,' Lady Henderson concluded, 'is a job in itself and a career. In some posts it is a full-time and exacting career.'[24] Other DSWA members warned younger wives against taking too belligerent an attitude towards the old ways. At the AGM in 1972, chairman Joan Wilford denigrated the 'militant' behaviour of Foreign Service wives in the USA and pleaded for more tolerant views to prevail amongst British wives. 'If the Head of Mission's wife should ask you to share in the preparations for the Queen's Birthday Party,' the report of her speech read, 'it was no moment to get up-tight and start sounding off. Poor woman probably needs all the help she can get.'[25]

Wilford was referring to the policy recently adopted by the US State Department to exempt spouses from all formal obligations towards the Service, meaning that wives were no longer expected to rustle up three-course dinners or buffet lunches, provide small-talk at official receptions or carry out worthy voluntary work on behalf of their countrymen. But if Wilford was ambivalent towards this emancipation of US wives 'from abuses to their liberty', almost the exact same sentiments were shortly to be expressed by Margaret Ibbott in a strongly worded letter published in the *Newsletter* in 1976. Ibbott declared herself incensed by the survival of old-fashioned assumptions which regarded the diplomatic wife as 'virtually an employee' of the Service and subject to its authority, even though she 'has not been trained, she is not paid, and perhaps most important, she has no real authority herself'. The diplomatic wife's position, Ibbott angrily pointed out, 'is entirely a courtesy one. Everything she has in the way of status and position is by virtue of her marriage. Any respect accorded to her is out of respect for her husband's position.' Ibbott deeply resented the pressures which had been applied by fellow wives to make her feel 'apologetic that I should wish to have a job of my own'. If others wished to devote themselves exclusively to helping their husbands in their work, that was their choice, but they should not victimise women who chose to follow a different path. Such intolerance, in Ibbott's experience, caused 'more unhappiness and resentment than anything else' in an overseas mission. The 'blunt truth', she insisted, 'is that wives owe the post and the Office nothing at all'.[26]

Unsurprisingly, Ibbott's letter drew a great deal of comment from other readers, who wrote both to echo her views heartily and to express profound disagreement. What the unfolding debate uncovered was a very real tension existing between those wives who, like Ibbott, wished to disavow the traditional duties of the diplomatic wife and strike out on their own, and others who genuinely found self-fulfilment and a sense of purpose in the conventional wifely role. Sheila Taylor wrote from San Salvador to second Ibbott's assertion that wives 'are not FCO employees and have as much right to preserve their individual identities overseas as at home'. Jean Reddaway, by contrast, who was then ambassadress in Warsaw, thanked the Foreign Office for having given her the opportunity to travel the world with her family and for looking 'after our every need, with good housekeeping, medicine, travel, and domestic help'. There was no doubt in Reddaway's mind that life had been 'infinitely the richer for taking on this job which is, after all, a family affair'. Anne Ponsonby in Mongolia concurred, adding that young women ought to 'understand the problems before they marry into the Service', and, if they cannot see their way to adapting to its demands, 'it would be better if they persuaded their future husbands to look towards another career'.[27]

Two related issues crept into the debate over working wives during the course of the 1970s, further polarising opinion. The first was the extent to which spousal behaviour could be said to have a material effect upon male officers' career prospects. Jill Pellew found this idea 'appalling', and expressed her sincere hope that it no longer had any root in reality. As late as 1979, however, DSWA chairman Margaret Heath acknowledged that, although the personnel department had assured them that it was only 'the officer who counts', it still appeared that a head of mission's attitude towards a member of staff could be influenced by 'the acceptance or non-acceptance of a traditional role by a wife'.[28] This fed into concerns about the burden which fell upon others when working wives chose to 'opt out' of entertaining or charitable work: if one wife refused to slave over her cooker for the Queen's birthday party, or collect second-hand toys for the local children's home, it necessarily followed that other wives would have to pick up the slack – and often with strong feelings of resentment.

The second theme exercising DSWA members was the profound status-consciousness which continued to characterise relations between wives in many overseas missions. Some younger women found casual references to 'junior' or 'senior' wives offensively anachronistic, whilst others deplored the practice – still common – of sitting at DSWA branch meetings in order of their husbands' seniority. Heath testified to the enquiries she received from wives anxious to know whether it was really necessary to submit to 'a "fagging" system which they regard as outdated, or risk getting "black marks"'. The traditional view that wives served under the authority of the ambassadress proved an especially emotive issue. Lady Henderson provoked a reaction in her 1976 'Going Abroad' speech by referring imperiously to 'her' wives, and one *Newsletter* correspondent was shocked to read that Lady H. had been openly discussing the 'problems' of two younger wives with the embassy doctor.[29]

The fact that wives were now posing such searching questions about their position was, of course, a sign of the times. Just as the Foreign Office was forced to reflect the realities of wider social changes in its treatment of female employees, so too was it under pressure to rethink its whole attitude towards wives. It was naive to believe that the model of unpaid spousal labour which had served British diplomacy so well in the past could survive the revolution taking place in women's lives in the 1970s unchanged. Combining work with marriage and mother-hood was no longer an unusual or daring choice: by 1981, nearly half of all married women in Britain were employed, more than double the proportion in the early 1950s. Moreover, the traditional image of the family unit headed by a male breadwinner was being further eroded by rising rates of marital breakdown following the introduction of 'no fault' divorce in 1969. Numbers of divorce petitions more than doubled after this date, whilst the proportion of marriages ending in divorce shot up dramatically, a trend which provided the DSWA with much food for thought, particularly when it came to the welfare of divorced or separated wives.[30]

Driving these trends was a range of complex influences, from the 'post-materialist' values of the baby-boomer generation to the fading moral authority of the Church, but, as was the case for women diplo-mats in this period, the impact of second-wave feminism had arguably the most consequential implications for the position of wives. The DSWA was hardly a hotbed of radical feminist thought, and there was little evidence amongst its membership of any active or sustained involvement with the Women's Liberation Movement, now on the march in Britain and other advanced Western democracies. 'The DSWA is still not militant,' Margaret Heath declared in 1979, 'I do not think we are women's libbers.'[31] And yet the presence of distinctly feminist values, such as autonomy and selfhood, was unmistakeable in the highly introspective debates over working wives and social duties which so dominated the DSWA in the 1970s. If, in earlier decades, wives had experienced similar conflicts of identity, they lacked the critical vocab-ulary required to put it into words. Second-wave feminism supplied a framework of analysis which enabled women like Margaret Ibbott and

Jill Pellew to articulate their frustrations with the traditional model of spousal service. Feminist sociologists even coined a specific term – the 'incorporated wife' – to describe the peculiar status of women whose identity after marriage became defined by their husband's occupation.[32] The diplomatic wife appeared to represent the paradigmatic case of this social phenomenon, with her right to an independent identity submerged beneath a weight of assumptions about her prior loyalties both to her husband and to his employer. The social anthropologist Hilary Callan, herself married to a diplomat, made these assumptions explicit in an influential essay of 1975 which pointed out the highly paradoxical nature of the diplomatic wife's obligations to an organisation with which she had 'accidental but no contractual links'.[33]

The DSWA implicitly acknowledged the stresses and strains which this paradox might produce when in 1976 it tentatively engaged the services of a professional sociologist, Dr Eric Miller, to help with the training of wives as counsellors. Miller persuaded the committee to allow him to initiate a much broader debate amongst the membership about the difficulties they experienced as diplomatic spouses, including conflicts of identity prompted by recent changes in the roles and aspirations of women in Western societies. He set the ball rolling with a short paper based on conversations with fifteen wives, which was published in the *Newsletter* in 1978. It brought to the surface problems with which many wives had been gallantly struggling alone for years: guilt about leaving their children in Britain; pain at losing friends every few years when their husbands were moved on; resentment towards the 'veiled moral pressure' exerted by higher-ranking wives; feelings of emptiness created by the absence of purposeful work and, perhaps worst of all, fears that admitting to any one of these problems would jeopardise their husbands' career prospects.[34]

Miller's paper generated a huge response. The DSWA office was inundated with letters on the subject, whilst many overseas branches formed special discussion groups to examine the issues he had raised. An open forum was held in London the following year and Miller was asked to write another paper, this time on the peculiar problems faced by wives of heads of mission.[35] As before, rather than proposing solutions, Miller urged DSWA members to speak openly about their feelings, creating conditions in which, as Margaret Heath suggested at the 1979 AGM, 'members felt freer to talk or write about what was on their minds'. It was impossible, she added, to 'talk easily with a Stiff Upper Lip . . . I think there is nowadays more readiness to discuss matters'. It was a departure which sadly came too late to help poor Diana Bromley, but it demonstrated just how anxious the DSWA remained to banish her ghost.

The British diplomatic wife of the early 1980s was thus a very different creature from her 1950s counterpart. In the first place, she was much more likely to work. One survey put the number of wives in paid employment overseas at just over forty per cent, nearly double the figure for 1975, and found that many more would have gladly taken a paying job if one were available.[36] Of those who did not work, the terms on which they were willing to attend to their traditional social duties had become far more conditional. Selfless devotion to husband and mission was rare. Wives now demanded that their contribution be formally recognised, in the form of more generous allowances and improved pension rights, perhaps even through cash payments for hostessing or compensation for loss of earnings. This newfound assertiveness began to displace the old stereotypes of feminine subordination which had been commonplace in media portraits of the diplomatic wife. One piece in *Homes & Gardens* described a 'new breed' of wife who was 'educated to independence' and saw 'no need for loyalty to, or total involvement with, their husbands' jobs'.[37] Journalist Simon Jenkins was similarly surprised by the frankness with which the wives he interviewed for a BBC documentary on the Foreign Office in 1984 criticised the Service and its treatment of spouses.[38] The days when wives feared being thought of as 'bolshie' had clearly gone for good.

In fact, by the mid-1980s, Foreign Office chiefs had gone some way towards meeting wives' demands for a better deal. In addition to free language tuition, wives were now included in country briefings and were promised preferential treatment for job vacancies within embassies where their skills and qualifications matched requirements. The DSWA managed to persuade a number of posts to employ wives on a part-time basis as community liaison officers, enabling them to get paid for welfare services which they would otherwise be providing for free. Another victory was won in 1985 when the Foreign Office agreed to pay a third fare, meaning that children could visit their parents in post during the summer, Christmas and Easter holidays, rather than just two of the three.

Other requests, however, stood little chance of success amidst the climate of austerity which set in after the election of Margaret Thatcher in 1979. Pressure to reduce expenditure had been felt for some years at the Foreign Office, but it was not until the early 1980s that the DSWA began to register serious alarm at the implications for the welfare of wives and children. The closure of embassies and consulates, together with job cuts, salary controls and early-retirement schemes naturally raised fears about husbands' career prospects, whilst the seemingly endless calls for savings threatened the existing system of allowances which wives relied upon to maintain a decent standard of living abroad. One member wrote anonymously to the *Magazine* in 1986, detailing the despairing mood of wives at her post, whose husbands were over-worked because of personnel shortages, and whose homes were run-down with no money to spare for new furnishings or repairs. And yet still they were asked to sacrifice more. 'Every Whitehall boffin who comes this way sucks his teeth, shakes his head in horror and seeks to shrink the only amenity that makes life bearable,' she wrote. Was it any wonder that women who had given up the chance of having their own careers were now asking 'why should I?'[39]

As the Thatcherite axe fell on public spending, morale within the Diplomatic Service took further knocks: from public criticism of alleged failings during the run-up to the Falklands War of 1982; from growing security threats to British civilians in conflict zones; and from chilling assassinations of British diplomats at the hands of Irish and Palestinian terrorist cells. Diplomats and their wives had faced mortal dangers in earlier times, of course, but could fall back for mental suste-nance on the thought that they served an enlightened global superpower whose mission was to make the world a safer and more civilised place. These moral certainties vanished in step with Britain's overseas colonies during the post-war decades, a loss which, combined with growing aspirations amongst women for jobs of their own, meant that by the mid-1980s some wives were pressing their husbands to switch profession, whilst many bachelor males were having difficulty finding wives willing to play the trailing-spouse role in the first place.[40] Catherine Hughes recalled working with two thirty-something male colleagues who were desperately trying to persuade their girlfriends to tie the knot. 'Both of them were having a very hard time, because you'd got to the phase where women wouldn't marry and follow, and they were distraught . . . I felt very sorry for them.'[41]

Husbands were, more generally, moving up the DSWA's agenda during these years. Male spouses of female diplomats began to materialise shortly after the abolition of the marriage bar, but they hardly rushed to beat down the DSWA's door, demanding entry to its membership. In fact, the earliest contribution to appear in the *Magazine* from a male spouse was in 1985, when Guy Digby set out a light-hearted proposal to form a Diplomatic Service Husbands' Association which would organise 'beer mornings' and 'poker afternoons'. Digby's letter was evidently not meant to be taken wholly seriously – a postscript revealed that it had been sent in as a 'dare'.[42] Yet only later that year the *Magazine* was reporting that the Danish equivalent of the DSWA had already recruited equal numbers of male and female members and was at present led by a male chairman.[43] In 1986, the DSWA Committee announced that the association's name and future policy on admitting men was actively under consideration. Two years later it was agreed at the AGM that husbands would be eligible for associate membership, and two years after that the DSWA was finally renamed the British Diplomatic Spouses' Association – or BDSA.*

This move did not, however, usher in a new era of spousal equality.

* It was renamed the Diplomatic Service Families Association in 1999.

The DSWA chairman calculated in 1988 that there were 214 men married to female officers who were not themselves also members of the Diplomatic Service – 'people', she suggested, 'who are potentially in exactly the same situation as us'.[44] But in reality, diplomatic husbands inhabited a very different world from wives. As men, they were not held to the same exacting standards of behaviour, as one DSWA member writing from Tokyo pointed out. Male spouses, she observed, 'have much greater freedom allowed them to get a job or follow whatever path they may choose. They are not expected to cater for cocktail parties, arrange flowers and *placements* for official dinners, or even necessarily accompany their wives to official engagements.'[45] This feeling of separateness was borne out in *Magazine* articles penned by husbands, which, like Digby's earlier letter, often struck a tone of semiamused embarrassment. Paul Hartley, a young husband who had accompanied his wife to Chile, opened his account of attending a DSWA meeting by noting that he did 'not wear a blouse and skirt because my Ambassador will not allow me to do so', and went on to describe how he was 'ribbed by all and sundry wherever I went' after word got out that he had agreed to join the wives.[46] Alex Sutherland, husband of Veronica, wrote of his experience of becoming the 'first ever British male Ambassadress' with similar levity. He attended the wives' session at a heads of mission training day in order to see 'what dragon Ambassadresses looked like in embryo', and had to stifle his giggles when told by the speaker 'that never, never, never should we leave the bedroom in the morning without having put on our make-up and our earrings'.[47]

Alongside male spouses, the DSWA also had to make up its mind as to where it stood vis-à-vis unmarried female officers, who, curiously, had been included as associate members from the earliest days of the Foreign Service Wives Association. The rationale for this was, as Margaret Heath noted in 1979, 'somewhat odd', although she suggested that the link between wives and 'single girls' – as female officers were persistently referred to regardless of age – was 'the experience of living and running our homes overseas'.[48] It was certainly true that friendships naturally developed between wives and female officers in many posts. 'Single girls' were known to get involved in the activities of local DSWA branches, and many ambassadresses took an interest in the welfare of female members of staff in the same way that they looked after young bachelor males newly arrived in post. But beyond this, it was nonsense to suggest that the two groups had anything in common. Unlike wives, female officers had a formal, contractual relationship with the Foreign Office, performing jobs which were clearly defined and properly remunerated. The 'homes' they ran overseas did not contain husbands or children, and most of the problems discussed in the pages of the *Newsletter* and *Magazine*, from boarding-school allowances to widows' pension rights, were therefore totally irrelevant to their lives.

Furthermore, tensions could arise between the two groups. Writing as a 'single girl' in 1983, Norma Reid described the loneliness she felt returning to an empty flat at the end of the working day, and the resentment with which she regarded the additional allowances and superior accommodation enjoyed by married colleagues.[49] Reid tired too of the prurient speculation she attracted as an unattached female. 'There will always be someone who, having spotted a certain car outside a certain flat, puts two and two together and makes five,' she wrote: 'Married, you are shielded, and the pressure is resultantly diminished.' This unwelcome scrutiny could develop into jealousy or even suspicion on the part of wives, who resented the peculiar kind of intimacy that grew up between colleagues of the opposite sex thrown together by the pressures of work. Eric Miller observed that some wives 'adopted' younger female secretaries or typists by regularly inviting them into their homes partly as a means of containing this threat.

The perceived danger was perhaps especially acute in the case of high-flying Branch A women, who were less amenable to being 'adopted' and who were pursuing the sort of professional career that many university-educated wives might once have hoped for themselves. Before going to The Hague on her first posting, Catherine Hughes recalled being told by a male superior, 'now, you won't have any problems with the members of the service, Catherine, the only problem could be the wives' – a statement which she read as a coded warning against getting romantically involved with any of her married male colleagues. Hughes thought this useful, if rather obvious, advice, but always made a point of befriending colleagues' wives and seeking out their views when serving in overseas posts. In Bangkok she was struck by how eagerly they asked her about their husbands' work, suggesting that many male diplomats told their wives very little about their day-to-day jobs. In these and other matters female officers had to tread carefully. As Margaret Rothwell reflected, 'you were still single, so you could be regarded as a danger. And you had to be aware of that and sensitive to it.'[50]

Thirty years after Diana Bromley murdered her sons and attempted to take her own life, the lot of the British diplomatic wife was still, in many important respects, unenviable. She lived a restless, roving exist-ence, moving to a new posting every few years where she had to make a new home in an entirely unfamiliar culture, often without speaking the language or having the faintest clue about how to get the telephone connected or where to buy a box of teabags. If she had young children, she started her hunt for playgroups, swimming pools and reliable babysitters; if they were older, she bravely said her farewells until the next school holiday. One wife told Eric Miller that these constant part-ings tore at her heart like a series of 'small-scale bereavements'. Returning to the UK could be just as disorientating, with the need to reclaim rented-out houses, track down doctors and dentists, and seek out former acquaintances. One wife likened it to getting out of prison, having felt on arrival back home utterly out of touch with a world she had once known so well. For many, hardest of all was the impossibility of pursuing a proper career, a frustration which the wives of the 1950s and '60s were largely spared, living as they did in an era when even university-educated women were not generally expected to work after marriage. 'It has become hard to live in someone else's shadow', as one wife put it, especially now that so many other women in Britain were emerging into the sunlight and laying claim to careers of their own.

Yet in other respects the ghost of Diana Bromley had been laid to rest. Wives who were miserable or depressed now had someone they could talk to, whether it was the liaison officer for the local DSWA branch, the family welfare officer at the Foreign Office in London, or simply a fellow wife with a sympathetic ear. Over the course of the post-war decades, the DSWA not only forced the Foreign Office to take wives' problems more seriously and devote proper resources to welfare and counselling, but encouraged its own members to reflect collectively upon their frustrations and to come up with their own solutions. Not all their dilemmas could be resolved; many still remained. But, as one wife looking back in 1992 on Eric Miller's earlier reflections on the role of the diplomatic spouse remarked, whilst the problems hadn't gone away, 'we are better able to confront them'.[51]

Epilogue

Members of the Club

Until the autumn of 1995, Pauline Neville-Jones's thirty-three-year career in the Diplomatic Service appeared enviable in practically every respect. She had been marked out as a high-flyer almost from the start, enjoying a string of overseas postings which any ambitious young officer – of either sex – would have been proud to advertise on their CV: third secretary in Rhodesia during the Unilateral Declaration of Independence; first secretary in Washington at the time of Watergate; chef de Cabinet to Christopher Tugendhat, Britain's European Commissioner in Brussels; number two in Bonn in the run-up to German unification. Her desk jobs in London were no less impressive. She was made head of Planning Staff, the Foreign Office's in-house think tank, at the age of forty-three, and ten years later became the first woman to chair the Joint Intelligence Committee (JIC), a body of top-ranking spooks, diplomats and defence chiefs with a remit to oversee all aspects of Britain's intelligence and security operations. After that came the post of political director, traditionally second in status only to the permanent secretary, in which capacity Neville-Jones led Britain's negotiators at the peace talks in Dayton, Ohio, which brought the long-running conflict in the Balkans to a close. To any casual onlooker, by the mid-1990s the star of the highest-ranking woman in the Foreign Office was well and truly in the ascendant.

Behind the scenes, however, things were not quite as they seemed. Neville-Jones was irked to discover on becoming political director that

the post had been subtly downgraded, with a loss of status and responsibility. Eager therefore to move on, she vacated the job in late 1995 in
the expectation of landing a top ambassadorship for her final overseas
posting before retirement at sixty. Two high-level spots in particular
were in play: Paris and Bonn – both grade one embassies of first importance to Britain's policy in Europe, where proposals for a single currency
and expansion of the European Union to the east were dominating the
political agenda. Neville-Jones made no attempt to disguise the fact
that she dearly wanted Paris. She was a confirmed Francophile and had
already served time in Germany. In any case, the Bonn job was not due
to fall vacant for at least a year, and Neville-Jones had already left her
post as political director. It had to be Paris.

The dream posting, however, was not to be. From time immemorial, Paris had been handed over to a seasoned diplomat as a
pre-retirement plum, but this time it fell to Michael Jay, a deputy
under-secretary some six years Neville-Jones's junior. She was duly
offered Bonn instead, but little thought had been given to how the
intervening year might be spent and her request for promotion in the
interim was refused. As this highly unsatisfactory scenario unfolded,
Neville-Jones realised that she had a tough decision to make: either to
take what was on the table and stick it out, in the knowledge that she
would soon become the first British woman ever to head a grade one
embassy, or to leave in search of pastures new, recognising that she
had got as far as she was likely to get in her diplomatic career. The
Prime Minister, John Major, stepped in at the eleventh hour to offer
her a job in Downing Street, and he also made her a dame in the New
Year's Honours list as a tribute to her contribution at Dayton. But
whilst these gestures were appreciated, they could not persuade
Neville-Jones to alter the course that she was now set upon. She
tendered her resignation and was swiftly snapped up by the NatWest
Bank, who made her managing director for international strategy in
its merchant banking arm, a move which, from one perspective,
symbolised the tying up of unfinished business. Deterred as a young
graduate from pursuing a corporate career by the macho culture of
the board room, thirty years on, Dame Pauline was now walking into

a senior executive position in one of the UK's leading banks (with a fat salary to match).

The news that the Foreign Office had lost its highest-ranking female diplomat quickly made its way into the national press under such predictably trite headlines as: 'Our Woman in Limbo', 'A Very Undiplomatic Incident', and 'Nothing Like a Dame'. Stories about squabbling mandarins in Whitehall were, of course, bread and butter for the hard-bitten political correspondents of Fleet Street, but the fact that the chief protagonist in this case was female inevitably invited special comment, much of it informed by briefings from unnamed sources within the Foreign Office. *The Times* diary referred to Neville-Jones's 'efficient, strong-willed manner', which certain of her colleagues regarded as not 'sufficiently emollient for the niceties of diplomatic life'.[1] The *Guardian*'s correspondent noted her 'poor organisational skills' and 'occasionally imperious manner', and cited one (female, as it so happened) official who described Dame Pauline as a 'brilliant and waspish' officer who had 'painted herself into a corner' over the Paris posting.[2] Other reports told of 'a strong-willed diplomat with a reputation for intimidating her staff', a 'respected but not popular figure in Whitehall', who had high-handedly dismissed the Bonn ambassadorship as if it were a mere consolation prize.[3] As one former minister quoted by the *Daily Mail* put it: 'The Foreign Office is not like opening a box of Black Magic and you just pick what you fancy.'[4] Francis Wheen of the *Guardian* even insinuated that Neville-Jones was looking to position herself as a 'feminist martyr' in order to dodge any bullets that might be fired in her direction by Lord Scott's soon-to-be-published report into arms to Iraq.[*5]

If those anonymous briefers hoped, however, to defend the Foreign Office's good name by portraying Neville-Jones as an egotistical troublemaker, their efforts badly misfired. Nearly every news report, even those which reproduced the hostile whispers against her, referred to the Foreign Office's dismal record on promoting women to top jobs

* Neville-Jones had been seconded to Downing Street as a senior foreign policy advisor at the time that John Major was summoned before the enquiry.

and reminded readers of its long history of masculine exclusivity. Furthermore, Dame Pauline was not without her own allies and sympathisers both in Whitehall and on Fleet Street. Polly Toynbee denounced the Foreign Office's behaviour in the *Independent*, noting how Neville-Jones had been 'winkled out' of her political director job and was now victim of 'snake whispers' designed to portray her as an irrational female bent on 'aggrieved revenge'.[6] As for the Paris ambassadorship, Toynbee cited a 'friend' in whose view there was 'absolutely no doubt at all that if she had been a man, she would never have been passed over'. Charlotte Eagar similarly took Neville-Jones's enemies to task in the *Observer*, describing their unattributed briefings as a 'classic male attack on a forthright woman'.[7] Dame Pauline's staunchest defender, however, was her own mother, Dr Celia Winn, a pioneering woman medic now in her eighties, who told the *Daily Mail* that her daughter had 'hit the glass ceiling' of the 'very male world' of the Foreign Office.[8]

For her own part, Neville-Jones said little to the press, making only a brief comment to the effect that she did not feel she had been discriminated against on grounds of sex. Six months later, however, she was ready to offer a less restrained account in a full-length interview in *The Times*. No, the Foreign Office was not a bastion of misogyny, she reiterated, but the tone of the briefings made against her was clearly sexist. 'It is true that I am strong-willed,' she said,

> But when a woman is in favour, she's called formidable. When she is out of favour, she's strong-willed. What I felt was they wanted to have their cake and eat it. They wanted all those qualities I had and some others which they thought I lacked. They wanted me ultimately to do what they wanted.

Setting the record straight, Neville-Jones revealed that she had been entertaining doubts about her future in the Service ever since the political director post was downgraded. 'That was sharp practice,' she felt; 'I can't think it was anything other than deliberate, but I don't know why they did it.' Being passed over for Paris and then refused promotion only confirmed her fears that she and the Foreign Office had reached the end of the road. 'But I don't want to believe that it was because I was a woman,' Neville-Jones added; 'I don't want to believe it was all deliberately schemed.'[9]

———

Foreign Office chiefs did not want anyone to believe that either. They watched the media storm brewing over the Neville-Jones affair with mounting dismay. In a bid to defuse this unwelcome publicity, the permanent secretary, John Coles, wrote to the press categorically refuting the claim that senior appointments were based 'on anything other than fair and open competition'. He declared his personal commitment to securing 'a better balance between men and women in the Diplomatic Service' and pointed to a range of equal opportunities and flexible working policies now in place. The paucity of senior female officials, he argued, was a legacy of the 'social attitudes prevailing in now distant periods of recruitment', and would in time be rectified. Fast-stream women entrants currently outnumbered men, Coles noted, and they did so 'entirely on merit'.[10] Any budding women diplomats out there should not feel discouraged.

Although intended to lower the heat over Dame Pauline's resignation – of which Coles himself had been publicly named as one of the instigators – these sentiments were nonetheless sincerely expressed. By the mid-1990s, new recruits to the Foreign Office joined an institution whose culture had been dramatically transformed since the post-war days of bowler hats and smoking coal fires. Alongside a greater abundance of women, non-white faces were now more regularly seen behind desks, whilst gay men and women could at last live openly with their sexuality, the 'security risks' having diminished as a result of changing social attitudes and the end of the Cold War.* Some of the

* Sherard Cowper-Coles tells a story in his memoirs from the mid-1980s of a gay colleague who was tricked into propositioning a Vice Squad officer in a nightclub, an incident which resulted in the withdrawal of his security clearance and his eventual resignation. As Cowper-Coles rightly observed: 'You would have thought that the Metropolitan Police had better things to do than hang around gay clubs.' (*Ever the Diplomat: Confessions of a Foreign Office Mandarin*, London, 2012, p. 90.)

administrative hierarchies were also beginning to break down, including the previously caste-like distinctions separating the elite Branch A high-flyers from their less starry Branch B colleagues. Also on the way out was the paternalistic system of overseas postings. These had for years been dealt out to employees with minimum consultation and almost zero transparency. Now securing a post abroad was a two-way negotiation in which officers had far greater scope to shape their own destinies (a development which would eventually see diplomats competitively 'bidding' for vacant posts in an almost entirely unfettered internal labour market).

As for women breaking through to the higher echelons of the Service, progress had admittedly been slow, but there were grounds for cautious optimism. The tally of female ambassadors was unmistakeably on an upward trajectory. Veronica Sutherland followed her earlier stint as head of mission in the Ivory Coast with a high-profile appointment to Dublin in 1995, whilst Maeve Fort set an important precedent for aspiring female Arabists three years earlier when she became ambassador to the Lebanon. Doubts about how women might fare in traditionalist Catholic countries were swept away when Maureen MacGlashan was appointed ambassador to the Holy See in 1995, the same year that Barbara Hay was despatched to Uzbekistan in central Asia as head of mission in Tashkent.[11] All the same, it was hard to argue against Celia Winn's claim that a 'glass ceiling' existed at the Foreign Office. Around the time of the Neville-Jones resignation, there were just five women (including Dame Pauline) in the top bracket of grades one to three, and only seven women ranked amongst Britain's 180-odd heads of mission overseas. Two years later, when John Major's Conservative government was on the brink of collapse, all twenty-two director-level posts in London (as departmental heads were now known) were occupied by men.[12]

These statistics shocked the incoming Foreign Secretary, Robin Cook, who strode bullishly into the Foreign Office after Labour's landslide election victory in May 1997 determined to shake things up. As part of a wider rethink of Britain's foreign policy aims and overseas representation, Cook ordered a stocktaking of current working

practices with a view to introducing more flexibility for women wishing to balance family and career. The fruits of this exercise included a
move to extend the maximum term of special unpaid leave (SUPL)
from five to ten years, plus new incentives to entice back talented
women who had recently left the Service. This latter policy was pushed
particularly hard by John Kerr, who had taken over from Coles as
permanent secretary and was keen – influenced, no doubt, by the fall-
out over the Neville-Jones affair – to push 'gender diversity' (to use the
new managerial parlance) up the list of departmental priorities. Under
Kerr's leadership, the Foreign Office acquired a Gender Diversity
Advisor, a Gender Action Plan and a Gender Advisory Group, with
board-level Gender Champions and a Gender Network added by his
successors, Michael Jay (the man who had beaten Dame Pauline to the
Paris job) and Peter Ricketts.[13]

A decade later, it would have been impossible to accuse Foreign
Office chiefs of complacency towards the position of women, or indeed
towards ethnic minority, gay, disabled and older employees, all of
whom became beneficiaries of dedicated networking initiatives,
mentoring schemes, 'talent management' programmes, 'learning sets'
and other 'diversity' measures which would have seemed bafflingly
alien to any recruit of the 1950s.[14] Slowly the number of women in the
top four grades (now re-badged the Senior Management Structure)
nudged up, from seventeen per cent in 2007 to eighteen per cent a year
later and subsequently to nearly twenty-two per cent by September
2009.[15] This not only meant more women presiding over departments
in London, but also more female heads of mission overseas, including
a fair few who had successfully balanced motherhood and career on
their way up. Judith MacGregor, for instance, joined the Service in
1976, married a fellow diplomat in 1982 and brought up four children
before winning her first ambassadorial posting in 2004 as head of
mission in Slovakia. She became Britain's woman in Mexico five years
later. Mariot Leslie, MacGregor's near-contemporary, similarly juggled
career with family (in her case, two daughters) through the 1980s and
'90s before being appointed ambassador to Norway in 2002. Eight
years later, Leslie was given the prestigious post of permanent repre-

sentative on the UK delegation to NATO in Paris. Half a dozen or so years her junior, Frances Guy, a mother of three, struck another blow for female Arabists when she was appointed ambassador to the Yemen in 2001 and later to the Lebanon in 2006, with a spell as head of the 'Engaging the Islamic World Group' in London in between.

―――――――

In truth, these success stories probably said as much about the transformed attitudes of British husbands as they did about the Foreign Office's conversion to the new managerial doctrines of gender diversity. As noted, the trailing male spouse had been slow to materialise after the removal of the marriage bar, notwithstanding the two well-known cases of Alex Sutherland and Alexander Campbell, who accompanied their wives as 'male ambassadresses' to the Ivory Coast and Luxembourg respectively in the late 1980s. By the era of New Labour there was evidence that the diplomatic husband was embracing domesticity in ways unimaginable ten or twenty years before. In 1998 the magazine of the British Diplomatic Spouses Association featured the story of Mark Kilroy, a former civil servant who had retrained as a furniture-maker in order to 'avoid a clash of careers' with his diplomat wife. Overseas, Kilroy willingly took on the role of house husband, devoting most of his time to childcare and housework but keeping his furniture business going in his spare hours, an arrangement which seemed to suit all concerned admirably.[16] Another example of the diplomatic 'new man' was Leigh Turner, who resigned from his job at the British embassy in Berlin in 2002 to become primary carer to his two children, whilst his diplomat wife, who had been working part-time, took over his vacated slot at the embassy. After returning to the Diplomatic Service in 2006, Turner described his stint of full-time fatherhood as 'possibly the best four years of my working life'.[17]

Just how common this new breed of male spouse has become in the present-day Diplomatic Service is, nonetheless, difficult to judge. Even after decades of feminism, men who leave their jobs to care for small children are frequently viewed with pity, bemusement or outright contempt – and not only by other men. Turner recalled bumping into a former embassy colleague during the school run in Berlin who immediately exclaimed, 'How the mighty have fallen!' On another occasion, he told a newly arrived female officer about his domestic set-up and was greeted with the withering reply, 'Oh, so you're the house-boy now, are you?'[18] Although British fathers today do far more childcare and housework than ever before, the proportion opting for full-time parenthood is still tiny, perhaps as low as four per cent amongst those with children of pre-school age.[19] It also remains the case that working mothers are overwhelmingly more likely than fathers to take advantage of 'flexible' working arrangements or to reduce their hours to fit in around childcare, decisions which can have serious consequences for career progress and earning power in the longer term. In this respect, provisions to enable women with children to stay in London-based posts for up to ten years arguably risk exacerbating the problem, as it is still overseas experience which counts for most when the top jobs are being handed out.*

These trends are as evident in the Diplomatic Service as in any other workplace. Indeed, given the peculiar demands this profession places upon its members – most critically, the expectation of regular overseas postings – it is perhaps hardly surprising that women's representation continues to lag behind the Home Civil Service and other comparable occupations. In 2013, women's share of the top jobs stood at twenty-three per cent, only a single percentage point rise over four years, whilst their presence in the feeder grades immediately below the Senior Management Structure crept up by a modest two per cent over the same period (from thirty-three per cent to thirty-five per cent).[20] The male monopoly over the most prestigious overseas posts looks worryingly robust. Anne Pringle made history by becoming ambassador to Moscow in 2008, two years before Mariot Leslie secured another 'top-ten' post as permanent representative to NATO. Still, there has never been a female chief sitting in Washington, Paris, Tokyo, Beijing or Delhi, or at the British delegations to the United Nations in New York

---

* In 2013, eighty-nine per cent of UK-based staff in the FCO who worked part time were female.

or the European Union in Brussels, all grade-one missions deemed of the highest strategic importance to Britain's foreign policy interests. Nor has a woman ever held the highest post of all: permanent secretary and head of the Diplomatic Service.

The challenges of juggling career and family go a long way towards explaining women's under-representation, but they do not, however, provide the whole story. Despite the changes which have taken place since the 1990s, including the enshrinement of 'diversity' as an organi-sational objective, at its higher levels the Diplomatic Service is still a male-dominated institution in which male behaviours, attitudes and assumptions inevitably prevail, and this affects *all* women, regardless of whether or not they have children. It is notoriously difficult to pin down what constitutes this 'male culture' with any precision. Some current Diplomatic Service members talk of 'blokeishness' or 'machismo', of a certain quality of intellectual aggression or tough talk-ing which many women are either unable or unwilling to emulate. (Think of Jonathan Powell's famously blunt instruction to Christopher Meyer before the latter took up his post as ambassador to Washington in 1997: 'We want you to get up the arse of the White House and stay there.' Would Powell have issued such an order to a woman?[21])

Naturally, not every female diplomat would necessarily endorse this picture. The 'masculine vigour' of Gertrude Bell and 'strong-willed' manner of Pauline Neville-Jones, after all, are proof that women can possess many of those qualities which are typically associated with men. And yet, the belief that real differences exist between the sexes has featured as a persistent theme ever since the question of women's suit-ability for diplomatic careers was first mooted in the early twentieth century. Advocates of equality held that distinctive 'feminine' qualities such as empathy, intuition and a feel for female public opinion would enrich the diplomatic profession, whilst opponents thought these qual-ities the very antithesis of what made for effective diplomacy. The experience of the immediate post-war decades failed to settle the issue because so few women were recruited, and so many of those forced to retire because of the marriage bar. Even today, it is very difficult to evaluate the collective impact that women might have made to British diplomacy when they occupy less than a quarter of higher-grade posts. Moreover, from the moment they stepped into the Foreign Office, many female diplomats were profoundly resistant to the idea that they had a 'special' contribution to make as women and were sceptical of the notion that they might bring a different set of perspectives and experiences to their work. It is arguably only since the internal reforms of the 1990s that it has become possible to talk seriously about gender diversity as a genuine asset rather than a threat to the effectiveness of Britain's diplomatic workforce.

It is sobering to see just how far women's under-representation is replicated when one looks beyond the diplomatic profession to the wider world of international politics, where male heads of state and foreign ministers continue to preside. Granted, a handful of women have made their mark at the regular summits of the global power elite: Margaret Thatcher, Angela Merkel, Madeleine Albright and Hillary Clinton most readily spring to mind. Yet their presence was, or remains still, exceptional. Even in the twenty-first century, a woman wielding serious power in the global political arena is an oddity, a phenomenon to be explained rather than taken for granted. Not only is her performance subject to closer scrutiny than her male peers, but it often comes to stand as a test of the ability of all women and to reflect, for good or ill, the wisdom of allowing a woman to do a 'man's' job.

This tendency to be held to a higher standard is not limited to the field of diplomacy. Few successful women, whatever their profession, can escape the dispiriting feeling of being always on trial. Yet the story of women diplomats remains a distinct one with its own twists and turns. For over a century it was assumed that the job of representing the nation overseas required qualities which only men possessed, or, more accurately, which only men could *acquire*, typically through a privileged upbringing and a public school and university education. Even after women had claimed their right to higher education, broken into the professions, won the vote and entered Parliament on equal terms with men, their suitability for diplomatic careers was viewed with deep scepticism. As late as the 1940s it was openly claimed that women were too emotional, too sentimental, too lacking in natural

EPILOGUE

authority to be entrusted with safeguarding British interests overseas. Well into the 1950s and '60s, as the first generation of women diplomats discovered, these attitudes died hard. Married women were barred until as late as 1973, whilst the accompanying male spouse remained an extraordinarily rare breed before the 1990s.

In short, the advance of women in the British Diplomatic Service has been painfully slow, much slower than in most other professional fields, and the Foreign Office is still today struggling to eradicate this legacy of under-representation and masculine privilege. Doing so will not be easy. If history teaches us anything, it is that throughout the ages the woman diplomat has struggled to resolve a fundamental and existential tension between being representative of her country and being herself. Britain might have won two world wars, lost an empire and sought new ways to exert influence as a second-rate global power in the course of the twentieth century, but this fact of diplomatic life appears to remains as true today as it ever was.

Notes

Berlin, 1878

1. For historical accounts of the congress see R. W. Seton-Watson, *Disraeli, Gladstone and the Eastern Question* (London, 1935); B. H. Sumner, *Russia and the Balkans, 1870–1880* (Oxford, 1937); W. N. Medlicott, *The Congress of Berlin and After: A Diplomatic History of the Near Eastern Settlement, 1878–1880* (London, 1938); M. S. Anderson, *The Eastern Question, 1774–1923* (London, 1966); Mai'a K. Davis Cross, *The European Diplomatic Corps: Diplomats and International Cooperation from Westphalia to Maastricht* (Basingstoke, 2007); and Jonathan Steinberg, *Bismarck: A Life* (Oxford, 2011). For a detailed contemporary press report of the opening of the congress, see *The Times,* 14 June 1878, p. 5.
2. Lord Frederick Hamilton, *The Vanished Pomps of Yesterday: Being Some Random Reminiscences of a British Diplomat* (London, 1919), p. 69.

Chapter 1: The Natural Order of Things

1. Esme Howard, *Theatre of Life: Volume I: Life Seen from the Pit, 1863–1905* (London, 1935), p. 48.
2. George Buchanan, *My Mission to Russia and Other Diplomatic Memories* (London, 1923).
3. H. J. Bruce, *Silken Dalliance* (London, 1946).
4. Vincent Corbett, *Reminiscences: Autobiographical and Diplomatic* (London, 1927).
5. Hamilton, *Vanished Pomps.*
6. Lord Hardinge, *Old Diplomacy: The Reminiscences of Lord Hardinge of Penshurst* (London, 1947).
7. Ibid., p. 14.

8. Evidence of Sir Edmund Hammond, *Report from the Select Committee on Diplomatic Service* (House of Commons, 1861), p. 26.

9. Evidence of Sir Andrew Buchanan, *First Report from the Select Committee on Diplomatic and Consular Services* (House of Commons, 1871), pp. 13 and 15.

10. Evidence of Sir Augustus Paget, ibid., p. 5.

11. Evidence of Sir Andrew Buchanan, *Report from the Select Committee on Diplomatic Service*, p. 128.

12. Evidence of Sir George Hamilton Seymour, *Report from the Select Committee on Diplomatic Service*, p. 210.

13. T. G. Otte, 'Outdoor Relief for the Aristocracy? European Nobility and Diplomacy, 1850–1914', in Markus Mösslang and Torsten Riotte, eds., *The Diplomats' World: A Cultural History of Diplomacy, 1815–1914* (Oxford, 2008), p. 27.

14. Ibid., p. 48.

15. Raymond Jones, *The British Diplomatic Service, 1815–1914* (Gerrards Cross, 1983).

16. Evidence of Sir Rutherford Alcock, *First Report from the Select Committee*, p. 79.

17. D. C. M. Platt, *The Cinderella Service: British Consuls Since 1825* (London, 1971).

18. Evidence of Earl of Clarendon, *Report from the Select Committee on Diplomatic Service*, p. 100.

19. John Tilley, *London to Tokyo* (London, 1942).

20. Sir James Rennell Rodd, *Social and Diplomatic Memories, 1884–1893* (London, 1922).

21. Evidence of Edmund Hammond, Earl of Clarendon, Sir Stratford de Redcliffe and Lord Malmesbury, *Report from the Select Committee on Diplomatic Service*, pp. 29, 114, 163, 184.

22. Evidence of Lord Wodehouse, ibid., p. 85.

23. Evidence of Henry Elliot, ibid., p. 149.

24. Evidence of George Strachey, ibid., p. 236.

25. David Kelly, *The Ruling Few: Or the Human Background to Diplomacy* (London, 1952), p. 76.

26. Bruce, *Silken Dalliance*, p. 40.

27. Evidence of Charles Spring Rice, *Report from the Select Committee on Diplomatic Service*, p. 273.

28. Charles Roland Middleton, *The Administration of British Foreign Policy 1782–1846* (Durham, North Carolina, 1977).

29. Evidence of Earl of Clarendon, *Report from the Select Committee on Diplomatic Service*, p. 101.

30. Corbett, *Reminiscences*, p. 30.

31. Ian Toplis, *The Foreign Office: An Architectural History* (London, 1987); Bernard Porter, *The Battle of the Styles: Society, Culture and the Design of a New Foreign Office, 1855–61* (London, 2011).

32. Ray Jones, *The Nineteenth-century Foreign Office: An Administrative History* (London, 1971).

33. John Tilley and Stephen Gaselee, *The Foreign Office* (London, 1933), pp. 130–1.

34. The description of Sanderson is from Robert Vansittart, *The Mist Procession: The Autobiography of Lord Vansittart* (London, 1958), p. 45.

35. J. D. Gregory, *On the Edge of Diplomacy: Rambles and Reflections, 1902–1928* (London, 1929), p. 255.

36. Vansittart, *Mist Procession*, p. 43.

37. Zara Steiner, *The Foreign Office and Foreign Policy, 1898–1914* (Cambridge, 1969).

38. Sir Minto Farquhar, *Report from the Select Committee on Diplomatic Service*, pp. 19–20.

39. Evidence of Sir Andrew Buchanan, *First Report from the Select Committee*, p. 13.

Chapter 2: Through the Mill

1. Mary Crawford Fraser, *A Diplomatist's Wife in Many Lands*, vol. II (London, 1910).

2. R. B. Wernham, *The Making of Elizabethan Foreign Policy, 1558–1603* (London, 1980); Wallace T. MacCaffrey, *Elizabeth I: War and Politics, 1588–1603* (Princeton, New Jersey, 1992); Susan Doran, *Monarchy and Matrimony: The Courtships of Elizabeth I* (London, 1996).

3. Stanley Weintraub, *Victoria: Biography of a Queen* (London, 1987), p. 427.

4. Theo Aronson, *Grandmama of Europe: The Crowned Descendants of Queen Victoria* (London, 1973).

5. Glenda Sluga, Giulia Calvi and Carolyn James, eds., *Women, Diplomacy and International Relations Since 1500* (London, forthcoming, 2014).

6. Mai'a K. Davis Cross, *The European Diplomatic Corps*.

7. Sarah Ellis, *The Women of England: Their Social Duties, and Domestic Habits* (London, 1839), cited in Kathryn Gleadle, *Borderline Citizens: Women, Gender, and Political Culture in Britain 1815–1867* (Oxford, 2009), p. 4. See also Anna Clark, 'Women in eighteenth-century British Politics' in Sarah Knott and Barbara Taylor, eds., *Women, Gender and Enlightenment* (Basingstoke, 2005), pp. 570–86; Amanda Vickery, 'Golden Age to Separate Spheres? A Review of the Categories and Chronology of English Women's History', *Historical Journal*, 36 (1993), pp. 383–414; and Sarah Richardson, *The Political Worlds of Women: Gender and Politics in Nineteenth-Century Britain* (London, 2013).

8. K. D. Reynolds, *Aristocratic Women and Political Society in Victorian Britain* (Oxford, 1998).

9. Cited in Reynolds, *Aristocratic Women*, p. 185.

10. John Charmley and Jennifer Davey, 'The Invisible Politician: Mary Derby and the Eastern Crisis' in John Fisher and Anthony Best, eds., *On The Fringes of Diplomacy: Influences on British Foreign Policy, 1800–1945* (Farnham, 2011), pp. 17–34.

11. Sir James Rennell Rodd, *Social and Diplomatic Memories, 1884–1893* (London, 1922), *Social and Diplomatic Memories, 1894–1901: Egypt and Abyssinia* (London, 1923); *Social and Diplomatic Memories, 1902–1919* (London, 1925).

12. Gregory, *On the Edge of Diplomacy*, p. 38.

13. Fraser, *Diplomatist's Wife in Many Lands*, p. 283.

14. Meriel Buchanan, *Ambassador's Daughter* (London, 1958), pp. 92–3.
15. John Tilley, *London to Tokyo* (London, 1942), p. 54.
16. Rennell Rodd, *Social and Diplomatic Memories, 1894–1901*, p. 63.
17. Mary Crawford Fraser, *A Diplomatist's Wife in Japan: Sketches at the Turn of the Century* (edited by Sir Hugh Cortazzi, New York, 1982), p. 125.
18. Lady Anne Macdonell, *Reminiscences of Diplomatic Life* (London, 1913).
19. See, for instance, Meriel Buchanan, *Diplomacy and Foreign Courts* (London, 1928).
20. Sir Thomas Hohler, *Diplomatic Petrel* (London, 1942), p. 3.
21. Buchanan, *Ambassador's Daughter*, p. 33.
22. Saho Matsumoto-Best, 'The Cultural Diplomacy of Sir James Rennell Rodd', in John Fisher and Antony Best, eds., *On the Fringes of Diplomacy: Influences on British Foreign Policy, 1800–1945* (Farnham, 2011), pp. 209–24.
23. Rennell Rodd, *Social and Diplomatic Memories, 1902–1919*, pp. 172–4.
24. The Dowager Marchioness of Dufferin and Ava, *My Russian and Turkish Journals* (London, 1916).
25. Rennell Rodd, *Social and Diplomatic Memories, 1884–1893*, p. 266.
26. Hamilton, *Vanished Pomps*, p. 75.
27. Dufferin, *Russian and Turkish Journals*.
28. Maneesha Lal, 'The politics of gender and medicine in colonial India: the Countess of Dufferin's Fund, 1885–1888', *Bulletin of the History of Medicine*, 68 (1994), pp. 29–66; Sean Lang, 'Saving India through its Women', *History Today*, 55(9), 2005.
29. Rennell Rodd, *Social and Diplomatic Memories, 1894–1901*, p. 21.
30. Ibid., p. 246.
31. Bruce, *Silken Dalliance*, p. 95.
32. Dufferin, *Russian and Turkish Journals*, pp. 76 and 77.
33. Fraser, *Diplomatist's Wife in Many Lands*, pp. 131 and 227.
34. Macdonell, *Reminiscences*, p. 143.
35. Dufferin, *Russian and Turkish Journals*, p. 8.
36. Fraser, *Diplomatist's Wife in Many Lands*, p. 248.
37. Dufferin, *Russian and Turkish Journals*, p. 57.
38. Cited in F. A. Wellesley, ed., *The Paris Embassy during the Second Empire: Selections from the Papers of Henry Richard Charles Wellesley, 1st Earl Cowley, Ambassador at Paris 1852–67* (London, 1928), p. 321.
39. Hardinge, *Old Diplomacy*, p. 54.
40. Cited in Matsumoto-Best, 'Cultural diplomacy', p. 215, n. 31.
41. Richard Davenport-Hines, 'Blackwood, Hariot Georgina Hamilton-Temple, Marchioness of Dufferin and Ava (1843–1936)', *Oxford Dictionary of National Biography* – hereafter *ODNB* – (Oxford, 2004).
42. Dufferin, *Russian and Turkish Journals*, pp. 23 and 60.
43. Hardinge, *Old Diplomacy*, p. 41.
44. Vita Sackville-West, *Pepita* (London, 1937).
45. Ibid., p. 164.

46. *Memoir of the Right Hon. Sir John McNeill and of his second wife Elizabeth Wilson, by their Grand-Daughter* (London, 1910), p. 76.

Chapter 3: War

1. Bertha Phillpotts to Ledsim (Maud) Phillpotts, 1 March 1917, GCPP Phillpotts 2/2/1, Girton College, Cambridge.
2. Phillpotts to her parents, 15 April 1917.
3. Phillpotts to Ledsim (Maud) Phillpotts, 24 January 1916.
4. Owen Phillpotts to Ledsim (Maud) Phillpotts, 30 June 1915. For Phillpotts's appointment, see typescript of a broadcast on Bertha Phillpotts, with covering letter from Mary Clover to Gilbert Murray, dated 21 April 1941, GCPP Phillpotts 1/1/9.
5. Sir Hughe Knatchbull-Hugessen, *Diplomat in Peace and War* (London, 1949), chapter 3.
6. Tilley and Gaselee, *Foreign Office*.
7. Ibid. See also Gregory, *On the Edge of Diplomacy*, chapter 3.
8. Hilda Martindale, *Women Servants of the State, 1870–1938: A History of Women in the Civil Service* (London, 1938), chapter 2; Tammy M. Proctor, *Female Intelligence: Women and Espionage in the First World War* (London, 2003), especially chapter 3.
9. Dorothy Evans, *Women and the Civil Service* (London, 1934).
10. Meta Zimmeck, 'The Mysteries of the Typewriter: Technology and Gender in the British Civil Service, 1870–1914', in Gertjan de Groot and Marlou Schrover, eds., *Women Workers and Technological Change in Europe in the Nineteenth and Twentieth Centuries* (London, 1995), pp. 67–96.
11. Tilley and Gaselee, *Foreign Office*; George P. Antrobus, *King's Messenger 1918–1940: Memoirs of a Silver Greyhound* (London, 1941), chapter 1.
12. Tilley and Gaselee, *Foreign Office*, p. 181.
13. For London in wartime, see Mrs C. S. Peel, *How We Lived Then: A Sketch of Social and Domestic Life in England during the War* (London, 1929); Michael MacDonagh, *In London during the Great War: The Diary of a Journalist* (London, 1935).
14. Buchanan, *Ambassador's Daughter*, p. 126.
15. Ibid., p. 131.
16. Rennell Rodd, *Social and Diplomatic Memories, 1902–1919*, p. 313.
17. Ibid., p. 314.
18. Lady Randolph Churchill, ed., *Women's War Work* (London, 1916).
19. Leah Leneman, *In the Service of Life: the Story of Elsie Inglis and the Scottish Women's Hospitals* (Edinburgh, 1994).
20. Viscountess D'Abernon, *Red Cross and Berlin Embassy, 1915–1926: Extracts from the Diaries of Viscountess D'Abernon* (London, 1946).
21. The best biography of Gertrude Bell published in recent years is Georgina Howell, *Daughter of the Desert: The Remarkable Life of Gertrude Bell* (London, 2006),

although also see Janet Wallach, *Desert Queen: The Extraordinary Life of Gertrude Bell, Adventurer, Adviser to Kings, Ally of Lawrence of Arabia* (London, 1996).

22. Gertrude Bell (GB) to Florence Bell, 1 December 1914, Gertrude Bell Archive, http://www.gerty.ncl.ac.uk/

23. GB to Florence Bell, 16 December 1914.

24. GB to Hugh Bell, 6 January 1915.

25. Ibid.

26. Cited in Howell, *Daughter of the Desert*, p. 253.

27. GB to Florence Bell, 8 January 1915.

28. GB to Florence Bell, 5 August 1915.

29. GB to Florence Bell, 20 August 1915.

30. GB to Florence Bell, 25 August 1915.

31. Cited in Howell, *Daughter of the Desert,* p. 255.

32. GB to Florence Bell, 16 November 1915.

33. GB to Florence Bell, 30 November 1915.

34. Bruce Westrate, *The Arab Bureau: British Policy in the Middle East, 1916–1920* (Pennsylvania, 1992). See also Priya Satia, *Spies in Arabia: The Great War and the Cultural Foundations of Britain's Covert Empire in the Middle East* (Oxford, 2008).

35. GB to Florence Bell, 13 December 1915.

36. GB to Hugh Bell, 24 January 1916.

37. GB to Florence Bell, 11 February 1916.

38. GB to Hugh Bell, 18 February 1916.

39. GB to Hugh Bell, 3 March 1916.

40. GB to Florence Bell, 27 April 1916.

41. GB to Hugh Bell, 14 May 1916.

42. Cited by Howell, *Daughter of the Desert,* p. 297.

43. GB to Florence Bell, 5 December 1918.

44. GB to Hugh Bell, 31 May 1916.

45. Cited by Liora Lukitz, *A Quest in the Middle East: Gertrude Bell and the Making of Modern Iraq* (London, 2006), p. 3.

46. David Hogarth, obituary of Gertrude Bell in the *Geographical Journal*, vol. 68, no. 4 (Oct 1926), p. 363. Obituary of Bell (written by Chirol), *The Times*, 13 July 1926, p. 10.

47. Mary Clover to Gilbert Murray, 21 April 1941, GCPP Phillpotts 1/1/9.

Paris, 1919

1. The best general history of the conference is Margaret Macmillan's *Peacemakers: The Paris Conference of 1919 and Its Attempt to End War* (London, 2001). Useful eyewitness accounts include Vernon Bartlett, *Behind the Scenes at the Peace Conference* (London, 1920); R. H. Beadon, *Some Memories of the Peace Conference* (London, 1933); Lord Hankey, *The Supreme Control at the Paris Peace Conference 1919* (London, 1963); Sir James Headlam-Morley, *A Memoir of the Paris Peace Conference 1919* (London, 1972);

Sisley Huddleston, *Peace-Making at Paris* (London, 1919); Harold Nicolson, *Peacemaking, 1919* (London, 1933); *Lord Riddell's Intimate Diary of the Peace Conference and After, 1918–1923* (London, 1933); James T. Shotwell, *At the Paris Peace Conference* (New York, 1937).

2. Vansittart, *Mist Procession*, p. 201.
3. Esme Howard, *Theatre of Life, Vol.2: Life Seen from the Stalls 1905–1936* (London, 1936), p. 374.
4. Nicolson, *Peacemaking*, p. 279.
5. A. J. P. Taylor, ed., *Lloyd George: A Diary by Frances Stevenson* (London, 1971), p. 171.
6. Frances Lloyd George, *The Years that Are Past* (London, 1967), p. 164.
7. Hankey, *Supreme Control*, p. 188.

Chapter 4: Ammunition

1. Circular letter from Charles Howard Smith to heads of missions, 27 September 1933, FO 366/915, National Archives, Kew.
2. Sir W. Lampson to Howard Smith, 10 November 1933, FO 366/917.
3. Sir N. Henderson to Howard Smith, 27 November 1933; A. C. Routh to Howard Smith, 23 November 1933, FO 366/916.
4. Sir Patrick Ramsay to Howard Smith, 14 October 1933, FO 366/915; Sir W. Seeds to Howard Smith, 30 November 1933, FO 366/917.
5. Sir C. Wingfield to Howard Smith, 11 October 1933, FO 366/915; AS Calvert to Howard Smith, 23 October 1933, FO 366/916.
6. Howard Smith to Sir E. Phipps, 10 November 1933, FO 366/916.
7. HMSO, *Report of the Sub-Committee appointed to consider the position after the war of women holding temporary appointments in Government Departments* (Cmd. 199, 1919).
8. *Hansard Parliamentary Debates* (Lords), 4 August 1919, Col. 265.
9. See note on 'Sex Disqualification (Removal) Bill. Deputation from Women's Societies to Mr Bonar Law and the Lord Chancellor, August 11th 1919' in Bonar Law Papers, BL/98/1/9, Parliamentary Archives, Westminster.
10. 'The Civil Service and the Sex Disqualification (Removal) Act', *Time and Tide*, 17 August 1923, p. 825.
11. HMSO, *Royal Commission on the Civil Service: Fifth Report of the Commissioners* (Cmd. 7748, 1914).
12. A. J. P. Taylor, *The Troublemakers: Dissent over Foreign Policy, 1792–1939* (London, 1957).
13. Union of Democratic Control, *How to Get a Permanent Peace* (London: leaflet no. 446, 1917), p. 5.
14. J. H. Hudson, 'Labour's Greatest Menace: The Foreign Office', *Foreign Affairs*, January 1920, p. 14.
15. *How to Get a Permanent Peace*, p. 6.

16. Of the sixteen men holding the posts of permanent under-secretary, deputy under-secretary, chief clerk and assistant under-secretary between 1919 and 1939, ten spent their entire careers in the Foreign Office; two went overseas only on their final postings as ambassadors; and four had spells abroad, but spent most of their careers in London. See Christina Larner, 'The Amalgamation of the Diplomatic Service with the Foreign Office', *Journal of Contemporary History,* 7 (1/2), 1972, pp. 107–26.

17. Alastair Kocho-Williams, 'Engaging the World: Soviet Diplomacy and Foreign Propaganda in the 1920s', (2007), paper available at http://www.uwe.ac.uk/hlss/history/sovietdiplomats1920s.pdf

18. Cited in Isabel de Palencia, *Alexandra Kollontay: Ambassadress from Russia* (London, 1947), p. 182.

19. William Strang to Howard Smith, 19 October 1933, FO 366/916.

20. Howard Smith to Strang, 27 October 1933, FO 366/916.

21. Sir C. Wingfield to Howard Smith, 11 October 1933, FO 366/915.

22. Archibald Clark Kerr to Howard Smith, 3 November 1933, FO 366/916.

23. 'Woman Red's New Post', *Daily Mirror,* 10 September 1926, p. 2.

24. Alexandra Kollontai, *The Autobiography of a Sexually Emancipated Communist Woman* (New York, 1971), p. 44.

25. Quoted in Barbara Clements, *Bolshevik Feminist: The Life of Aleksandra Kollontai* (London, 1979), p. 247.

26. Alastair Kocho-Williams, 'The Soviet Diplomatic Corps and Stalin's Purges', *Slavonic and East European Review,* 86(1), 2008, pp. 90–110.

27. The early history of women in the State Department is covered in detail in Homer Calkin, *Women in the Department of State: Their Role in American Foreign Affairs* (Washington, DC, 1978).

28. See Calkin, *Women in the Department of State,* pp. 69, 70, 76 and 78.

29. Written submission from Council of Women Civil Servants to the Inter-Departmental Committee on the Admission of Women to the Diplomatic and Consular Services, March 1934, FO 366/933.

30. 'These names make news', *Daily Express,* 23 January 1934, p. 6.

31. 'Woman's Gift of Diplomacy', *Daily Mirror,* 9 August 1933, p. 5.

32. Tom Clarke, 'Her First Year as a Woman Diplomat', unidentified press clipping in FO 366/929.

33. Ruth Bryan Owen, *Leaves from a Greenland Diary* (New York, 1935), p. 4.

34. Philip Nash, 'America's First Female Chief of Mission: Ruth Bryan Owen, Minister to Denmark, 1933–36', *Diplomacy and Statecraft,* 16 (2005), pp. 57–72.

35. Hugh Gurney to Howard Smith, 29 November 1933, FO 366/916.

36. Howard Smith to Hugh Gurney, 5 December 1933, FO 366/916.

37. Editorial, *New York Times,* 1 September 1936, p. 20.

38. HMSO, *Report of the Royal Commission on the Civil Service (1929–31)* (Cmd. 3909, 1931). The minutes of evidence can be found in series T 169 at the National Archives.

39. Statement submitted by the Council of Women Civil Servants (Higher Grades), dated October 1930, T 169/20, p. 7.

40. Statement submitted by the London and National Society for Women's Service, dated October 1930, third volume of minutes, T 169/18, p. 982.

41. Evidence of Miss GEM Jebb, 23 February 1931, third volume of minutes, T 169/18, p. 1485.

42. Evidence of the Association of Headmistresses, 17 October 1930, third volume of minutes, T 169/18, p. 1005.

43. Evidence of the London and National Society for Women's Service, 15 October 1930, third volume of minutes, T 169/18, p. 993.

44. Evidence submitted by the National Union of Societies for Equal Citizenship, February 1930, first volume of minutes, T 169/17, p. 460.

45. Statement submitted by the Council of Women Civil Servants (Higher Grades), dated October 1930, T 169/20, p. 13.

46. Evidence of Sir C. H. Montgomery, 1 and 2 July 1930, second volume of minutes, T 169/17.

47. Eunan O'Halpin, *Head of the Civil Service: A Study of Sir Warren Fisher* (London, 1989).

48. Evidence of Sir Warren Fisher, 17 December 1930, third volume of minutes, T 169/18.

49. *Report of the Royal Commission on the Civil Service (1929–31).*

50. Howard Smith to Robert Vansittart, 21 September 1933, FO 366/915.

51. Ibid.

52. Howard Smith's minute of conversation with James Rae, dated 13 December 1933, FO 366/917.

53. Evidence of Sir Claud Schuster, 15 December 1930, third volume of minutes, T 169/18.

54. Sir Claud Schuster to J. W. Nicholls, 19 January 1934, FO 366/929.

55. Sir Joseph Addison to Howard Smith, 27 November 1933, FO 366/916; Sir William Tyrrell to Howard Smith, 11 October 1933, FO 366/915.

Chapter 5: Women of Exceptional Gifts

1. Lady Astor's evidence to the Inter-Departmental Committee on the Admission of Women to the Diplomatic and Consular Services (hereafter Schuster Committee), 28 February 1934, FO 366/928.

2. 'Personalities and Powers: Dame Edith Lyttelton, DBE', *Time and Tide*, 24 October 1924, p. 1026.

3. Edith Lyttelton's letters to unidentified recipient, 1–6 February 1931, Churchill Archives Centre, Cambridge, CHAN II/4/22.

4. Hebe Spaull, *Women Peace-Makers* (London, 1924), p. 121.

5. Vera Brittain, 'Personalities at the Fourth Assembly. 2. Some European Delegates', *Time and Tide*, 21 September 1923, p. 954.

6. Helena Swanwick, *I Have Been Young* (London, 1935), p. 386.

7. Ibid., p. 385.

8. Dame Edith Lyttelton's evidence to the Schuster Committee, 1 March 1934, FO 366/928.

9. Evidence of the Council of Women Civil Servants to the Schuster Committee, 22 March 1934, FO 366/928.

10. Barbara Metzger, 'Towards an International Human Rights Regime during the Inter-War Years: the League of Nations' Combat of Traffic in Women and Children', in Kevin Grant, Philippa Levine and Frank Trentmann, eds., *Beyond Sovereignty: Britain, Empire and Transnationalism, c.1880–1950* (Basingstoke, 2007), pp. 54–79.

11. Rachel Crowdy, 'The Humanitarian Activities of the League of Nations', *Journal of the Royal Institute of International Affairs*, 6 (3), May 1927, p. 156.

12. Little has been known to date about this intermediate layer of female employees, but historians are now beginning to explore the personnel files available for the League and the ILO. See, for example, Jaci Eisenberg, 'American women in international Geneva, 1919–1939: a prosopography', *Women's History Magazine*, 71, Spring 2013, pp. 4–11.

13. As it happened, Wilson was replaced by a Dutchman rather than a German, whilst the decision to terminate her contract was strongly denounced by many of the women's societies in Geneva, but to no avail. See Doris Cruger Dale, 'An American in Geneva: Florence Wilson and the League of Nations Library', *Journal of Library History*, 7 (2), 1972, pp. 109–29.

14. Evidence of the Association of Headmistresses to the Schuster Committee, 15 March 1934, FO 366/928.

15. Swanwick, *I Have Been Young*, p. 415.

16. J. H. Whitley to D. K. Monteith, 14 February 1929, India Office Records, British Library, London, L/PO/263, f. 424.

17. Letters to unknown recipient dated 16 October 1930; 22 October 1930; 7 December 1930, in Beryl Power Papers, Girton College, Cambridge, GCPP Powers B2/4.

18. Letter dated 16 October 1930.

19. J. H. Whitley to Margaret Bondfield, 10 December 1930 in GCPP Powers B1/4.

20. Typescript memo dated 14 November 1945, GCPP Powers, B1/5.

21. 'Some notes on a Brief Russian Trip Taken in October 1932', GCPP Powers, 2/7.

22. Statement submitted by H. J. Crawford on behalf of the University of London Appointments Board, 13 April 1934, FO 366/934.

23. Written evidence of the London and National Society for Women's Service to the Tomlin Commission, dated 15 October 1930, T 169/18, third volume of evidence, p. 975.

24. Jane Potter, 'Livingstone, Dame Adelaide Lord (c.1881–1970)', *ODNB* (2004).

25. Alix Meynell, *Public Servant: Private Woman: An Autobiography* (London, 1988), p. 81.

26. Evidence of the Council of Women Civil Servants to Schuster Committee, 22 March 1934, FO 366/928.

27. Copy of letter from Ruth Bryan Owen to Lady Astor, dated 9 February 1934, forwarded to Committee, FO 366/932.

28. Memorandum Submitted by the Women's Freedom League to the Schuster Committee, 2 March 1934, FO 366/932.

29. The women appointed to consular positions were Miss Olga de la Barra, who served in Glasgow from 1927 to 1930 and was subsequently promoted to the post of consul-attaché at the Chilean legation in London; Miss Ines Ortuzar, who took over de la Barra's post in Glasgow, having previously served as Consul in Hull; and the Irish-born Miss Katherine Duffy, who represented Chile at the Consulate in New York. The first two names were provided by Frances Melville, a former suffragist and Mistress of Queen Margaret College, a women-only institution within the University of Glasgow.

30. Evidence of National Union of Societies for Equal Citizenship before the Tomlin Commission, 26 February 1930, first volume of minutes, T 169/17, p. 460.

31. Evidence of Council of Women Civil Servants to Schuster Committee, 22 March 1934, FO 366/928.

32. Evidence of Ruth Fry to Schuster Committee, 17 March 1934, FO 366/928.

33. Written statement of Association of Headmistresses submitted to Schuster Committee, 20 February 1934, FO 366/929, p. 194.

34. Statement submitted to the Schuster Committee by the London and National Society for Women's Service, March 1934, FO 366/930, p. 238.

35. Dame Edith Lyttelton's evidence to the Schuster Committee, 1 March 1934, FO 366/928.

36. Ibid.

37. Evidence of the London and National Society for Women's Service to Schuster Committee, 16 March 1934, FO 366/928.

38. Evidence of the Council of Women Civil Servants to Schuster Committee, 22 March 1934, FO 366/928.

39. Memo submitted to the Schuster Committee by the National Association of Women Civil Servants, dated 4 April 1934, FO 366/934.

Chapter 6: Foiled!

1. *Sunday Times*, 4 May 1958.

2. Norman Rose, *Vansittart: Study of a Diplomat* (London, 1978).

3. Memorandum by Sir Robert Vansittart, 30 January 1934, FO 366/929.

4. Howard Smith to Chilton, 7 March 1934, FO 366/932.

5. Sir Henry Chilton's evidence to the Schuster Committee, 16 March 1934, FO 366/928.

6. R. C. S. Stevenson's evidence to the Schuster Committee, 21 March 1934, ibid.

7. D. J. Scott and Mr McLean's evidence to the Schuster Committee, 22 March 1934, ibid.

8. Memo from H. C. Swan, 24 January 1934, FO 366/931.

9. Howard Smith to Alexander Hutcheon, 16 February 1934, ibid.

10. Howard Smith to Sir Edward Crowe, 7 March 1934, FO 366/932.

11. Howard Smith to Lady Granville, 7 March 1934, ibid.

12. Lady Granville's evidence to the Schuster Committee, 21 March 1934, FO 366/928.

13. Mrs V. MacDonnell's evidence to the Schuster Committee, 16 March 1934, ibid.

14. Marjorie Graves's evidence to the Schuster Committee, 28 February 1934, ibid.

15. Mary Pickford's evidence to the Schuster Committee, 1 March 1934, ibid. There is a rather tragic coda to Pickford's appearance before the committee, as she dropped dead five days later of pneumonia.

16. Mary Agnes Hamilton, 'Women in Politics', *Political Quarterly*, 3 (1932), p. 231.

17. Margaret Yates's evidence to the Schuster Committee, 16 March 1934, FO 366/928. See also her written submission, dated 19 February 1934, in FO 366/932.

18. Archibald Clark Kerr to Howard Smith, 3 November 1933, FO 366/916.

19. Edward Crowe to Howard Smith, 6 April 1934, FO 366/932.

20. Ibid. For Willis's career, see Philip Nash, '"A Woman's Touch in Foreign Affairs"? The Career of Ambassador Frances E. Willis', *Diplomacy & Statecraft*, 13 (2), 2002, pp. 1–20.

21. See letters to Howard Smith from Sir Charles Wingfield, 28 March 1934, FO 366/934; Rowland Sperling, 12 March 1934, and Patrick Ramsay, 14 March 1934, FO 366/933.

22. James Morgan to Howard Smith, 27 January 1934, FO 366/929; Sir George Grahame to Howard Smith, 14 March 1934, FO 366/932.

23. London and National Society for Women's Service's evidence to the Schuster Committee, 16 March 1934, FO 366/928.

24. Evidence of Council of Women Civil Servants to the Schuster Committee, 22 March 1934, ibid.

25. Sir William Seeds to Howard Smith, 30 November 1933, FO 366/917.

26. Question asked during Nancy Astor's evidence to the Schuster Committee, 28 February 1934, FO 366/928.

27. Evidence of Oxford University Appointments Committee to the Schuster Committee, 15 March 1934, ibid.

28. Evidence of St Joan's Social and Political Alliance to the Schuster Committee, 15 March 1934; evidence of Nancy Astor to the Schuster Committee, 28 February 1934, both in FO 366/928.

29. Evidence of Council of Women Civil Servants to the Schuster Committee, 22 March 1934, ibid.

30. Statement of Evidence submitted by the London and National Society for Women's Service, n.d., FO 366/930.

31. Howard Smith to Sir Samuel Hoare, 19 June 1935 (and Hoare's scribbled reply of 23 June), FO 366/954.

32. It was published as *Documents Relating to the Admission of Women to the Diplomatic and Consular Services* (Cmd. 5166, 1936).

33. See letter from heads of women's colleges in *The Times*, 26 May 1936; for Evans, see 'Women Better Than Men in Diplomacy?', *Daily Mirror*, 30 April 1936, p. 8.

34. 'Women as Diplomats', *Manchester Guardian*, 30 April 1936.

35. *The Times*, 'Women in Diplomacy', 29 April 1936, p. 15.

San Francisco, 1945

1. For a vivid portrait of San Francisco in wartime see Kevin Starr, *Embattled Dreams: California in War and Peace, 1940–1950* (Oxford, 2002).

2. Cited in Glenda Sluga, '"Spectacular Feminism": The international history of women, world citizenship and human rights', in Francisca de Haan, Margaret Allen, June Purvis and Krassimira Dasklova, eds., *Women's Activism: Global Perspectives from the 1890s to the Present* (London, 2012).

3. Virginia Gildersleeve, *Many a Good Crusade* (New York, 1954), p. 350.

4. Letter from Bertha Lutz to Margery Corbett Ashby, 11 August 1945, in Margery Corbett Ashby Papers, 7MCA/C/02 (file marked 6B/106/7/MCA/C2), The Women's Library, London.

5. 'Reminiscences of the San Francisco Conference that Founded United Nations, Bertha Lutz Brazilian Plenipotentiary Delegate', typescript, n.d., (but *c.*1970) in Corbett Ashby Papers, 7MCA/C/03.

6. Margery Corbett Ashby, 'Women out-numbered fifty to one by men', *International Women's News*, vol. 40, no. 5, February 1946, p. 51.

Chapter 7: Woman Power

1. David Garnett, *The Secret History of the PWE: the Political Warfare Executive, 1939–1945* (London, 2002)

2. Interview with Rowena Vining, 11 November 2010.

3. The papers of the Woman Power Committee are held at the British Library of Social and Economic Sciences, London School of Economics, London, COLL MISC 0548.

4. *House of Commons Debates*, 7 August 1941, col. 373.

5. Vera Douie, *The Lesser Half: A survey of the laws, regulations and practices introduced during the present war which embody discrimination against women* (London, 1943).

6. Information derived from the *Foreign Office List and Diplomatic and Consular Year Book*, 1939–1945.

7. F. T. A. Ashton-Gwatkin to A. P. Waterfield, 16 June 1942, FO 366/1277.

8. Anthony Eden to Thelma Cazalet, 5 January 1942, FO 366/1277.

9. Memo entitled 'Women Administrative and Executive Officers in the Foreign Service', and date-stamped 3 November 1945, in FO 366/1519.

10. See memo by F. T. A. Ashton-Gwatkin, dated 18 November 1941, and response by 'IM', FO 366/1277.

11. Enid McLeod, *Living Twice: Memoirs* (London, 1982).

12. Mary Agnes Hamilton, *Up-Hill All the Way: A Third Cheer for Democracy* (London, 1953), p. 113.

13. Juliette Pattinson, *Behind Enemy Lines: Gender, Passing and the Special Operations Executive in the Second World War* (Manchester, 2007).

14. Penny Summerfield, *Reconstructing Women's Wartime Lives: Discourses and Subjectivities in Oral Histories of the Second World War* (Manchester, 1998); Gail Braybon and Penny Summerfield, *Out of the Cage: Women's Experiences in Two World Wars* (London, 1987); Harold Smith, ed., *War and Social Change: British Society in the Second World War* (Manchester, 1986); Sonya Rose, *Which People's War? National Identity and Citizenship in Britain, 1939–1945* (Oxford, 2003).

Chapter 8: Two Attachés

1. Stark to Herbert Young, 2 September 1939, in Caroline Moorehead, ed., *Over the Rim of the World: Freya Stark: Selected Letters* (London, 1988), p. 165.

2. Freya Stark, *East is West* (London, 1945), p. 2. Stark always spelt Bedouin without the 'o'.

3. Stark to Sydney Cockerell, 8 October 1939, in *Over the Rim*, pp. 166 and 167.

4. Freya Stark tells her early life story in *Traveller's Prelude* (London, 1950); see also Jane Fletcher Geniesse, *Freya Stark: Passionate Nomad* (London, 1999), and Molly Izzard, *Freya Stark: A Biography* (London, 1993).

5. See letters from Freya Stark to Flora Stark for 19 October 1916 and 20 November 1916 in *Over the Rim*.

6. Stark to Flora Stark, 4 February 1917, in ibid., p. 22.

7. Geniesse, *Freya Stark,* p. 84.

8. I am grateful to Professor John Gurney for clarifying this reference for me.

9. 'Three Women in Arabia: Hadhrami Folk II – Brigandage and the RAF', *The Times,* 19 July 1938, p. 15, and 'Part III – A Journey with a Caravan', 20 July 1938, p. 15.

10. Stark to Halifax, 29 January 1940, in Caroline Moorhead, ed., *Freya Stark, Letters: Volume Four: Bridge of the Levant, 1940–43* (Salisbury, 1977), p. 7.

11. Stark to Flora Stark, 26 January 1940, ibid., p. 5.

12. Freya Stark, *Dust in the Lion's Paw: Autobiography 1939–1946* (London, 1985; first published 1961), p. 20.

13. Stark to Stewart Perowne, 15 February 1940, ibid., p. 26.

14. Ibid., p. 26.

15. Ibid., p. 25.

16. Ibid., p. 48.

17. Stark to Cockerell, 11 June 1940, in Moorhead, ed., *Bridge of Levant*, p. 72.

18. Stark, *Dust*, p. 50.

19. Ibid., p. 56.

20. Freya Stark to Gerald de Gaury, 15 August 1940, ibid., p. 82.

21. Stark to Flora Stark, 4 July 1941, ibid., p. 138.

22. Stark to Flora Stark, 30 June 1941, Moorhead, ed., *Bridge of Levant*, p. 136.

23. Stark to Walter Monckton, 2 December 1941, *Dust*, p. 174.

24. Freya Stark, 'In Iraq during the Crisis: Leisure at the Baghdad Embassy, the Charm of Danger', *The Times*, 30 June 1941, p. 5.

25. Stark, *Dust*, p. 92.

26. Stark, 'In Iraq during the Crisis'.

27. Stark, *Dust*, p. 120.

28. Ibid., p. 139.

29. Stark to Flora Stark, 28 September 1942, Moorhead, ed., *Bridge of the Levant*, p. 249.

30. Stark to Cockerell, 25 October 1941, ibid., p. 160.

31. Stark to Cockerell, 7 September 1940, ibid., p. 89.

32. Stark to Perowne, 12 February 1940; and Stark to Nigel Clive, 25 December 1943, both in *Dust*.

33. Stark to Rushbrook Williams, 27 August 1940, in Moorhead, ed., *Bridge of the Levant*, p. 87.

34. Stark to Perowne, 27 January 1941, ibid., p. 115.

35. Stark to Perowne, 8 March 1941, ibid., p. 122.

36. Stark to Perowne, 7 March 1940, ibid., p. 37.

37. This story is told by both Geniesse, *Passionate Nomad*, and Izzard, *Freya Stark*.

38. Stark to Cockerell, 21 May 1943, in Moorhead, ed., *Bridge of the Levant*, p. 289; Stark to Perowne, 27 April 1944, ibid., p. 88.

39. Bullard to his family, 8 February 1943, in E. C. Hodgkin, ed., *Letters from Tehran: A British Ambassador in World War II Persia* (London, 1991), p. 175.

40. Bullard to Nancy Lambton, 26 October 1945, in the papers of Professor A. K. S. Lambton (hereafter Lambton Papers), University Library, Durham, 52/2.

41. Lambton to Violet Rhodes, 20 March 1941, 48/1; Lambton to Nelly Cecil, 12 June 1941, 51/8; Lambton to Nelly Cecil, 27 May 1941, 51/8, all in Lambton Papers.

42. Cited in Hodgkin, *Letters from Tehran*, p. xv.

43. Diary entry for 1 September 1939, 16/36.

44. Lambton to Nelly Cecil, 3 August 1941, 51/8.

45. Burzine K. Waghmar, 'Lambton, Ann Katherine Swynford (1912–2008)', *ODNB* (2012).

46. Lambton to Rhodes, 22 January 1940, 47/7.

47. Lambton to Robert and Nelly Cecil, 10 January 1941, 51/8.

48. Bullard to family, 6 August 1941, in Hodgkin, *Letters from Tehran*, p. 67.

49. Lambton to Rhodes, 11 September 1941, 48/1.

50. Lambton to Nelly Cecil, 1 September 1941, 48/1; Lambton to Rhodes, 11 September 1941, 48/1.

51. Obituary of Professor Ann Lambton by Hugh Arbuthnott, *Journal of the Iran Society*, 2(7), 2008, pp. 37–40; Lambton to Robert Cecil, 21 September 1941, 48/1. See Massoumeh Torfeh, 'The BBC Persian Service, 1941–1979', paper presented at

The European Communication Research and Education Association Biannual Conference, November 2008.

52. Ann Lambton, 'Recollections of Iran in the mid-twentieth century', *Asian Affairs,* 19(3), October 1988, pp. 273–88.

53. Bullard to family, 6 August 1941, in Hodgkin, *Letters from Tehran,* p. 67.

54. Lambton to Nelly Cecil, 1 December 1941, 51/8.

55. Lambton to Rhodes, 2 March 1945, 48/1.

56. *The Times,* 7 December 1943, p. 3.

57. Lambton to Robert and Nelly Cecil, 2 March 1941, 51/8.

58. Bullard to family, 10 December 1944, in Hodgkin, *Letters from Tehran,* p. 262.

59. Lambton to Rhodes, 1 January 1940, 47/7; see also account in letter to Robert Cecil, 1 January 1940, 51/8, and for Bullard's version see Hodgkin, *Letters from Tehran,* pp. 6–7.

60. Lambton to Rhodes, 28 January 1941, 48/1.

61. Lambton to Nelly Cecil, 10 July 1940, 51/8; Lambton to Rhodes, 21 September 1941, 48/1.

62. Lambton to Rhodes, 4 August 1942, 48/1; Lambton to Rhodes, 29 November 1940, 47/7.

63. Lambton to Rhodes, 21 January 1941, 48/1.

64. Lambton to Rhodes, 27 November 1942, 48/1; Lambton to Nelly Cecil, 8 February 1940, 51/8.

65. Lambton to Nelly Cecil, 1 April 1940, 51/8.

66. Lambton to Rhodes, 8 September 1942, 48/1; Lambton to Nelly Cecil, 3 August 1941, 51/8.

67. Stark, *Beyond Euphrates,* p. 184.

68. Lambton to Rhodes, 2 March 1941, 48/1.

69. David O. Morgan, 'Ann K. S. Lambton (1912–2008) and Persian Studies', *Journal of the Royal Asiatic Society,* 21(1), 2011, pp. 99–109.

70. Wm Roger Louis, 'Musaddiq, oil, and the dilemmas of British Imperialism', in *Ends of British Imperialism: The Scramble for Empire, Suez and Decolonization* (London, 2006), pp. 727–87.

Chapter 9: Ambassadors of British Women

1. 'Text of address to be delivered by Miss Caroline Haslett, CBE, adviser to the British Ministry of Labor on Women's Training, at the 15th Annual Friendship Dinner November 17, 1941 at the Hotel Biltmore, New York at 7pm', Haslett Papers, Institution of Engineering and Technology, London, NAEST 33/10/2.2.

2. Rosalind Messenger, *The Doors of Opportunity* (London, 1967).

3. Nicholas Cull, *Selling War: the British propaganda campaign against American 'neutrality' in World War II* (Oxford, 1995); Susan A. Brewer, *To Win the Peace: British Propaganda in the United States during the Second World War* (Ithaca, 1997).

4. John Wheeler-Bennett, *Special Relationships: America in Peace and War* (London,

1975), p. 74; Freya Stark, *Dust*, p. 187. On Berlin, see Michael Ignatieff, *Isaiah Berlin: A Life* (London, 1998).

5. Robert Marett, *Through the Back Door: An Inside View of Britain's Overseas Information Services* (London, 1968), p. 84. For Hayes, see letter from Barbara Hayes to Caroline Haslett, 1 March 1942, NAEST 10/2/6.

6. R. E. M. Bowden, 'Cullis, Winifred Clara (1875–1956)', *ODNB* (2004).

7. 'Professor Cullis's lists of activities in the United States from September, 1941 to the end of June, 1942', Papers of Professor Winifred Cullis, The Women's Library, 7WCU/1.

8. *New York Times,* 20 January, 1942.

9. 'Letters of appreciation received', dated 5 February 1942, 7WCU/1.

10. Wheeler-Bennett, *Special Relationships*, p. 68.

11. Stark, *Dust*, p. 181.

12. Ibid., p. 177.

13. Moorhead, ed., *Bridge of the Levant*, p. 46; and Stark, *Dust,* p. 191.

14. For Lee's wartime diary, see Jennie Lee Collection, Open University Library, Milton Keynes, JL/2/3/2/12.

15. See, for example, typed text of an undated broadcast entitled 'The Spirit of British Women in Wartime', in NAEST 33/10/2.2.

16. Haslett to Mr Hall of the British Embassy in Washington, 23 December 1941, NAEST 10/2/5. For radio broadcasts, see letter from Marjorie Walters to Haslett, 25 November 1941, enclosing typed 'Script for NBC', in NAEST 33/10/2.2.

17. See clippings from *Illustrated Leicester Chronicle*, 23 September 1944, and *Sunday School Chronicle*, October 1944, both in NAEST 10/3/7.

18. Letter from David E. Lilienthal to Sir Stafford Cripps, 27 July 1944 in NAEST 10/3/2; Louise Franklin Bache to Haslett, 21 July 1944, NAEST 10/3/1.

19. See clipping from *Christian Science Monitor*, Boston, 19 January 1943, p. 8, in NAEST 33/10/2.4.

20. 'Text of address to be delivered . . . Friendship Dinner'.

21. Typed copy of speech made at Winnipeg, 6 July 1944, NAEST 10/3/3.

22. Ernest Owen to Haslett, 3 March 1942, NAEST 10/2/6.

23. See correspondence between Haslett and Judson in NAEST 10/3/2.

24. Cited in Mary Kinnear, *Woman of the World: Mary McGeachy and International Cooperation* (Toronto, 2004), p. 51.

25. Nicholas J. Cull, 'Lord Halifax, 1941–46', in Michael F. Hopkins, Saul Kelly and John Young, eds., *The Washington Embassy: British Ambassadors to the United States, 1939–1977* (Basingstoke, 2009), pp. 33–51.

26. H. G. Nicholas, ed., *Washington Despatches 1941–45: Weekly Political Reports from the British Embassy* (London, 1981), introduction by Isaiah Berlin, p. x.

27. Anne Whiteman, 'Lucy Stuart Sutherland, 1903–1980', *Proceedings of the British Academy*, vol. 69, 1983, p. 619. I am grateful to Oliver Mahony at Lady Margaret Hall for directing me to this information.

28. Copy of letter from Mary McGeachy to Sir Gerald Campbell, 11 August 1941, in NAEST 10/2/5.
29. Haslett to Hall, 23 December 1941.
30. McGeachy to Campbell, 11 August 1941.
31. *The Times*, 2 October 1942, p. 4.
32. 'Britain's first woman diplomat', *New York Times,* 11 April 1943.
33. See Kinnear, *Woman of the World*, p. 119.
34. 'Britain's first woman diplomat'.
35. Cited in Kinnear, *Woman of the World*, p. 125.
36. Stark, *Dust*, p. 167.
37. For US attitudes towards the British Empire during the war, see Wm Roger Louis, *Imperialism at Bay: The United States and the Decolonisation of the British Empire, 1941–1945* (Oxford, 1977).
38. Freya Stark's American Diary (which she sent to Monroe), 10 December 1943, quoted in Stark, *Dust*, p. 179.
39. Stark to Perowne, 15 December 1943; and Stark to Monroe, 28 December 1943, in *Dust*, pp. 180, 183.
40. Stark to Jock Murray, 6 January 1944, in *Dust*, p. 188.
41. Stark to Sydney Cockerell, 6 January 1944, in Stark, *Letters*, p. 43.
42. Freya Stark's American Diary, 9 December 1943, in *Dust*, p. 179.
43. Michael Wright, British Embassy, Washington, to Baxter, FO, 15 May 1944, FO 371/40131; and Halifax to Eden, 9 June 1944, FO 371/40131.
44. Only the *Manchester Guardian* made an explicit link between the plight of European Jewry under Nazism and British policy in Palestine, arguing in an editorial of 26 April 1945 for the creation of a Jewish state in the Palestinian Mandate. See Joanne Reilly, *Belsen: The Liberation of a Concentration Camp* (London, 1998), p. 75.

Chapter 10: Equally Eligible

1. Price had, in fact, also served in the USA – as consul in Kansas City and Los Angeles – and had married an American wife, with whom he had two daughters. It is tempting to speculate on the possible effects of this feminine influence in shaping Price's views on women.
2. Written statement by John Playfair Price, 15 September 1945, FO 366/1519.
3. The change thesis is best represented by Paul Addison, *The Road to 1945: British Politics and the Second World War* (London, 1977), and Arthur Marwick, ed., *Total War and Social Change* (Basingstoke, 1988). For revisionist perspectives see Steve Fielding, Peter Thompson and Nick Tiratsoo, *England Arise! The Labour Party and Popular Politics in 1940s Britain* (Manchester, 1995); James Hinton, *Women, Social Leadership, and the Second World War: Continuities of Class* (Oxford, 2002); and Ross McKibbin, *Classes and Cultures: England, 1918–1951* (Oxford, 1998).

4. Council of Women Civil Servants to Anthony Eden, 2 March 1943, Records of the Council of Women Civil Servants, 6CCS/3/07, The Women's Library, London, in file marked '1939–', ff. 43–5.
5. A. P. Waterfield to Sir David Scott, 27 February 1945, FO 366/1497.
6. Alan Barlow to David Scott, 21 March 1945, and Barlow to Scott 23 March 1945, FO 366/1497.
7. Herbert Morrison to Anthony Eden, 26 March 1945, FO 366/1497.
8. Minutes of a preliminary meeting of the Committee to Review the Question of Admission of Women to the Foreign Service, 14 September 1945, FO 366/1499.
9. Bevin to Eden, 5 June 1942, Bevin Papers, Churchill Archives Centre, Cambridge, BEVN 3/2 f. 13.
10. Copy of memo by Anthony Eden circulated to the Cabinet, 15 March 1945, in FO 366/1588.
11. *Proposals for the Reform of the Foreign Service* (Cmd. 6420, 1943).
12. Hansard, Parliamentary Debates (Commons), 18 March 1943, col. 1371.
13. Harold Nicolson, 'Marginal Comment', *Spectator,* 23 January 1942, p. 81.
14. Hansard, Parliamentary Debates (Commons), 18 March 1943, col. 1390.
15. Evidence of Sir David Scott, 23 November 1945, FO 366/1521.
16. Evidence of Sir Alexander Cadogan, 23 November 1945, FO 366/1521.
17. Evidence of G. V. Kitson, 21 September 1945, and evidence of Sir Humphrey Prideaux-Brune, 28 September 1945, both in FO 366/1519.
18. Evidence of Lord Killean, Sir Maurice Peterson, Sir Reader Bullard, Sir H. Stonehewer-Bird, Mr L. B. Grafftey-Smith, Mr T. A. Shone and Sir Walter A. Smart, 18 September, 1945, FO 366/1519.
19. Evidence of Sir William McCallum, 10 October 1945, FO 366/1519; and evidence of Sir Montague Eddy, 16 November 1945, FO 366/1521.
20. Evidence of Mr I. A. Kirkpatrick, 28 September 1945, FO 366/1519; written evidence of Sir David Scott, 19 November 1945, FO 366/1521.
21. Evidence of Lady Reading, 19 October 1945, FO 366/1520.
22. Evidence of Miss I. A. Strong, 26 October 1945, FO 366/1520.
23. Letter submitted by Hilda Martindale and received 27 October 1945, and see also her oral evidence, 9 November 1945, FO 366/1520.
24. Memo submitted by the Council of Women Civil Servants, 1 December 1945, FO 366/1590.
25. Hansard, Parliamentary Debates (Commons), 18 March 1943, col. 1386.
26. Evidence of Caroline Haslett, 19 October 1945, FO 366/1520.
27. Freya Stark to F. C. Mason, 12 December 1945, FO 366/1588.
28. Evidence of Mary McGeachy, 12 October 1945, FO 366/1519.
29. Evidence of F. E. Evans, 14 September 1945, FO 366/1499; evidence of Mr W. H. Montagu-Pollock, 29 November 1945, FO 366/1521; and written memo by D. B. Woodburn, 22 October 1945, FO 366/1520.
30. Memo submitted by the Cambridge University Women Appointments Board, 19 November 1945, FO 366/1521.

31. Statement from H. V. Markham on behalf of the Admiralty, 28 November 1945, FO 366/1521.
32. Evidence of M. G. Kendall, 2 November 1945, FO 366/1520.
33. Minutes of the seventeenth meeting of the Gowers Committee, 4 January 1946, FO 366/1588.
34. Report of the Committee to Re-Examine the Question of Admission of Women to the Foreign Service, 20 February 1946, FO 366/1588.
35. Eva Hartree of the Status of Women Committee to Bevin, 26 March 1946; Florence Barry of St Joan's Alliance to Bevin, 28 March 1946, both in FO 366/1595.

Mexico City, 1975

1. Draft 'Magazine Article on IWY Conference 19 June –2 July 1975', by Millie Miller and Kay Carmichael, in FCO 61/1424.
2. For the official account of the conference, see *Meeting in Mexico: The Story of the World Conference of the International Women's Year,* Mexico City, 19 June–2 July 1975 (United Nations, 1975).
3. Note by Millie Miller, 'International Womens' [sic] Year Conference, Mexico June 1975', FCO 61/1424.
4. See 'Brief No. 1. The World Conference of the International Women's Year, 19 June – 2 July 1975. Steering Brief', dated 10 June 1975, FCO 61/1423. For more on the politics of the conference, see Virginia R. Allan, Margaret E. Galey and Mildred E. Persinger, 'World Conference of International Women's Year', in Anne Winslow, ed., *Women, Politics, and the United Nations* (Westport, Connecticut, 1995), pp. 29–4.
5. R. B. M. King, Permanent Secretary at Overseas Development Ministry to Sir Thomas Brimelow, 19 August 1975, FCO 61/1427.
6. Tessa Solesby to John Macrae, 16 June 1975, FCO 61/1426.
7. John Macrae to Ivan Callan, 21 July 1975, ibid.

Chapter 11: Pioneers

1. Interview with Mary Moore, 5 April 2011. Moore went on to pursue a freelance career as a fiction-writer before serving as Principal of St Hugh's College, Oxford, between 1980 and 1990.
2. A. P. Waterfield to David Scott, 21 March 1946, FO 366/1589.
3. Enid McLeod, *Living Twice: Memoirs* (London, 1982), p. 132.
4. David Scott to A. P. Waterfield, 15 August 1946, FO 366/1591.
5. Alex May, 'Salt, Dame Barbara', in *ODNB* (2004). Another ex-SOE recruit was Barley Alison, who had worked with the French in Algiers before being 'loaned to the Foreign Office', where she stayed until moving into the publishing industry in 1956 (interview in *The Times,* 27 April 1968, p. 21). Michael Butler (ambassador to

UKREP, 1979–85) worked with her in Western Department in 1950 when a telegram came through from the Paris embassy conveying Robert Schuman's invitation to Britain to join the negotiations to set up the European Coal and Steel Community (the forerunner of the European Union). The Francophile Barley, he recalled, was 'tearing her hair out' because she couldn't interest any ministers or senior officials in the contents of the telegram (interview with Sir Michael Butler, 1 October 1997, British Diplomatic Oral History Project, Churchill Archives Centre).

6. 'Recruitment of Men and Women to the Senior Branch of the Foreign Service and the Administrative Class of the Home Civil Service', memo dated 23 August 1963, FO 366/3325.
7. Joan Macintosh (née Burbidge), *Origin of a Species* (unpublished family history).
8. Interview with Dame Margaret Anstee, 23 October 2010.
9. Viola Klein, 'The Demand for Professional Womanpower', *British Journal of Sociology*, 17(2), June 1966, pp. 183–97.
10. Interview with Anne Stoddart, 16 November 2010; interview with Margaret Rothwell, 23 November 2010.
11. Interview with Baroness Neville-Jones, 4 April 2011.
12. Interview with Dame Veronica Sutherland, 8 November 2010.
13. A. H. Halsey, 'Further and Higher Education', in A. H. Halsey with Josephine Webb, eds., *Twentieth-Century British Social Trends* (Basingstoke, 2000), pp. 221–53.
14. See Carol Dyhouse, 'Graduates, mothers and graduate mothers: family investment in higher education in twentieth-century England', *Gender and Education*, 14 (2002), pp. 325–36.
15. Interview with Patricia Lever, 24 May 2011.
16. 'Recruitment of Men and Women', FO 366/3325.
17. Elizabeth Adams, 'Britain's women diplomats battle for promotion . . . with their 749 male colleagues', *Evening Standard*, 23 August 1955, p. 9, clipping in the records of the Council of Women Civil Servants, 6CCS/3/26, File 6.
18. Cambridge appears to be less well represented, supplying only six Branch A recruits (of the total number for whom educational background can be established) for this period.
19. Interview with Catherine Hughes, 26 July 2010.
20. Moore's father was V. H. H. Galbraith, Regius Professor of Modern History at Oxford, 1948–57. Rothwell's father was H. R. Rothwell, Professor of Medieval History at the University of Southampton.
21. They were Lorna Heaton and Judy Newton, although Newton joined the B rather than A stream.
22. The proportion of new entrants to Branch A educated at public schools between 1950 and 1954 was eighty-three per cent and the proportion holding degrees from Oxford or Cambridge was even higher at almost ninety per cent. Twenty years later, these figures had dropped considerably – to fifty-six per cent and sixty-eight per

cent respectively. See 'Recruitment to the Administrative Grades of the Diplomatic Service: Memorandum by a former head of Recruitment, Personnel Policy Department of FCO (D50)', in *Fourth Report from the Expenditure Committee (Defence and External Affairs Sub-Committee), Session 1977–78 on the Central Policy Review Staff Review of Overseas Representation, Volume II: Minutes of Evidence and Appendices*, pp. 284–5.

23. Madge M. McKinney, 'Recruitment of the Administrative Class of the British Civil Service', *Western Political Quarterly*, 2 (3), 1949, pp. 345–57. See also Richard Chapman, *Leadership in the British Civil Service: A Study of Sir Percival Waterfield and the Creation of the Civil Service Selection Board* (London, 1984).

24. The Home Civil Service ran both methods in tandem, but Method II was used exclusively by the Foreign Office until 1957, after which Method I was reinstated as an alternative route into Branch A, and thereafter twenty-five per cent of vacancies were reserved each year for this method. HMSO, *Recruitment to the Administrative Class of the Home Civil Service and the Senior Branch of the Foreign Service: Statement of Government Policy and Report by the Civil Service Commission* (Cmnd. 232, 1957); HMSO, *The Method II System of Selection (for the Administrative Class of the Home Civil Service): Report of the Committee of Inquiry* (Cmnd. 4156, 1969).

25. 'Qualities for a Civil Servant', in *The Times*, 24 May 1948, p. 2.

26. Interview with Dame Anne Warburton, 25 October 2010.

27. Interview with Sarah Squire, 12 January 2011.

28. Viola Klein, *Britain's Married Women Workers* (London, 1965); Political and Economic Planning, *Women and Top Jobs: An Interim Report* (London, 1967); Rhona Rapoport and Robert N. Rapoport, *Dual Career Families Re-examined: new integrations of work and family* (London, 1976).

29. Interview with Juliet Campbell, 1 November 2010.

30. The quote is from Geoffrey Moorhouse, *The Diplomats: The Foreign Office Today* (London, 1977), p. 8.

31. Keith Hamilton, 'Accommodating Diplomacy: The Foreign and Commonwealth Office and the Debate over Whitehall Redevelopment', *Contemporary British History*, 18 (3), 2004, pp. 198–222.

32. Sir Alan Campbell, 'From Carbon Paper to E-mail: Changes in Methods in the Foreign Office, 1950–2000', *Contemporary British History*, 18 (3), 2004, pp. 168–76.

33. Interview with Sir Rodric Braithwaite, 1 November 2011.

34. See Anstee's obituary of Patricia Hutchinson, *The Times*, 1 January 2009.

35. Interview with Dame Margaret Anstee, 23 October 2010. The story is also related in Anstee's memoirs, *Never Learn to Type: A Woman at the United Nations* (Chichester, 2003), p. 70.

36. Interview with Katherine Smith, 7 October 2012.

37. 'Women in the Foreign Service' agreed note of the deputation from the Council of Women Civil Servants to see Head of Personnel, Major J. P. E. C. Henniker-Major,

6 December 1956, Records of the Council of Women Civil Servants, 6CCS/3/26, File 6.

38. E. J. Howes to Information Policy Department, 2 November 1948, enclosing 'Final report by Mrs E. Pemberton on Publicity Work among Women in the Middle East', FO 1018/43; Elizabeth Waller to Mr Champion, 5 May 1967, FCO 61/1428.

39. Anne Pimlott Baker, 'Elwell [*née* Glass], Ann Catherine (1922–96)', in *ODNB* (2004); Charles Elwell, *Ann Catherine Elwell: A Memoir* (King's Lynn, 1997).

40. James Craig, *Shemlan: A History of the Middle East Centre for Arabic Studies* (Basingstoke, 1998).

41. Interview with Dame Veronica Sutherland, 19 April 2005, as part of the British Diplomatic Oral History Project. Transcript available at http://www.chu.cam.ac.uk/archives/collections/BDOHP/

42. The situation was probably tougher in Branch B, where women were more plentiful. One official from the personnel department noted in 1963 'the great difficulty which we are experiencing in getting women officers, however good their record, accepted by Heads of Mission for posts overseas. This is, in fact, a problem peculiar to Branch B, as the number of women officers in Branch A has been kept to a small proportion of the total by the nature of the competitions for entry . . .' Minute by [Mr Young?], 17 July 1963, FO 366/3322.

43. Interview with Rowena Vining, 11 November 2010.

44. *Daily Express*, 27 November 1953, p. 2; *Daily Mirror*, 27 November 1953, p. 16.

45. *Sunday Times*, 20 December 1953. Clipping in records of the Council of Women Civil Servants, 6CCS/3/26, File 6.

46. Adams, 'Britain's Women Diplomats'.

Chapter 12: Diplomatic Women's Lib

1. G. E. Sorenson to the Home Secretary, dated 31 January 1973, forwarded by Peter Canovan to J. S. Whitehead, 15 February 1973, FCO 79/278.

2. J. Davidson's reply to Canovan on Whitehead's behalf, 22 February 1973, FCO 79/278.

3. Interview with Katherine Smith, 7 October 2011.

4. Memoranda submitted by the Fawcett Society, the British Federation of Business and Professional Women and the National Council of Women, forwarded to the Plowden Committee on 10 July 1963, FO 366/3322.

5. *Report of the Committee on Representational Services Overseas appointed by the Prime Minister under the Chairmanship of Lord Plowden 1962–63* (Cmnd. 2276, 1964), p. 33.

6. Minute by F. B. A. Rundell, 19 August 1963, FO 366/3322.

7. Copy of a circular dated 11 August 1965, FO 366/3550.

8. See file marked 'Policy on retention of married women, 1968–9', FCO 79/105.

9. *Report of the Committee on Representational Services*, p. 33.

10. Interview with Mary Moore, 5 April 2011.

11. L. A. Coales of Civil Service Commission to Harold Berners Walker, 18 February 1969; Walker to Coales, 25 March 1969, memo from R. Rendall, dated 13 March 1969, and memo from R. Russell, dated 14 March 1969, FCO 79/90.

12. See copies of *Diplomatic Service Careers* (1972) and *Graduate Careers in the Diplomatic Service* (1971) in FCO 79/278.

13. Rodney Lowe, *The Official History of the British Civil Service: Reforming the Civil Service, Vol. I: The Fulton Years, 1966–81* (London, 2011), chapter 9.

14. 'Record of Administration Planning Committee Meeting on 5 July 1972', FCO 79/356.

15. J. Davidson to Mr Gordon-Smith, 9 May 1973, FCO 77/226.

16. Minutes of the AGM, May 1988 in *Diplomatic Service Wives Association (DSWA) Magazine*, Autumn 1988.

17. Draft enclosed in letter from Mrs B. Williams, assistant secretary of the Diplomatic Service Association, to R. O. Miles in personnel department, 3 January 1974, FCO 79/355.

18. Interview with Sir Rodric Braithwaite, 1 November 2011.

19. At the 1988 AGM of the Diplomatic Service Wives Association, it was claimed that thirty-two female officers were on joint postings abroad with their husbands, although it can be assumed that this figure relates to all grades (including secretarial and clerical) rather than just Branches A and B. See Minutes of the AGM, May 1988 in *Diplomatic Service Wives Association (DSWA) Magazine*, Autumn 1988.

20. Interview with Georgina Butler, 3 June 2011.

21. Interview with Sarah Squire, 12 January 2011.

22. Sutherland was appointed to the Ivory Coast in 1987. Campbell became ambassador to Luxembourg in 1988.

23. Statistics supplied by J. Davidson in response to a request from Mr Gregory of Dorking, 11 March 1974, FCO 79/355.

24. *The Times*, 12 March 1976, p. 8.

25. Interview with Sir Michael Palliser, 4 October 2011.

26. Interview with Dame Anne Warburton, 25 October 2010.

27. 'The not so diplomatic wives', by Shirley Harrison, *Homes & Gardens*, February 1978, pp. 80–2, copy in records of the International Alliance of Women, The Women's Library, London, 2/IAW/2/B/7.

28. 'Note of a meeting on 8 September 1972 to discuss implications for DS of the Kemp-Jones report on women in the Home Civil Service', FCO 79/279.

29. 'Defensive Brief on the Employment of Women in the Diplomatic Service' (unsigned) for Whitley Council Meeting on 1 May 1974, FCO 79/355.

30. Interview with Anne Stoddart, 16 November 2011.

31. Although Sutherland was not the first Branch A woman to be posted there: Joan Burbidge served at the UK High Commission in Delhi from July 1951 until her resignation the following year.

32. Interview with Dame Veronica Sutherland, 8 November 2010.

33. Anne Stoddart was posted to Ankara in 1970; Rosalind Marsden was posted to Tokyo in 1977; Glynne Evans was posted to Buenos Aires in 1972. Hutchinson had been posted earlier in 1964 to Lima as first secretary, so was not a stranger to South America.

34. See Anstee's obituary of Patricia Hutchinson, *The Times,* 1 January 2009.

35. Iran introduced women's suffrage in 1963 and Yemen in 1970. In Kuwait women first voted in 2005. Women still cannot vote in Saudi Arabia.

36. Interview with Margaret Rothwell, 23 November 2010.

37. Interview with Baroness Neville-Jones, 4 and 6 April 2011.

38. Interview with Sophia Lambert, 8 February 2011.

39. Draft enclosed in letter from Mrs B. Williams to R. O. Miles, 3 January 1974, FCO 79/355.

40. Homer Calkin, *Women in the Department of State: Their Role in American Foreign Affairs* (Washington, DC, 1978).

41. This included one career diplomat and five political appointees; see Calkin, *Women in the Department of State,* appendix P.

42. Cited in Nancy E. McGlen and Meredith Reid Sarkees, *Women in Foreign Policy: The Insiders* (London, 1993), p. 19.

43. Ibid., p. 116, although Calkin states that Palmer was in fact appointed to Addis Ababa in Ethiopia, but was required to serve in an executive – rather than political – position; see *Women in the Department of State,* p. 149.

44. Calkin, *Women in the Department of State*; Joan Hoff-Wilson, 'Conclusion: of Mice and Men', in Edward P. Crapol, ed., *Women and American Foreign Policy: Lobbyists, Critics, and Insiders* (London, 1987), pp. 173–88.

45. See *Guardian,* 5 October 1986, p. 3 and 25 November 1986, p. 3; *Daily Express,* 25 November 1986, p. 15; *The Times,* 6 October 1986 and 25 November 1986.

46. Deputy Under-Secretary William B. Macomber Jr, as cited in Calkin, *Women in the Department of State,* p. 157.

47. Although Glaspie's record as ambassador was controversial, most notably for her now famous meeting with Saddam Hussein in July 1990 when she allegedly intimated that the US would not act in the event of an Iraqi invasion of Kuwait.

48. For a useful overview of pressures on British diplomacy in this period, see John W. Young, *Twentieth-Century Diplomacy: A Case Study of British Practice, 1963–1976* (Cambridge, 2008).

49. This remark was made in a minute drafted by Scrivener which he suggested the Foreign Secretary should send to the Prime Minister in response to a request from Barbara Castle, Secretary of State for Social Services, for Foreign Office funding to be made available for International Women's Day activities. See confidential memo from R. S. Scrivener to PUS, dated 9 July 1974, FCO 26/1674.

50. This view was expressed at the permanent under-secretary's planning committee in July 1974. See J. R. James's memo to C. Meyer, dated 27 November 1974, FCO 26/1675.

51. Ibid., and H. J. Spence to C. Meyer, 31 December 1974, FCO 26/1675.

52. For Waller's report of the conference, see 'UN International Women's Year – Conference and Tribune', FCO 61/1424.

Chapter 13: Still Married to the Job

1. Sources for this murder case include *The Times*, 20 December 1958, p. 4, 22 December 1958, p. 12, 19 February 1959, p. 6, and 2 July 1960, p. 8; *Daily Mirror*, 20 December 1958, p. 1, 19 February 1959, p. 4, 26 February 1959, p. 11; *Daily Express*, 20 December 1958, p. 1, 19 February 1959, p. 4; *Guardian*, 26 February 1959, p. 3; Robert Bartlett, *The Working Life of the Surrey Constabulary, 1851–1992* (Open University, 2012).
2. *Daily Mirror*, 20 December 1958, p. 1.
3. Masha Williams, 'Foreign Service Wives' Association: How it started', *DSWA Magazine*, Autumn 1985, pp. 52–4.
4. Betty Friedan, *The Feminine Mystique* (New York, 1963).
5. For women's experiences in post-war Britain, see Jane Lewis, *Women in Britain Since 1945* (London, 1992); Marcus Collins, *Modern Love: An Intimate History of Men and Women in Twentieth-Century Britain* (London, 2003); Dolly Wilson, 'A New Look at the Affluent Worker: The Good Working Mother in Post-War Britain', *Twentieth-Century British History*, 17 (2), 2006, pp. 206–29; Angela Davis, *Modern Motherhood: Women and Family in England, 1945–2000* (Manchester, 2012).
6. Lady Henderson, 'Representing Your Country Abroad', *DSWA Newsletter*, Spring 1976, pp. 23–9.
7. Sally James, *Diplomatic Moves: Life in the Foreign Service* (London, 1995), p. 44.
8. 'Foreign Service Wives' Association: How it started'.
9. Minutes of the Plowden Committee, 13 May 1963, FO 366/3302.
10. *Report of the Committee on Representational Services Overseas appointed by The Prime Minister under the Chairmanship of Lord Plowden 1962–63* (Cmnd. 2276, 1964), p. 34.
11. Report of the AGM held on 13 May 1964, *DSWA Newsletter*, no. 9, July 1964, pp. 3–4.
12. 'Is it all Glamour?', *DSWA Newsletter*, Autumn 1968, pp. 20–2.
13. *DSWA Newsletter*, Spring 1969, p. 6.
14. Report of a DSWA panel on working wives, *DSWA Newsletter*, Autumn 1970, p. 31. In 1981 a bilateral arrangement was reached with the US government to allow dependents of embassy personnel with diplomatic immunity to undertake paid employment outside the embassy.
15. 'Working Wives', *DSWA Newsletter*, Spring 1976, pp. 17–23.
16. Interview with Bridget Cowper-Coles, 22 November 2011.
17. Letter from Cathune Cape, *DSWA Newsletter*, Spring 1973, p. 23; 'Keeping the Pot Boiling in Tripoli', *DSWA Newsletter*, Spring 1974, pp. 68–70.
18. Letter from Jane Reid, *DSWA Newsletter*, Spring 1977, p. 44.

19. 'Questionnaire on work for wives: Report', *DSWA Magazine*, Spring 1983, pp. 15–21.

20. Replies to DSWA Questionnaire, *DSWA Magazine*, Autumn 1986, p. 73.

21. 'Kindergarten in Bangkok', *DSWA Newsletter*, Spring 1972, pp. 23–5; 'Keeping the Pot Boiling in Tripoli'.

22. Letter from Elizabeth Fawcett, *DSWA Newsletter*, Autumn 1974, p. 27.

23. Letter from Mrs M. E. Pellew, *DSWA Newsletter*, Autumn 1970, pp. 27–8.

24. 'Representing your country abroad'.

25. AGM report, *DSWA Newsletter*, Autumn 1972, p. 13.

26. Margaret Ibbott, 'The Role of the Foreign Service Wife: A Personal View', *DSWA Newsletter*, Spring 1976, pp. 43–5.

27. See replies to Ibbott in *DSWA Newsletter*, Autumn 1976, pp. 53–4, and Spring 1977, p. 43.

28. Report of the AGM, *DSWA Newsletter*, Autumn 1979, p. 16.

29. Letter from Sheila Taylor, *DSWA Newsletter*, Autumn 1976, p. 54.

30. In the period 1966–70, there was an average of 57,089 divorce petitions filed each year in England and Wales. For the period 1971–5, this figure shot up to 121,772. The risk of divorce within twenty years for couples who married in 1951 was seven per cent. For those marrying in 1966, the risk had risen to twenty-four per cent and of couples marrying in 1971, 27.5 per cent were divorced within twenty years. David Coleman, 'Population and Family', in A. H. Halsey with Josephine Webb, eds., *Twentieth-Century British Social Trends* (Basingstoke, 2000), pp. 63–4.

31. Report of the AGM, *DSWA Newsletter*, Autumn 1979, p. 17.

32. Hilary Callan and Shirley Ardener, eds., *The Incorporated Wife* (London, 1984).

33. Hilary Callan, 'The Premiss of Dedication: Notes towards an Ethnography of Diplomats' Wives', in Shirley Ardener, ed., *Perceiving Women* (London, 1975), p. 97. Margaret Ibbott actually cited Callan's work in her letter to the *DSWA Newsletter*.

34. Eric Miller, 'Some reflections on the role of the diplomatic wife', in *From Dependency to Autonomy: Studies in Organisation and Change* (London, 1993), pp. 132–45.

35. 'The Role of the Wife of Head of Mission: a note prepared for the Diplomatic Service Wives' Association', by Eric J. Miller, *DSWA Magazine*, Spring 1981, pp. 13–23.

36. 'Questionnaire on work for wives: Report', *DSWA Magazine*, Spring 1983, pp. 15–21.

37. Harrison, 'The not so diplomatic wives'.

38. 'With Respect Ambassador', interview with Simon Jenkins, *DSWA Magazine*, Autumn 1984, pp. 47–53.

39. 'Opinion: the Service in Decline', *DSWA Magazine*, Spring 1986, pp. 24–5.

40. See feature by Lindsay Knight, 'Married to affairs of state', *The Times*, 5 November 1986, and reproduced in *DSWA Magazine*, Spring 1987, pp. 61–3.

41. Interview with Catherine Hughes, 26 July 2011.

42. Letter from Guy C. Digby, *DSWA Magazine,* Spring 1985, pp. 103–4.
43. 'Two-day Conference of Spouses' Associations, Rome 10/11 June 1985', *DSWA Magazine,* Autumn 1985, pp. 42–3.
44. Report of AGM, *DSWA Magazine,* Autumn 1988, p. 31.
45. Letter from Tina Pinnell, *DSWA Magazine,* Spring 1986, pp. 89–90.
46. 'Letter from South America – by a reluctant DSWA member!', *DSWA Magazine,* Spring 1989, pp. 60–1.
47. Alex Sutherland, 'The Ambassador's Husband', *DSWA Magazine,* Autumn 1990, pp. 44–7.
48. Report of AGM, *DSWA Newsletter,* Autumn 1979, p. 21.
49. Norma Reid, 'A thorn among the roses?', *DSWA Magazine,* Spring 1983, pp. 39–41.
50. Interview with Margaret Rothwell, 23 November 2010.
51. Quoted in Miller, 'Some reflections'.

Epilogue: Members of the Club

1. *The Times,* 3 January 1996, p. 1.
2. *Guardian,* 6 February 1996, p. 9.
3. 'FO's top woman quits to join bank', *The Times,* 8 February 1996, p. 1.
4. 'Why the FO chaps wouldn't make my daughter our lady in Paris: Mandarins accused of sexism over Dame Pauline', *Daily Mail,* 5 February 1996, p. 6.
5. 'Wheen's World: Scott's leading actors step into the limelight', *Guardian,* 7 February 1996, p. 5.
6. 'A very undiplomatic incident', *Independent,* 6 February 1996, p. 17.
7. 'Executive equality: When high-flying women bump into a glass ceiling. Britain's men's-room culture is still preventing women in the fast stream from reaching the top of their professions', *Observer,* 11 February 1996, p. 17.
8. 'Why the FO chaps', *Daily Mail,* 5 February 1996, p. 6.
9. 'Sharp practice at the Foreign Office', *The Times,* 23 September 1996, p. 1.
10. 'Sexual diplomacy', *Independent,* 8 February 1996, p. 18.
11. Other female heads of mission from this period include: Margaret Rothwell, ambassador to the Ivory Coast (1990–7); Rosemary Spencer, ambassador to the Netherlands (1996–2001); Kaye Oliver, ambassador to Rwanda (1995–8); Glynne Evans, ambassador to Chile (1997–2000); Jessica Pearce, ambassador to Belarus (1996–9). Maeve Fort had been ambassador to Mozambique (1989–92) and after her Lebanon posting went on to become high commissioner in South Africa (1996–2000).
12. Ruth Dudley Edwards, *True Brits: Inside the Foreign Office* (London, 1994); John Dickie, *The New Mandarins: How British Foreign Policy Works* (London, 2007).
13. Dickie, *The New Mandarins,* p. 25.
14. FCO, *Diversity @ FCO: The Foreign and Commonwealth Office's First Annual Diversity Report* (2007).
15. See FOI release, 'Information on gender equality in the FCO', dated 4 September 2009.

16. 'Career Profiles: the furniture maker', *BDSA Magazine*, Spring 1998, pp. 20–1.

17. Leigh Turner's profile on FCO website: http://blogs.fco.gov.uk/leighturner/about-leigh/ (accessed 20 July 2012).

18. Leigh Turner, 'From Herr to Maternity', *Financial Times*, 8 May 2003, and 'Behind Every Great Woman', *Financial Times,* 1 August 2003.

19. The Fatherhood Institute cites research which finds that only one per cent of fathers in two-parent families with babies a year old or younger are on 'sole charge' for more than thirty hours per week, whilst in families with three to four year olds, four per cent of the fathers take on that role. http://www.fatherhoodinstitute.org/2011/fi-research-summary-fathers-mothers-work-and-family/ (accessed 20 July 2012).

20. *Foreign and Commonwealth Office (FCO) Diversity and Equality Report 2013 in response to the Equality Act 2010*, p. 4.

21. Christopher Meyer, *DC Confidential* (London, 2005), p. 1.

Bibliography

UNPUBLISHED SOURCES

Manuscripts

British Library, London
India Office Records, files relating to Royal Commission on Indian Labour (L/PO/263)

British Library of Social and Economic Sciences, London School of Economics
Records of the Woman Power Committee (COLL MISC 0548)

Churchill Archives Centre, Cambridge
Papers of Alfred Lyttelton and Dame Edith Lyttelton, and their son Oliver Lyttelton (CHAN)
Papers of Ernest Bevin (BEVN)
British Diplomatic Oral History Project, Transcribed Interviews: Sir Michael Butler, 1 October 1997; Juliet Campbell, 3 March 2003; Rosamund Huebener, 11 May 2000; Dame Veronica Sutherland, 19 April 2005

Girton College, Cambridge
Papers of Bertha Phillpotts (GCPP Phillpotts)
Papers of Beryl Power (GCPP Powers)

Institution of Engineering and Technology, London
Papers of Dame Caroline Haslett (NAEST 033)

The National Archives, Kew

FO/366/915–7, FO/366/928–34, FO 366/954, FO 366/1277, FO/366/1497–9, FO 366/1519–21, FO/366/1588–90, FO 366/1595, FO 366/3302, FO/366/3322, FO/366/3325, FO 366/3550, FO 371/40131, FO 1018/43, FCO/26/1674–5, FCO 61/1423–4, FCO 61/1426–8, FCO 77/226, FCO 79/90, FCO 79/105, FCO 79/278–9, FCO 79/355–6, T 169/17–20

University of Newcastle

Gertrude Bell Archive, digitised material available at http://www.gerty.ncl.ac.uk/

Open University, Milton Keynes

Jennie Lee Collection (JL)

Palace Green Library, University of Durham

Papers of Professor A. K. S. (Nancy) Lambton

The Parliamentary Archives, Westminster

Bonar Law Papers (BL)

The Women's Library, London

Papers of Dame Margery Corbett Ashby (7MCA)
Papers of Professor Winifred Cullis (7WCU)
Records of the Council of Women Civil Servants (6CCS)
International Alliance of Women (2IAW)

Other

Author interviews: Dame Margaret Anstee, 23 October 2010; Sir Rodric Braithwaite, 1 November 2011; Georgina Butler, 3 June 2011; Juliet Campbell, 1 November 2010; Sir Hugh Cortazzi, 15 September 2011; Bridget Cowper-Coles, 22 November 2011; Catherine Hughes, 26 July 2010; Sophia Lambert, 8 February 2011; Patricia Lever, 24 May 2011; Ann Lewis, 10 November 2010; Mary Moore, 5 April 2011; Sir Alan Munro, 19 June 2012; Baroness Neville-Jones, 4 and 6 April 2011; Sir Michael Palliser, 4 October 2011; Margaret Rothwell, 23 November 2010; Richard Samuel, 5 January 2012; Katherine Smith, 7 October 2012; Sarah Squire, 12 January 2011; Anne Stoddart, 16 November 2010; Dame Veronica Sutherland, 8 November 2010; Nina Veitch, 7 January 2011; Rowena Vining, 11 November 2010; Dame Anne Warburton, 25 October 2010

Private correspondence: Joan Macintosh (neé Burbidge)

PUBLISHED SOURCES

Primary Sources

Newspapers and periodicals
British Diplomatic Spouses Association Magazine; *Carousel* (organ of the Diplomatic Service Families Association); *Daily Express*; *Daily Mail*; *Daily Mirror*; *Diplomatic Service Wives Association Magazine*; *Diplomatic Service Wives Association Newsletter*; *Evening Standard*; *Financial Times*; *Foreign Affairs* (organ of the Union of Democratic Control); *Independent*; *Manchester Guardian*; *New York Times*; *Observer*; *Spectator*; *Sunday Times*; *Time and Tide*; *The Times*

Official Publications
Cheke, Marcus, *Guidance on foreign usages and ceremony, and other matters, for a Member of His Majesty's Foreign Service on his first appointment to a Post Abroad* (FCO, 1949)
Foreign and Commonwealth Office, 'Information on gender equality in the FCO' (Freedom of Information release dated 4 September 2009)
Foreign and Commonwealth Office, *Foreign and Commonwealth Office (FCO) Diversity and Equality Report 2013 in response to the Equality Act 2010*
Foreign and Commonwealth Office, *Diversity @ FCO: The Foreign and Commonwealth Office's First Annual Diversity Report* (FCO, 2007)
Foreign Office List and Diplomatic and Consular Year Book
Fourth Report from the Expenditure Committee (Defence and External Affairs Sub-committee), Session 1977–78 on The Central Policy Review Staff Review of Overseas Representation, Volume II: Minutes of Evidence and Appendices
Hansard Parliamentary Debates
—— *Report from the Select Committee on Diplomatic Service* (House of Commons, 1861)
—— *First Report from the Select Committee on Diplomatic and Consular Services* (House of Commons, 1871)
HMSO, *Royal Commission on the Civil Service: Fifth Report of the Commissioners* (Cmd. 7748, 1914)
—— *Report of the Sub-committee appointed to consider the position after the war of women holding temporary appointments in Government Departments* (Cmd. 199, 1919)
—— *Report of the Royal Commission on the Civil Service (1929–31)* (Cmd. 3909, 1931)

—— *Documents Relating to the Admission of Women to the Diplomatic and Consular Services* (Cmd. 5166, 1936)

—— *Proposals for the Reform of the Foreign Service* (Cmd. 6420, 1943)

—— *Recruitment to the Administrative Class of the Home Civil Service and the Senior Branch of the Foreign Service: Statement of Government Policy and Report by the Civil Service Commission* (Cmnd. 232, 1957)

—— *Report of the Committee on Representational Services Overseas appointed by the Prime Minister under the Chairmanship of Lord Plowden 1962–63* (Cmnd. 2276, 1964)

—— *Report of the Review Committee on Overseas Representation 1968–1969* (Cmnd. 4107, 1969)

—— *The Method II System of Selection (for the Administrative Class of the Home Civil Service): Report of the Committee of Inquiry* (Cmnd. 4156, 1969)

Memoirs, diaries and other contemporary texts

Anstee, Margaret Joan, *Never Learn to Type: A Woman at the United Nations* (Chichester, 2003)

Antrobus, George, *King's Messenger 1918–1940: Memoirs of a Silver Greyhound* (London, 1941)

Ashby, Margery Corbett, 'Women out-numbered fifty to one by men', *International Women's News*, vol. 40, no. 5, February 1946, p. 51

Bartlett, Vernon, *Behind the Scenes at the Peace Conference* (London, 1920)

Beadon, R. H., *Some Memories of the Peace Conference* (London, 1933)

Bruce, H. J., *Silken Dalliance* (London, 1946)

Buchanan, George, *My Mission to Russia and other Diplomatic Memories* (London, 1923)

Buchanan, Meriel, *Diplomacy and Foreign Courts* (London, 1928)

—— *Ambassador's Daughter* (London, 1958)

Callan, Hilary, 'The Premiss of Dedication: Notes towards an Ethnography of Diplomats' Wives', in *Perceiving Women*, ed. Shirley Ardener (London, 1975), pp. 87–104

Callan, Hilary, and Ardener, Shirley, eds., *The Incorporated Wife* (London, 1984)

Churchill, Lady Randolph, ed., *Women's War Work* (London, 1916)

Corbett, Vincent, *Reminiscences: Autobiographical and Diplomatic* (London, 1927)

Cowper-Coles, Sherard, *Ever the Diplomat: Confessions of a Foreign Office Mandarin* (London, 2012)

Crowdy, Rachel, 'The Humanitarian Activities of the League of Nations', *Journal of the Royal Institute of International Affairs*, 6 (3), May 1927, pp. 153–69

D'Abernon, Helen, *Red Cross and Berlin Embassy, 1915–1926: Extracts from the Diaries of Viscountess D'Abernon* (London, 1946)

De Palencia, Isabel, *Alexandra Kollontay: Ambassadress from Russia* (London, 1947)

Douie, Vera, *The Lesser Half: A Survey of the Laws, Regulations and Practices Introduced during the Present War which Embody Discrimination Against Women* (London, 1943)

Dowager Marchioness of Dufferin and Ava, *My Russian and Turkish Journals* (London, 1916)

Evans, Dorothy, *Women and the Civil Service* (London, 1934)

Fraser, Mary Crawford, *A Diplomatist's Wife in Many Lands, Volume II* (London, 1910)

—— *A Diplomatist's Wife in Japan: Sketches at the Turn of the Century* edited by Sir Hugh Cortazzi (New York, 1982)

Friedan, Betty, *The Feminine Mystique* (New York, 1963)

Gildersleeve, Virginia, *Many a Good Crusade* (New York, 1954)

Gregory, J. D., *On the Edge of Diplomacy: Rambles and Reflections, 1902–1928* (London, 1929)

Hamilton, Lord Frederick, *The Vanished Pomps of Yesterday: Being Some Random Reminiscences of a British Diplomat* (London, 1919)

Hamilton, Mary Agnes, 'Women in Politics', *Political Quarterly,* 3 (1932), pp. 226–44

—— *Up-Hill All the Way: A Third Cheer for Democracy* (London, 1953)

Hankey, Lord, *The Supreme Control at the Paris Peace Conference 1919* (London, 1963)

Hardinge, Charles, *Old Diplomacy: The Reminiscences of Lord Hardinge of Penshurst* (London, 1947)

Headlam-Morley, James, *A Memoir of the Paris Peace Conference 1919* (London, 1972)

Hodgkin, E. C., ed., *Letters from Tehran: A British Ambassador in World War II Persia* (London, 1991)

Hogarth, David, Obituary of Gertrude Bell, *Geographical Journal,* vol. 68, no. 4 (Oct 1926), pp. 363–8

Hohler, Thomas, *Diplomatic Petrel* (London, 1942)

Howard, Esme, *Theatre of Life: Volume I: Life Seen from the Pit, 1863–1905* (London, 1935)

—— *Theatre of Life: Volume II: Life Seen from the Stalls, 1905–36* (London, 1936)

Huddleston, Sisley, *Peace-Making at Paris* (London, 1919)

James, Sally, *Diplomatic Moves: Life in the Foreign Service* (London, 1995)

Jenkins, Simon, and Sloman, Anne, *With Respect, Ambassador: An Inquiry into the Foreign Office* (London, 1985)

Keenan, Brigid, *Diplomatic Baggage: The Adventures of a Trailing Spouse* (London, 2005)

Kelly, David, *The Ruling Few: Or the Human Background to Diplomacy* (London, 1952)

Klein, Viola, *Britain's Married Women Workers* (London, 1965)

—— 'The Demand for Professional Womanpower', *British Journal of Sociology*, 17 (2), June 1966, pp. 183–97

Knatchbull-Hugessen, Hughe, *Diplomat in Peace and War* (London, 1949)

Kollontai, Alexandra, *The Autobiography of a Sexually Emancipated Communist Woman* (New York, 1971)

Lambton, Ann, 'Recollections of Iran in the mid-twentieth century', *Asian Affairs*, 19 (3), October 1988, pp. 273–88

Lloyd George, Frances, *The Years that Are Past* (London, 1967)

MacAlister, Florence, *Memoir of the Right Hon. Sir John McNeill and of his second wife Elizabeth Wilson, by their Grand-Daughter* (London, 1910)

MacDonagh, Michael, *In London during the Great War: The Diary of a Journalist* (London, 1935)

Macdonell, Lady Anne, *Reminiscences of Diplomatic Life* (London, 1913)

McKinney, Madge, 'Recruitment of the Administrative Class of the British Civil Service', *Western Political Quarterly*, 2 (3), 1949, pp. 345–57

McLeod, Enid, *Living Twice: Memoirs* (London, 1982)

Marett, Robert, *Through the Back Door: An Inside View of Britain's Overseas Information Services* (London, 1968)

Martindale, Hilda, *Women Servants of the State, 1870–1938: A History of Women in the Civil Service* (London, 1938)

Meyer, Christopher, *DC Confidential* (London, 2005)

Meynell, Alix, *Public Servant: Private Woman: An Autobiography* (London, 1988)

Miller, Eric, 'Some reflections on the role of the diplomatic wife', *From Dependency to Autonomy: Studies in Organisation and Change* (London, 1993), pp. 132–45

Moorehead, Caroline, ed., *Over the Rim of the World: Freya Stark: Selected Letters* (London, 1988)

—— *Freya Stark, Letters: Volume Four: Bridge of the Levant, 1940–43* (Salisbury, 1977)

Nicholas, H. G., ed., *Washington Despatches 1941–45: Weekly Political Reports from the British Embassy* (London, 1981)

Nicolson, Harold, *Peacemaking, 1919* (London, 1933)

Owen, Ruth Bryan, *Leaves from a Greenland Diary* (New York, 1935)

Peel, C. S., *How We Lived Then: A Sketch of Social and Domestic Life in England during the War* (London, 1929)

Political and Economic Planning, *Women and Top Jobs: An Interim Report* (London, 1967)

Rapoport, Rhona, and Rapoport, Robert, *Dual Career Families Re-examined: New Integrations of Work and Family* (London, 1976)

Lord Riddell's Intimate Diary of the Peace Conference and After, 1918–1923 (London, 1933)

Rodd, Sir James Rennell, *Social and Diplomatic Memories, 1884–1893* (London, 1922)

—— *Social and Diplomatic Memories, 1894–1901: Egypt and Abyssinia* (London, 1923)

—— *Social and Diplomatic Memories, 1902–1919* (London, 1925)

Sackville-West, Vita, *Pepita* (London, 1937)

Shotwell, James, *At the Paris Peace Conference* (New York, 1937)

Spaull, Hebe, *Women Peace-Makers* (London, 1924)

Stark, Freya, *East is West* (London, 1945)

—— *Traveller's Prelude: Autobiography 1893–1927* (London, 1950)

—— *Dust in the Lion's Paw: Autobiography 1939–1946* (London, 1961)

Swanwick, Helena, *I Have Been Young* (London, 1935)

Taylor, A. J. P., ed., *Lloyd George: A Diary by Frances Stevenson* (London, 1971)

Tilley, John, *London to Tokyo* (London, 1942)

Tilley, John, and Gaselee, Stephen, *The Foreign Office* (London, 1933)

Union of Democratic Control, *How to Get a Permanent Peace* (London: leaflet no. 446, 1917)

United Nations, *Meeting in Mexico: The Story of the World Conference of the International Women's Year, Mexico City, 19 June–2 July 1975* (New York, 1975)

Vansittart, Robert, *The Mist Procession: The Autobiography of Lord Vansittart* (London, 1958)

Wellesley, F. A., ed., *The Paris Embassy during the Second Empire: Selections from the Papers of Henry Richard Charles Wellesley, 1st Earl Cowley, Ambassador at Paris 1852–67* (London, 1928)

Wheeler-Bennett, John, *Special Relationships: America in Peace and War* (London, 1975)

Wiskemann, Elizabeth, *The Europe I Saw* (London, 1968)

Secondary Sources

Addison, Paul, *The Road to 1945: British Politics and the Second World War* (London, 1977)

Allan, Virginia, Galey, Margaret and Persinger, Mildred, 'World Conference of International Women's Year' in Anne Winslow, ed., *Women, Politics, and the United Nations* (Westport, Connecticut, 1995), pp. 29–44

Anderson, M. S., *The Eastern Question, 1774–1923* (London, 1966)

Arbuthnot, Hugh, Obituary of Professor Ann Lambton, *Journal of the Iran Society*, 2 (7), 2008, pp. 37–40

Aronson, Theo, *Grandmama of Europe: The Crowned Descendants of Queen Victoria* (London, 1973)

Baker, Anne Pimlott, 'Elwell [*née* Glass], Ann Catherine (1922–1996)', *Oxford Dictionary of National Biography* (Oxford, 2004)

Barker, Alex, 'Britain's first female diplomats', *Financial Times*, 6 November 2009

Black, Annabel, 'The changing culture of diplomatic spouses: some fieldnotes from Brussels', *Diplomacy & Statecraft*, 6 (1995), pp. 196–222

Bowden, R. E. M., 'Cullis, Winifred Clara (1875–1956)', *Oxford Dictionary of National Biography* (Oxford, 2004)

Braybon, Gail and Summerfield, Penny, *Out of the Cage: Women's Experiences in Two World Wars* (London, 1987)

Brewer, Susan, *To Win the Peace: British Propaganda in the United States during the Second World War* (Ithaca, 1997)

Calkin, Homer, *Women in the Department of State: Their Role in American Foreign Affairs* (Washington DC, 1978)

Campbell, Sir Alan, 'From Carbon Paper to E-mail: Changes in Methods in the Foreign Office, 1950–2000', *Contemporary British History*, 18 (3), 2004, pp. 168–76

Chapman, Richard, *Leadership in the British Civil Service: A Study of Sir Percival Waterfield and the Creation of the Civil Service Selection Board* (London, 1984)

Charmley, John and Davey, Jennifer, 'The Invisible Politician: Mary Derby and the Eastern Crisis' in *On The Fringes of Diplomacy: Influences on British Foreign Policy, 1800–1945*, eds. John Fisher and Anthony Best (Farnham, 2011), pp. 17–34

Clark, Anna, 'Women in eighteenth-century British Politics' in *Women, Gender and Enlightenment*, eds. Sarah Knott and Barbara Taylor, (Basingstoke, 2005), pp. 570–86

Clements, Barbara, *Bolshevik Feminist: The Life of Aleksandra Kollontai* (London, 1979)

Coleman, David, 'Population and Family' in *Twentieth-Century British Social Trends*, ed. A. H. Halsey with Josephine Webb (Basingstoke, 2000), pp. 27–93

Collins, Marcus, *Modern Love: An Intimate History of Men and Women in Twentieth-Century Britain* (London, 2003)

Craig, James, *Shemlan: a History of the Middle East Centre for Arabic Studies* (Basingstoke, 1998)

Crapol, Edward, ed., *Women and American Foreign Policy: Lobbyists, Critics, and Insiders* (London, 1987)

Cross, Mai'a K. Davis, *The European Diplomatic Corps: Diplomats and International Cooperation from Westphalia to Maastricht* (Basingstoke, 2007)

Cull, Nicholas, *Selling War: the British Propaganda Campaign Against American 'Neutrality' in World War II* (Oxford, 1995)

—— 'Lord Halifax, 1941–46' in *The Washington Embassy: British Ambassadors to the United States, 1939–1977*, eds. Michael F. Hopkins, Saul Kelly and John Young (Basingstoke, 2009), pp. 33–51

Dale, Doris Cruger, 'An American in Geneva: Florence Wilson and the League of Nations Library', *Journal of Library History*, 7 (2), 1972, pp. 109–29

Davenport-Hines, Richard, 'Blackwood, Hariot Georgina Hamilton-Temple, Marchioness of Dufferin and Ava (1843–1936)', *Oxford Dictionary of National Biography* (Oxford, 2004)

Davis, Angela, *Modern Motherhood: Women and Family in England, 1945–2000* (Manchester, 2012)

Dickie, John, *The New Mandarins: How British Foreign Policy Works* (London, 2007)

Doran, Susan, *Monarchy and Matrimony: The Courtships of Elizabeth I* (London, 1996)

Dudley Edwards, Ruth, *True Brits: Inside the Foreign Office* (London, 1994)

Dyhouse, Carol, 'Graduates, mothers and graduate mothers: family investment in higher education in twentieth-century England', *Gender and Education*, 14 (2002), pp. 325–36

Eisenberg, Jaci, 'American women in international Geneva, 1919–1939: a prosopography', *Women's History Magazine*, 71, Spring 2013, pp. 4–11

Elwell, Charles, *Ann Catherine Elwell: A Memoir* (King's Lynn, 1997)

Fielding, Steve, Thompson, Peter and Tiratsoo, Nick, *England Arise! The Labour Party and Popular Politics in 1940s Britain* (Manchester, 1995)

Firkatian, Mari, *Diplomats and Dreamers: The Stancioff Family in Bulgarian History* (Lanham, MD, 2008)

Foreign and Commonwealth Office, *Women in Diplomacy* (London, 1992, and revised ed. 1999)

Garnett, David, *The Secret History of the PWE: the Political Warfare Executive, 1939–1945* (London, 2002)

Geniesse, Jane Fletcher, *Freya Stark: Passionate Nomad* (London, 1999)

Gleadle, Kathryn, *Borderline Citizens: Women, Gender, and Political Culture in Britain 1815–1867* (Oxford, 2009)

Halsey, A. H., 'Further and Higher Education', *Twentieth-Century British Social Trends*, ed. A. H. Halsey with Josephine Webb (Basingstoke, 2000), pp. 221–53

Hamilton, Keith, 'Accommodating Diplomacy: The Foreign and Commonwealth Office and the Debate over Whitehall Redevelopment', *Contemporary British History,* 18 (3), 2004, pp. 198–222

Hickman, Katie, *Daughters of Britannia: The Life and Times of Diplomatic Wives* (London, 1999)

Hinton, James, *Women, Social Leadership, and the Second World War: Continuities of Class* (Oxford, 2002)

Howell, Georgina, *Daughter of the Desert: The Remarkable Life of Gertrude Bell* (London, 2006)

Huck, James, 'Palma Guillén, Mexico's First Female Ambassador and the International Image of Mexico's Post-Revolutionary Gender Policy', *MACLAS: Latin American Essays,* 13 (1999), pp. 159–71

Ignatieff, Michael, *Isaiah Berlin: A Life* (London, 1998)

Izzard, Molly, *Freya Stark: A Biography* (London, 1993)

Jones, Raymond, *The British Diplomatic Service, 1815–1914* (Gerrards Cross, 1983)

—— *The Nineteenth-century Foreign Office: An Administrative History* (London, 1971)

Kinnear, Mary, *Woman of the World: Mary McGeachy and International Cooperation* (Toronto, 2004)

Kocho-Williams, Alastair, 'Engaging the world: Soviet diplomacy and Foreign Propaganda in the 1920s' (2007): paper available at http://www.uwe.ac.uk/hlss/history/sovietdiplomats1920s.pdf

——————'The Soviet Diplomatic Corps and Stalin's Purges', *Slavonic and East European Review,* 86 (1), 2008, pp. 90–110

Lal, Maneesha, 'The politics of gender and medicine in colonial India: the Countess of Dufferin's Fund, 1885–1888', *Bulletin of the History of Medicine,* 68 (1994), pp. 29–66

Lang, Sean, 'Saving India through its Women', *History Today,* 55 (9), 2005

Larner, Christina, 'The Amalgamation of the Diplomatic Service with the Foreign Office', *Journal of Contemporary History,* 7 (1/2), 1972, pp. 107–26

Leneman, Leah, *In the Service of Life: the Story of Elsie Inglis and the Scottish Women's Hospitals* (Edinburgh, 1994)

Lewis, Jane, *Women in Britain Since 1945* (London, 1992)

Louis, Wm Roger, *Imperialism at Bay: The United States and the Decolonisation of the British Empire, 1941–1945* (Oxford, 1977)

—— 'Musaddiq, oil, and the dilemmas of British Imperialism' in *Ends of British Imperialism: The Scramble for Empire, Suez and Decolonization* (London, 2006), pp. 727–87

Lowe, Rodney, *The Official History of the British Civil Service: Reforming the Civil Service, Vol. I: The Fulton Years, 1966–81* (London, 2011)

Lukitz, Liora, *A Quest in the Middle East: Gertrude Bell and the Making of Modern Iraq* (London, 2006)

MacCaffrey, Wallace, *Elizabeth I: War and Politics, 1588–1603* (Princeton, New Jersey, 1992)

McCarthy, Helen, 'Petticoat Diplomacy: The Admission of Women to the British Foreign Service, c.1939–1946', *Twentieth Century British History*, 20 (2009), pp. 285–321

McGlen, Nancy and Sarkees, Meredith Reid, *Women in Foreign Policy: The Insiders* (London, 1993)

McKibbin, Ross, *Classes and Cultures: England, 1918–1951* (Oxford, 1998)

Macmillan, Margaret, *Peacemakers: The Paris Conference of 1919 and its Attempt to End War* (London, 2001)

Marwick, Arthur, ed., *Total War and Social Change* (Basingstoke, 1988)

Matsumoto-Best, Saho, 'The Cultural Diplomacy of Sir James Rennell Rodd', *On the Fringes of Diplomacy: Influences on British Foreign Policy, 1800–1945*, eds. John Fisher and Antony Best (Farnham, 2011), pp. 209–24

May, Alex, 'Salt, Dame Barbara', *Oxford Dictionary of National Biography* (Oxford, 2004)

Medlicott, W. N., *The Congress of Berlin and After: A Diplomatic History of the Near Eastern Settlement, 1878–1880* (London, 1938)

Messenger, Rosalind, *The Doors of Opportunity* (London, 1967)

Metzger, Barbara, 'Towards an International Human Rights Regime during the Inter-War Years: the League of Nations' Combat of Traffic in Women and Children' in *Beyond Sovereignty: Britain, Empire and Transnationalism, c.1880–1950*, eds. Kevin Grant, Philippa Levine and Frank Trentmann (Basingstoke, 2007), pp. 54–79

Middleton, Charles, *The Administration of British Foreign Policy 1782–1846* (Durham, North Carolina, 1977)

Moorhouse, Geoffrey, *The Diplomats: The Foreign Office Today* (London, 1977)

Morgan, David, 'Ann K. S. Lambton (1912–2008) and Persian Studies', *Journal of the Royal Asiatic Society*, 21 (1), 2011, pp. 99–109

Mori, Jennifer, *The Culture of Diplomacy: Britain in Europe, c.1750–1830* (Manchester, 2010)

Mösslang, Markus and Riotte, Torsten, eds., *The Diplomats' World: A Cultural History of Diplomacy, 1815–1914* (Oxford, 2008)

Nash, Philip, '"A Woman's Touch in Foreign Affairs"? The Career of Ambassador Frances E. Willis', *Diplomacy & Statecraft*, 13 (2), 2002, pp. 1–20

—— 'America's First Female Chief of Mission: Ruth Bryan Owen, Minister to Denmark, 1933–36', *Diplomacy and Statecraft*, 16 (2005), pp. 57–72

O'Halpin, Eunan, *Head of the Civil Service: A Study of Sir Warren Fisher* (London, 1989)

Pattinson, Juliette, *Behind Enemy Lines: Gender, Passing and the Special Operations Executive in the Second World War* (Manchester, 2007)

Pellew, Jill, 'Married to a British Diplomat in Washington, DC, 1983–1989', *Britain and the World*, 2 (2010), pp. 282–5

Pernet, Corinne, 'Chilean Feminists, the International Women's Movement, and Suffrage, 1915 to 1950', *Pacific Historical Review*, 69 (2000), pp. 663–88

Platt, D. C. M., *The Cinderella Service: British Consuls Since 1825* (London, 1971)

Porter, Bernard, *The Battle of the Styles: Society, Culture and the Design of a New Foreign Office, 1855–61* (London, 2011)

Potter, Jane, 'Livingstone, Dame Adelaide Lord (*c.*1881–1970)', *Oxford Dictionary of National Biography* (Oxford, 2004)

Proctor, Tammy, *Female Intelligence: Women and Espionage in the First World War* (London, 2003)

Reilly, Joanne, *Belsen: The Liberation of a Concentration Camp* (London, 1998)

Reynolds, K. D., *Aristocratic Women and Political Society in Victorian Britain* (Oxford, 1998)

Richardson, Sarah, *The Political Worlds of Women: Gender and Politics in Nineteenth-Century Britain* (London, 2013)

Rose, Norman, *Vansittart: Study of a Diplomat* (London, 1978)

Rose, Sonya, *Which People's War? National Identity and Citizenship in Britain, 1939–1945* (Oxford, 2003)

Satia, Priya, *Spies in Arabia: The Great War and the Cultural Foundations of Britain's Covert Empire in the Middle East* (Oxford, 2008)

Seton-Watson, R. W., *Disraeli, Gladstone and the Eastern Question* (London, 1935)

Sluga, Glenda, Calvi, Giulia and James, Carolyn, eds., *Women, Diplomacy and International Relations Since 1500* (London, forthcoming, 2014)

Sluga, Glenda, '"Spectacular Feminism": The international history of women, world citizenship and human rights', in Francisca de Haan, Margaret Allen, June Purvis and Krassimira Dasklova, eds., *Women's Activism: Global Perspectives from the 1890s to the Present* (London, 2012)

Smedley, Beryl, *Partners in Diplomacy* (Ferring, 1990)

Smith, Harold, ed., *War and Social Change: British Society in the Second World War* (Manchester, 1986)

Starr, Kevin, *Embattled Dreams: California in War and Peace, 1940–1950* (Oxford, 2002)

Steinberg, Jonathan, *Bismarck: A Life* (Oxford, 2011)

Steiner, Zara, *The Foreign Office and Foreign Policy, 1898–1914* (Cambridge, 1969)

Summerfield, Penny, *Reconstructing Women's Wartime Lives: Discourses and Subjectivities in Oral Histories of the Second World War* (Manchester, 1998)

Sumner, B. H., *Russia and the Balkans, 1870–1880* (Oxford, 1937)

Taylor, A. J. P., *The Troublemakers: Dissent over Foreign Policy, 1792–1939* (London, 1957)

Toplis, Ian, *The Foreign Office: An Architectural History* (London, 1987)

Torfeh, Massoumeh, 'The BBC Persian Service, 1941–1979', paper presented at the European Communication Research and Education Association Biannual Conference, November 2008

Vickery, Amanda, 'Golden Age to Separate Spheres? A Review of the Categories and Chronology of English Women's History', *Historical Journal*, 36 (1993), pp. 383–414

Waghmar, Burzine, 'Lambton, Ann Katherine Swynford (1912–2008)', *Oxford Dictionary of National Biography* (Oxford, 2012)

Wallach, Janet, *Desert Queen: The Extraordinary Life of Gertrude Bell, Adventurer, Adviser to Kings, Ally of Lawrence of Arabia* (London, 1996)

Weintraub, Stanley, *Victoria: Biography of a Queen* (London, 1987)

Wernham, R. B., *The Making of Elizabethan Foreign Policy, 1558–1603* (London, 1980)

Westrate, Bruce, *The Arab Bureau: British Policy in the Middle East, 1916–1920* (Pennsylvania, 1992)

Whiteman, Anne, 'Lucy Stuart Sutherland, 1903–1980', *Proceedings of the British Academy*, vol. 69, 1983, pp. 612–30

Wilson, Dolly, 'A New Look at the Affluent Worker: The Good Working Mother in Post-War Britain', *Twentieth-Century British History*, 17 (2), 2006, pp. 206–29

Young, John, *Twentieth-Century Diplomacy: A Case Study of British Practice, 1963–1976* (Cambridge, 2008)

Zimmeck, Meta, 'The Mysteries of the Typewriter: Technology and Gender in the British Civil Service, 1870–1914' in *Women Workers and Technological Change in Europe in the Nineteenth and Twentieth Centuries*, eds. Gertjan de Groot and Marlou Schrover (London, 1995), pp. 67–96

Acknowledgements

Like every author, I have, in the process of writing this book, accumulated a long list of debts – material, intellectual, emotional, and in some cases a mix of all three – which will never be repaid. I started the project as a Junior Research Fellow in the tranquil environs of St John's College, Cambridge, and finished it at my current home at Queen Mary in London's East End. Both institutions have provided the stimulating company and time for quiet reflection which are so necessary for book-writing, whilst an Early Career Fellowship from the Arts and Humanities Research Council gifted me a precious six months in which to draft much of the final manuscript. My old friend and mentor, David Cannadine, read the draft in its entirety, as did my agent Andrew Gordon, Professor Patrick Salmon, and former diplomat and interviewee Sophia Lambert. Smaller sections of the book received a thorough going-over from Laura Beers, Deborah Cohen, James Ellison, John Gurney, James Mather, Jill Pellew and Dan Todman. Every one of these generous readers saved me from a multitude of schoolgirl errors and the book is all the better for it. The official historians at the Foreign and Commonwealth Office, most importantly Patrick Salmon and Isabelle Tombs, backed the project from the start and put their unrivalled institutional knowledge at my disposal. Thanks also to Philip Barclay, Helen Hughes-McKay and Andy Pike at the FCO, and to Oliver Mahoney, Burzine Waghmar, Ruth Dudley Edwards, Rodney Lowe, Sophia Lambert, Sir Rodric Braithwaite and Sir Sherard

Cowper-Coles, who helped join the dots in several of the extraordinary lives featured in this book. Academic colleagues at seminars and conferences in Cambridge, Keele, London, Brighton and the European University Institute, Florence, offered challenging questions and observations which pushed me to refine my ideas, as did individual exchanges with Neil Armstrong, Philip Nash, Corinne Pernet and Glenda Sluga. Working with Michael Fishwick at Bloomsbury has been a pleasure from the start; I could not have wished for a more enthusiastic or attentive editor. Likewise Anna Simpson has steered the production process through with exceptional efficiency and cheerfulness.

My most heartfelt thanks, however, are reserved for the extraordinary group of women and men who shared their memories with me, in many cases going much further by offering warm hospitality or providing introductions to ex-colleagues whom I would never have found by myself. It was a privilege to spend time with every one of these brilliant individuals, and it was with great sadness that I learned of the deaths of three of them: Sir Michael Palliser, Richard Samuel and Rowena Vining. I only wish I could have devoted more space to telling their stories of lifelong public service.

The final mention is, of course, for James, Florence and Beatrice, to whom this book is dedicated with love.

Index

A NOTE ON THE AUTHOR

Helen McCarthy is Senior Lecturer in History at Queen Mary, University of London. She studied as an undergraduate at Gonville & Caius College, Cambridge, and as a Kennedy Scholar at Harvard University. She worked briefly for the think tank Demos before embarking on doctoral studies at the University of London. Her first book, *The British People and the League of Nations* (Manchester University Press, 2011), explores the vibrant popular cultures of internationalism in interwar Britain. Before taking up her post at Queen Mary, Helen was a Research Fellow of St John's College, Cambridge. She lives in London with her husband and two daughters.